Taking the fear out of eating

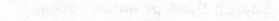

Taking the fear out of eating

A nutritionists' guide to sensible food choices

CHARLETTE R. GALLAGHER

JOHN B. ALLRED
The Ohio State University

CAMBRIDGE
UNIVERSITY PRESS

Published by the Press Syndicate of the University of Cambridge
The Pitt Building, Trumpington Street, Cambridge CB2 1RP
40 West 20th Street, New York, NY 10011-4211, USA
10 Stamford Road, Oakleigh, Victoria 3166, Australia

© Cambridge University Press 1992

First published 1992
Reprinted 1992

Printed in the United States of America

Library of Congress Cataloging-in-Publication Data
Gallagher, Charlette R.
Taking the fear out of eating: a nutritionists' guide to sensible food choices /
  Charlette R. Gallagher and John B. Allred.
    p. cm.
Includes index.
ISBN 0-521-43124-7. – ISBN 0-521-43728-8 (pbk.)
1. Nutrition. I. Allred, John B. II. Title.
RA784.G35   1992
613.2–dc20   92-8737
                                                                  CIP

A catalog record for this book is available from the British Library.

ISBN 0-521-43124-7 hardback
ISBN 0-521-43728-8 paperback

Contents

Preface

Nutrition has become a hot topic!

> cholesterol
> saturated fat
> salt
> sugar
> vitamins
> pesticides
> fiber prevents cancer
> broccoli causes cancer
> broccoli prevents cancer

What's hype? What's not? How much of what the public hears should it believe? We are given daily media reports and advertisements about what should and should not be eaten, many of which offer contradictory advice. It is no wonder that surveys reveal that consumers' most common complaint is that they do not know what to believe. There are literally hundreds of books available to the consumer about the role of nutrition in health and disease and – in spite of them or, more likely, because of them – public confusion is accelerating! And in the process, consumers are being scared to death about what to eat and what not to eat. *Taking the fear out of eating* offers consumers a way out of this dilemma.

You will find that this book is different from all the others because:

It is authoritative and comprehensive

With few exceptions, books on diet, nutrition, and health are written by professional writers, not professional scientists. Professional scientists normally spend their time communicating with one another in language that is usually unintelligible to the average consumer. Writers then attempt to translate this information for the public. The result often is books that are readable and usually provide ideas that sound reasonable. Unfortunately, and all too often, they are inaccurate and incomplete.

Such lapses of veracity are often excused as simplifications on the grounds that the public is too unsophisticated to understand complex issues. Conventional wisdom has it that consumers do not want to be bothered with details; they just want to know the final judgment – "eat this food" or "avoid that food." In our many years of working with the public, we are convinced that it is time to quit treating consumers as simpletons waiting for the next scientific "breakthrough." Some people may benefit from following a cholesterol-lowering diet or eating less salt, just as some people may benefit from merely eating less, but obviously not everyone will. We will give you the information that lets you decide your own cost-to-benefit ratio.

It assumes that the public wants the truth – not gimmicks

We have been repeatedly advised that in order for a book on nutrition to sell, it is necessary to have a ploy that "grabs the public's imagination." The problem with gimmicks is that they always overpromise and underdeliver. A healthy imagination can solve the world's problems, but only if the problems are also imaginary. The real world is much more demanding. We have no gimmick – unless you take the position that there has been so much hype and misinformation fed to the public that the truth has now become one.

It is not intended as a "self-help" book but, rather, as a means to make you a participating partner with health professionals

Books on nutrition are often neatly arranged on bookstore or library shelves labeled *self-help*. They usually admonish us to "take control of our health." This might sound like a good idea, but it isn't. Such an attitude encourages self-diagnosis and self-treatment, which are never good ideas. For healthy hypochondriacs, the consequence of such behavior may simply be money needlessly spent on vitamin supplements or magical elixirs, assuming that these people don't poison themselves, but for those who have serious health problems, self-treatment can be life threatening if it replaces or delays professional help. Rather than "taking control of your health," we urge you to form a partnership with health professionals. At the same time, you need to have some basic information about nutrition if you are going to be more than a silent partner. This book will give you that information.

It is a book that physicians and dietitians can recommend to their clients

Consumers often rely on physicians for information about nutrition, whereas physicians often have neither the inclination nor the time to be nutrition educators. Physicians as well as dietitians have expressed a need for an authoritative book on nutrition that they can recommend to their clients. We have written this book to meet that need. As you read it, you will soon discover a feature that you will not find in other nutrition books written for the public – a large number of references to the scientific literature in the form of end notes for each chapter. Many of the citations are of papers written in language that nonprofessionals can understand, others refer to "hard-core" science journals. We have included references to the scientific literature to demonstrate that this book is based on science, not imagination, as well as to provide health professionals with the reasons for our conclusions, particularly in regard to controversial topics.

It puts general public "knowledge" about nutrition – myths, misconceptions, and all – into a historical context

Is it important for the consumer to know that many of the current television advertisements for cereal grains as "health foods" could have been written by Rev. Sylvester Graham 150 years ago or by Dr. John Harvey Kellogg shortly after the end of the Civil War? We think so because, as others have said, those who do not know history are destined to repeat it or, more succinctly, "what goes around, comes around." These forefathers of "healthy eating" used hype and imagination to tout their products. What has changed? Don't bet the farm that "truth in advertising" laws have made a difference!

This book is dedicated to helping the public eat for both health and plea-sure. It provides a rational basis for choosing foods that supply necessary nutrients and that contribute to the quality of life. It presents what is known and, equally important, what is not known about nutrition. We think you will agree after you read *Taking the fear out of eating* that food should be enjoyed and not feared.

Introduction: What are we supposed to eat?

The greatest enemy of the truth is very often not the lie – deliberate,
contrived and dishonest – but the myth – persistent, persuasive and
unrealistic.
John F. Kennedy

We recently encountered a frail, well-dressed, elderly lady scrutinizing row
after row of prepared breakfast cereals in a large supermarket. She was
thin, almost to the point of emaciation, and looked perplexed. She gave
us a clue to the basis of her bewilderment when she remarked, to no one
in particular: "It is so confusing. What are we supposed to eat?"

Her question was not based only on intellectual curiosity. It was obviously coming out of fear. To her and millions of other consumers of all
ages, the question of what we should eat has taken on a significance of
life-and-death importance. In recent years, there has been an explosion of
media reports and advertisements that imply that an early demise awaits
those who do not choose their food properly. If you are one of those who
fear that any lapse in eating the wrong food will bring disaster, this book
will give you good news to the contrary! The diet and nutrition information
available to the modern consumer is often based much more on hype than
on science. Both the benefits ascribed to eating the right foods and the
hazards of eating the wrong ones are routinely overstated for the great
majority of us.

Not that nutrition is not important. It is. But there are limits on what
it can do for you. The assertion "Eat right and stay healthy" makes a good
slogan, but it is not entirely true. You can eat right and still not stay healthy
– if you are exposed to the wrong germ or fall from a ladder. Germs and
ladders have notoriously little respect for what you had for breakfast.

On the other hand, people who try to exist for long periods of time on
a limited variety or quantity of food will not stay healthy. Indeed, the
scientific research spanning much of this century has established that our
cells require certain chemical substances that must come from our diet if
we are to remain alive and healthy. Fortunately, research has also established that adequate amounts of these substances can be obtained by the

1

simple practice of eating a variety of foods. The problem with telling people that the secret of good nutrition is to eat a variety of foods in moderate amounts is somewhat like telling teenagers that playing the stereo too loudly will damage their hearing. Although both assertions are true, after you have heard them a thousand times, the message they convey tends to become boring and not to be heard. In the present climate, diet and health issues generate many deep feelings, but boredom is not usually one of them.

Diet and chronic diseases

In all probability, the lady in the supermarket was not as worried about the nutrient content of foods as she was about the possibility that a wrong choice might leave her more vulnerable to one of the dreaded chronic diseases. It is easy to understand such fear. Heart disease, cancer, and stroke are currently the three leading causes of death in developed countries. In the United States, these diseases now account for about 70 percent of all deaths. Statistically, most of us and our relatives and friends will die from one of these diseases. In addition, these diseases account for a major part of our nation's burgeoning health care costs. These emotional and financial tolls have put enormous pressure on health professionals and politicians to do something, but because of the complexities of the diseases and the mysteries that continue to surround them, it is not obvious what that something should be. One solution to this dilemma has been to promote dietary changes that might decrease the incidence of these diseases.[1]

Wouldn't it be nice if eating right would make heart disease, cancer, and stroke just go away? Unfortunately that's too good to be true, as much as all of us might wish otherwise. The reality is that no one has discovered any magical diet that will eliminate these diseases. Indeed, the only societies in which they are not the major causes of death are, or were, those whose members died too young to succumb to them. If dietary modification cannot eradicate heart disease, cancer, and stroke, can it at least reduce their incidence? Perhaps, but even this has its limitations. Both the benefits and the costs of dietary modification vary substantially from one person to the next. The task for each of us is to assess the cost–benefit ratio for our own lives. One purpose of this book is to give you the necessary information to do just that.

Virtually everyone is now aware of the statistical connection between high blood cholesterol levels and heart disease. Indeed, "cholesterolphobia" has been called the most prevalent disease of our time. If a newly arrived group of Martians spent a few hours watching American television, they would undoubtedly conclude that we are in the midst of an epidemic of heart disease. The fact is that the death rate from heart disease has

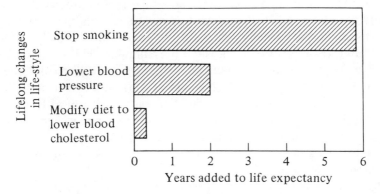

Figure I.1. Calculated increase in life expectancy of a 20-year-old male smoker with high blood pressure and high blood cholesterol levels. (For the calculations, it was assumed that cigarette smoking, blood pressure, and blood cholesterol levels all were above the 90th percentile. The reduction in blood pressure and blood cholesterol level were assumed to be 14.3 and 6.7 percent, respectively.) *Source:* W. C. Taylor, T. M. Pass, D. J. Shepard and A. L. Komaroff, "Cholesterol Reduction and Life Expectancy," *Annals of Internal Medicine* 106 (1987): 605–14.

declined about 2 percent per year over the last two decades.[2] Although some of this decline can be attributed to changes in life-style and improved health care, much of it has occurred for unknown reasons.[3] We must be doing something right, even though we don't know what it is.

The *Executive Summary* of *The Surgeon General's Report on Diet and Heath*[4] tells us that if we do not smoke and do not have high blood pressure, the most important thing that we can do to decrease our chance of developing heart disease is to modify our diet to reduce our blood cholesterol level. It is true that smoking, high blood pressure, and high blood cholesterol all are statistically associated with an increased incidence of heart disease, but the three are not equal in their effects on longevity. Figure I.1 shows the estimated effects on life expectancy by a change in life-style by a 20-year-old male smoker with high blood pressure and high blood cholesterol levels.[5]

Although this report is not without critics,[6] it serves to illustrate the disparity in results of various changes in life-style even if the absolute numbers are not accurate. This information also exemplifies a major problem with trying to educate the public about complex health issues, by means of mass communication.

The Surgeon General's Report was intended to inform the public, but it is important that consumers recognize that the specific words used in such governmental reports, as well as those by private health groups, are carefully chosen[7] and must be read with equal care to avoid being misunderstood. Unfortunately, the public doesn't usually have access to the unabridged report and so must rely on secondhand accounts for information. The problem is that when lengthy reports are condensed into twenty seconds in a broadcast or into a few lines in the print media or an advertisement, the consumer can easily, even if unintentionally, be misled. More often than not, the result is the oversimplification of complex issues that usually exaggerates the benefits or hazards of a particular course of action. We are told daily which foods or nutrients to eat and which to avoid, mostly on the basis of speculation rather than hard facts. Consequently, the lists of prescribed and proscribed foods may change from one newscast or commercial to the next, depending on the point of view of the speculator. It is no wonder that consumers have been left confused and fearful about what to eat.

Food production and processing

One often hears, with a large dose of nostalgia, about the "good old days" when food was tastier, fresher, and uncontaminated with synthetic chemicals, but this is, to a large extent, based on myth, not facts. The fact is that only two or three generations ago, our ancestors had a difficult time obtaining enough food to keep body and soul together. It was not uncommon for city dwellers a century ago to spend three-fourths of their meager income on food for the family. Today, the cost of food, as a percentage of income, has never been lower.

The availability of relatively inexpensive food, regardless of the season, is directly attributable to a revolution in agriculture, beginning about the end of World War II. However, some people question whether the benefits derived from modern food production, processing, and transportation methods are worth the cost in terms of contamination of our environment and the safety of our food supply. It is true that present-day food production methods depend on the use of synthetic chemicals as fertilizers as well as to control insects and weeds, but without them our food supply would not be nearly so plentiful, and it would cost significantly more.

It is also true that much of our modern food supply has undergone considerable processing between field and table, which has resulted in increased convenience, but at the same time chemicals in the form of additives have been added to our diet. And the public's fear of additives and preservatives is exploited by some manufacturers as a marketing ploy. For example, it is often asserted that eating natural food is healthier than eating food containing additives. Yet some of those additives are there to prevent natural things, like microorganisms, from killing us. In the final analysis, the question for consumers to answer, individually as well as collectively, is whether the benefits are worth the potential costs of modern food production methods. Chapters 8 and 10 give you information to make your own judgment about this cost–benefit ratio.

Myths and misconceptions about foods and nutrition

At one time or another, a dietary treatment for virtually every real or imagined malady known to humans has been recommended. Many of these myths are still with us. Have you heard that the amino acid lysine will prevent herpes? (It won't.) That vitamin C will prevent colds and cancer? (It will do neither.) That vitamin E will increase your sex drive? (It won't unless you think it will and then it might.) That nucleic acids or vitamin E will prevent aging? (They won't unless you consume enough of them to kill you and thus stop your aging.)

Our candidate for the most bizarre myth about diet and disease is that dysfunctions of organs can be cured by eating analogous dried organs of animals.[8] The absurd idea, perhaps originating from a literal interpretation of the slogan "You are what you eat," is that if your pancreas is not producing enough insulin, you can solve the problem by eating a desiccated pig pancreas. Diabetics who are still alive know better! But someone must buy desiccated pig ovary and uterus powder (helpfully labeled "for female trouble") or desiccated pig testes and prostate gland powder (labeled "for male trouble") because these and other dried body parts continue to be available at specialty stores and even many pharmacies and supermarkets.

Other erroneous ideas about our diet are not so easily spotted. One of these is that "good nutrition" means "vitamins." Some manufacturers of prepared food continually tell us that all of our daily vitamin needs should be met by a single food. Vitamin and mineral supplement manufacturers want us to believe that we should get our vitamins and/or minerals by consuming a pill "just in case." Purveyors of vitamins and minerals tell us that for all kinds of reasons – stress, pollution, and "life in the fast lane" – our diet is no longer adequate to supply needed nutrients. The fact is that with the exception of a very few people who have specific medical problems, we can obtain all of the vitamins and minerals that we need by eating a variety of foods. It is still true that it is better to get your nutrients from food rather than from a bottle. Vitamin or mineral supplements are not only expensive; they can be dangerous. Indeed, it is possible to get too much of a good thing.[9]

Proposed solutions for curing the problem of weight control, almost all of which are ineffective, can be found in advertisements, books, magazines, and those "periodicals" displayed beside the candy at the checkout counter of your local supermarket. They promise to provide the right pill, the right formula, or the right combination of foods so that the body of any over-weight person will magically be transformed into one that would be the envy of any Hollywood personality. They are empty promises – as those who have tried them know. There is a way to reduce body fat stores, but it isn't easy. We have devoted Chapter 13 to the problem of weight control and include a discussion of why it is difficult to change one's body weight and factors to consider before attempting to do so. If you are hoping that this chapter includes a plan to "eat your way to a slimmer you," you will be disappointed. We believe that the most important ingredients for successful weight reduction are motivation and perseverance. If you have them, you can do it!

Finally, it is often assumed that the old adage "anything that we enjoy is illegal, immoral, or unhealthy" is valid. It isn't in the case of food; food should be enjoyed! In spite of what you may have heard, it is simply not true that a genuinely nutritious diet must contain some foods that don't taste good and should never include those that do. We will show you how easy it is to choose tasty, popular foods that meet our vitamin, mineral, and protein needs and still leave room for another helping of a favorite food or a scrumptious dessert without exceeding caloric needs and without guilt or fear.

A healthy perspective on eating

It seems to us that the publicity about diet and health has provided mixed blessings. It has undoubtedly raised our nation's conscience about how our life-style might affect our health. On the other hand, overzealous reporting and interpretation of the dangers of a wrong choice have needlessly scared the daylights out of too many people. It is time to get things back into perspective.

The purpose of this book is to provide information about food and nutrition – what it will and will not do for you. We have chosen an intermediate path between the proponents and opponents of making general dietary recommendations. Rather than simply telling you what to eat and what not to eat, we give you the facts of what is known, what is suspected, and what is not known about nutritional issues and let you decide on a course of action. Our premise is that living is risky – everything that one does or does not do has a certain level of risk associated with it. The pragmatic approach to diet is to obtain the facts from which we can calculate our own cost–benefit ratio. We will, to the best of our ability, give you the necessary facts.

Many of the issues, particularly those associated with the possible role of diet in preventing chronic diseases, are complex. In addition, all of us have daily encounters with fallacies, misinformation, or, in some cases, even disinformation to sell products, books, or ideas. Knowledge is the consumers' only real defense against these. The old adage "Let the buyer beware" is still alive and well. For these reasons, we have devoted the next several chapters to the information on basic nutrition and physiology necessary to be an enlightened consumer.

Part I

Deciding what to have for dinner

After you get through the advertisements and the media reports of the day touting this food or panning that one, each of us is left with the question, "What shall we have for dinner?" We have therefore chosen to begin our discussion of nutrition with some basic information that will help answer that question.

If you have gotten the idea from a multitude of sources that choosing an appropriate pattern of food intake is complicated, you are only partly right. Nutrition is complicated but becomes much less mysterious when broken down into its component parts. Actually, nutrition and food can be considered on at least three different levels.

First and foremost, food must nourish us. That is, our food must provide the cells of our body with chemical substances – nutrients – that are necessary to keep our cells alive and functioning.

But food is more than simply a source of nutrients. Food is a part of our social makeup. It is used to celebrate important events in our lives – weddings, holidays – as well as more ordinary times, like a business lunch, a good time out at a nice restaurant, or a relaxing evening meal at home. Eating food gives us pleasure. It can be an important component of the quality of life but only if we enjoy the foods that we consume.

There is a third level at which nutrition can be considered – the possible role of diet in the prevention and treatment of chronic diseases. Although this aspect of nutrition is a relative newcomer, it is the one that receives the most publicity and is, at the same time, the most controversial.

In the following two chapters, we concentrate on selecting combinations of foods that provide all of the nutrients that our bodies require and still offer the pleasure of eating the foods that we enjoy. The simple truth is that even though our body requires certain nutrients, we need not – and indeed, should not – rely on any one particular food to provide them, nor do we have to eat foods that we don't like. We have a very wide choice of foods to supply necessary nutrients and, at the same time, satisfy our taste buds.

1 Meeting nutrient needs from food: The simple nutrition truths

Obviously, food has supplied humans with nutrients since they have been on earth, but no one knew it until well into the twentieth century. Until then, food choices were made on the basis of availability and, presumably, trial and error. The discovery of nutrients quickly led the avant garde, including some nutritionists, to take up the cause of scientific eating, in which nutrients, not food, received the emphasis. For the most part, however, people simply continued to select their food in the same way that their ancestors did.

In practice, there is no real conflict between scientific eating and the tradition of eating a variety of foods, because either way, our nutrient needs can be met. Still, the concept of scientific eating, with its emphasis on nutrients instead of food, is helpful in understanding basic nutrition. According to this idea, it follows that nutrients, not specific foods, are essential to life. The nutrients required by our body's cells are carbohydrates, fats, proteins, vitamins, minerals, and water. Our need for them can be met by consuming a variety of foods. You might protest that the difference between food and nutrients is simply semantics, but the difference is important for several reasons. Consider:

1. Food never gets inside the body; nutrients do. The gastrointestinal (GI) tract is a hollow tube with both ends open to the outside of the body. Food in the GI tract is broken down into nutrients by means of digestion, and the nutrients released by that process enter the blood when they are absorbed from the GI tract.
2. All cells of the body require nutrients in order to live, but these cells do not care what foods provide those nutrients. For example, cells (with the possible exception of the taste buds in your mouth) do not care one whit whether the vitamin C they require was consumed as orange juice, potatoes, or a vitamin C tablet or even whether the vitamin C was injected into the bloodstream.
3. Emphasis on nutrients instead of foods makes it clear that you have a wide choice of foods, which means that you can select a diet that satisfies your nutrient needs as well as your taste buds. In other words, it is not necessary to eat brussels sprouts or spinach if you sicken at the mention of them. Rather, you can obtain the nutrients that they supply from many other foods.

9

What are all those nutrients used for?

In order to live, humans depend on complex biochemical systems operating within and between cells. When these systems fail, our cells, and consequently we, die. The systems in our body require literally thousands of chemical compounds, most of which are made in the body from the carbohydrates, fats, and proteins that we eat. Some chemicals, including minerals, vitamins, certain amino acids, and certain fatty acids, cannot be made in the body and therefore must come directly from the diet. These chemicals are said to be *essential nutrients*. A nutrient is a dietary essential if you have an absolute physiological requirement for it (meaning that you will die without it) and your cells either cannot manufacture it or cannot manufacture it in large enough quantities to supply your body's needs.

Carbohydrates and fats have the important function of producing the chemical energy necessary to keep the cells alive. Chemical energy is measured as calories. Another way of saying this is that carbohydrate and fat provide *calories*. Energy needs are usually stated in terms of *Calories*, with a capital C, to distinguish it from the scientific term *calorie* with a lowercase c. Actually, the more proper term is *kilocalorie*, in which a kilocalorie = 1 Calorie, and a Calorie = 1,000 calories.[a] Even though *calories* has become a bad word in our society, we need them for survival as much as we need the oxygen we breathe and the water we drink.

Dietary protein serves several functions. One is to furnish certain amino acids that are required for our bodies to make protein. Of the twenty or more amino acids, nine of them are *essential* to the diet of adult humans. This means that your cells must have a supply of these nine amino acids to make new protein to replace those proteins lost in the process of just staying alive. Because none of the cells in your body can make these nine amino acids, your diet must supply them. Two other amino acids are said to be *semiessential*, because if your diet does not supply enough of them to meet your requirement, they can be made from two of the nine essential amino acids. The remaining amino acids are called *nonessential* because they can be made in the body from carbohydrates and other amino acids. Many amino acids are used by cells of the body to make specialized compounds. For example, adrenalin (the so-called fight-or-flight hormone) is made from an amino acid.

Another function of dietary protein – but one that is not essential – is that amino acids, like carbohydrates and fats, may be used to produce

---

[a] A calorie is defined as the amount of heat necessary to increase the temperature of 1 gram of water by 1 degree C. Starch is said to provide 4 kilocalories per gram (equal to 4,000 calories, or 4 Calories), because when 1 gram of it is burned in a flame, enough energy is produced to raise the temperature of 4,000 grams (slightly more than a gallon) of water by 1 degree C.

chemical energy (calories). There is nothing biochemically wrong with this (assuming that your kidneys function properly to rid the body of nitrogen that must be eliminated), but getting calories from meat is an expensive way to get what you could have obtained from carbohydrate-containing foods; that is, steak costs more than potatoes.

Earlier when we identified the six classes of nutrients that our bodies require in order to stay live (carbohydrates, fats, proteins, vitamins, minerals, and water), we left out fiber. Fiber is a special case, because even though it is a natural component of our diet and has some important functions, it is not absolutely essential. In fact, fiber has been called a *nonnutrient* because it is not absorbed and therefore never really enters our bodies. Chapter 3 on digestion and Chapter 7 on fiber provide more information about this nonnutrient.

How much of each nutrient is needed?

Now that we have told you which nutrients your body requires, the next question is, How much of each do you need? The answer is not simple. The exact amounts required can vary considerably from one person to another and are determined by genetics, the environment, and ever-changing physiological conditions, such as growth, reproduction, and responses to the stresses of injury or disease.

It is important to understand how the amount of each nutrient needed in our diet has been determined. Scientists working at colleges and universities and at government and other laboratories around the world have for years studied human nutrient requirements. Both animal and human studies have been used to decide which nutrients, and approximately how much of each, are required to maintain life. Classical nutrition experiments involve studying a particular vitamin, mineral, essential amino acid, or essential fatty acid by leaving it completely out of the diet of a group of human subjects, waiting until the subjects become deficient, and then slowly feeding it back in increasing amounts until the deficiency is corrected. The amount of the particular nutrient that begins to correct the deficiency is then said to be the requirement for that nutrient.

There are thousands of research papers in the scientific literature describing the results of such studies. It is neither practical nor possible for any one person to review all of these papers to calculate how much of a particular nutrient should be consumed by each individual. Therefore, the literature has been reviewed and summarized by a committee of experts in the field of nutrition and nutrient requirements. Members of the Committee on Dietary Allowances are appointed by the Food and Nutrition Board of the National Research Council, whose members are drawn from the National Academy of Sciences, the National Academy of Engineering, and the Institute of

Medicine. The committee is given the responsibility for establishing the Recommended Dietary Allowances, which are defined as "the levels of intake of essential nutrients considered, in the judgment of the Committee on the basis of available scientific knowledge, to be adequate to meet the known nutritional needs of practically all healthy persons."[1]

The Recommended Dietary Allowances, called the RDA, are reviewed periodically, usually every five years, by a new Committee on Dietary Allowances. The purpose of these reviews is to incorporate the results of new research into the recommendations. Members of this committee serve without pay and are carefully selected to avoid the possibility or even the appearance of a vested interest in the values recommended. Every effort is made to ensure that the recommendations are scientifically correct, with sound research to support each of the values identified. The forty-four-year-old system has worked well, with one notable exception.[b]

Note that there is a significant difference between the nutrient requirements and the Recommended Dietary Allowances. The committee that sets the RDA first establishes a value for the necessary intake of a given nutrient that will prevent the symptoms of deficiency of that nutrient. This is the requirement for that nutrient. A factor is then added to this minimum requirement to account for genetic variations among individuals, called the *individuality factor*. Finally, a *safety factor* is included to account for variations in the quantity of nutrients in food and the potential loss of those nutrients during processing, storage, and food preparation. The final value is the RDA.

As an example of establishing the RDA, let's look at vitamin C. Classic research studies show that the requirement for vitamin C (the amount that will prevent or begin to treat the deficiency disease called *scurvy*) is 10

[b] The tenth edition of the RDA was due to be published in 1985 but was not because it was embroiled in controversy. The Committee on Dietary Allowances differed with the leadership of the National Research Council–National Academy of Sciences on the RDA values for vitamins A and C. The committee wanted to reduce each of these relative to the 1980 recommendation, based on the newer research indicating that less of each nutrient was needed to maintain body stores and prevent deficiencies. Although the reduction in the RDA was ostensibly opposed on scientific grounds, an underlying reason for opposition appears to be that such a recommendation was not consistent with public policy. For one thing, the recommendation was felt to be inconsistent with the controversial position of the National Cancer Institute that consumption of vegetables high in these nutrients may reduce the risk of some types of cancer (see Chapter 15). Nonetheless, on October 7, 1985, Dr. Frank Press, president of the National Academy of Sciences and chairman of the National Research Council (who, incidentally, is a geologist by training), in a move unprecedented in the forty-four-year history of the RDA, informed Dr. James Wyngaarden, then director of the National Institutes of Health, that the tenth edition of the RDA would not be published. (The fascinating details can be found in *Nutrition Today*, November–December 1985, pp. 4–23.) A portion of the 1985 committee's work was published in 1987 as "Recommended Dietary Intakes," *American Journal of Clinical Nutrition* 45 (1987): 661–716. In the meantime, a new RDA committee was appointed and subsequently published the tenth edition of the Recommended Dietary Allowances in 1989.

milligrams (mg) daily for the healthy adult. The RDA was set in 1989 at 60 mg per day, which included 50 mg for the individuality and safety factors. The RDA in this case is six times the requirement.

"If a little is good, a lot is better" is a popular misconception that the Committee on Dietary Allowances must avoid when making its recommendations. At some high level of intake, most nutrients become toxic; that is, they cause adverse physiological effects. Fortunately, however, you would have to work awfully hard to get toxic amounts of nutrients when consuming food alone, although it is possible.[c] In addition, there is the problem of imbalance, particularly relevant to minerals, some amino acids, and some vitamins. An imbalance occurs when the intake of too much of one nutrient interferes with the absorption and/or utilization of another necessary nutrient. For example, an excessive intake of vitamin E interferes with the functions of vitamins A and K. You can create a toxic or imbalance problem by the excessive use of nutritional supplements, which is one of the reasons that we urge you not to take supplements unless they are prescribed and monitored by a physician.

The latest version of the RDA is given in Appendix A. Your intuition might tell you that the amount of each nutrient that you need varies according to age, sex, and physiological condition, such as pregnancy and lactation. Note that the Committee on Dietary Allowances has taken into account each of these factors in its recommendations.

Humans require several vitamins and minerals in addition to those for which RDA values have been established. Many of these are listed in Appendix B, along with an estimated range of the safe and adequate amounts needed in our diet. These are listed separately from the RDA, not because they are unimportant, but because scientific understanding is not yet sufficient for the committee to specify more exact recommendations.

Scientific eating – the hard way

Now that you have the information in Appendixes A and B, you know how many grams, milligrams, or micrograms of the twenty-six nutrients you need to consume daily. You can calculate what foods you need to eat to meet these values if you want to. All that you need is a scale to weigh the food that you eat and a food composition table. Food composition tables, such as that published by the U.S. Department of Agriculture,[2] list the average nutrient content of various foods. Oh yes, you will also need a good calculator and plenty of paper for record keeping. Work fast,

---

[c] We have not ever been served polar bear liver as an hors d'oeuvre, but if you ever are, our advice is to turn it down. A few ounces of this Eskimo delicacy contains enough vitamin A to kill within hours.

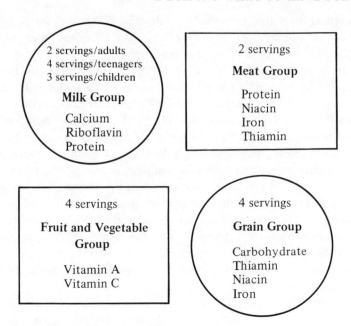

Figure 1.1. Daily food guide.

because by the time you finish calculating your nutrient intake for one meal, it will be time for another.

Actually, the RDA is designed for use in planning diets for groups of people (such as the U.S. military). It was never intended to be routinely used by consumers to plan their meals or to determine the adequacy of their nutrient intake.[3] No one that we know, including even the most dedicated nutrition devotee, goes to all of the trouble to do the calculations proposed in the preceding paragraph, for home use. An easier way to plan a nutritious diet is to use the Daily Food Guide.

Semiscientific eating – the easy way

Dietary guides based on food groups have been available for over sixty-five years in order to help consumers plan diets that meet the RDA for essential nutrients. The best known and most widely used of these guides is the Daily Food Guide (Figure 1.1), also commonly referred to as the basic four food groups, which was developed at Harvard University and introduced to the American public in 1957 by the U.S. Department of Agriculture. The most common form in which the Daily Food Guide is currently found is in a popularized version, called the Guide to Good Eating, developed by the National Dairy Council.

Table 1.1. *Milk and milk products group, appropriate choices for 1 serving (kilocalories in parentheses)*

Whole milk, 8 oz. (150)
2% milk or buttermilk, 8 oz. (130)
Skimmed milk or buttermilk, 8 oz. (90)

Hard cheeses, 1 oz. (110)
Processed cheeses, 1½ oz. (150)
Processed cheese spread, 1¾ oz. (150)
Cottage cheese, 1⅓ c. creamed (239)
Cottage cheese, 2 c. dry curd (225)

Yogurt, plain, 8 oz., made from partially skimmed milk (125)
Yogurt, fruit, 10 oz., made from 2% milk (300)

Pudding or custard, 8 oz., made from 2% milk (315)
Cream puffs with custard filling, 2½ med. (760)
Cream soups, 1½ c., made from skim milk (225–325)
Ice cream, 1½ c. (380)
Ice milk, 1½ c. (300)

Source: C. F. Adams, "Nutritive Value of American Foods in Common Units," *Agriculture Handbook* 456 (Washington, DC: U.S. Government Printing Office, 1975).

In the Daily Food Guide, foods are classified into groups according to their similarity in vitamin, mineral, and protein (but not calorie) composition. Thus, instead of calculating each day's intake of vitamins, minerals, and proteins to make sure you satisfy your requirements, you need only select, each day, any of a number of foods from each food group in order to obtain adequate nutrients to sustain health. The four basic food groups are as follows:

1. Milk and/or milk products

The milk group is a major source of calcium. Because calcium is needed in greater amounts during the growth period, it is recommended that children consume three servings per day, teenagers four servings per day, and adults two servings a day. Amounts of foods equivalent in calcium to one serving are given in Table 1.1. As you can see, serving sizes vary according to their calcium content and may be different from the usual portion size. Foods also vary in their calorie content, which is related to their fat content.

Mothers' milk is said to be an almost perfect food because it alone can sustain the life of an infant for the first few months of life. Milk and milk products, however, cannot sustain the life of either growing children or adults, but they are an important part of our diet. When items from the milk group are consumed in recommended amounts, they supply most of our calcium, riboflavin, and phosphorus needs as well as significant amounts of protein, thiamin, and niacin. Because most milk sold is fortified with vitamins A and D, it is also a major source of these important nutrients. The label on the milk container must tell you if the milk has been fortified with either or both of these vitamins. The milk group does not supply much iron or vitamin C.

When determining how many servings of the milk group that you have consumed on a given day, remember to include "hidden" servings. For example, it is obvious that the cheese on pizza and in macaroni and cheese contributes to your consumption of the milk group, but so does the milk used in preparing foods such as puddings, cream pies, cream soups, delectable cream puffs, and milk gravy.

Nutrients in milk are very stable when exposed to heat, freezing, or drying, although the riboflavin content can be significantly reduced if milk is left out of the refrigerator and exposed for several hours to sunlight or air. With proper refrigeration, milk and milk products will retain their nutrient content for many days. Neither homogenization nor pasteurization alters the nutrient content of milk. The fat content of whole milk is normally standardized at about 3.5 percent. Removing fat from milk reduces the amount of calories but not other important nutrients, including protein, minerals, or vitamins, except for vitamins A and D. By law, the manufacturer must add back any vitamin A that is lost, but the replenishment of vitamin D is optional, although it is usually done. The label must tell you if vitamin D has been added.

2. Meat, fish, poultry, eggs, and meat substitutes

The meat, fish, poultry, eggs, and meat substitutes group provides our best sources of protein. In addition, the meat group supplies thiamin, niacin, iron, zinc, and vitamins B_{12} and B_6. Recommendations for daily intake are three to four ounces for children and four to five ounces for adolescents and adults. The amounts of various foods equivalent to one to three ounces of meat or meat substitutes are given in Table 1.2. In general, proteins from animal sources, such as meat, fish, poultry, eggs, and milk, contain a well-balanced mixture of the essential amino acids and are therefore said to be high-quality proteins. Meat substitutes provide proteins from nonanimal sources like vegetable proteins, especially legumes. Peanuts, peas, and soybeans are legumes that are high in proteins but low in one or more of the essential amino acids. Thus, these foods are said to supply lowquality proteins. When meat substitutes are used extensively, care should be exercised to mix them with foods from the grain, meat, or milk groups

Table 1.2. *Meat, fish, poultry, eggs, and meat substitutes group,*
appropriate choices for 1- to 3-ounce serving (kilocalories in parentheses)

1-ounce serving
Egg, 1 chicken, med. (72)
Chicken leg, 1 fried with skin (64)
Tofu (soybean curd), 1, 2½ × 2½ × 1 in. (66)
Legumes, dried beans or peas, ½ c. cooked (110)
Peanut butter, 2 tbsp. (188)
Nuts, 1 oz. (average 175)

2-ounce serving
Chicken thigh, 1 med. fried with skin (122)
Oysters, 5 med. (40)
Shrimp, 10 lg. (67)

3-ounce serving
Tuna, ½ c. water-packed (127)
Chicken breast, ½ lg. fried with skin (160)
Hamburger patty, 3 oz. cooked lean with 15% fat (200)
Roast beef, 3 oz. (177)
Pork chop, 3 oz. baked (308)
Ham, 3 oz. baked (318)
Fish, 3 oz. broiled (average 156)
Liver, beef, 3 oz. fried (222)
Turkey, 3 oz. roasted white meat, no skin (150)
Turkey, 3 oz. roasted dark meat, no skin (173)
Lamb, 3 oz. roasted (237)
Shellfish, 3 oz. (average 90)

Source: C. F. Adams, "Nutritive Value of American Foods in Common Units,"
Agriculture Handbook 456 (Washington, DC: U.S. Government Printing Office,
1975).

in order to ensure an adequate supply of all of the essential amino acids
(see Chapter 2 on vegetarian diets). Those who are concerned about their
intake of calories and/or fat in relation to weight reduction (see Chapter
13) or chronic degenerative disease (see Chapters 14 and 15) should select
lean cuts of meats.

Contrary to popular opinion, gelatin is not a good source of protein,
and it is not included in the meat group. When mixed with water and sugar,
cooled, and allowed to solidify, as it is usually prepared, the proper food
group classification is "other" because it supplies calories and little else.
We should also caution you that if you are consuming gelatin in order to
increase the growth or strength of your fingernails, don't rush to get an
appointment with a manicurist. Gelatin will do neither.

3. Fruits and vegetables

The fruit and vegetable group is a major source of vitamins and minerals. Four servings (two fruits and two vegetables) per day are recommended. One serving should be a citrus fruit or juice (such as orange, lemon, lime, or grapefruit) to supply vitamin C. A second serving every other day should be a dark green leafy or orange vegetable (broccoli, spinach, other greens, carrots, sweet potatoes, squash, pumpkin, or vegetable juice) to supply vitamin A.[d] Table 1.3 gives some options for foods that are included in this group and also the size of an equivalent serving.

The fruit and vegetable group supplies vitamin K, magnesium, and iron, in addition to vitamins C and A. Some fruits and vegetables can also be important sources of fiber. Canning, freezing, or cooking does not significantly reduce the fiber content unless the skin of the fruit or vegetable is removed and thrown away. Canning and freezing do not change the vitamin and mineral content either, but the exposure of pared fruits and vegetables to light and oxygen causes the loss of vitamins C and E. When you eat at salad bars and smorgasbords, check to see whether the fruits and vegetables have retained their color. If they are colorful and appear fresh, they are, no doubt, highly nutritious. Cooking fruits and vegetables may decrease some of the vitamin and mineral content. The loss of vitamins and minerals can be minimized, however, if these foods are cooked quickly and with little water.

4. Grains including breads and cereals

The grain group supplies thiamin, niacin, riboflavin, vitamin B_6, iron, and trace minerals, as well as fiber. Four servings daily are recommended. Table 1.4 lists several foods in this group and gives equivalent serving sizes.

Notice that this group includes breakfast cereals as well as other grain products, one of which is bread. A popular misconception is that white bread is not nutritious, whereas whole-grain bread is. Actually, white bread made with enriched flour contains just as much of the major B vitamins and iron as whole-grain bread does, because these nutrients have been added back to the enriched flour. It is true that whole-wheat bread contains more fiber than white bread does and that it has more of some trace minerals, but you can get trace minerals, other nutrients, and fiber from other foods that are commonly eaten. Whether you choose white or whole-wheat bread should generally be determined by your taste buds rather than on nutritional grounds. If you avoid eating breads and cereals because you

---

[d] Actually, vitamin A occurs only in animal products. Fruits and vegetables do not contain vitamin A, but they do contain a compound called *carotene* that is converted into vitamin A in the body.

Table 1.3. *Fruit and vegetable group, appropriate choices for 1 serving (kilocalories in parentheses)*

Citrus fruits
Orange juice, ½ c. (56)
Fresh orange, 1 med. (64)
Grapefruit juice, ⅔ c. (64)
Grapefruit, 1 sm. or ½ lg. (75)
Lemon juice, fresh or frozen, ½ c. (33)
Lime juice, fresh or frozen, ¾ c. (50)
Tangerine, 2 lg. (92)
Tangelos, 2 lg. (94)

Green leafy or deep yellow-orange vegetables
Broccoli, 1 med. stalk cooked (about 1 c.) (47)
Spinach, ¼ c. cooked (10)
Other greens, ½ c. cooked (15)
Carrots, ½ lg. fresh (15)
Pumpkin, ¼ c. (20)
Sweet potato, ¼ c. canned (54)
Squash, winter mashed, baked, ½ c. (65)
Squash, summer mashed, baked, 4 c. (136)
Vegetable juice cocktail, 2 c. (83)

Other fruits
Apple, 1 med. (123)
Apricots, 2 med. (36)
Banana, 1 sm. (81)
Cantaloupe, ¼ sm. (40)
Peach, 1 med. (38)
Pear, 1 med. (86)
Pineapple, ½ c. (40)
Strawberries, 5 med. (15)
Tomato, ½ sm. (10)
Watermelon, 1 c. diced (42)

Other vegetables
Lima beans, ½ c. (106)
Green beans, ½ c. (15)
Lettuce, 2 c. chopped (14)
Green peas, ½ c. frozen, cooked (55)
Asparagus, 3 spears, canned (14)
Potato, 1 med. (150)
Corn, ½ c. cooked (105)

Source: C. F. Adams, "Nutritive Value of American Foods in Common Units," *Agriculture Handbook* 456 (Washington, DC: U.S. Government Printing Office, 1975).

Table 1.4. *Grain group, appropriate choices for 1 serving (kilocalories in parentheses)*

Breads or toast
Bread, white enriched, or whole-grain or raisin, 1 slice (average 72)
Tortilla, 1, 6-in. diameter (100)
Taco shell, 2 (150)

Cereals
Hot cereals:
    Cream of Wheat (Farina), ½ c. cooked (75)
    Oatmeal or grits (enriched), 1 c. cooked (average 130)
Ready-to-eat cereals:
    Bran, 2 tbsp. (25)
    Bran type, ½ c. (95)
    Flake type, 1 c. (120)
    Flake type, sugar-coated, 1 c. (120)
    Granola type, ¼–½ c. (90–130)
    Puffed type, 1 c. (120)

Rolls, quick breads, crackers
Sweet roll, 1 Danish pastry, plain, 4-in. diameter, 1-in. height (275)
Dinner roll, 1 med. cloverleaf (119)
Frankfurter bun or small hamburger bun, whole (120)
Muffin, plain enriched, 1, 2½-in. diameter (118)
Biscuit, 1, 2-in. diameter (103)
Waffle, ¼ whole, 9 × 9 in. (138)
Pancake, 1, 6-in. diameter (164)
Doughnut, 1 cake-type plain, 3½-in. diameter (227)

Pastas and rice
Macaroni, spaghetti, noodles, ½ c. cooked (100)
Rice, converted white, ½ c. cooked (111)
Rice, brown, ¾ c. cooked (174)
Rice, wild and long grain, ⅔ c. cooked (120)

Cookies
Sugar, soft, thick, 5, 2-in. (180)
Oatmeal-raisin, 4, 2-in. (235)

Source: C. F. Adams, "Nutritive Value of American Foods in Common Units," *Agriculture Handbook* 456 (Washington, DC: U.S. Government Printing Office, 1975).

think grains are fattening, we encourage you to reconsider. Four servings of the grain group may contain only about 300 kilocalories, which is not very much of your daily energy needs. Without grains in the diet, it is difficult to consume enough B vitamins.

5. "Other" category

A fifth food group, "others," includes the foods not in the previous four basic groups. Fats, oils, sugar, and alcohol comprise this group. These foods primarily add calories and variety to the diet, but they also can add some important nutrients. For example, fats and oils can supply essential fatty acids, vitamin E, and vitamin K. Alcoholic beverages often contain B vitamins, and beer contains iron. All of the nutrients that this food group supplies, however, can be obtained from the other four groups. Therefore no recommendations are set for consumption of foods from the "other" category.

Example of meeting the RDA using the Daily Food Guide

Using the Daily Food Guide to ensure that we meet our nutrient needs is simple. Consider the following menu for adults:

Breakfast	*Lunch*	*Dinner*
1 egg	2 ounces chicken	2 ounces beef
½ cup orange juice	1 small banana	1 baked potato
1 cup dry cereal	1 slice white bread	¼ cup carrots
8 ounces 2% milk	½ cup rice	¼ cup green beans
	8 ounces 2% milk	1 slice whole-wheat bread

In terms of the daily food guide, this menu provides:

> *2 servings Milk Group:* 2 cups (16 ounces) 2% milk.
> *2 servings Meat Group:* 1 egg, 2 ounces chicken and 2 ounces beef.
> *4 servings Fruit and Vegetable Group:* ½ cup orange juice (the citrus requirement), 1 small banana (the second fruit), 1 medium baked potato (a vegetable), and ¼ cup cooked frozen carrots (½ the requirement for ½ cup dark green leafy or orange vegetable which should be eaten every other day) plus ¼ cup cooked frozen green beans (to finish the second ½ cup vegetable serving).
> *4 servings Grain Group:* 1 cup dry cereal, 1 slice white bread, 1 slice whole wheat bread, and ½ cup cooked rice.

Caution! We are not recommending this menu as your total daily food intake. In fact, it is short of calories, unless you are either trying to lose weight or you are less than four and a half feet tall. This menu contains only 1,225 kilocalories. Because the average caloric requirement is about 2,900 kilocalories for men and 2,200 kilocalories for women to maintain body weight, this diet meets less than half the daily calorie needs for men and about 60 percent of those for women. Thus, the good news is that you get to eat considerably more food than this.

We have calculated the quantity of nine nutrients provided by the foods in this menu in relation to the RDA for adult men (Figure 1.2) and women (Figure 1.3). Notice that even with this small amount of food, such a menu

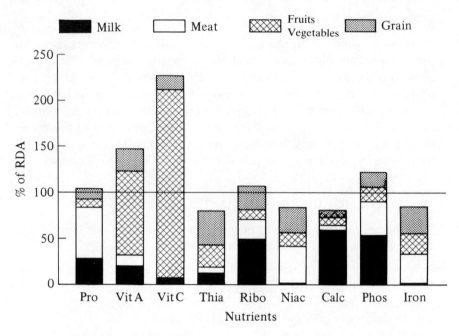

Figure 1.2. Percentage of RDA for selected nutrients for males aged 23 to 50 years.

provides sufficient major nutrients to exceed or almost meet the RDA for both men and women, with the possible exception of iron for women.[e]

Now for some more good news! Healthy adults have a great deal of latitude when selecting foods to meet the remainder of their daily caloric needs. For example, you could decide to increase the portion size of the foods listed. The average man could consume twice the quantities of each food, and the average woman could eat one and one-half times the amount specified without exceeding caloric needs. Either sex could, of course, opt for consuming items from the "other" food group. This means that you could choose doughnuts from the coffee cart at work or popcorn in the evening to meet some of your additional caloric needs, without worrying that you are depriving your body of essential nutrients. Many might prefer to add servings from the grain group and the fruit and vegetable group to increase fiber consumption. Indeed, all of these snack foods add to your intake of nutrients and also include a source of calories.

Look again at Figures 1.2 and 1.3 and notice that they show which foods

---

[e] Even this level of iron intake from this particular menu may be sufficient to prevent iron deficiency anemia in most women. The reason is that iron is generally poorly absorbed from plant sources, but the chemical form of iron present in meat is absorbed much better. Note that in this menu, meat provides about one-third of the total iron. Because of the consequences of excessive iron in the body, the indiscriminate use of iron supplements "just for insurance" is not recommended unless appropriate medical tests indicate the need for supplemental iron. See Chapter 6 for details.

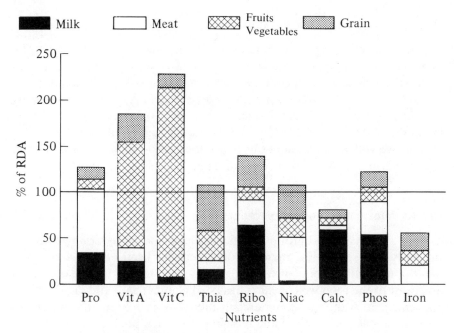

Figure 1.3. Percentage of RDA for selected nutrients for females aged 23 to 50 years.

provide which nutrients. In this example, the milk and the meat groups provide the major sources of protein, riboflavin, calcium, and phosphorus. Fruits and vegetables provide the major sources of vitamins A and C, and the grain group is an important source of the B-complex vitamins – thiamin, riboflavin, and niacin. As you can see, it is easy to meet your nutrient needs by consuming a variety of foods, but the task becomes more difficult if food selection is limited.

This brings us to another important point – there is nothing magical about the foods chosen for this analysis. You could select entirely different foods, still meet the food group recommendations, and obtain the same results. For example, the following three meals and snack that might be selected by busy people also nearly meet or exceed the RDA for major nutrients:

Breakfast	*Lunch*	*Dinner*
½ cup orange juice	large chef salad	3 ounces hamburger
1 whole bagel	4 saltine crackers	whole hamburger bun
2 tablespoons cream cheese	12-ounce diet cola	tomato slice and lettuce leaf
		1 medium apple
		8 ounces 2% milk

Mid-morning snack: 8 ounces vanilla yogurt

Note that this meal pattern is also short of calories, which can, as before, be obtained from a variety of food choices.

What about nutrients not listed in the food groups?

You may have noticed that some of the twenty-nine nutrients required by humans, listed in Appendixes A and B, are not mentioned in the previous discussion. Those nutrients not specifically mentioned – which include some of the B vitamins and trace minerals – are needed in very small amounts by humans. (*Trace minerals* are so named because we only need a trace of them in our diet.) It turns out that if we eat the variety suggested in the basic food groups, we will not only meet our needs for the so-called major nutrients, but we will also consume plenty of those needed in small amounts.

Helpful information on food packages

The idea of basic food groups was introduced into an agrarian society in the early 1900s when the majority of Americans lived on farms and prepared almost all of their own food. Today very few of us live on farms, and most of the food we consume has been commercially prepared for our convenience. Although commercialization has increased the variety of foods available year around and has simplified food preparation, there are costs to be paid. One of them is that we have to decide how to categorize foods such as combination dishes, casseroles, and some commercially prepared foods into one or more of the food groups. For example, when you picked green beans from the garden, it was obvious that they were in the fruit and vegetable group, but how do you classify "Campbell's Chunky Soup, Old Fashioned Vegetable Beef"? Help is available on the food package label.

Most packaged foods must contain two types of information on the label. The first is called the *food label*, and it must be on all food packages and canned goods but is not necessary on fresh meat and produce. A second type, called the *nutrition label*, must appear on most foods. To differentiate between the two labels, let's consider them one at a time.

Food labels

Food labels provide basic information, including the food's name, the name and address of the manufacturing or processing company, and the net weight of the contents. The most important information on a food label in terms of classifying the food for nutritional purposes is the list of ingredients. The ingredients in the package are listed in decreasing order of amount, which means that the ingredient present in the largest amount by weight must be listed first, followed by the ingredient present in the second largest amount, and so forth. (Notice that an ingredient list must include all additives, artificial colors, and artificial flavors. These may be of concern to you and are discussed in Chapter 10.)

You can use the list of ingredients to get some idea of what food groups a specific packaged food represents. For example, the first five ingredients listed on "Campbell's Chunky Soup, Old Fashioned Vegetable Beef" are beef stock, carrots, potatoes, cooked lean beef, and tomatoes. This tells you that this soup contributes to the meat and the fruit and vegetable groups. The number of servings of each group depends on how much soup you eat. You can get a much better idea and more quantitative information about the nutrient content of the soup if it has a nutrition label.

Nutrition labels

As the name indicates, the nutrition label is designed to describe a food's nutrient content. The FDA created the nutrition label to make it easier for consumers to compare food brands for their nutrient content. Under FDA regulations, most packaged foods must have a nutrition label. In addition, grocery stores are encouraged to display nutrition information for twenty of the most frequently consumed raw fruits, vegetables, and fish.

The nutrition label on packaged foods must state the size of an individual serving as well as the number of servings in the container. Whereas serving size is often stated in metric measures (e.g., grams or milliliters) and U.S. measures (e.g., ounces or fluid ounces), the Nutrition Labeling Act of 1990 and subsequently proposed FDA rules make it mandatory that the serving size be stated in metric and common household measures (e.g., 1 cup), effective in 1993. In addition, serving sizes have been standardized for a large number of foods.

Traditionally, the nutrition label also stated the number of kilocalories (Calories) in a serving as well as the number of grams of carbohydrate, protein, and fat and the number of milligrams of sodium. Additional information required by the Nutrition Labeling Act of 1990 and subsequently proposed FDA rules includes the number of kilocalories derived from fat and the amounts of

> Saturated fat and cholesterol
> Complex carbohydrates and sugars
> Dietary fiber
> Vitamins A and C
> Calcium and iron

The actual quantity of specific vitamins and minerals present in a serving of a food is not as important to most of us as knowing how that food contributes to our daily nutrient needs. To make the information more useful, the FDA established the term *U.S. Recommended Daily Allowances*, or *U.S. RDA*, for use in nutrition labeling. Simply stated, the U.S. RDA is an esti-

mate of the percentage of a food's contribution to meeting our needs for protein and certain vitamins and minerals. The term U.S. RDA should not be
confused with Recommended Dietary Allowances (RDA), discussed earlier
in this chapter. In fact, the terms U.S. RDA and RDA are so likely to be
confused that the FDA has proposed that "U.S. RDA" be replaced with
"Reference Daily Intake" (abbreviated RDI) on nutrition labels. Although
the terms are different, U.S. RDA and RDI mean the same. The U.S. RDA
(or RDI) are based on the RDA but are used only when referring to nutrition labels. The reason that the U.S. RDA were devised is that the RDA
vary depending on age, sex, and other factors. To have included all of these
values on a nutrition label would have been exceedingly cumbersome and
confusing; in addition, food packages would have to be a foot square on each
side to include all the information! Thus, a single value was established (the
U.S. RDA or RDI), which in most cases is the highest RDA value for each
nutrient. For example, the RDA for protein for an adult female is 50 grams
and for an adult male is 63 grams. The U.S. RDA for protein uses the value
of 56 grams, which is above the amount needed for women and children. In
addition to protein, the FDA established in the same way a U.S. RDA value
for nineteen vitamins and minerals. In each case, the U.S. RDA meet or exceed the RDA (except for pregnant or lactating women).

To illustrate how the system works, let's look at the nutrition label for
the "Campbell's Chunky Soup" mentioned earlier.

Nutritional Information Per Serving

Serving size (305 grams): 10 ¾ oz.
   servings per container: 1
   Calories (kilocalories): 190
   protein (grams): 13
   carbohydrates (grams): 20
   fat (grams): 6
   sodium (milligrams): 1,090

Percentage of U.S. Recommended Daily Allowances (U.S. RDA)

protein	25	riboflavin	10
vitamin A	120	niacin	10
vitamin C	10	calcium	6
thiamin	4	iron	15

The nutrition label tells you that if you ate the entire contents of the
can, you would have consumed 190 kilocalories. You would have also
consumed 13 grams of protein, which amounts to 25 percent of the U.S.
RDA. It also shows that you would have obtained 120 percent of the U.S.
RDA for vitamin A; 15 percent of the U.S. RDA for iron; 10 percent of
the U.S. RDA for vitamin C, niacin, and riboflavin; 6 percent of the U.S.
RDA for calcium; and 4 percent of the U.S. RDA for thiamin. How does
this information help you decide how much of what food groups you just

consumed? First, recall that the ingredients in the soup listed on the food label were beef stock, carrots, potatoes, tomatoes, and cooked beef. Second, note that you have consumed a large amount of protein and vitamin A, as shown on the nutrition label. (You probably suspected this even without looking at the nutrition label, because you remember that beef is high in protein and carrots are high in vitamin A.) Third, look at Figure 1.1 (the Daily Food Guide) or recall that you need 4 to 5 ounces (two 2- to 3-ounce servings) of meat or meat substitute daily and one serving of a dark green leafy or orange vegetable every other day. Because the soup provided 25 percent of the U.S. RDA for protein, you can assume it supplied 1 to 1½ ounces of meat (25 percent of 4 to 5 ounces) or about one-half of a 2- to 3-ounce meat serving. Because the soup provided 120 percent of the U.S. RDA for vitamin A, it met the recommendation for one serving of a dark green or orange vegetable. Thus, in the language of the Daily Food Guide, the beef and vegetable soup fulfilled one-half serving of meat and one serving of a dark green or orange vegetable.

The nutrition label can be used to compare products from different manufacturers. In addition, if many of the foods that you consume in a day have nutrition labels, they can be used to determine whether you have obtained the allowance for a given nutrient, by simply adding the percentages for that nutrient in all the foods you have eaten during the day. By the end of the day, you should have consumed close to 100 percent for each nutrient. If you have not met the 100 percent on a given day, don't worry about it – yet. Instead, read on.

What if I skip a few servings?

Suppose that you awaken at two o'clock in the morning and suddenly remember that you are out of orange juice. If you don't drink orange juice for breakfast, how will you meet your vitamin C requirement? You have several options, but the simplest is to skip your breakfast orange juice. But if you do that, can you expect to be stricken with scurvy before lunchtime? Will you have bleeding gums and lose seven teeth before daybreak tomorrow? Of course not! Why? Two reasons. First, there are other sources of vitamin C in your diet. Second, and more important, your body's cells, unbeknownst to you, have been storing vitamin C for some time. In fact, healthy persons with a good store of vitamin C in tissues (such as after consuming the RDA for vitamin C daily for one month), can go for three to six months without any vitamin C before they develop scurvy.[4]

The fact that we do store vitamin C in our bodies may come as a surprise to many of you and may contradict what you have previously been told. Despite what is often said, water-soluble vitamins are stored in the body. We do not store as much of the water-soluble vitamins as we store of the fat-soluble vitamins, but we do not need to fear deficiency symptoms to-morrow if we fail to consume the RDA for any vitamins today. It is important to remember that the RDA are deliberately set high to provide us with stores that will last for weeks or months (and years for some nutrients). The human body is a marvelous machine that can maintain health despite a wide range in nutrient intake.

Our best nutrition advice

The best advice that we can give you for meeting your basic nutrition needs is as follows:

1. Select a wide variety of foods from each of the major food groups (dairy products, meats or meat substitutes, fruits and vegetables, and breads and cereals) in order to ensure a high probability of consuming adequate amounts of all essential nutrients.
2. Adjust the quantity of the variety of foods you eat in order to achieve and maintain a reasonable weight for height. To lose weight, eat less of all foods, especially foods such as alcohol, fats, oils, and sugars that tend to be high in calories but low in other essential nutrients. Also increase physical activity when medically advisable.
3. If you have a medical problem, consult a physician. Do not attempt to treat yourself by altering your diet or taking nutrition supplements. If you have a nutrition-related problem, consult a professional (such as a registered dietitian, or R.D.) who is trained to evaluate your nutrition status and, if a problem exists, advise you of ways to correct it. Your physician can refer you to a registered dietitian, or you can locate one by calling a local hospital or looking in the telephone directory of major cities. In addition, the National Center for Nutrition and Dietetics at the American Dietetic Association (1–800–366–1655) maintains a telephone hot line and is an excellent source of food and nutrition information.

Each of these nutrition suggestions is discussed in more detail in later chapters.

Note added in proof

In April 1992 the United States Department of Agriculture reintroduced the food groups in the form of a pyramid. This new food guide differs from the basic four food groups (Figure 1.1) in that it separates fruits and vegetables into two groups. In addition, it increases the recommended number of servings per day of fruit from two to 2–4, vegetables from two to 3–5, and grains and cereals from four to 6–11. As we have demonstrate in this chapter, consuming the recommended number of servings of the basic four food groups will meet nutrient requirements except for calories. The rationale for recommending additional servings of fruit, vegetables, and grains and cereals in the pyramid food guide is that such a food consumption pattern may reduce the risk of heart disease (see Chapter 14) and cancer (see Chapter 15) in some people.

2   Alternative eating styles:
The vegetarian diets

Many people believe that our prehistoric ancestors were vegetarians and that because of this genetic heritage, such a life-style is healthier. On the other hand, the tendency of at least some of our ancestors to be messy housekeepers (or was it cavekeepers?) provides ample evidence, in the form of bones, that they ate meat as well as grains and plants.[1] Actually, no one knows with certainty what foods our prehistoric ancestors consumed, but we do have evidence that cattle were domesticated between 4000 and 3000 B.C., presumably for reasons other than companionship as cave pets. There is too much uncertainty to argue convincingly that humans were meant to be vegetarians.

Regardless of our ancestors' culinary habits, it is possible to obtain the necessary nutrients from a vegetarian diet. As with any eating pattern, the more limited the food choices are, the harder it becomes to meet nutrient needs. Thus, the difficulty in obtaining necessary nutrients with a vegetarian diet depends on how strictly one chooses to follow the vegetarian philosophy.

Some people prefer not to eat meat for moral, religious, ethnic, social, or perceived health reasons. We have no quarrel with any of these. Those people who avoid eating meat from animals as a way to reduce world hunger, however, might want to rethink their position. Much of the meat in our diet comes from cattle and sheep. These species are ruminants who have the capability of turning foods inedible for humans, such as grass or fodder, into nutritious products. Thus, the use of cattle and sheep as sources of food can increase, not decrease, the world's food supply. It is true that swine and poultry compete with people for grain but, at least in modern times and in much of the world, grain has not been in short supply. The hunger problem in Third World countries is not due to a worldwide shortage of food but, rather, to economics and distribution.

Because there are a number of reasons that people choose to be vegetarians, it follows that there are various vegetarian diets, generally based on the animal foods included. The simplest vegetarian diet (which, it might be argued, is not vegetarian at all) includes fish and/or poultry but excludes

29

meat from cattle, swine, and sheep. Those who eat fish are called *pesco-vegetarians* ("pesco" meaning fish), and those who eat poultry are called *pollovegetarians* ("pollo" meaning poultry). People who follow this type of diet can easily obtain needed nutrients by following the Daily Food Guide recommendations discussed in Chapter 1. The only nutrient that might be adversely affected by not eating meat from cattle, swine, and sheep is iron, because the chemical form of iron in these so-called red meats, called heme-iron, is more easily absorbed than are other chemical forms of iron.

A more restrictive type of vegetarianism is practiced by *ovolactovegetarians* ("ovo" meaning eggs, "lacto" meaning milk). These vegetarians, as the names imply, consume eggs, milk, and milk products, as well as plant foods, but abstain from meat, fish, and poultry. Many Seventh-Day Adventists practice this form of vegetarianism. People who consume milk but not eggs are called *lactovegetarians*. This form of vegetarianism is practiced in the United States by groups such as the so-called Hare Krishnas, some yoga groups, and Trappist monks. Practitioners of these types of vegetarianism should not have a great deal of difficulty obtaining necessary nutrients, but they should be aware that by eliminating all meat from their diet, they lose excellent sources of protein, thiamin, niacin, vitamin B_{12}, iron, and zinc. However, when milk and milk products are consumed, their needs for protein, niacin, and vitamin B_{12} can be met. Eggs, eaten by ovovegetarians, are a good source of these same nutrients as well as iron and zinc. Increasing the intake from the fruit and vegetable group and the grain group and consuming meat substitutes such as legumes (soybean products, dried beans, and peas) and nuts, can provide additional protein as well as an adequate amount of vitamins and minerals.

Milk substitutes and meat substitutes are available commercially.[a] These products are generally made from soybean protein that has been spun into a variety of meatlike textures. This "textured vegetable protein" is then formulated to taste and look like beef, ham, turkey, chicken, bacon, frankfurters, sausage, cold cuts, seafood, milk, eggs, or whatever. Egg white is used in many of these substitute products in order to shape them to resemble the original product. Depending on the amount of egg white that is added, the nutritional value may or may not be similar to meat. Wheat gluten is also mixed with some products to improve texture. These additions provide a good source of methionine, the essential amino acid largely missing from soybeans.

The most restrictive type of vegetarianism is practiced by pure vegetarians who consume a *vegan* diet that contains only plant foods and avoids

[a] Check with your local supermarket. Companies that produce meat substitutes include Worthington Foods, 900 Proprietors Rd., Worthington, OH 43085; and Loma Linda Foods, 11503 Pierce St., Riverside, CA 92505.

all animal products. When a wide variety of plant foods is consumed, a pure vegetarian diet can be nutritionally adequate but requires very careful planning. The key to adequate nutrition, for the vegetarian and nonvegetarian alike, is variety. When choices of foods are extremely restricted, as they are, for example, in the more disciplined stages of the Zen macrobiotic diet, health can be significantly endangered.

Example of meeting nutrient needs with a vegetarian diet

The task of the pure vegetarian is to meet nutrient requirements using essentially only two of the four basic food groups. Substitutes for the milk group and meat group are available and should be consumed by the pure vegetarian. As an example, consider the following menu for adults that we would consider a reasonable vegetarian diet:

Breakfast	*Lunch*	*Dinner*
½ cup orange juice	¾ cup black-eyed	2 (2 inch) soybean
1 cup cooked oatmeal	peas	burgers
2 tablespoons peanut	½ cup brown rice	½ cup coleslaw
butter	¼ cup broccoli	1 slice whole wheat
1 slice whole wheat	(cooked)	bread
toast	1 medium tomato	nut-mix (10 almonds
1 cup soybean milk	1 2½ inch square	+ 2 tablespoons
	cornbread	each of raisins and
		sunflower seeds)
		2 whole apricots
		1 cup soybean milk

In terms of the daily food guide, this menu provides:

2 servings Milk Substitute Group: 2 cups (16 ounces) soybean milk.
3 servings Meat Substitute Group: 1 cup cooked oatmeal and 2 tablespoons peanut butter; ¾ cup cooked black-eyed peas and ½ cup cooked brown rice; and 2 2-inch diameter soybean burgers.
4 servings Fruit and Vegetable Group: ½ cup orange juice (the citrus requirement); 2 whole apricots (the second fruit); ¼ cup cooked broccoli and 1 medium tomato (the requirement for a dark green leafy or orange vegetable); and ½ cup coleslaw (the second vegetable).
4 servings Grain Group: 2 slices whole wheat bread; 1 2½ inch square piece cornbread; and 10 roasted almonds and 2 tablespoons sunflower seeds (mixed with 2 tablespoons raisins).

We have calculated the quantity of nine nutrients provided by the foods in this vegetarian menu in relation to the Recommended Dietary Allowances (RDA) for adult men (Figure 2.1) and women (Figure 2.2). Note that even with the exclusion of animal products, this menu meets the RDA for men, with the possible exception of riboflavin and calcium, much of which is usually provided by milk. For women, the RDA is met except for

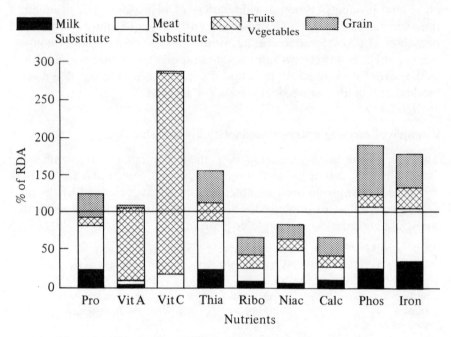

Figure 2.1. Percentage of RDA for selected nutrients, vegetarian diet, for males 23 to 50 years.

calcium, again reflecting the lack of foods from the milk group.[b] The menu described provides 1,650 kilocalories and therefore does not meet the caloric needs of the average person (2,900 kilocalories for men, 2,200 for women). This means that additional foods should be eaten, and as with a standard diet, there is a wide choice as to the form in which these additional calories can be consumed.

Potential pitfalls of the pure vegan diet

Low calorie intake

For some people, one of the problems associated with vegetarian diets is that plant foods tend to have a low-nutrient density; that is, one must eat quite a lot of food to obtain sufficient nutrients. Although adequate calorie intake is not commonly a problem for adult vegetarians, infants and children fed pure vegan diets often are smaller and grow more slowly than do children who eat less restrictive vegetarian diets or who eat meat.[2] One

---

[b] The low calcium intake from the vegetarian diet for both men and women relative to the RDA is of concern because the calcium is from plant sources, which is less easily absorbed than is calcium from dairy products.

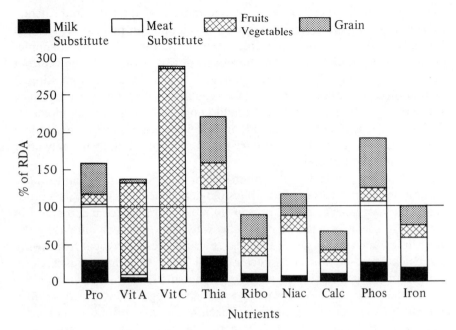

Figure 2.2. Percentage of RDA for selected nutrients, vegetarian diet, for females 23 to 50 years.

possible reason for the smaller size may be that pure vegetarian diets tend to be so high in fiber and bulk that the child may be unable to eat enough to satisfy the need for calories to support rapid growth.

Reduced vitamin and mineral intake or absorption

In addition, feeding a vegan diet to a child is fraught with possibilities of deficiencies, especially vitamin B_{12}, vitamin D, riboflavin, iron, and calcium. Plants do not contain vitamin B_{12} and are relatively poor sources of vitamin D and riboflavin in comparison with milk. Although plants do contain calcium and iron, they also contain other naturally occurring chemicals, such as phytates and oxalates, that can bind minerals and thereby decrease their absorption. Thus, clinical signs of rickets from vitamin D and calcium deficiency[3] and anemia from iron and/or vitamin B_{12} deficiencies,[4] are not uncommon in vegan children.

Decreased intake and/or decreased absorption of vitamins and minerals may also pose a problem for some adults. Anemia (from iron and/or vitamin B_{12} deficiency) and osteoporosis (from calcium deficiency) can occur in ill, pregnant, or lactating vegan adults whose nutrient needs may be higher than those of other adults and whose intakes may be limited. One solution to this problem is to eat more foods high in iron, vitamin B_{12}, and calcium as well as to obtain sufficient exposure to sunlight to produce vitamin D (see Chapter 5). Taking a multiple-vitamin and multiple-mineral supplement equal to the RDA may be necessary during periods of high nutrient need, though only after consultation with a physician. Calcium supplementation is particularly important for vegetarian women during pregnancy and lactation. Vegetarians also should consider taking iron supplements during pregnancy, early childhood, and adolescence, and if any major loss of blood occurs, including voluntary blood donation, but again, only after appropriate medical consultation.

The fact that plants do not contain vitamin B_{12} poses a problem for pure vegetarians, regardless of age or physiological state. Vitamin B_{12} is a product of microorganisms and is present in meat and milk from cattle and in meat from sheep because of its synthesis by the organisms inhabiting the gastrointestinal tract of these animals. It also is present in meat from swine and chickens, as well as eggs, because feed for these animals must include the vitamin. Fortunately, we need only very small amounts of vitamin B_{12} in our diet, but what we do need is critical. Vegetarians can develop a vitamin B_{12} deficiency that manifests itself as anemia and, unless correctly and promptly treated, can result in neurological damage. Neurological damage primarily affects the spinal cord, causing an often-permanent curvature of the back.

Most of us obtain the vitamin B_{12} needed for life by eating meat. Although ovovegetarians and lactovegetarians can obtain vitamin B_{12} by eating eggs, milk, and other dairy products, pure vegetarians must find alternative sources. Vitamin B_{12} can be obtained from fortified soybean milk, tofu, miso, tempeh, brewer's yeast, fortified breakfast cereal, or a vitamin B_{12} supplement. Vegetarians must always be sure to cook soybeans and brewer's yeast in order to obtain digestible and absorbable nutrients. Uncooked yeast, legumes, and grains can cause gas and diarrhea and can limit the absorption of many nutrients.

Imbalanced amino acid intake

Another nutritional concern for pure vegetarians is the need to ensure an adequate intake of all the essential amino acids in the amounts required for the growth, maintenance, and repair of body tissues. Remember that proteins from animal and plant sources differ in quality. Animal products contain the highest quantity of protein, and because they contain all nine of the amino acids essential to the human diet, animal proteins are of the highest quality. In contrast, the proteins in plant foods are generally of lower quality because plant proteins are low in at least one of the essential amino acids. The three amino acids most likely to be in low concentration in plant proteins relative to the human's requirement for them are lysine, methionine, and tryptophan. Fortunately, which of these amino acids is in short supply varies, depending on the source of the plant protein. For example, grains tend to be low in lysine but high in methionine. Legumes – with the exception of peanuts – are low in methionine and tryptophan and high in lysine. Nuts and seeds are primarily low in lysine.

Vegetarians can meet their needs for essential amino acids by carefully choosing protein sources other than dietary supplements. To obtain the required amount of each of the nine essential amino acids in a vegetarian diet, a combination of legumes, grains, and nuts should be consumed each day. Such a combination is said to contain *complementary* protein sources. For complementation, a food low in one of the essential amino acids is combined with another food that is high in that amino acid. For example, grains low in the amino acid lysine should be combined with legumes high in lysine. Therefore, two good complementary protein foods are whole-grain bread and baked beans. Other food combinations that provide complementary proteins are bread and peanut butter; rice and lentil soup; cornbread and black-eyed peas; corn tortillas and red beans; sesame or sunflower seeds and peanuts; cereal and milk; macaroni and cheese; and beans and cheese. Note that combining any grain or legume with milk or cheese automatically makes the meal high in protein quality because dairy products are excellent sources of all of the essential amino acids. Pure vegetarians should learn how to complement proteins, preferably by obtaining advice from a registered dietitian. In addition, books are available[5] that give information on selecting protein sources to ensure an appropriate intake of essential amino acids. Attempts to balance the essential amino acids by using amino acid supplements are strongly discouraged. For example, sprinkling lysine (which can be purchased) on grains to try to make up for a deficiency might sound like a good idea, but it isn't. Too little will have limited value and give the user a false sense of security. Too much can interfere with the absorption and utilization of other amino acids and lead to their deficiency.

Are there health benefits for pure vegetarians?

Throughout recorded history, some people have asserted that a vegetarian life-style is healthier – physically, mentally, or spiritually (or combinations of these) – than are the more conventional food choices of most of us. Present-day supporters of vegetarianism usually concentrate on claims of improved physical health, and often the advocacy is subtle. Advertisements of products made from cereal grains or plant fats and oils seem to imply that these foods, which are important to the diet of vegetarians, are inherently more healthy than animal products. Are they?

We do not know of convincing scientific evidence indicating that vegetarians are more healthy or live longer than do those people who choose a more varied diet. Advocates of vegetarianism usually focus their health claims on two nutrients: fiber and fat. It is true that many plants are good sources of dietary fiber, which has some definite advantages in gastrointestinal function. Indeed, the large amount of fiber in the diet of vegetarians makes it unlikely that they will need to take laxatives. In addition, it has been contended that some types of fiber may lower the risk of coronary heart disease and may decrease the risk of some forms of cancer in some people, although the importance of fiber in preventing these chronic diseases remains controversial (see Chapters 14 and 15). Regardless of the reasons for including fiber in the diet, it is not necessary to become a vegetarian to obtain adequate amounts of it. Indeed, as we shall explain in Chapter 7, it is possible to consume too much fiber.

The fat connection has to do with the chemical form of plant versus animal fat. Consumption of the type of fat present in most plants has been associated with a decrease in blood cholesterol, whereas consumption of animal fats has been associated with a higher blood cholesterol level. In turn, blood cholesterol concentration has been related to the risk of coronary heart disease in some people. In addition, animal products contain cholesterol, whereas plants do not. One might conclude from this that the consumption of any animal fat is more risky, but note that the dietary recommendations by the American Heart Association[6] and the National Institutes of Health[7] is to reduce – not eliminate – cholesterol and the type of fat found in animal products. Thus, people at risk for heart disease who wish to follow those dietary recommendations can do so without becoming vegetarians. Occasionally, it is asserted that a vegetarian diet is an automatic weight-reducing diet. Unfortunately for the overweight people of the world, this is not true. Adults can obtain a large amount of calories without ever consuming animal products. Indeed, our example of a vegetarian diet in this chapter has about one-third more kilocalories than does the more conventional diet shown in Chapter 1.

The choice is yours

In the early part of this chapter, we asserted that people choose a vegetarian life-style for various reasons. Some people follow a vegetarian diet because they prefer the taste of plants compared with that of animal products or because such a diet makes them feel better. If either of these describes you, our advice is to enjoy! Other people may have chosen a vegetarian life-style because they think that it is healthier, perhaps out of fear of cancer, heart disease, or some other malady that might affect their physical well-being. If this describes you and you are satisfied with your decision, it is not our purpose to try to change your mind. However, in keeping with our pragmatic approach to nutrition, we suggest that you may want to reconsider your position after you have finished reading this book, especially Chapters 7, 14, and 15 on fiber, heart disease, and cancer, respectively, particularly if being a vegetarian requires a substantial sacrifice on your part. As with any other choice in life, the final decision can be made on the basis of the cost–benefit ratio.

Regardless of the reason for your choice, it is clear that the necessary nutrients can be obtained from a vegetarian diet that is varied and follows the recommendations in this chapter. The fact that the vegetarian alternative can be nutritionally sound again illustrates that on a biochemical level, the body needs nutrients, not foods. We have a wide choice of foods to provide those nutrients. Taste, knowledge, and practicing what we know are keys to good nutrition.

Part II

The nutrients: What they do

In the preceding chapters, we described how to combine the information available from food labels with a knowledge of the contribution of each of the food groups in order to design a diet that can meet all of our nutrient needs. If deciding what to have for dinner is the only question, we – and you – could stop here. But becoming a knowledgeable consumer requires substantially more digging into the basic details. It is now time to take the next step.

In the next five chapters, we describe the processes by which carbohydrates, fats, proteins, vitamins, and minerals are extracted from food, how the products of their digestion are transported to the cells of the body, and what they do when they arrive there. Fiber – which differs from other nutrients because it is not absorbed but, rather, stays in the digestive tract – is discussed in Chapter 7.

3 Extracting nutrients from food: Digestion and absorption

In the previous chapters, we discussed the fact that although our bodies need nutrients, we eat food. *Digestion* is the process of converting the usable chemicals in food into nutrients that meet our nutritional needs. *Absorption* is the process of transporting nutrients from the outside of the body (from the digestive tract) to the inside of the body (into the intestinal mucosal cells).

To understand digestion, it is necessary to understand the anatomy of the digestive tract and how it works. Without this, our view of the process would differ very little from that of primitive people, who observed that after food was inserted into the mouth and swallowed, it disappeared. At some later time, the food emerged as a foul-smelling fecal mass no longer fit for anything except as fertilizer for plants. About all that primitive humans knew about digestion was that between the time food was put in one end and came out the other, some magical transformation occurred that was necessary for survival. Thus, food took on magical properties in their eyes.

Knowledge of the process of digestion remained limited until an unfortunate, chance event occurred in northern Michigan on June 6, 1822. On that day, a 28-year-old French Canadian named Alexis Bidagan dit St. Martin was lounging in a local trading post of the American Fur Company on Mackinac Island after a long arduous winter of trapping. It was his misfortune to be wounded by the accidental discharge of a shotgun at a distance of 2 to 3 feet. The only physician available for hundreds of miles, a 36-year-old army surgeon named William Beaumont stationed at Fort Mackinac, was called. Beaumont found a gaping hole under St. Martin's left breast. Indeed, the injuries to his chest and abdomen were so severe that Beaumont predicted death within 36 hours, but as it turned out, St. Martin lived for another 58 years to the ripe old age of 86. In fact, the patient outlived the surgeon by nearly a quarter of a century.

Beaumont attempted to close St. Martin's wound by suture but to no avail: Too much tissue was missing. This left a hole in the abdomen as well as in the stomach, although eventually a flap of skin grew over the

abdominal orifice. Because St. Martin stayed in Beaumont's home so that
he could receive constant care, Beaumont decided to study the digestive
process, using the hole that remained in St. Martin's abdomen and stomach.

St. Martin cooperated with Beaumont's experiments on digestion as best
he could, but it was such an unpleasant task that he could not take it as a
steady diet (so to speak) for long periods. At irregular intervals, St. Martin
would disappear back into Canada for months and, in one case, four years,
before returning to be studied further. Nonetheless, based on his observations, Beaumont published the first definitive papers on the digestive
process. The lack of understanding of digestion before Beaumont's work
is illustrated by a suggestion for research addressed to Beaumont by his
mentor, Dr. Joseph Lovell, who then was surgeon general of the army:

It is stated that if several articles of food were taken into the stomach, that it would
digest all of one kind first, then all of a second, and so on, and that this is the
cause of the bad effects of a variety of foods at the same meal. Suppos[ing] a man
eats beef, potatoes, fish, cabbage and pudding, it is expected that he will first digest
the beef, the others in the meantime remaining untouched; then all the pudding;
then all the potatoes, and lastly, the cabbage. Now it is thought if he eats a dozen
articles, by the time the stomach has disposed of eight or ten, it will become
exhausted and the rest will be left to ferment and produce indigestion and the
consequent evils.[1]

Even though Beaumont clearly established that when St. Martin was fed
various foods, no such sequence of digestion occurred, variations of this
erroneous interpretation of digestion can still be found even today in books
on weight control written for the public. It became clear from the work of
Beaumont, and of others who followed, that the digestive tract can best
be considered as a tube that runs through the body, the contents of which
are as external to the body as is the dirt on your hands. This is important
because in practical terms, it means that even though you put food in your
mouth and swallow it, it is not in your "body."

All organisms in the world that utilize food can be basically classified as
either internal or external digesters. *Internal* digesters are more primitive
and are represented by single-celled organisms, such as amoebae, which
consume food by surrounding it. Enzymes within the cell break down the
food into its simplest parts, which are then used by the cell. *External*
digesters secrete digestive enzymes into their surrounding environment,
where they break down food into the simplest parts. These products are
then absorbed into cells where they take part in processes that keep the
body alive. Humans, as well as animals, including dogs, cats, and even
guppies have this sort of nonprimitive digestion system.

The digestive process

The digestive tract is very simple anatomically, yet it is poorly understood
by most people. It is conveniently divided into three parts: upper (including

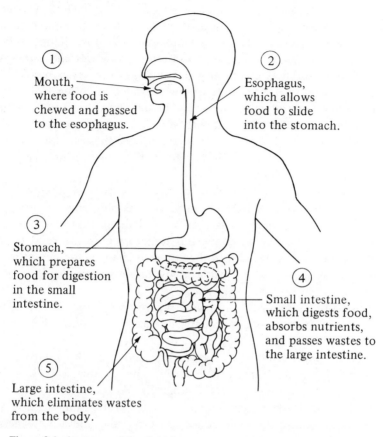

1. Mouth, where food is chewed and passed to the esophagus.

2. Esophagus, which allows food to slide into the stomach.

3. Stomach, which prepares food for digestion in the small intestine.

4. Small intestine, which digests food, absorbs nutrients, and passes wastes to the large intestine.

5. Large intestine, which eliminates wastes from the body.

Figure 3.1. Anatomy of the digestive tract.

the mouth, esophagus, and stomach), in which food is prepared for digestion; middle (small intestine), where digestion occurs; and lower (large intestine), where the residue is processed for excretion (see Figure 3.1).

The major function of the mouth is the grinding of food by the teeth, which mixes the food with saliva. The only digestion that occurs in the mouth is that of starch by enzymes in the saliva. Normally, because food is in contact with the saliva for only a short time before it is swallowed, even very little starch is actually digested in the mouth. In any case, the action of this salivary enzyme ceases when the swallowed food reaches the acid environment of the stomach. Indeed, the digestion of starches in the mouth is so insignificant that you would not notice if it did not happen, which is the reason that some patients can be successfully fed through a tube going directly into the stomach.

The esophagus has no digestive function. It simply serves as a tube to connect the mouth to the stomach. There is a valve between the esophagus and the stomach that normally allows food to pass into, but not back out of, the stomach. This valve, called the *esophageal sphincter*, can sometimes open inappropriately for a variety of reasons, which allows the acidic contents of the stomach to reenter the esophagus. When this happens, belching can be the result, and a burning sensation in the lower chest area is often felt. This symptom is commonly called *heartburn* or, in medical terms, *reflux esophagitis*. It does not, of course, have anything to do with the heart, except that the pain can be severe, and because it occurs in the chest area, it can be mistaken for a heart attack. Because the consequence of a heart attack can be disastrous, if you experience these symptoms, it is only prudent to obtain expert medical opinion as to whether the symptoms are due to heartburn or heart pain!

Contrary to its reputation, the stomach is responsible for surprisingly little actual digestion of food. In fact, there is only one digestive enzyme that is really active there. This enzyme, called *pepsin*, breaks some of the bonds in proteins, thereby converting large proteins into smaller ones. In addition, the acid secreted into the stomach changes the structure of proteins so that they can be attacked by digestive enzymes in the small intestine.

The small intestine is the real site of digestive action. By the time food arrives there, it is no longer recognizable as specific items, because of the grinding by the teeth and the effect of the stomach acid. This food mass is called a *bolus*. A bolus of food is released from the stomach in small measured amounts. Release is controlled by a valve, called the *pyloric sphincter*, at the lower end of the stomach. The presence of the bolus of food, and the stomach acid with it, initiates certain biochemical signals. These signals cause the gallbladder to release the bile acids necessary to aid in digesting fats and the pancreas to secrete pancreatic juice into the small intestine. Pancreatic juice is a concentrated solution of digestive enzymes responsible for breaking down carbohydrates, proteins, and fats. This solution also contains bicarbonate, which neutralizes the stomach acid that accompanied the bolus of food as it entered the small intestine from the stomach. Note that digestive enzymes are secreted into the interior of the small intestine where digestion occurs and that the process must be completed before the products of digestion can enter the body.

The absorption process

Absorption is the process by which materials present in the external environment (the interior of the small intestine) are transported into the body. The small intestine is lined with specialized cells called *mucosal cells*. Although the final steps of the digestion of some carbohydrates and proteins occur in the outer membrane of these intestinal mucosal cells, which is in contact with the contents of the small intestine, the primary function of the outer mucosal cell membrane is to provide a barrier between the interior of the body and the outside world. This membrane is very selective about what it allows to enter the body, and so only a few of the chemicals that a person consumes are permitted to cross this barrier and actually enter the body.[a] Those that are allowed in include water, vitamins, minerals, and the digestion products of carbohydrates, fats, and proteins. In addition, a few other compounds that the body can use − like nucleic acids or their chemical cousins, such as caffeine − are also permitted entry. Fiber is not allowed in.

The exclusion properties of the small intestinal mucosal cell membranes are efficient, but they are not perfect; that is, they do permit the entry of some chemicals that we would prefer to remain outside the body. This lack of perfection has to do with the chemical properties of the unwanted substances as well as the chemical properties of the membrane. For example, the toxic minerals cadmium and mercury are chemically so closely related to the required mineral zinc that all three are permitted entry. In addition, some small chemicals that are soluble in fat, like the now-banned insecticide DDT, can sneak across the membrane because this barrier includes a layer of fatty materials that fat-soluble chemicals can penetrate. Even though it is not perfect, the exclusivity of the membranes of the small intestine gives the body a remarkable degree of protection from unwanted constituents of the environment.

On the other hand, the anatomy of the small intestine is designed not to miss the digestion and absorption of those dietary nutrients required for survival. To the touch, a fresh small intestine feels smooth and even slippery because of the mucus that coats the surface in contact with the digestive contents. Upon closer examination, this surface is found to be covered with very small protrusions, called *villi*, pointing toward the contents of the small intestine, which make it look like velvet. Each of the cells making up the villi has an estimated 1,000 short rodlike structures extending from its surface that can be seen only with a microscope. These are called *microvilli*. Even though the small intestine is only 9 to 18 feet long and 1 to 2 inches in diameter, the folds and protrusions greatly increase its absorptive surface. In fact, if the small intestine of an average man could be made perfectly flat, it would cover much of the surface area of a

---

[a] When we talk about obtaining nourishment from food, we usually are referring to those nutrients required by our body, but it takes little reflection to realize that foods contain literally thousands of other chemicals, almost all of which are present naturally. To a large extent, it is these nonnutritive constituents of food that are responsible for the odor, taste, color, and even texture of food, all of which affect appetite. These other chemicals make peas taste like peas and potatoes taste like potatoes. It requires very little experimentation to conclude that eating freshly prepared corn on the cob is far different from eating cooked pure cornstarch. After they have done their job of interacting with our senses, however, almost none of these nonnutritive chemicals are absorbed into the body but instead eventually end up in the sewer system.

football field! To put it in another way, the average person has the capacity to absorb daily the digestive products of the equivalent of almost 12 pounds of starch. This is equivalent to more than 21,000 kilocalories! Nobody eats that much, even the people you know who seem to eat all the time. This remarkable capacity for digestion and absorption is the reason that the digestion of cooked starch is virtually 100 percent. Similarly, when moderate amounts of fat are consumed, 95 percent or more of it is absorbed. The digestion of protein is often less efficient and is much more variable than is the digestion of starch and fat, depending on the particular protein ingested and its preparation. In general, cooking improves the digestibility of protein, particularly that from plants.

After the slight modification of some of them in the small intestine, vitamins and minerals also are absorbed into the intestinal mucosal cells. Many vitamins and minerals have specific absorption carriers to ensure that they do not escape absorption. On the other hand, the absorption of some, such as iron, is carefully regulated by these absorption mechanisms to decrease the possibility of an overdose.

The large intestine

By the time the bolus makes its way through the small intestine and enters the large intestine, it contains indigestible leftovers from the diet (including fiber, some protein, a small amount of fat, and a very small amount of carbohydrate), the residue of materials secreted by the body into the intestinal tract, and mucosal cells sloughed off from the small intestine. (Note that even if you are fasting, you will still have bowel movements because of these latter two contributions.) This residual material is accompanied by a copious amount of water, and one of the major functions of the large intestine is to reabsorb much of this water. If it is not reabsorbed, diarrhea is the result. But if too much water is removed, constipation is the consequence.

Malfunctions of the large intestine: Diarrhea and constipation

Diarrhea can be caused by any of several factors, all of which decrease water reabsorption in the large intestine. For example, the consumption of relatively large amounts of a poorly absorbed material like sorbitol, a sugar alcohol found in "sugar-free" candy, attracts water into the large intestine and causes what is called *osmotic diarrhea*. A similar effect can occur when some kinds of raw vegetables are eaten, because of the limited digestion of uncooked starch in the small intestine. The starch that escapes this normal digestive process enters the large intestine and can be degraded by the hungry microbial inhabitants normally found there. The microbial degradation products cause osmotic diarrhea. Unfortunately, the microorganisms also produce gas, called *flatus* in polite society, from these degradation products. Diarrhea and gas (particularly the gas) occur after the consumption of raw vegetables such as broccoli and cauliflower – popular at cocktail parties as snack foods. Beans, which are well known as gas producers, do so because they contain carbohydrates that our digestive enzymes cannot degrade but microorganisms in the large intestine can. We can only hope that these microorganisms do not decide to have their own party, horn tooters and all, at the same time we have ours.

Constipation can be a problem for some people under some circumstances. Often a problem during pregnancy, constipation can be exacerbated by the consumption of iron supplements. It is also a frequent problem for the elderly. For those of us with the excuse of neither pregnancy nor age, we can cause constipation by simply ignoring the "call of nature" because we are too busy. When we do that, additional water is reabsorbed from the contents of the large intestine, and the fecal material that should be soft becomes increasingly hard and more difficult to eliminate. Fortunately, when constipation becomes a problem, there are a number of non-prescription medications available, all of which depend on reducing water reabsorption in the large intestine, thereby allowing the water in the bowel to remain and form a soft stool. Care should be taken with this approach, however, because self-treatment with any type of laxatives for more than a few days is not a good idea without close monitoring by a physician. And long-term reliance on laxatives to prevent constipation can result in permanent impairment in the function of the gastrointestinal musculature. Normally, the incidence of constipation can be minimized by forming the habit of regularity, exercise, and the consumption of a diet that includes adequate fiber and fluid.

Movement of food and residue through the digestive tract

Even though the mouth is normally farther from the center of the earth than is the site of elimination, when we consume food, it does not move through the intestinal tract by means of gravity. (If it did, astronauts would be in serious trouble!) Rather, the bolus of food moves downward because of rhythmic contractions of the smooth muscle that surrounds the gastrointestinal tract. Vomiting occurs when the direction of this *peristalsis* is reversed.

As the bolus of food is forced along the digestive tract, usable nutrients are released by digestive enzymes and are absorbed into the mucosal cells lining the small intestine. The unwanted residue remains in the GI tract for elimination. The nutrients that enter the mucosal cells are transported via the blood to tissues, where they undergo metabolism. In the next chapter, we discuss the chemistry, function, and metabolic fate of carbohydrates, fats, and proteins.

4　The major nutrients: Carbohydrates, fats, and proteins

When you think of the word *carbohydrate*, what do you think of? Sugar? Fattening? When you think of the word *protein*, what do you think of? Muscle? Good for you? When you think of the word *fat*, what do you think of? Bulges? Bad for you? If these words quickly come to your mind, you've been "myth informed."

Carbohydrates, fats, and proteins are the key nutrients around which all other nutrients revolve. Except for water, carbohydrates, fats, and proteins are, by far, the most abundant constituents of our diet. One of the most important functions of carbohydrates and fats is to provide calories. Proteins can also provide calories, but they have other functions as well.

To say that we have a requirement for calories is a gross oversimplification compared with what is really happening. If you remember your physics (or even if you don't), the term *calorie*, by definition, is a measure of heat. Based on this definition, you might think that the word *calorie* would be more at home in the business section of a newspaper in a story on OPEC than in the food section. It isn't. The caloric (energy) content of a food is a convenient way to determine how much chemical energy can be produced by our body's cells from the carbohydrates, fats, and proteins that we eat.

The form of this chemical energy is the same in all living organisms. It is called *ATP*, derived from the initials of the chemical name for it. It keeps our heart beating, and it lights the tail of a firefly hunting for a mate. Every cell in our body must have a continuous supply of ATP in order to live. Eating ATP itself does no good, as it is destroyed by digestive enzymes. In addition, it must be made by each cell for that cell's own use. This means that the ATP needed in a heart cell must be made in that heart cell. The ATP needed in a brain cell must be made in that brain cell. ATP is not a shared commodity.

Because ATP does not travel between tissues, the carbohydrates, fats, and amino acids from proteins – necessary to generate it – must be available to all cells from the bloodstream. Because ATP production

49

almost always requires oxygen, this too must be supplied by the blood. If the blood supply to cells in a section of the heart is interrupted, so that nutrients and oxygen are no longer available, ATP cannot be generated in those cells. The result is a heart attack. Without ATP, the deprived cells die quickly. If the blood flow to a section of the brain stops, the cells in that section will be deprived of the oxygen and nutrients to make ATP. The result is a stroke, and without ATP, the affected cells will die within three to five minutes.

When ATP is used to keep cells alive, it is destroyed. This means that there must be a continuous supply of nutrients and oxygen available to each cell to generate ATP. Because we do not eat continuously, the GI tract does not provide a constant supply of nutrients. In fact, contrary to popular opinion, nutrients are available for absorption from the intestinal tract for only a relatively short time after a meal is consumed. For example, after a meal high in carbohydrates, digestion and absorption are virtually complete within one to two hours. A mixed meal of carbohydrates, proteins, and fats may lengthen the time for the digestion and absorption process to three to four hours. This is why you feel fuller longer after you've eaten proteins and fats than after you've eaten primarily carbohydrates. The expression that proteins and fats will "stick to your ribs" is a graphic description of this concept. Although the physiology of the statement is fairly accurate, the anatomy is terrible! The body is clever, however, and avoids a potential problem by storing nutrients, in the form of carbohydrates, fats, and proteins, during the period when nutrients are available from digestion. These nutrients are then taken from storage a few hours later to feed cells during those periods when nutrients are not available from the intestinal tract.

Carbohydrates: Dietary glucose and starch

The simplest carbohydrates are conveniently called *simple sugars*. There are some two hundred of these known in nature. The chemical popularly called *sugar, table sugar*, or *sucrose* is not a simple sugar. Sucrose is actually composed of two different simple sugars, glucose and fructose.

The most common simple sugar is *glucose*, which is also called *blood sugar*, because it is by far the most abundant sugar in our blood. In fact, glucose is the most abundant sugar in all of nature. Glucose molecules can be hooked together chemically to make what are called *polymers*. A polymer ("poly" meaning many) is a large molecule made up of many small, repeating units. Starch is a polymer of glucose because it is made of hundreds, or perhaps thousands, of glucose molecules chemically hooked together. During digestion, the bonds holding these glucose units together are broken by the chemical addition of water in the presence of digestive enzymes. The glucose molecules released are absorbed into intestinal mucosal cells and then into the blood. In this way, when starch is consumed, whether it is from corn, potatoes, poi, artichoke flour, or any other food, it increases the amount of sugar in the blood. When glucose enters the mucosal cells and then the blood, it is the same, regardless of the food it came from.

Glucose is present in other polymers. In fact, these words are printed on paper composed primarily of a polymer of glucose, called *cellulose*. If you are wearing clothing that is made from fabric containing cotton, you are wearing a polymer of glucose; cotton is cellulose.

Cellulose is also present in food we eat. Even though cellulose is composed of glucose, as starch is, it is not a source of glucose for the body, because we do not have a digestive enzyme that can free the glucose from cellulose.[a] Thus, for us, cellulose is indigestible. Even though it cannot contribute its glucose for our use, as starch can, cellulose does have another important function – it is the most common form of dietary fiber. (The importance of cellulose as fiber and the chemical composition of paper and cloth has led to the facetious suggestion that if you do not have enough fiber in your dinner, you can always eat your napkin!)

Glucose that is released from starch through digestive processes is absorbed into the intestinal mucosal cells and then enters the blood. The blood supply that picks up glucose and other water-soluble nutrients from the intestinal mucosal cells goes directly to the liver before it goes to other tissues of the body, such as those of the muscle, heart, and brain. This is important because it means that everything you consume and absorb (except for some large fat-soluble compounds) goes through the liver before it goes anywhere else. This makes the liver an extremely important organ for survival.

One of the principal functions of the liver is controlling the amount of glucose in the bloodstream. If the glucose in blood is too high, diabetes mellitus and all of its complications can result. If blood glucose is too low, the brain will suffer because it must have glucose as well as oxygen to produce chemical energy in the form of ATP. The liver, under the direction

---

[a] Cattle, sheep, goats, deer, and other similar animals have a segment in their digestive tract called a *rumen* that is filled with microorganisms. These microorganisms have the necessary enzymes to free glucose from cellulose, but alas, the little varmints use the released glucose for their own metabolism. Fortunately (for the animal, not the microbes), the animal's intestinal tract can digest these well-fed microorganisms, which is why animals with a rumen can survive very well on grass and hay, whereas others like pigs and people cannot. It is too bad that Uncle George did not understand this when the goat ate his cotton drawers off the clothesline. The goat did not do it out of mischief; it was simply a way to feed the microbial hordes that populated his digestive tract.

of hormones such as insulin, prevents blood glucose from getting too high, by taking glucose out of the bloodstream when it is coming from the digestive tract.

Some of the glucose taken out of the blood by the liver is used to make ATP within liver cells. Some of it is stored as a polymer of glucose similar to starch, except that the polymer of glucose found in the liver, muscles, and other organs of the body is called *glycogen*. In fact, the chemical structures of starch and glycogen are so similar that any glycogen present in the meat that we eat is digested in the same way and with the participation of the same digestive enzymes as starch is. The digestion product from glycogen, as it is from starch, is glucose.

The liver uses the remainder of the glucose that it removes from the bloodstream to make fat. Some of this fat stays in the liver, but most of it is exported by way of the blood to be stored in specialized cells called *fat cells* or *adipose tissue*. Overfilling of these fat cells can result in over-weight or, in more extreme cases, obesity. There is a limit to how much glucose can be stored in the liver (and muscles) as its polymer, glycogen. Unfortunately, for a large (no pun intended) segment of our population, there appears to be no practical limit to how much fat can be stored in our fat cells! If you consume more starch or other sources of glucose than that required for your energy needs and to fill glycogen stores, the re-mainder will be made into and stored as fats.

The effectiveness of the liver in taking glucose out of the blood when we have eaten starch is shown by the fact that the concentration of glucose *in* the blood coming to the liver from the small intestine is two to three times higher than the concentration of glucose in blood coming *from* the liver. Even so, the concentration of glucose in blood from your arm, for example, is higher after a meal of carbohydrates than it will be a few hours later when glucose is no longer coming from digestive processes.

Where does glucose in the blood come from during periods when it is not coming from the digestion of consumed carbohydrates? You guessed it! The liver! When the blood glucose concentration decreases because it is no longer available from digestion, hormones send a signal to the liver to release the glucose stored earlier as glycogen. In addition, the liver has the capability of making glucose from such things as amino acids that have been previously stored as protein.

Much of the glucose coming from the liver under such circumstances is saved for the brain, because when blood glucose is low, less of it is used by the liver and less of it is allowed entry into muscle or fat cells. At the same time, low blood glucose initiates hormonal signals that result in the breakdown of fats stored in fat cells. The products from stored fats (fatty acids) are used, instead of glucose by liver, muscle, and other tissues (except brain) to make ATP. In this way, glucose is saved for the brain.

So, you see, we store as fats some of the carbohydrates we eat, not to make our life miserable, but to give our tissues a source of nourishment between meals in the form of fatty acids. The storage and mobilization of nutrients is a normal and essential cycle to keep each of our cells continuously supplied with nutrients that produce ATP. Through such a process, we are kept alive. An inability to store and mobilize fats could have disastrous results.

Other dietary carbohydrates

Starch is the major, but not the only, dietary source of glucose. Some foods, such as fruits, contain glucose, and glucose is often added to prepared foods, but you are not likely to find it under that name in the list of ingredients on the label. Instead, it is listed using one of its many pseudonyms, usually dextrose or corn sugar. A compound closely related to dextrose, called *dextrin*, is also added to food. Like starch, dextrin is a polymer of glucose and, in fact, is made from starch by chemically breaking some of the bonds holding the glucose units together. In this sense, dextrin is partially predigested starch. Corn syrup and corn syrup solids represent other sources of glucose (dextrose) and dextrin in our diet. Regardless of the source, the glucose in food, and that produced by further digestion of these glucose polymers, is absorbed into intestinal mucosal cells and used by the body in the same way as is glucose from starch digestion.

Another simple sugar that may be in our diet goes by the chemical name of *fructose*. Fructose is also called *levulose* or *fruit sugar*. As the name implies, one source of fructose is fruit. Fructose can have a very sweet taste in some foods, and indeed, it accounts for most of the sweetness and almost half of the carbohydrates in honey (most of the remainder is glucose). In recent years, a process has become available commercially to convert some of the glucose in corn syrup into fructose. The product, called *high-fructose corn syrup*, is used in prepared foods to provide a sweet taste because it can be less expensive than table sugar. Fructose from all three sources is absorbed into intestinal mucosal cells, from which it enters the blood and travels directly to the liver. In the liver, it is used to produce ATP, is made into fats, or is converted into glucose. When it is eaten, fructose as fructose does not get past the liver. That is why it is not normally found in the blood.

Two other sugars account for almost all of the remaining carbohydrates in our diet. Both of them are called *disaccharides* ("di" meaning two, "saccharide" meaning sugar) because they each contain two simple sugars.

Of the two, one gets a lot more publicity (most of it bad) than the other does. Everyone has heard of sucrose, also called table sugar. The two simple sugars in sucrose are glucose and fructose. The bond holding these two simple sugars together must be broken by an enzyme in the digestive tract before the products will be allowed entry into the intestinal mucosal cells. Thus, table sugar never enters the body as such; the constituent simple sugars, glucose and fructose, enter instead. These, like glucose or fructose from any other source, travel directly to the liver where they are used as just described.

The other disaccharide likely to be in our diet in significant amounts is the carbohydrate present in milk, called *lactose* ("lac" meaning milk, "ose" meaning sugar), or *milk sugar*. The two simple sugars in lactose are glucose and a closely related cousin of glucose called *galactose*. When lactose is digested, glucose and galactose enter the intestinal mucosal cells and then the blood, to travel directly to the liver. The glucose from lactose is, of course, chemically identical to that from starch or any other source and is used in the same way as is glucose from the other sources. Galactose, like fructose, is used in the liver to produce ATP, to be made into fats, or to be converted into glucose. Again, like fructose, galactose ingested in the diet goes to the liver and no farther.

Finally, we should mention a substance called *sorbitol* present in some commercially prepared foods, particularly "sugar-free" candy, gum, and soft drinks. Foods that contain sorbitol instead of glucose, fructose, or table sugar can be advertised as "sugar free" because technically sorbitol is not a sugar; it is a sugar alcohol. Manufacturers may or may not realize that many people erroneously equate "sugar free" with "calorie free." The fact is, sorbitol has the same number of calories, weight for weight, as does starch, table sugar, or any other carbohydrate. When sorbitol is consumed and absorbed, it is transported to the liver where it is converted directly into fructose. Because this fructose is identical to that from fruit, honey, or table sugar, it is used in the same way as is the fructose from these other sources.

Fats

The biochemistry of fats can become very complicated very quickly, mostly because of the language necessary to describe it. If we first define a few terms, it will be easier to understand fats.

The first term that needs to be defined is the word *fat* itself. When people use this word, whether they are referring to the white stuff so visible on bacon or the material that causes those bulges on the body, they mean the substance known chemically as *triglyceride*. It is called *tri*glyceride because it contains *three* fatty acids chemically bound to a glycerol backbone, like:

```
G – FATTY ACID
L
Y
C – FATTY ACID
E
R
O
L – FATTY ACID
```

The word *fat* is often used interchangeably with the word *lipid*, but actually lipid is a generic term that includes triglyceride and other fatty substances such as cholesterol.

The term *fatty acid* needs some explanation. Fatty acids, like people, come in a variety of sizes. They usually have an even number of carbon atoms (2, 4, 6, 8, etc.) and have two oxygen atoms bound to one of the end carbons, which is what makes them acids. The simplest fatty acid, containing two carbons, is called *acetic acid* and is the principal component (except for water) in vinegar. The fatty acid containing four carbons is called *butyric acid* because of its presence in butter. The formulas of these fatty acids are as follows (C stands for a carbon atom, O for oxygen, and H for hydrogen):

```
    H    O              H   H   H    O
    |   //              |   |   |   //
H – C – C          H – C – C – C – C
    |    \              |   |   |    \
    H    OH             H   H   H    OH
```

    Acetic Acid   Butyric Acid

The next three larger fatty acids, containing six, eight, and ten carbon atoms are called the *goat acids* because they are responsible for the characteristic odor of goats and goat milk. Most of the fatty acids in the triglycerides in our diet are called *long-chain fatty acids* because they contain from sixteen to twenty carbon atoms hooked together in a chain.

The terms *saturated* and *unsaturated* fat are often used in the media and in advertisements. These adjectives refer to the number of hydrogen atoms associated with the fatty acids that make up the fats. When the carbon atoms of a long-chain fatty acid have all of the hydrogen atoms that they can hold, the fatty acid is said to be saturated, whereas a fatty acid missing some hydrogen atoms is said to be unsaturated. Hydrogen atoms must be removed, or added, in pairs. When only one pair of hydrogen atoms is missing, the fatty acid is said to be *monounsaturated* ("mono" meaning one). When two or more pairs of hydrogen atoms are missing, the fatty acid is said to be *polyunsaturated* ("poly" meaning many). Animals and humans can make saturated and monounsaturated but not polyunsaturated fatty acids. Although plants can make all three types, polyunsaturated fatty acids are usually predominant in plant fats. Examples of the structures of all three types of fatty acids are as follows:

Saturated Fatty Acid

Monounsaturated Fatty Acid

Polyunsaturated Fatty Acid

An estimate of the degree of a fat's saturation can be made at a glance because the number of hydrogen atoms attached to the fatty acids affects the fat's melting point. Plant fats, like corn oil, are liquid at room temperature (which is why they are called oils), because most of the fats contain polyunsaturated fatty acids. Animal fats, like lard, are solid at room temperature because they contain a higher amount of saturated fatty acids. Margarine is made from plant fats, and if you listen carefully to advertisements or read the label, you will be told that the product is partially hydrogenated vegetable oil. This means that some of the hydrogen atoms missing in the vegetable oil's polyunsaturated fatty acids have been added chemically. This so-called hydrogenation makes the margarine firm so that it can be put into a tub or be made into the shape of a stick.

Lecithin is another type of lipid that has received more publicity than its importance in our diet warrants. It is one of a class of compounds called *phospholipids* because in addition to fatty acids, they contain phosphorus. Although it is true that lecithin is used as an emulsifying agent in food preparations, it plays no such role in our digestive processes – bile acids perform that function. It also is true that lecithin is an important component of all cellular membranes, but this does not mean that it is needed in our diet – the body makes all that is needed. Indeed, any lecithin that we consume is degraded into its constituent parts during the digestive process.

Thus, the claims that lecithin prevents heart disease or aging or that it aids in weight reduction are simply untrue.

Getting fat from eating fat

Regardless of whether the fats in your diet come from animal or vegetable sources, they are a highly digestible, concentrated source of dietary energy. In fact, fats, on the average, contain two and a quarter times as many calories, weight for weight, as do carbohydrates or proteins. The digestion of triglyceride involves the chemical addition of water to the bonds holding the three fatty acids to the glycerol backbone. In order to be digested, the triglyceride must first be emulsified, that is, physically made into very small droplets. Bile acids (made in the liver from cholesterol, stored in the gallbladder, and secreted into the small intestine when fats arrive there from the stomach), do this in exactly the same way that a detergent emulsifies fats when it is used to wash dishes or clothes. The small droplets of emulsified triglyceride can then be broken down in the small intestine to their constituent parts – glycerol and three fatty acids – by means of an enzyme that came from the pancreas.

The glycerol and three fatty acids from triglyceride digestion are then absorbed into the intestinal mucosal cells where the fatty acids are used to remake a triglyceride. At this point, the mucosal cells encounter a physical problem. The triglyceride that they just made is not soluble in blood or any of the other water-based body fluids, and so it cannot get out of the mucosal cell without help. This problem is resolved by adding protein, which is at least compatible with water, to the triglyceride. The result is a small particle called a *chylomicron* ("chylo" rhymes with silo, as found on a farm). Because the particle is now composed of fat and protein, it can also be called a *lipoprotein* ("lipo" meaning lipid, rhymes with hippo, as found in a zoo). This chylomicron particle makes its way out of the back side of the intestinal mucosal cell, and instead of entering the blood as all other nonlipid materials do, it enters the lymph that is subsequently dumped into the blood near the carotid artery in the neck. Remember that the blood supply from the intestinal area first goes to the liver before it goes anywhere else, so that nonlipid material goes through the liver before it goes to the rest of the body. Chylomicrons that carry fat bypass the liver. The triglyceride in the chylomicron can be removed by various tissues, including those of the heart, kidneys, and muscles and is used in these tissues to produce ATP. However, much of it (depending on how much fat and whatever else you ate) is taken out of the blood and stored in fat cells. There it waits patiently to be called forth later during periods when you are not eating and not digesting food. If you eat all the time, this fat is never summoned, and thus your fat cells grow bigger. And bigger! And bigger!

Getting fat without eating fat

It is not necessary to eat fat in order to deposit large quantities of it in fat cells. If you paid attention in the discussion of carbohydrates, you will have noted that any of the dietary carbohydrates can be readily converted into fat in the liver. The fat made in the liver from carbohydrates is either saturated or monounsaturated, never polyunsaturated.

Fat made in the liver from carbohydrates enters the blood as particles of fat bound to protein. These particles, like chylomicrons, are properly called lipoproteins, but they are much smaller than chylomicrons. The triglyceride in these lipoprotein particles from the liver can be removed by a variety of tissues, but like that in chylomicrons, most of it is removed and stored in fat cells. That is how dietary carbohydrates can contribute to the body's stores of fat.

Proteins

Excluding water, proteins are the most abundant class of chemicals in the body. Each of the literally thousands of enzymes in the body is a protein, and proteins are responsible for most of the structure of cells and therefore tissue. All of these proteins, at one time or another, came from amino acids in your diet.

Proteins are the usual source of amino acids in our diet. Their structures are difficult to describe because there are so many different ones. Nonetheless, proteins are always made up of amino acids hooked together in chains such as the following:

```
AMINO–AMINO–AMINO–AMINO–AMINO–AMINO– – – –
  A        A        A        A        A        A
  C        C        C        C        C        C
  I        I        I        I        I        I
  D        D        D        D        D        D
 (1)      (2)      (3)      (4)      (5)      (6)
                     Protein
```

The number of amino acids in proteins can vary from a few dozen to thousands. Add to this the fact that there are about twenty amino acids that can be hooked together in any sequence, and you can appreciate that there is almost an infinite variety possible. Regardless of the source or composition of the protein, its digestion occurs in the small intestine and requires the action of several enzymes that come from the pancreas. During digestion, amino acids are released by the chemical addition of water to the bonds holding them together. Proteins themselves are not absorbed to any extent.[b] Instead, amino acids are absorbed into intestinal mucosal cells and, like glucose and other water-soluble compounds, travel via the blood directly to the liver.

We have known for a long time that proteins, like all of the constituents of the body, are continually being degraded and reformed. The process is called *turnover*. If turnover did not occur, once you became an adult and would grow no larger, your cells would have all of the protein that they would ever need, and you would never have to eat it again. But turnover does occur; proteins are destroyed, and some of the amino acids are used to make glucose or other metabolites, oxidized to generate ATP, or excreted instead of being made into proteins. You must eat a source of amino acids to replace those lost by these processes.

This normal turnover and resynthesis of proteins takes place most of the time without our knowledge. Unfortunately, the effects of it are noticed at a most inopportune time – when we are trying to lose weight. Not that it is bad for our physiology, but rather, our psyche might suffer if we don't understand what is happening. If you have ever tried to lose weight by reducing your calorie intake, have you observed that success comes quickly for the first three to five days, but then the diet "doesn't work any more"? Blame it on protein turnover. Here's what happens.

Storing protein in cells requires chemical energy in the form of ATP. This translates into a need for dietary calories. If you are consuming fewer calories, particularly in the form of carbohydrates, than your body needs to maintain your weight, less protein is made in your cells, but its degradation continues. If your body is making less protein than is being broken down, obviously the total amount in your body will be reduced (but not muscle, as the protein in muscle fibers is preserved). Because protein is stored in cells with three times its weight of bound water, its loss, along with its bound water, will result in substantial, rapid weight loss. To add to this apparent success of the diet, glycogen (which is also stored with three times its weight of bound water) is also being lost. Taken together, the protein, glycogen, and the water stored with them can amount to 3 to 5 percent of body weight.

After the first few days of a low calorie intake, the stored protein and glycogen are depleted, and the weight loss progresses much more slowly (see Figure 4.1). The initial rapid weight loss was a sham – often thought to be a cruel trick of nature. The goal of the dieter is, of course, to reduce body fat stores, not protein, glycogen, and water, but the scales cannot

[b] The qualifier "to any extent" is added because some proteins such as botulism toxin can get through the mucosal cell membrane in very small amounts, but the botulism toxin is such a potent toxin that it takes only very little of it to kill a person if left untreated.

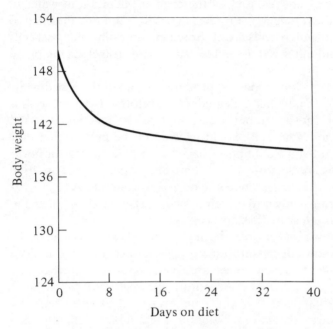

Figure 4.1. Typical weight pattern with a calorie-reduced diet.

tell the difference. If the dieter sticks with a reduced calorie intake, fat stores will be lost, but only very slowly. If the dieter is fooled into believing that the diet doesn't work anymore and returns to a normal caloric intake, the protein, glycogen, and water – and the weight they represent – will be regained very quickly. The dieter is left with a feeling of failure again, and another diet to add to the long list of those that did not work. Reducing body fat stores is difficult but not impossible (see Chapter 13).

The protein that is quickly lost during periods of reduced caloric intake is called *labile protein stores*. Labile simply means that some proteins are rapidly degraded. Two questions might be asked by people on a weight-reduction diet: (1) Is there any way to avoid this loss of protein? (2) Is the loss of the protein hazardous to one's health? The answer to both questions is no! Because the net loss of proteins is a consequence of decreased caloric intake, the only way to avoid it is to consume a diet with sufficient calories to meet the body's daily energy needs, but if that is done, it will no longer be a weight-reducing diet. Despite what television commercials imply, eating protein does not prevent this loss, unless you eat enough to make up the caloric deficit of the diet. Fortunately, substantial research by numerous scientists over several years has failed to demonstrate that losing these protein stores has any negative effects on health.[1] This loss of protein does not compromise the immune system (which would make one more susceptible to disease), nor does it diminish the capacity of muscles to do work. Thus, our advice is to be aware that it is happening and not to worry about it.

Ordinarily, if you are eating a nutritionally balanced diet (including sufficient calories to meet your daily energy needs), amino acids obtained from the digestion of proteins in a mixed meal will be used simply to replace the proteins lost since the last meal. There is a limit to the amount of protein that can be made in these tissues. If you consume more than enough to replace these protein losses and fill labile protein stores, the remainder, like glucose, will be made into fats and stored in your fat stores.

Metabolism of carbohydrates, fats, and proteins

The word *metabolism* can be defined as the process by which the digestive products of carbohydrates, fats, and proteins are converted into products that keep the cells alive. The process requires the participation of enzymes and, in many cases, vitamins. In the next chapter, we explore the field of vitamins – what they are, what they do, and how to be sure to get enough in our diet.

5   Vitamins

The discovery of vitamins in the early years of the twentieth century marked the beginning of a new area of scientific inquiry that we now call nutrition. Unfortunately, it seems that vitamins have always been misunderstood, and surveys reveal that they still are, by much of the public.

Before the discovery of vitamins, government scientists were urging that precious resources of time, land, and money not be wasted on the production or purchase of foods with "low nutrient content," such as green vegetables, tomatoes, and sweet corn.[1] At that time, scientists only knew about protein and calories – not the need for vitamins.

It is not surprising that the pendulum swung far in the opposite direction when vitamins were discovered. The ability of vitamins to cure and, more important, to prevent certain diseases that had plagued humans since prehistoric times was so spectacular that the word vitamin became almost synonymous with the word nutrition. Overzealous people again misunderstood because they became mistakenly convinced that it was vitamins, instead of protein and calories, that were most important in the diet.

It is easy to imagine a young enthusiast of the new field of nutrition telling an old farmer that he should grow and consume lettuce and kale instead of meat and potatoes. The farmer would likely retort that "a man could starve to death eating lettuce," and of course, the farmer would be right. In fact, he would have had to consume about 40 pounds of lettuce each day to obtain 2,500 kilocalories. As if that were not enough bad news, consider that the consumption of that much lettuce would require the daily elimination from the body of 4 gallons of water. The dilemma faced by the farmer and the public in general was that the foods that scientists said were the best sources of vitamins contained little sustenance.

American ingenuity quickly came to the rescue in the form of a new industry, the vitamin business. Rumors were widely circulated that as soon as the technology was perfected, no one would eat food. Rather, a meal could consist of a pill and a glass of water. Many Americans succumbed to the exorbitant promises of the vitamin industry. They sprinkled vitamins, yeast cake, and wheat germ on everything and swallowed pills for good measure. These practices became so widespread that by the early 1930s, the medical profession decried the use of "shot-gun" vitamin therapy as both a waste of money and dangerous.[2] The medical profession and the nutrition community are still saying the same thing today, but nonetheless the vitamin industry has grown to be a multibillion-dollar business. Vitamins are not only used to sell foods ranging from soup to nuts, but incredibly, they are also used to sell hair shampoo, body lotions, and treatments for burns and skin abrasions. Many of the advertisements for vitamin supplements and all of those for vitamins in nonfood products are based on the fact that most of the public misunderstands what vitamins do and what they do not do.

Who takes supplements and why

We showed you in Chapter 1 that it is relatively easy to meet your vitamin needs simply by eating a variety of foods. Even so, surveys reveal that at least 40 percent to probably more than half of adult Americans routinely take nutritional supplements, mostly in the form of vitamins or vitamin and mineral combinations.[3] Generally, higher rates of supplement consumption have been found to be associated with women, whites, older age, and higher educational levels.[4] Although people with higher incomes are more likely to buy supplements, consumers with a small family income do so also. Ironically, people who take supplements have generally higher nutrient intakes from food than do those who do not take supplements.

People take supplements for a variety of reasons. The idea that vitamins give a person pep is pervasive. Even though vitamins do not themselves provide any dietary calories, more than three-fourths of those included in a random survey thought that vitamins did provide energy.[5] Unfortunately, advertisers and media reports often encourage this erroneous idea. For example, when a breakfast cereal is advertised as being nutritious and full of energy, the claim is often bolstered by a description of its vitamin content. When athletes do well in the 100-yard dash, high jump, pole vault, or shot put, the sportscaster may glibly announce that they must have taken their vitamins that day.

Whether or not athletes "take" vitamins on the day of an athletic event is totally irrelevant to their performance. Had they not consumed sufficient vitamins in the days, weeks, and months prior to the event, they would be in no condition to perform. This is not because vitamins provided the chemical energy necessary for muscle contraction; vitamins themselves do not provide calories. Instead, they play a role in the chemical reactions by which the chemical energy necessary for muscle contraction is produced from the carbohydrates, proteins, and fats in the diet. Vitamins are absolutely necessary to our well-being, but they are not the stars of nutrition; they play only supporting roles.

You can't tell the vitamins without a program

The definition of a vitamin is very specific. It includes three basic components that must be satisfied before a substance can correctly be called a vitamin:

1. A vitamin is a complex chemical substance needed by the body in small amounts.
2. It must be obtained in the diet because the body either cannot make it at all or cannot make it in sufficient quantities to satisfy our need for it.[a]
3. In order for a substance to be called a vitamin, a lack of it must produce a deficiency disease, and supplying the vitamin must cure that deficiency.

Only thirteen chemicals fit all three criteria and are therefore properly classified as vitamins for humans. These are vitamins A, C, D, E, K, and the B-complex vitamins, which include pyridoxine (B_6), cyanocobalamin (B_{12}), thiamin (B_1), niacin, riboflavin (B_2), folic acid, biotin, and pantothenic acid. This list of vitamins required by humans may surprise you because you may have heard or read of other substances that have been advertised as vitamins. Sometimes these substances wrongly appear on the list of essential nutrients for humans because they are essential to some other organism. For example, a compound called *carnitine*, which is necessary for the production of chemical energy from the metabolism of fat, is sometimes touted to be a vitamin. Because of its function, its consumption by athletes is often encouraged. But carnitine is, in fact, a vitamin for the cornmeal worm and a few other insects. It is not a vitamin for humans because our cells can make it themselves.

Another case of mistaken identity is a chemical whose initials are PABA, which is required as a vitamin by some bacteria but not by humans. In fact, however, humans do need PABA in their diet, not in the free form in which it is sold, but as a constituent of folic acid, one of the B vitamins. It does us no good to consume PABA or the other constituents of folic acid because our cells are not capable of putting the parts together. The only use of PABA for humans is as a component of sun screen. It functions there not as a vitamin but as an externally applied chemical that can absorb ultraviolet light and thus help prevent sunburn. Bioflavonoids, or "vitamin P," are mistakenly called a vitamin for humans. Bioflavonoids are not a

[a] This statement needs to be qualified in the case of two vitamins. First, the requirement for vitamin D can be met in whole or in part if one receives adequate exposure to the sun, which results in the formation of vitamin D from cholesterol in the skin. Second, niacin (one of the B-complex vitamins) can be made to some degree in the body from the essential amino acid tryptophan. Tryptophan, however, like other essential amino acids, must be obtained through the diet because the cells cannot make it.

single substance but a group of some two hundred chemical compounds occurring in plants. Some of these compounds may be required by crickets and other insects, but none has ever been found to be essential to human health. Two constituents of bioflavonoids that have been called vitamins are *rutin* and *hesperidin*, but a need for them by humans has not been demonstrated.

Over the past several years, a lot has been written about two other "vitamins" that in fact have not been shown to be required by any organism. One of these is vitamin B_{17}, also called *laetrile* or *amygdalin*. You may remember hearing about this substance, which is often promoted as a "cancer cure," a claim that is as unproven as the claim that it is a vitamin.[6] The other nonvitamin "vitamin" has sometimes been called vitamin B_{15}, or *pangamic acid*. Depending on who makes it, it can be a harmless substance, or in the hands of other manufacturers, it can contain a substance with the initials DIPA that can be toxic if consumed in large amounts. Regardless of its composition, claims that pangamic acid can detoxify toxic products formed in the human body or that it can be used to treat heart disease, diabetes, gangrene, alcoholism, schizophrenia, cirrhosis, and other conditions are not supported by scientific evidence.[7]

Even though the need for these mislabeled "vitamins" has not been proved, is there any harm in taking them "just in case"? In some cases, ingesting them as supplements is dangerous. For example, if you are taking sulfonamides (sulfa drugs), consuming PABA can counteract their antibacterial action.[8] An even greater mistake is to take these substances in large amounts. Unfounded claims have been made that PABA can cure infertility and impotence and, in massive doses, can darken graying hair. It can do none of these, but large amounts can cause nausea, vomiting, and acidification of the blood. When laetrile is degraded in the body, it produces a substance that no one wants or needs to consume, cyanide. Cyanide kills. We have already discussed the toxic nature of some preparations of "pangamic acid." We hope you'll agree that it is definitely not wise to take any of these unproven "vitamins" in any amount.

This does not, however, exhaust the list of all of the known nonvitamin "vitamins." Claims have been made in the past, and no doubt will be made in the future, that other chemicals belong on the list of vitamins required by humans. It is extremely likely, however, that if the chemical is not among the thirteen known vitamins, such claims will not be substantiated by facts. How can we be so sure? History is on our side.

Searching for other vitamins

After the initial discovery of some of the vitamins, the search for others began and became increasingly intensive as each one was found. The rewards for scientists who discovered a new vitamin could be great and, for some, meant a trip to Sweden to collect a Nobel Prize. Because of the potential payoff, laboratories around the world continued to look for unidentified factors necessary in the diets of both animals and humans well after 1948 when vitamin B_{12} was discovered. As it turned out, vitamin B_{12} was the last chemical found that met all three of the criteria for being a vitamin, but of course, no one knew that at the time, and so the search went on. As the years go by without the discovery of any more chemicals that meet these criteria, the chance that one or more have escaped our attention becomes increasingly remote.

Another reason for the doubt that any new vitamins will be found is that a system was developed years ago to feed people, through their veins, a purely chemical diet containing all of the known essential nutrients. The system, called *total parenteral nutrition* (*TPN*), has been used as the sole source of nutrients to sustain the life of some patients for years without the development of any nutritional deficiency diseases. For those of us who can eat food, the probability of succumbing to some heretofore unknown nutritional deficiency is extremely remote and is, in fact, close to zero if a variety of foods are consumed.

If you are thinking that some of the diseases that bedevil humans (such as the common cold) or threaten lives (such as cancer) may be symptoms of a deficiency of some known or unknown nutrient, believe us, this has been thought of before. Unfortunately, the cultivation of such ideas has so far raised nothing but false hopes for some and cash for others.

What do vitamins do?

There are literally thousands of chemical reactions that must occur in our cells all of the time in a coordinated fashion, in order to keep us alive. Almost all of these reactions would occur too slowly to do us any good if it were not for the fact that we have specialized proteins, called *enzymes*, to increase the speed of these reactions. Most of the time these enzymes work alone, but in a few dozen cases, they need the help of other chemicals to do their job. These other chemicals are called *coenzymes* because they cooperate with enzymes. Coenzymes are made from vitamins.

After vitamins are consumed, they are absorbed into the mucosal cells of the small intestine and then enter the blood. The blood carries vitamins to all cells of the body. After entering each cell, most vitamins undergo some sort of chemical alteration to become a true coenzyme. The coenzyme then becomes bound, either physically or chemically, to the enzyme with which it is a coenzyme. The combination of the enzyme and coenzyme into a *holoenzyme* ("holo" meaning whole), means it is now ready to accomplish its assigned task, that of speeding up a particular reaction.

Note that enzymes that require coenzymes cannot do their job alone and that coenzymes cannot accomplish the task without the enzyme. Enzyme and coenzyme must work together. This is the reason that if your cells become deficient in a particular vitamin, the reactions for which that vitamin is necessary as a coenzyme will stop. If enough of these critical reactions cease, the cells will die.

In the scheme of things, the enzyme is made first, under direction of our genes, and then the coenzyme is added. Each molecule of enzyme needs one, and only one, molecule of coenzyme. Additional molecules of coenzyme do not cause the cell to make additional enzyme. Because your cells contain a certain amount of enzyme and can therefore use only an equivalent amount of coenzyme, this means that you need to consume only enough of a particular vitamin to make that much coenzyme and to maintain a small reserve.[b] The Recommended Dietary Allowances (RDA) have been set high enough to accomplish both of these (see Chapter 1). A significantly greater vitamin intake than the RDA will do you no good and can do you harm.

Harmful effects of too many vitamins

A small excessive intake of vitamins is not hazardous because once the cells have a sufficient supply to satisfy their immediate and reserve needs, the remainder will be excreted. Thus, you are not likely to experience a vitamin toxicity from eating foods alone. Even if you take vitamin supplements that, when added to the vitamins in your food, amounts to as much as twice the RDA, you are still not likely to have a problem. However, because such vitamin supplements are expensive, you may want to consider the economics of buying vitamins which, for the most part, will become part of the diet of bacteria in the sewage treatment plant.

The ability of the body to excrete excess vitamins is limited, however. When more vitamins are consumed than can be excreted, they build up in cells, interfere with the function of other vitamins, and disrupt normal cell activities. In fact, the vitamin concentration in cells can become so high that the excess is no longer functioning as a vitamin but, rather,

---

[b] Some reserve of vitamins, in the free, coenzyme, or holoenzyme form, is normally present in the body. This is necessary for our survival because cells need a constant supply of nutrients, including vitamins, and we do not eat all of the time in order to meet that need. For example, the body contains three times the amount of the coenzyme form of niacin than the minimum that we absolutely need. That is why we can go for weeks without ingesting an adequate amount of niacin before developing pellagra. Because other biochemical lesions could occur earlier, it is obviously prudent not to count on this reserve too heavily. The reserves for vitamins A, D, E, and K are larger than for the others, and so they do not have to be consumed as often.

becomes a drug with harmful effects. For example, the overingestion of vitamin A in supplemental form can exceed the liver's ability to store it by binding it to a specific protein. When so much vitamin A is consumed that it is present in a free rather than a protein-bound form, it can attack and rupture liver cell membranes. The resulting liver damage can be fatal.

It is ironic that people who are sufficiently health conscious that they feel they must take vitamin supplements may run the risk of poisoning themselves by taking too much of too many. In our society, vitamin toxicity is more of a threat than vitamin deficiency is. How much is too much? Some of the vitamins, particularly A, D, and perhaps E, have been shown to produce toxic effects when continually consumed at a level of five to ten (or more) times the RDA. If you are buying vitamin supplements, read the label. It should tell you the quantity of each vitamin in a daily dose in two ways: (1) (usually) in milligrams or micrograms and (2) as a percentage of the United States Recommended Daily Allowances (U.S. RDA). If percentages of U.S. RDA are given, look for any value of 500 percent or more. If one or more of the vitamins is found to be this high, our advice is to buy another brand that does not contain such excessive amounts. For those vitamins that have a footnote saying that a RDA has not been established, compare the number of milligrams or micrograms in a daily dose with the level recommended as Safe and Adequate in Appendix B. Again, if the suggested daily dose of the supplement provides five times or more than the highest recommended Safe and Adequate value, consider another brand of vitamins. Because vitamin supplements are legally classified as foods and not drugs, the manufacturers are not required to establish safety and effectiveness, as they are required to do for drugs.

Vitamin supplements: What to buy if you buy

If you decide to buy vitamin supplements, there is some basic information that you might want to consider besides the quantity in a daily dose. First, you have a choice of whether to buy vitamins individually or as a multiple-vitamin supplement. Buying vitamins individually is generally not a good idea unless a particular vitamin has been prescribed by your physician. There are three reasons for this: (1) Vitamins are usually more expensive when several are bought individually, as opposed to combinations of them in a multiple-vitamin supplement; (2) it is more convenient to take one tablet containing all of the vitamins than it is to take a tablet or capsule for each; and (3), most important, the quantity of vitamins in individual tablets or capsules is more likely to exceed the RDA by considerably more than do multiple-vitamin tablets or capsules.[c]

Marketing vitamin supplements

Vitamins are easily sold with a clever marketing strategy and boast a high profit margin because they are inexpensively produced. Supplements are frequently marketed with the descriptors "pure," "natural," and/or "organic." Are these products better for you than other vitamin supplements? In a word, no. The fact is that vitamins are specific chemicals with specific, defined structures that do not vary, regardless of their source. When a vitamin is consumed and converted into a coenzyme in the cell, the enzyme with which it works does not or cannot detect any difference in its structure or function, whether the vitamin came from a plant or was made in the laboratory. For example, vitamin C, known chemically as ascorbic acid, is a specific, defined compound whether it is made from glucose in a citrus plant or (pardon the pun) in a chemical plant. Chemically and physiologically, the vitamin C from each of the two sources is identical. The only difference is price: You can pay as much as two hundred times more for "natural" vitamin C in "rose-hip tea tablets" than for "synthetic" vitamin C purchased in bulk amounts.[d] Federal law requires that if a product is labeled as "100 milligrams vitamin C per tablet," it must contain that amount of vitamin C. To comply with the law, you will find a statement on the label that the vitamin C content of each rose-hip tea tablet has been standardized to contain a certain amount of the vitamin. What it may or may not tell you is that to achieve this standardization, enough extra synthetic vitamin C may have been added to provide the stated quantity.

Another marketing strategy for some vitamin preparations is that "the vitamins have been extracted from natural sources and processed under mild conditions." The error here is that if extraction and processing changed the structure, the resulting chemical would no longer be the vitamin and could not legally be sold as such. Again, a vitamin is a vitamin, and a compound with a different structure is not.

Finally, some vitamin preparations are marketed as being good for you

[c] We suspect that most people buy these preparations of individual vitamins for the self-treatment of real or imagined medical problems. If you are doing this, we encourage you to remember the old adage that "a lawyer defending himself has an idiot for a client." Self-treatment is never a good idea. If you have a real or perceived medical problem, consult a physician.

[d] An additional claim is usually made that rose-hip tea tablets contain bioflavonoids, but as we pointed out earlier, there is no evidence that bioflavonoids are essential to humans.

because they have something else added, usually a mineral. If our diet is adequate, most of us will be unlikely to need the supplemental minerals in such preparations. (Read Chapter 6 to decide whether you need supplemental minerals.) Because "vitamins plus minerals" cost more than vitamins alone, unless you actually need the minerals supplied, you are wasting money to purchase the combined product.

How to play the vitamin "numbers game"

To play the "numbers game" successfully, all you have to do is remember the magic number 100 percent of the RDA or the U.S. RDA. To review some of the material in Chapter 1, the term RDA stands for Recommended Dietary Allowances, and the term U.S. RDA – derived from the RDA for purposes of nutritional labeling only – stands for United States Recommended Daily Allowances. Consumption of a vitamin, counting all sources, in an amount that meets 100 percent of the RDA or U.S. RDA means that you have consumed the amount recommended for that day. When counting vitamins from all sources, remember to include those in your food plus those in any vitamin supplement that you may be taking. For example, if your food supplies 100 percent of the RDA on a given day and you also take a vitamin pill that supplies another 100 percent, you have obviously consumed 200 percent of the RDA. An intake of 200 percent of the RDA (or U.S. RDA) means that you have consumed several times the minimum amount that your body must have (remember that the RDA is set much higher than your "requirement") and twice the amount that is recommended. The excess beyond what your cells can actually use is wasted through excretion if you are lucky and may be hazardous to your cells if you are not.

Marketing strategies for vitamin supplements are frequently based on the possibility that for you, the magic number of 100 percent may instead be 597 percent, 983 percent, or 1,455 percent because of stress, pollution, cigarette smoking, modern food production and processing methods, or other reasons too numerous to mention here.

Let's take stress as an example. All of us are under stress to some degree, and all of us need vitamins. But it is incorrect to argue that stress increases the magic number to greater than 100 percent. The RDA are set high enough to meet the needs of healthy people, even during periods of stress. Scientists who do studies of nutrient requirements did and continue to do them in regard to people living in the real world. Stress, pollution, smoking, and modern methods of food production and processing all are considered when the RDAs are established. The rules are still the same, and the magic number is still 100 percent.[e]

[e] The RDAs are for healthy people and may not meet the needs of people who are ill. Some

The low cost of vitamins

In 1986, Americans who supplemented their diet with vitamins and minerals spent about $32 each, whereas they could have purchased a perfectly adequate one-a-day vitamin/mineral supplement for less than $10.[9] Those who consume a varied diet could have saved all of this money because they do not need such supplements. Those who still choose to buy supplements can save money by shopping carefully. As an aid in your comparison shopping, remember that the manufacturer must, by law, truthfully list on the label which vitamins and how much of each are present in each capsule or tablet. The quality and structure of the vitamins must be the same, regardless of the brand name. All you have to do is to read the label to compare various brands, especially to determine whether a brand meets 100 percent of the U.S. RDA for each of the five major vitamins.

The major vitamins for which it is most difficult to meet the RDA from food are vitamins A and C, thiamin, riboflavin, and niacin. Notice that these are the only vitamins whose adequacy we calculated (see Chapters 1 and 2). Vitamins K, E, and B_6 (also called pyridoxine), folic acid, pantothenic acid, and biotin are not of concern because they are present in copious amounts in a wide variety of foods and are needed in such small amounts that deficiencies are extremely unlikely. Vitamin D should be of concern only if fortified milk is not consumed and exposure to the sun is avoided for long periods. Vitamin B_{12} need be of concern only to vegetarians who do not eat any animal or fermented products.

Information about specific vitamins

We have already discussed vitamins generally. To emphasize that each vitamin has unique idiosyncracies and functions, we next shall talk about individual vitamins. Additional information about each vitamin is also presented in tabular form (Table 5.1). Deficiency symptoms are not included in the table because the occurrence of vitamin deficiencies in developed countries is rare. In addition, these symptoms are often so general (feeling tired, loss of appetite, rough or red skin, difficulty sleeping) that they happen to most of us at one time or another. Indeed, reading the list while experiencing some of these problems may encourage some people to supplement their diet unnecessarily.

diseases, including some inborn errors of metabolism, require treatment with vitamins in amounts greater than the RDA. People with such disorders should be under the close supervision of a physician.

Table 5.1. *Summary of vitamins in human health*

Vitamin	What it does for us	Food sources
Vitamin A (retinol)	Essential to vision. Maintains normal skin, bones, teeth, urinary tract, and lining of nervous, respiratory, and digestive systems. Essential to reproduction, lactation, and resistance to infection.	*Vitamin A:* liver, egg yolk, fish liver oils, butter, margarine, whole or fortified milk, cheese. *Carotene:* dark green leafy and yellow vegetables and fruits, especially carrots, greens, squash, sweet potatoes, pumpkin, cantaloupe, apricots.
B-complex Thiamin (vitamin B_1)	Essential to releasing energy from carbohydrates, proteins, fats, and alcohol. Important to fat and nucleic acid synthesis. Helps nervous system and heart function normally.	Pork, liver, organ meats, lean meat, fish, poultry, eggs, dried beans and peas, yeast, whole-grain and enriched breads and cereals, nuts, potatoes.
Riboflavin (vitamin B_2)	Essential to releasing energy from carbohydrates, proteins, fats, and alcohol. Essential to growth, repair of tissues, and healthy skin and eyes.	Milk, cheese, yogurt, organ meats, lean meat, eggs, whole-grain and enriched breads and cereals, green leafy vegetables.
Niacin (nicotinic acid)	Essential to releasing energy from carbohydrates, proteins, fats, and alcohol. Important to fat synthesis. Helps maintain healthy skin, nervous system, and digestive tract.	Milk, eggs, liver, lean meat, organ meats, fish, poultry, dried beans and peas, nuts, yeast, whole-grain and enriched breads and cereals.
Pyridoxine (vitamin B_6)	Essential to releasing energy from proteins and glycogen. Important to maintaining cellular immunity, forming red blood cells, and maintaining healthy teeth, nerves, and blood vessels.	Whole-grain breads and cereals, liver, meat, dried beans and peas, soybeans, nuts, yeast, wheat germ.
Pantothenic acid	Essential to releasing energy from carbohydrates, proteins, fats, and alcohol. Important to synthesis of cholesterol, steroid hormones, fat, and red blood cells.	All plants and animals; its name means "widespread." Eggs, liver, organ meats, salmon, whole-grain breads and cereals, nuts, dried beans and peas, yeast.

Table 5.1 (*cont.*)

Vitamin	What it does for us	Food sources
Biotin	Essential to releasing energy from carbohydrates, proteins, fats, and alcohol. Important to fat and cholesterol synthesis. Helps maintain healthy skin.	Eggs, liver, organ meats, meat, milk, nuts, whole-grain breads and cereals, most vegetables and fruits, yeast.
Folacin, folic acid, folate	Essential to synthesis of DNA, RNA, nucleic acids, and red blood cells. Prevents macrocytic anemia of pregnancy, of infancy, and of sprue. Corrects pernicious anemia but not nervous system lesions.	All foods, especially green leafy vegetables, liver, organ meats, meat, fish, poultry, dried beans and peas, whole-grain breads and cereals, fruits.
Cyanocobalamin (vitamin B_{12})	Essential to synthesis of DNA, RNA, nucleic acids, and red blood cells. Prevents and cures pernicious anemia and nervous system lesions.	Only foods of animal origin, such as liver, organ meats, meat, fish, poultry, eggs, milk, and cheese. Not found in foods of plant origin unless fortified or fermented, such as fermented soybean products.
Vitamin C (ascorbic acid)	Essential to healthy gums, teeth, bones, and blood vessels. Important to wound healing, resistance to infection, hormone synthesis, and iron absorption. Acts as an antioxidant in tissues.	Citrus fruits, liver, green leafy vegetables, potatoes, tomatoes, green peppers, cabbages, strawberries, guavas, papayas, currants.
Vitamin D (cholecalciferol, ergocalciferol)	Essential to normal formation and mineralization of bones and teeth. Important to absorption of calcium and phosphorus.	Fish liver oils, whole and fortified milk, cheese, butter, cream, eggs, liver, tuna, salmon, sardines.
Vitamin E (tocopherol)	Helps prevent oxidation of fatty acids in cell membranes and other tissues.	Vegetable oils, whole-grain breads and cereals, wheat germ, nuts, dried beans and peas, eggs, green plants, liver, meat, fish, margarine.

Table 5.1 (*cont.*)

Vitamin	What it does for us	Food sources
Vitamin K (phylloquinone, menaquinone)	Essential to normal blood clotting.	Green leafy vegetables, liver, whole-grain breads and cereals, vegetable oils, eggs, cheese, fish oil, wheat germ, cauliflower, tomatoes.

Vitamin A

Vitamin A deficiency is extremely rare in the United States now, but it did occur in earlier times, resulting in skin disorders and "nutritional croup" when membranes of the throat were affected. The fortification of milk and the increased availability of green and yellow vegetables throughout the year have made vitamin A deficiency almost nonexistent. Unfortunately, vitamin A deficiency is still common in many less developed countries, where it is a major cause of blindness, a condition that could be prevented by taking a few cents' worth of vitamin A per year.

Ironically, the most serious problem that we have with vitamin A in well-developed countries is not a deficiency of it but, instead, overconsumption to the point of causing toxicity.[10] Three erroneous concepts conspire to cause this problem. First, because a deficiency of vitamin A causes skin problems, some people assume that any skin problem can be treated by ingesting this vitamin. Second, many people believe that "if a little is good, a lot is a lot better." Third, it is assumed that anything "natural," like a vitamin, can cause no harm and may do some good.

The most common cause of vitamin A toxicity is its consumption as a self-prescribed treatment for a common problem of puberty – acne. It is never wise to self-treat for any medical problem, and because of the high probability of vitamin A toxicity, it is certainly not wise to take vitamin A in supplemental amounts in order to treat acne. Liver damage is worse than acne, whether or not adolescents believe this. In addition, vitamin A probably won't help acne anyway. There is a synthetic compound similar to vitamin A, called *cis-retinoic acid*, still undergoing study, that has been reported to help treat acne without causing vitamin A toxicity. If you are interested, ask your physician about it.

To become slowly poisoned by vitamin A, all you have to do is consume five to ten times the RDA each day for several weeks or months. Such excessive intake of vitamin A can cause irreparable liver damage, pseudotumor cerebri (similar to a water-filled brain tumor but not malignant), headaches, nosebleeds, skin rash, hair loss, nausea, vomiting, weakness, bone and joint pain, and, eventually, death.

The good news is that eating plants that contain large amounts of carotene does not cause vitamin A toxicity in humans because the amount that is converted to vitamin A is well regulated by the healthy body. The bad news is that if you eat enough carrots, you will begin to look like one. Your skin will turn as yellow as a canary because carotene is stored in the fat in your skin cells. Liver damage, which can occur after an excessive intake of vitamin A or because of diseases such as hepatitis, can be distinguished from excessive carotene consumption because liver damage causes the yellowing of both the skin and the white of the eye. Carotene consumption affects only the skin. Of course, vitamin A toxicity and *hypercarotenemia* ("hyper" meaning excessive and "emia" meaning blood, therefore excessive carotene in the blood) may certainly occur together if one eats a large amount of carotene-containing foods daily and also supplements the diet with vitamin A.

Vitamin B Complex

Vitamin B complex, once thought to be only a single vitamin, is really a combination of eight vitamins: thiamin (B_1), riboflavin (B_2), niacin, pyridoxine (B_6), cyanocobalamin (B_{12}), folic acid, biotin, and pantothenic acid. In the early years of this century, deficiencies of two of these, thiamin and niacin, prompted the investigation of the role of diet in preventing some diseases and, ultimately, led to the discovery of all of the vitamins. In fact, the word *vitamin* was coined because of the chemical properties of thiamin. After thiamin was discovered in rice hulls, investigation of its chemical properties indicated that it belonged to a nitrogen-containing class of chemicals called *amines*. Because this "amine" was "vital" to life, a Polish chemist named Casimir Funk proposed that this and similar substances be called *vitamines*. The name, proposed in 1912, stuck until it became apparent that all "vitamines" were not chemically "amines." The final "e" was dropped, and the word vitamin entered our vocabulary for the first time in 1920.

The B-complex vitamins are needed in every cell of the body in order to make coenzymes. In general, the number and size of cells in an adult's body does not change from day to day; thus you have about the same total number of cells today as you did yesterday. The minimum amount of each of the B-complex vitamins that you need to consume daily is equal to the amount that is lost by means of excretion or chemical destruction. If you continually consume less than this amount, your cells will eventually become depleted.

The RDA for some of the B-complex vitamins are calculated on the basis of caloric need, the reason being that caloric need is proportional to body size. Thus, in general, the larger you are, the more calories and B-complex vitamins you will need.

When muscle mass increases, as it does during the growth spurts of children and adolescents and even adults undergoing weight training, additional B-complex vitamins are needed to stock this new tissue with coenzymes. At the same time, additional caloric and protein intake is required. Parents of active teenagers often conclude that they could sell the family refrigerator because food does not stay in the house long enough to spoil. The active and sports-minded person can be assured that if the additional caloric and protein needs are satisfied by the consumption of a variety of foods, higher vitamin needs will automatically be met.

Generally, members of the B-complex family are not toxic when taken in amounts a few times greater than the RDA. The amounts of B vitamins in "stress" and "high-potency" formulas are thus a greater threat to your economic health than to your physiological health. However, these amounts can interfere with the action of some drugs that you may be taking. For example, supplemental folic acid antagonizes the protective effect of anticonvulsive drugs in patients who have seizures. If you are taking any prescribed medications and if you also are taking vitamin supplements, it is wise to discuss your vitamin usage with your physician.

A more serious problem is the consumption of massive amounts of some of the B-complex vitamins. For example, gram amounts of niacin, representing two hundred times or more of the RDA, are recommended by some people to treat or prevent any number of disorders. There is no scientific basis for most of these claims, and worse, such self-treatment is dangerous. In large amounts, niacin acts like a drug and causes an increase in blood pressure, nervousness, itching of the skin, tingling of the hands and feet, flushing (characterized by a very red face and a feeling of being hot), and possibly cardiac arrhythmias. The prolonged consumption of such large amounts of niacin can cause goutlike arthritis, peptic ulcers, and liver damage. If high doses of niacin are prescribed by a physician, it is only prudent to ask about the side effects. (See Chapter 14 for treatment of high blood cholesterol levels with niacin.)

The same is true of large amounts of vitamin B_6. High doses are sometimes urged for women taking oral contraceptives and for the treatment of premenstrual syndrome, but such claims are unfounded. Massive doses of vitamin B_6 cause sleepiness, and prolonged consumption can result in liver damage. Further, the continual consumption of high doses can lead to deficiency symptoms if the intake of these large amounts is suddenly stopped.

There are toxic effects associated with very high levels of consumption of most of the other members of the B-complex family. To reiterate an important point, when massive doses of vitamins are consumed, the excess – over and above that used for normal needs – acts like a drug. Self-treatment with any drug, especially those whose side effects are unknown to you, is never wise.

Vitamin C

The chemical name for vitamin C is *ascorbic acid*, and the only known disease that it prevents, and cures, is *scurvy*. The vitamin was once and occasionally still is called the "antiscorbutic" factor ("scorbutic" meaning scurvy in Latin). Scurvy is virtually unknown in developed countries because vitamin C is fairly widely distributed in nature, and only a very small amount is needed to prevent the disease.

Studies have shown that as little as 5 to 15 milligrams of vitamin C each day is all that is needed to prevent scurvy. To illustrate how small an amount this is, consider that this is the quantity in either 2 tablespoons of orange or other citrus juice, 1 small tomato, ½ a medium-sized baked potato, 2 large strawberries, 1 medium spear of cooked broccoli, 1½ ounces of baked liver, 1 large raw apple, 1 medium banana, or ¾ cup raw cherries. Even though this small amount of vitamin C will prevent scurvy, the RDA is set at 60 milligrams daily so as to provide a margin of safety.

Some people have argued that stress and smoking may increase the need for vitamin C. If stress increases the requirement at all, it is small and is surely met by the margin of safety included in the RDA. Although some studies have suggested that smoking may substantially increase the need for vitamin C, other studies indicate that if there is an increased need, it is minimal.[11]

If you compare the RDA for each vitamin, it is apparent that vitamin C is needed in the greatest amount. In fact, the RDA for vitamin C is twenty thousand times that for vitamin B_{12}. The reason for this is that unlike most vitamins, vitamin C is "used up" doing its job. Even so, the amount needed to perform its function is relatively small compared with our intake when a variety of foods are consumed.

The assertion that vitamin C can prevent and/or cure the common cold was made popular by a book by Linus Pauling.[12] Since then, there have been numerous scientific studies showing that when experiments included proper controls, vitamin C had no effect on the development or course of colds.[13] Still, there are people who swear that taking large doses of vitamin C makes them "feel better," but this is most likely attributable to the placebo[f] effect. That is, the difference disappears when studies are con-

[f] The medical definition of placebo (pronounced pla-see-bo) is "any harmless substance given

ducted under conditions in which only a third party, and neither the subject nor the investigator, knows whether the subject was receiving vitamin C or a placebo. The assertion that vitamin C cures cancer has also been successfully refuted by controlled scientific studies.[14] In the absence of data indicating benefit, the issue is whether the ingestion of the amounts recommended, ranging from 1 to 40 grams per day, is safe. The answer for most of us is no.

The short-term effects of consuming a large dose of vitamin C may be uncomfortable but are not likely to be life threatening. Common effects include diarrhea, nausea, and abdominal pain. For those undergoing medical tests, the side effects can be more serious, because excess dietary vitamin C can result in false positive laboratory test results for glucose in blood and urine and a false negative test for blood in feces.

For some segments of our population, however, large doses of vitamin C (ten times the RDA) can be life threatening. For example, in patients with sickle-cell anemia (common in blacks), taking massive amounts of vitamin C can cause a sickle-cell crisis. For approximately 13 percent of American blacks and an even larger percentage of Sephardic Jews, Asians, and other ethnic groups who have a different congenital enzyme deficiency, a high vitamin C intake can cause severe hemolytic anemia and death. For all of us, an extremely excessive intake of vitamin C, if continued over a period of time, can cause kidney stones and kidney failure, precipitate gout, and result in anemia. Ironically, taking large doses of vitamin C can cause, of all things, scurvy if the excessive intake is suddenly stopped. The reason is that the destruction and excretion systems for ridding the body of excess vitamin C increase when massive doses are consumed. Because the excretion system is maintained for a few days even after the massive intake is discontinued, the body's stores of vitamin C become depleted, and this results in "rebound scurvy." Anyone taking massive doses of vitamin C should therefore taper off, that is, reduce the amount of intake by one-half each week until it is below 250 milligrams per day. Then the intake of supplementary vitamin C can be safely discontinued so that foods, not pills, supply the body's need for the vitamin.

Vitamin D

Before World War II, vitamin D deficiency was common in the United States. In fact, it has been suggested that the supplementation of milk with vitamin D was a necessary prerequisite to the popularity of miniskirts and shorts in the 1960s. Before vitamin D supplementation, almost everyone – and particularly those living in northern climates with long periods of

to humor a patient or as a test in controlled experiments on the effects of drugs." Translation: a substance that will not work unless the patient thinks it will.

limited sunshine – had experienced a deficiency of it. The disease caused by a lack of vitamin D in the young is called *rickets* and results in the legs being permanently bowed like those of a Hollywood cowboy.

Vitamin D is involved with calcium in several different ways and is therefore essential to the development of healthy bones and teeth. Vitamin D is unique because it can be made in the skin from cholesterol when the skin is exposed to ultraviolet light from the sun. If this source of vitamin D is insufficient to meet our needs,[g] vitamin D will have to be incorporated into our diet. From either source, it must undergo chemical modification, first in the liver and then in the kidneys, before it can do its job. Its job, in part, is to regulate the amount of calcium absorbed from the diet, the amount deposited in teeth and bone, and the amount excreted in urine.

Naturally occurring vitamin D in fish-liver oils is the same compound as the synthetic one used to fortify milk. Unless a person is never exposed to sunlight; is unable to consume milk, milk products, or fish-liver oils; and has a vitamin D deficiency, taking vitamin D supplements is unwise, owing to its high degree of toxicity.

Unlike vitamin C, vitamin D is not found in large amounts in many foods. This is fortunate because if it were, it would be easy to get too much of a good thing, and the safety range for vitamin D is very small. The RDA is 400 international units (10 micrograms of cholecalciferol) for an adult male, and it can be toxic at levels above 800 international units. The effects on bone of too much vitamin D are surprisingly similar to those of too little. Too much or too little vitamin D results in bone softening. In the case of vitamin D toxicity, calcium is removed from bone and deposited in soft tissue, where it normally belongs in very small amounts. This unwanted soft tissue deposition can result in arthritislike pain and kidney damage.

Vitamin K

Vitamin K is essential to blood clotting and got its name from the German word for coagulation (*koagulation*). Deficiencies of this vitamin are rare, occurring mainly in people who have had long-term difficulty absorbing fat. Most of us need only a small amount of vitamin K, and it is widely distributed in nature. Further, we can absorb some of the vitamin K that is produced by bacteria in our digestive tract.

Physicians sometimes give vitamin K to women before childbirth, to prevent bleeding in the newborn baby, but self-treatment with supple-

---

[g] The amount of vitamin D formed by the interaction of ultraviolet (UV) light with the skin depends on several factors. Heavily pigmented skin can limit the penetration of UV light and therefore reduce the synthesis of vitamin D. Cloudy skies and air pollution, which absorb UV light, also cut down the amount formed in the skin.

mental vitamin K is unwise. Like vitamins A and D, large amounts of vitamin K can be dangerous. Excessive consumption has been reported to cause anemia. More important, vitamin K can interfere with medications such as anticoagulants.

Vitamin E

We have saved vitamin E for last because we want to give it special attention, in order to save at least a smidgen of its besmirched reputation. Vitamin E is by far the most abused, confused, and misused vitamin known to humankind.

The reputation of vitamin E was first sullied at the time of its discovery. The first mistake was that one of the symptoms of vitamin E deficiency in mice and rats was that the males became sterile. Vitamin E thereafter became known as "the antisterility vitamin." This was unfortunate because mice and rats, it turned out, were the only animals to suffer such a fate. No evidence has ever turned up that a lack of vitamin E can cause sterility in humans or any other animals.

As if it were not bad enough to be called an antisterility vitamin, the word *sterility* became confused with the word *virility*, and vitamin E gained the unwarranted reputation of being an aphrodisiac. Vitamin E has been the darling of the impotent and semi-impotent ever since. Being an aphrodisiac puts it in the same class as powdered rhinoceros horn and ginseng root, hardly fitting company for a self-respecting vitamin. In fact, vitamin E can make no claim to being even remotely connected to sex drive on the basis of evidence – discounting, of course, the possible placebo effect. The real function of vitamin E – a member of a family of chemicals called *tocopherols* – is to prevent fat in the body from being attacked by oxygen. It does this, basically, by being so chemically vulnerable that oxygen attacks the vitamin E instead of the fat. Vitamin E is destroyed by the unprovoked attack of oxygen, and the product is then excreted. Fortunately, this does not happen very often. Our vitamin E requirement is therefore very small, and the substance is widely distributed in foods.

Vitamin E's reputation of being an "antioxidant" led to another misuse of it: It is added to deodorants and is widely distributed among the armpits of the world. The theory, we presume, is that when unsaturated fatty acids – which may be present in sweat and/or bacteria that reside under the arm – are attacked by oxygen, the products smell bad. It was reasoned that if vitamin E were present, the oxygen would attack it instead of the unsaturated fatty acids, but alas, when vitamin E is attacked by oxygen, it smells, too. Not only that, the vitamin E is soon used up, and oxygen is again free to attack the fatty acids.

For unstated reasons, vitamin E can also be found residing in body lotions for beautifying the skin and in ointments for burns, bruises, and abrasions. In all of these cases, if vitamin E has any benefit, it is because it is an oil. (Oils are not, however, usually recommended for first-aid treatment of traumas to the skin. Check a good first-aid book or with your physician.) One thing that you can bet on is that the vitamin E in these products is not functioning as a vitamin. In fact, because vitamins function as vitamins only inside cells and because the prescribed way of getting them to that site is via the intestinal mucosal cells and blood, the external application of vitamins to perform the function of vitamins makes no sense. Such a practice is analogous to taping an aspirin to your forehead when you have a headache.

The continual consumption of too much vitamin E does have unwanted side effects. These include vision problems, because vitamin E can interfere with the actions of vitamin A, and bleeding problems, because vitamin E can interfere with the action of vitamin K. In addition, an excessive consumption of vitamin E can cause headaches, nausea, tiredness, giddiness, and inflammation of the mouth. With all of these possible side effects, why would any one want to take this substance in large quantities? The answer is that it has been claimed as an aphrodisiac, as discussed, and also to cure or prevent any number of human conditions, including aging. But that is another story, and we've saved it for Chapter 12.

6   Minerals

Sometime in the dim distant past, our ancestors decided that all physical things in their world could be placed in one of two classifications: living and nonliving. Later scholars refined this primitive classification system by coining the word *organic* to describe things that were currently living or had lived and using the word *inorganic* to describe those things that had never lived. Eventually, the realization that living things were composed primarily of chemicals containing carbon led to the use of the word organic to describe carbon-containing chemicals (with a few exceptions like carbonate) and the use of the word inorganic to describe all other chemicals. It probably came as a surprise to early chemists to find that the remains of living things contained not only organic chemicals but inorganic ones as well. The inorganic chemicals are called *minerals*.

What's really in Uncle Edgar's ash urn?

We are told that in some circles it was at one time popular to remember the dearly departed by placing their cremated remains in an "ash" urn, which was given a place of honor on the fireplace mantle. Children who mustered enough courage to look in the urn may have imagined seeing Uncle Edgar's ghost, but what they actually saw was a light gray powder, representing the minerals that Uncle Edgar's cells had hoarded during his life. Obviously, because our bodies cannot make minerals, any present in Uncle Edgar's cells must have come from his diet.

The reason that only minerals are present in the urn is that when the body is subjected to an extremely high temperature, as in cremation, the organic compounds either volatilize and escape as gases or react with oxygen to form carbon dioxide. Water is lost as steam.

The human body is 3 to 4 percent minerals by weight. Thus, if Uncle Edgar had been an average-sized man of 155 pounds (men were smaller in those days), his ashes would have weighed about 5 pounds – enough to fill a shoe box or a respectable-sized urn. The major minerals by weight in the body are (in order of highest to lowest amount present): calcium, phosphorus, potassium, sulfur, chloride, sodium, magnesium, iron, zinc, and iodide. These minerals are the ones found in the body in the largest amounts, but as we shall see, they are not the only minerals essential to life. Of all the minerals known, only a relatively small number have been confirmed as being necessary to support human life. A few of the others have a bad habit of killing people.

Minerals

Nutritionists classify the minerals that the body requires for life as either *macrominerals* ("macro" meaning large) or *microminerals* ("micro" meaning small). This classification has nothing to do with the sizes of the mineral molecules, their essentiality, or their functions. Each mineral in both classes is essential, and each has its own indispensable functions. Rather, the classification is based on the amount of the mineral required by the body. Macrominerals are required in the diet in relatively large amounts, whereas microminerals are needed in very small quantities. In fact, microminerals are also called *trace minerals* because we need to consume only a trace amount of them. Table 6.1 lists the macrominerals and trace minerals required in our diet, their known functions in the human body, and the most commonly consumed foods that supply our needs. Other minerals that occur in the body as environmental contaminants – such as cadmium, lead, mercury, arsenic, boron, lithium, and aluminum – have no known function essential to the life of humans.

What do minerals do?

There are more functions of minerals in the body than there are minerals. Minerals, in fact, are so busy that many serve dual (or even triple) roles. As expected, minerals, like vitamins, were often misunderstood when first discovered. An example of such misunderstanding led to the expression that fish are "brain food."[1] This expression came from the discovery that certain phosphorus-containing compounds are abundant in the brain. From this observation, a German physiologist stated: "*Ohne Phosphor, kein Gedanke*," which translated means "Without phosphorus, no thought." Professor Louis Agassiz, a chemist at Harvard University, connected this idea to the fact that fish contain considerable phosphorus, and he urged in a speech that fish be eaten for the benefit of the brain, to say nothing of the benefit to the Fish Commission in Massachusetts which, perhaps coincidentally, sponsored his lecture. This erroneous concept probably would have died with the members of the audience that heard the speech, except that Mark Twain spread the idea far and wide by making fun of it in *Galaxy*,[2] in which he suggested that "he knew a few people who might

Table 6.1. *Summary of minerals in human health*

Mineral	What it does for our health	Food sources
Macrominerals		
Calcium	Major mineral in bone, vertebrae, and teeth. Essential to muscle contraction, nerve irritability, and blood coagulation. Activator for some enzymes.	Milk, cheese, yogurt, cottage cheese, some dark green vegetables, sardines, salmon, oysters, shrimp, clams.
Phosphorus	Major mineral in bone and teeth. Essential to energy production and normal acid–base balance. Component of DNA, RNA, nucleic acids, and several enzymes.	Milk, cheese, meat, eggs, poultry, fish, nuts, legumes, breads, cereals, carbonated beverages with phosphoric acid.
Magnesium	Component of bone and teeth. Activator for enzyme systems in energy production. Essential to protein synthesis, water and mineral balance, muscle contraction, and nerve function.	All vegetables, whole grains and cereals, nuts, legumes, meat, seafood, milk, seeds.
Sodium	Essential to all body cells and fluid spaces for enzyme activity, nerve function, and muscle contraction. Regulates water and mineral balance.	Table salt, seasoning salts, cured meats, salted snack foods, most processed foods.
Potassium	Essential to all body cells and fluid spaces for enzyme activity. Regulates water and mineral balance.	All fruits, all vegetables, legumes, meat, cereals.
Chloride	Component of gastric juices. Essential to acid–base balance and red blood cell uptake of oxygen and release of carbon dioxide.	Table salt, meat, fish, poultry.
Microminerals		
Iron	Essential part of hemoglobin, myoglobin, and all cells. Carries oxygen in blood. Needed in energy production.	Liver, eggs, meat, dried fruits, legumes, enriched and whole-grain breads and cereals, dark green leafy vegetables, blackstrap molasses.

Table 6.1 (*cont.*)

Mineral	What it does for our health	Food sources
Iodide	Essential part of thyroid hormones that influence basal metabolic rate. Needed for growth, maturation, and nerve function. Prevents goiter.	Iodized salt, seafood, fish, marine oils, commercially baked breads.
Zinc	Essential part of insulin and several enzymes involved in alcohol metabolism, protein digestion and synthesis, acid–base balance, immunity, vitamin A utilization, and taste acuity.	Shellfish, seafood, liver, meat, nuts, legumes, milk and milk products, eggs, whole-grain breads and cereals, oatmeal, corn, wheat germ.
Copper	Essential to red blood cell synthesis, iron utilization, bone formation, nerve function, and energy production. Part of many enzymes.	Liver, organ meats, shellfish, nuts, legumes, cocoa, whole-grain breads and cereals, dried fruits.
Manganese	Essential part of some enzymes in energy production, cholesterol synthesis, bone growth, and glucose utilization.	Whole-grain breads and cereals, nuts, legumes, leafy vegetables, cloves, tea.
Chromium	Works with insulin to regulate blood glucose.	Whole-grain breads and cereals, meat, seafood, cheese, dried beans and peas, brown sugar, bran, yeast.
Fluoride	Helps resist dental caries and bone demineralization.	Fluoridated water, fish, tea.
Selenium	Component of myoglobin and muscle. Important to energy production and nucleic acid synthesis. Acts with vitamin E as nonspecific antioxidant to protect cell membranes and tissues.	Whole-grain breads and cereals, onions, organ meats, eggs, seafood, cabbages, and yeast. Vegetable content depends on soil's selenium content.
Molybdenum	Essential to nucleic acid breakdown.	Meat, grains, and legumes. Food content depends on soil's molybdenum content.

benefit by the consumption of two, middling-sized, whales." Unfortunately, the humor has been forgotten, but people still remember and quote the expression of the Harvard chemist.

Actually no one has ever demonstrated that brain power can be limited or enhanced by taking phosphorus, but phosphorus is nonetheless essential to life. Phosphorus, in the form of phosphate or its chemical derivatives, functions in all cells of the body, including those of the brain. Most of the phosphate in the body, however, is in the bones and teeth, where its abundance is second only to that of calcium. Without these two minerals, our bones would be like the cartilage in infants, and we would resemble rag dolls.

Other minerals, like sodium, potassium, and chloride, function to maintain the balance of minerals and water (fluid and electrolytes) as well as the proper acidity of our blood and cells. Several other minerals work with enzymes and coenzymes, described in the previous chapter, to help speed up chemical reactions. Finally, some minerals are important as constituents of other compounds, such as iron in hemoglobin, cobalt in cyanocobalamin (hence the often-shortened name *cobalamin* for vitamin B_{12}), zinc in insulin, and iodine in thyroid hormone.

Minerals given public attention, past and present

It seems to be a part of humans' nature to have a relatively short attention span. Minerals that were featured in the media and advertisements yesterday have virtually disappeared from public attention today. Calcium is currently a popular mineral. Before that it was zinc, and before that, iron. Fluoride preceded iron, and iodide was perhaps the first mineral to be given such attention. Salt (sodium chloride) has also had its share of publicity over the last several years, not because of too little, but because of, by some standards, too much. This fickleness has nothing to do with changes in our physiological needs, but it is a measure of our focus of attention. Let's look at the importance of these minerals to our health.

Calcium

Calcium is the center of attention now because of the discovery that some people, especially postmenopausal women, may develop a serious medical problem: the loss of calcium from bone. This disease is called *osteoporosis* ("osteo" meaning bone, "porosis" meaning porous).

Although we think of calcium as a necessary constituent of bones and teeth because most of it in the body is located in these tissues, calcium has another important function as a regulator of metabolism. The significance of this role is illustrated by the fact that the blood calcium level is carefully controlled, and an increase or decrease of more than 10 percent from normal can cause death. We don't have to worry consciously about the calcium concentration in our blood because it is automatically regulated by the interplay of hormones and vitamin D. What we do have to worry about is that if the concentration in blood begins to drop, calcium is pulled out of bone to maintain the critical blood level. This weakens bones and causes them to break more easily – especially during our later years. It is also the reason for compressed vertebrae that cause us to become bent over as we age.

Attempts to slow the removal of calcium from bone after the symptoms of osteoporosis have appeared have been met with such limited success that it is somewhat analogous to locking the barn door after the horse has been stolen. The solution is prevention, and the best way that we know to minimize the problem in old age is to enter the "golden years" with "high-density" bone. High-density bone has more calcium than does low-density bone. Because genetics is a major factor in determining bone density, the most effective way of ensuring highly dense bone is to inherit the right genes. This option is, of course, not now available to us, but other factors, including diet, may help.

There are complex interrelationships among bone, blood, and dietary calcium. If our intake of calcium is habitually low, we will absorb a greater percentage of it from the gastrointestinal tract and excrete less in the urine. However, the mineral will likely still be removed from bone storage in order to maintain blood levels. Thus, an inadequate intake of calcium during early life may cause problems in later years.

The consumption of more calcium than the RDA of 800 milligrams per day for adults has generally not been shown to be of value in preventing osteoporosis,[3] although the question of whether or not a higher intake of calcium can increase bone density is not easily answered.[4] Part of the reason for this is that as calcium consumption rises above the RDA, its absorption declines, so that very little of the extra actually gets into the body.[5] Although unabsorbed calcium remaining in the GI tract can interfere with the absorption of other minerals, especially iron and zinc, part of what does enter the blood is excreted in the urine and can lead to the formation of kidney stones in some people. These potentially negative consequences of excess calcium intake must be weighed against the possibility, still unproven, that at least a small amount of the excess that is absorbed will find its way into bone, thereby increasing bone density. As an upper limit, calcium intake amounting to more than twice the RDA is not recommended.[6]

Calcium is generally more often absorbable from animal sources, especially milk and milk products, than from plant sources. For example, green leafy vegetables contain a considerable amount of calcium, but they also contain oxalate, an organic chemical that interferes with calcium absorption. The RDA for calcium takes into account the low availability of much of the calcium in food.[7]

For people who are unable to consume foods high in calcium, calcium supplements may be advisable. Of the several types available, calcium carbonate supplements provide the highest percentage of calcium, by weight. Most of the preparations are about equally absorbable. Calcium supplements in the form of antacids or as calcium carbonate, however, can make the upper small intestine so alkaline that it can interfere with calcium absorption as well as the absorption of iron and other trace minerals. The repeated consumption of such supplements can thus lead to iron-deficiency anemia. Such interference does not seem to occur, however, when the same quantity of calcium is obtained from milk and milk products. Some calcium supplements are less desirable choices because they may be contaminated with toxic metals; these include dolomite, bone meal, and calcium phosphate preparations. Many people become constipated when they take calcium in pill form. If this happens to you, we advise you not to eat more fiber to try to overcome the problem. Fiber will not only decrease the amount of calcium absorbed but can also result in small bowel obstruction if too much is consumed. Instead, drink more fluids and exercise more, limit your calcium supplement to no more than the RDA, and take any pills with meals.

Zinc

Misinformation about zinc is as plentiful as the mineral itself. Zinc deficiency, however, has been reported to occur in humans in the Middle East, in which chemicals naturally present in the foods normally consumed bind zinc and prevent its absorption. The deficiency symptoms include dwarfism and limited growth of male reproductive organs. Although there are regions in the United States where zinc supplements added to the feed of young growing animals have been found to be beneficial to their growth, the need for supplemental zinc in human diets is much less clear.

Zinc is present in a variety of foods (see Table 6.1), but it, like most other minerals, is more often absorbable from animal than plant sources. Because the best sources of available zinc (meat, milk, milk products, and eggs) are relatively more expensive than other foods are, it is perhaps not surprising that a zinc deficiency is more likely in low-income families. There have been some reports that young children from low-income families may benefit from additional dietary zinc.[8] At the same time, zinc supplementation for a vegan diet may be needed, especially for children. On the other hand, it is highly unlikely that zinc supplements are needed for anyone consuming a varied diet that meets the recommended servings of the four food groups (see Chapter 1).

It has been popular to advertise zinc supplements as a cure for stress, but there is no evidence to support such a claim. Several other claims have also been made for the wonders of zinc that are not supported by the evidence. You may be surprised to learn that

> Zinc cannot help the elderly improve their appetite unless they have an underlying zinc deficiency.
> Zinc supplementation cannot increase the rate of wound healing unless a zinc deficiency is present.
> Zinc is not an aphrodisiac, and it cannot cure sexual dysfunction.
> Zinc cannot prevent or cure baldness.

Zinc can be toxic when consumed in large amounts. The symptoms of toxicity include loss of appetite, nausea, vomiting, diarrhea, dizziness, muscle pain, lethargy, and bleeding gastric ulcers. Zinc supplementation at levels well above the RDA, in addition to wasting money, can interfere with the absorption of other trace minerals such as copper. In fact, a case of zinc-induced copper deficiency inappropriately diagnosed as preleukemia has been reported.[9] Thus, if you decide to take a supplement containing zinc, it is best to consume only the equivalent of the RDA, about 15 milligrams per day for adults.

Iron

Which, if any, of the following statements is true?

> "I'm tired after I exercise; I must have sports anemia. I need an iron supplement."
> "I need more iron in order to 'pump iron' in weight lifting."
> "I don't need iron now that I've gone through menopause."
> "I'm a vegetarian, and so I can't get enough iron from food."
> "I get more iron in my diet when I cook with cast-iron skillets."

The correct answer is none of the above. These commonly made statements represent misinformation about iron.

We normally think of iron in connection with blood, and it is an important constituent of red blood cells because it is a part of hemoglobin, the red pigment that carries oxygen. Iron also is present in virtually all other cells of the body.

All of us have a need for dietary iron, although the amount that we need varies throughout life. Because we need iron to make new cells, especially red blood cells, we need the most (1) when we are growing the fastest (in utero, from birth to age 2 years, during early childhood, and during adolescence) and (2) when we are making a lot of red blood cells because of a loss of blood (during menstruation or after a blood donation).

The common anemias of pregnancy, infancy, childhood, and adolescence attest to these periods of increased iron need.

Participation in sports that require heavy, strenuous physical activity may result in a condition commonly termed *sports anemia*. This condition is not a true anemia, but it is characterized by lower than normal hemoglobin and hematocrit levels despite normal iron stores. The condition does not seem to interfere with athletic performance, and it is not the cause of fatigue or "hitting the wall," which are due to a lack of energy. Because sports anemia is not a true anemia, iron supplementation is therefore not an appropriate therapy.[10]

Athletes should have a complete physical examination, including a blood test to measure iron and iron stores, before athletic training and yearly during their active years. These tests reveal the athlete's iron status, and only if iron stores are low should iron be supplemented. It is not wise to take iron supplements without such tests in the belief that extra iron is needed to make "muscle of iron."

Middle-aged and elderly adults still require iron in the diet because red blood cells do not live forever. Our bodies are constantly breaking down old red blood cells and making new ones. Even though most of the iron is conserved when old red blood cells are destroyed, some iron is nonetheless lost and must be replaced from dietary sources.

The absorption of iron into intestinal mucosal cells is, fortunately, carefully controlled, as too much or too little absorption can have deleterious effects. In general, our absorption of iron is not very good. On the average, we absorb about 10 percent of the iron we ingest, although the organic iron in animal tissue (especially red meat), called *heme-iron*, is better absorbed. The RDA has been adjusted to take poor absorption into account.

Several naturally occurring chemicals in plants decrease our absorption of iron. For example, whole-grain breads and cereals (containing phytate), leafy green vegetables (containing oxalate), cola beverages and milk (containing phosphate), and tea (containing tannin) hamper the absorption of iron when consumed at the same time as high iron-containing foods. On the other hand, when vitamin C and acid-containing foods such as fruits and fruit juices are consumed at the same meal with foods high in iron, they improve the absorption of iron.

Vegetarians who eliminate excellent sources of iron such as eggs, fish, poultry, or other meats and meat products from their diets may, but not necessarily, have difficulty obtaining enough absorbable iron. When vegetarians eat vegetables, nuts, and legumes high in iron, they should also eat fruits or drink fruit juices at the same meal. Despite advertisements to the contrary, cast-iron skillets are not a good source of dietary iron, and so cooking with them in hopes of leaching iron into food is merely wishful thinking.

If an inadequate amount of iron is consumed or absorbed, iron-deficiency anemia can result. The best test for iron status is to measure the amount of iron in blood bound to its transporting protein, called *transferrin* (usually expressed as *TIBC*). Iron status can also be measured by determining the quantity of its storage protein, called *ferritin*. If tests of blood drawn by your physician indicate high levels of TIBC or low levels of ferritin, then iron supplementation is appropriate.

Self-treatment with iron at any stage of life (even during the reproductive years) without your physician's advice and without proper blood testing is unwise because the absorption of large amounts of iron over time can be toxic to the liver, spleen, and other organs. And large amounts of unabsorbed iron may cause constipation. Different people absorb iron at different rates, because of many factors. Even if advertisements for iron supplements seem to describe your situation perfectly, check out your iron stores with your physician before taking supplements. We cannot stress too much that iron can be dangerous when too much is consumed! You will not know if this is happening until the damage has been done. Without proper iron testing, you cannot correctly determine whether or not you need iron supplementation.

Fluoride

The discovery of the protective effects of fluoride against dental cavities was made from an experiment performed by nature. Many areas in the southwestern portion of the United States have a relatively high concentration of fluoride in the soil, and therefore the water consumed in this region contains high amounts of fluoride. One result of excessive fluoride consumption is mottled teeth, which is a cosmetic disadvantage, but an advantageous result is the virtual absence of dental cavities. Such a finding eventually led to the addition of small amounts of fluoride to the drinking water of many communities throughout the United States.

Opponents to the fluoridation of water were very vocal in many cities, their objections ranging from political to physiological.[11] Politically, the opponents saw the fluoridation of a municipal water supply as a form of socialized medicine, whereas the proponents saw it as responsible public health policy. A physiological objection by opponents was the assertion that fluoride caused cancer, but there has never been the least amount of evidence that this charge is valid. The charge that fluoride is toxic is a more serious charge because it is true – if you consume too much of it.

The amount of fluoride added to drinking water is the quantity that will provide a final concentration of one part per million. The amount is equivalent to the addition of 1 teaspoon of fluoride to about 1,250 gallons of water. At this level of fluoride in water, the intake of fluoride by adults from the water, and the food prepared with it, is about 2 to 4 milligrams per day, which is considered a safe and adequate amount. A chronic intake of 20 milligrams per day can lead to toxic effects. Notice that the safety factor (the amount that is toxic divided by the amount usually consumed) is 5 to 10. The charge by antifluoridation forces that when water is boiled the fluoride is concentrated is true, but this does not tell the whole story. In order for this to become a problem, one would have to boil routinely a gallon of water long enough to reduce it to a pint and then use this concentrated water as the sole source for drinking and preparing food.

Fortunately for our teeth, the antifluoridation forces lost the battle in most areas.[12] As a result of fluoridating drinking water, fluoride toothpastes, and fluoride application by dentists, the incidence of dental cavities today is only a small fraction of what it was only a few years ago.[13] Another likely benefit from increased fluoride consumption, a decrease in osteoporosis, may not become apparent for several more years. The reason for this is that fluoride is deposited not only in the teeth to harden them but also in bone. Thus, there is reason to believe that as the generation that grew up drinking fluoridated water ages, the loss of bone calcium may be slowed.

Iodide

Iodide is often erroneously called *iodine*, but there is a major difference between the two. Iodine is an element, and iodide is the salt of that element. Iodine is often used as an antiseptic for minor cuts and abrasions on the skin and, as the bottle says, is for external use only. The salt, iodide, is the form needed in our diet. At one time, the iodide deficiency disease, goiter, was common in those parts of the United States where soils contained inadequate amounts of this mineral. Now, unless it can be attributed to some other medical problem, goiter has virtually disappeared because of the widespread use of iodized salt. Interestingly, because iodized salt is such an important dietary source of iodide for many of us, the practice of ingesting less salt in an effort to prevent high blood pressure may bring goiter back into vogue again.

Iodide did make the news in recent years, not because of a deficiency of it, but because of a surplus. An excess of iodide, like an iodide deficiency, has the effect of increasing the size of the thyroid gland, located in the neck. When the disaster at the Chernobyl nuclear power plant in the Soviet Union occurred in 1986, one of the radioactive products released was radioactive iodine. Because iodine, converted to iodide, is concentrated in the thyroid gland, radioactive iodide can produce thyroid cancer. Some measure of protection can be achieved by consuming nonradioactive iodide, which competes with the radioactive form for absorption and storage. Thus, when radioactive iodine was detected in rainwater in the Pacific Northwest, some people started taking iodide tablets to give them protection. However, the amount of radioactive iodine was so small that it was unlikely a health hazard, and public health officials warned that taking excessive iodide was much more likely to cause a problem than was the radioactivity. The moral of the story, as always, is that supplements should be taken in moderation and only if there is adequate reason to justify a need.

Salt: Sodium and chloride

The substance commonly called salt or table salt provides two minerals, sodium and chloride, both of which are essential to our survival. Sodium is the most abundant mineral in the blood and fluids surrounding each cell in the body. Without it, it would be impossible to live because sodium, working with potassium, creates an optimal chemical environment for all the body's vital processes within and around cells. Small changes outside the normal range of sodium or potassium prevent enzymes from functioning properly. If vital enzyme processes are not carried out, cells will die within minutes, and death will quickly follow.

Because sodium is such a critical nutrient, our body has numerous control systems to regulate its concentration. If we ingest and absorb more sodium than we need, our kidneys normally will excrete the excess. If we do not ingest enough sodium, we have mechanisms to conserve as much as possible. The amount of sodium lost from the body, which must be replaced by dietary sources, varies widely. For most adults most of the time, an intake of sodium equivalent to 500 to 750 milligrams of salt per day is sufficient to replace the sodium lost from the body. Under some conditions, however, sodium losses may be much greater. For example, vomiting, diarrhea, some antihypertensive medications or diuretics, or profuse sweating due to fever, strenuous exercise, or a hot environment can result in very large losses of sodium. It therefore is possible for persons to become sodium deficient if their sodium losses are high or if they restrict their dietary intake of sodium too much.

Although we know salt provides essential sodium in our diet, we often forget that salt also provides chloride. Chloride has several important functions, but perhaps its most critical one is to help maintain the proper acidity of blood and body fluids.[a] If the diet meets the sodium requirement, it is extremely likely also to provide sufficient chloride.

---

[a] Some religious sects believe so strongly in fasting on certain days of the year that they not

Salt has always been associated with the sea. In fact, many older persons still maintain that when food does not contain enough salt, it tastes "too fresh." Often promoters try to take advantage of this association by claiming that foods are more natural if they contain sea salt, thereby implying that sea salt is more healthful than table salt. Sea salt is primarily sodium chloride, but it also contains small amounts of other minerals. The amounts of these other minerals are, however, quite small compared with those in foods included in the average diet. More important, we remind you again that the body does need nutrients, including minerals, but that the origin of these nutrients has nothing to do with their nutritional properties. Accordingly, sea salt is no more nutritious than table salt and, in at least one respect, may be less so. Seawater does contain iodide, but most of this is lost during the drying process. Thus, most commercial sea salt contains less iodide than does iodized table salt. Sea salt would not be a good choice for consumption by people living in the goiter regions of the United States, including the northern states.

Does our taste for salt cause health problems?

Salt was the first mineral recognized to be essential to the diet of humans, probably because it is the only one for which we have developed a detection system – our taste buds. The usual concern about excessive salt intake is its potential relationship to high blood pressure, also called *hypertension*. One can easily gain the impression from media reports and television commercials that all of us are in danger of developing high blood pressure unless we eat less salt. This is such an oversimplification that it is wrong. With all the talk of salt's causing high blood pressure, it may surprise you to learn that evidence of this effect has not been found for most of us, as indicated by a statement by the Nutrition Committee of the American Heart Association: "Obviously, the relatively high consumption of salt by the U.S. public does not cause hypertension in the majority of people."[14] The term *majority* represents about 85 to 90 percent of us, and thus it is estimated that only about 10 to 15 percent of us are sensitive to salt.

The relationship between blood pressure and salt intake is complex. In the first place, high blood pressure is not a disease but a symptom that can have any number of underlying causes. Its potential for negative consequences is so high that any one with high blood pressure should be under the care of a physician. The complexity of the problem is illustrated by the fact that some people being treated for high blood pressure are advised

only avoid food and beverages, they also avoid swallowing their own saliva. To avoid swallowing saliva, it is necessary to spit continuously, but this depletes the body of fluids and also of the chloride that is abundantly present in saliva. The result may be that the blood becomes too alkaline, and death can occur. Thus, excessive spitting can be dangerous to one's health. Professional baseball players might take note.

by their physician to reduce their salt intake significantly, whereas others are advised *not* to limit their salt consumption. The reason is that for some people with high blood pressure, consuming less salt may decrease their blood pressure, whereas for others, consuming less may increase it, depending on the underlying cause of the symptom.[15]

The questions of whether and how much the majority of us would benefit from eating less salt have not been clearly answered.[16] Some, although not all,[17] epidemiological studies across cultural groups have suggested that a severe restriction of salt intake is associated with a decreased incidence of hypertension. For example, high blood pressure is very rare in subjects from primitive societies who habitually consume limited amounts of salt, whereas it is much more common in members of industrialized societies, who, on the average, consume more salt. Does this mean that the higher salt intake in industrialized populations caused an increase in blood pressure? Perhaps, but not necessarily.

The interpretation of such observations is confounded by the fact that in addition to consuming less salt, members of primitive societies are usually smaller, leaner, and more physically active than are members of industrialized societies, and they are likely to have a different intake level of other nutrients (e.g., more potassium). Any or all of these could affect blood pressure. Further, epidemiological studies within industrialized populations have almost always failed to show any statistical correlation between habitual salt intake and blood pressure, but again, this does not prove that no such relationship exists.

Experimental studies with animals and humans have also failed to provide clear-cut answers. Although it is possible to induce some forms of hypertension in animals by increasing their salt intake, the amount required to do so is generally far in excess of that usually consumed by humans. Dozens of clinical trials have been conducted with humans, but almost all of these involved subjects who already had higher than normal blood pressure, ranging from mild to severe hypertension. The results of such studies have been variable. In general, the effectiveness of dietary salt restriction in reducing blood pressure was found to depend on how high it was in the first place. That is, although salt intake restriction was more likely to have the greatest effect on subjects with severe hypertension, it was less likely to have as much effect on those with milder forms of hypertension.[b]

Far fewer studies have attempted to determine whether salt restriction affects blood pressure in subjects with normal blood pressure. A recent study of individuals with normal blood pressure reported that the restriction

[b] Again, we caution that some forms of high blood pressure are adversely affected by salt restriction. See J. H. Laragh, "Two Forms of Vasoconstriction in Systemic Hypertension," *American Journal of Cardiology* 60 (1987): 826–36. Thus, treatment should be prescribed only by a physician; high blood pressure should never be self-treated.

of salt intake to less than 4 grams per day (less than one-half their usual intake) produced a small average decrease in blood pressure, but individual responses varied widely.[18] Although salt restriction resulted in lower blood pressure in some, it resulted in higher blood pressure in others. However, the magnitude of the effect in either direction was so small that there is reason to doubt that such changes had any consequences, positive or negative, in terms of health.[c] These results are hardly surprising, as most of us have functional kidneys and proper hormonal balance, so that any excess salt we consume is simply eliminated, mostly in the urine.

Despite the lack of evidence that consuming less salt will provide health benefits to the great majority of us, several reports have recommended that we reduce our salt intake.[19] The primary basis for this recommendation is that on the average, we consume far more salt than is necessary to meet our nutritional needs for sodium and chloride. We agree that this is true, with the exception of people taking some kinds of medication (e.g., diuretics) or those engaged in activities that produce excessive amounts of perspiration.[20]

On the other hand, most of us adjust our salt intake not on the basis of nutritional needs for sodium and chloride but according to the dictates of our taste buds. Should we retrain our taste buds to prefer foods with less salt? It seems to us that the pragmatic approach is to determine our own cost–benefit ratio. The cost cannot simply be evaluated in terms of the bottom line of a financial balance sheet. Indeed, the financial difference is very small in either direction. A much more important consideration is how much changing our salt intake will affect our quality of life. The answer will be different for each of us because the importance of the taste of salt to the enjoyment of food is highly variable. Some people like the taste of salt so much that they are conditioned to use the salt shaker even before they taste their food, whereas others would be perfectly content to eat food without adding any salt. It seems reasonable to us that members of the former group, assuming that they are not among those who are salt sensitive, might want more evidence of its benefits than is now available before they reduce their salt intake. On the other hand, members of the

[c] Although high blood pressure increases the risk for heart disease and stroke, the relationship is not linear but curvilinear. See J. D. Neaton, L. H. Kuller, D. Wentworth, and N. O. Borhani, "Total and Cardiovascular Mortality in Relation to Cigarette Smoking, Serum Cholesterol Concentration, and Diastolic Blood Pressure Among Black and White Males Followed up to Five Years," *American Heart Journal* 108 (1984): 759–69. This means that small changes in the blood pressure, up or down, that remain within the normal range have virtually no discernable effect on a person's risk for these diseases, whereas changes in the blood pressure of those with overt hypertension does affect their risk. In the United States, a diagnosis of hypertension is usually made after diastolic readings of 90 mm Hg or more on two successive examinations, but the World Health Organization defines hypertension as a systolic-to-diastolic pressure of 160/95 mm Hg. See National Dairy Council, "Dietary Factors and Blood Pressure," *Dairy Council Digest*, September–October 1981, pp. 25–30.

latter group may choose to reduce their salt intake on the chance that it may be beneficial. Most of us fall somewhere between the two extremes. Our decision on what to do about salt intake, in the absence of specific medical advice, can reasonably be based on the importance of the taste of salt to our quality of life, weighed against the evidence of any benefits from lowering our salt intake.

Lesser-known minerals

A comparison of the list of minerals known to be required by humans (Table 6.1) with those previously discussed will quickly tell you that there are many important minerals that have not received a lot of public attention. The primary reason for this lack of publicity is that our diet contains plenty of them. Macrominerals, including potassium, phosphorus, and magnesium, and trace minerals, including manganese, copper, selenium, chromium, and molybdenum, are so abundant in foods and our environment, and our need for them is so small that there is little reason to worry about possible deficiencies. Indeed, concern is more often expressed that our diet contains some of these in excess. Let's look at some important information about these minerals.

Potassium

If our diet is varied, we will not be in danger of potassium deficiency, despite recent reports suggesting that it is too little potassium rather than too much sodium that leads to high blood pressure. The evidence for the assertion is very general and is unequivocally circumstantial.[21] The problem in this case is that there is far more reason to believe that potassium supplements can be harmful[22] than that they can be beneficial. In addition to the fact that potassium in supplemental form tastes terrible, too much potassium causes diarrhea, irritability, and muscle cramps. More important, if so much potassium is consumed that blood levels become too high, an irregular heartbeat can result that can end in death. Because of the established hazards, potassium supplements should never be taken unless they are prescribed by a physician for a specific reason.

Phosphorus

With the exception of being mistakenly associated with fish as a brain food, the reputation of phosphorus has remained relatively unscathed. Too little or too much consumption is rare. Phosphorus depletion, albeit uncommon, can occur in humans as a result of prolonged consumption of excessive amounts of antacids of the aluminum hydroxide and/or magnesium hydroxide types.

Once in a while the view is expressed that our diets may contain too much phosphate and thereby interfere with the absorption and utilization of calcium as well as some of the trace minerals. Although there is evidence that a specific, optimal ratio of calcium to phosphorus is needed in the diet of some animals to maximize the utilization of both minerals, there is much less evidence that there is such a close relationship in the diet of humans.[23]

One source of phosphorus in our diet is colas, which in earlier times were called *phosphates*. Assuming a reasonable intake of these refreshing drinks, there is no reason to believe that their consumption can lead to excessive phosphate intake. In fact, we have no reason to believe that colas or, for that matter, other soft drinks are injurious to health when consumed in reasonable amounts as a part of a varied diet.[d]

Trace minerals: Chromium, selenium, and molybdenum

A certain mystique has grown around some trace minerals, in some cases because of their reported function and, in other cases, because of myths. Chromium is an example of the first of these. It is true that chromium is thought to work with insulin to aid glucose entry into certain cells, but the quantity needed in relation to its abundance in a varied diet makes the possibility of a chromium deficiency extremely remote. Specifically, there is no evidence that diabetes mellitus or other disorders are caused by a chromium deficiency, despite such an assertion in the popular press.

Advertisements to the contrary, selenium cannot prevent the aging process or cure cancer, heart disease, sexual dysfunction, arthritis, poor eyesight, or skin and hair problems. The usual American diet contains an adequate amount of this mineral for its normal functions unless one consumes food and water only from geographical locations that have selenium-deficient soils. In this age of modern food distribution systems, such limited intake is highly unlikely, but it can occur, especially in certain ethnic or religious communities in which only locally grown foods are consumed. On the other hand, selenium poisoning is a real possibility because this mineral is very toxic in relatively small amounts. The repeated consumption

---

[d] One exception to this is that colas can increase the incidence of dental cavities because of their acid content. Phosphoric acid is used to acidify carbonated water, which results in the release of carbon dioxide to provide the "fizz." Noncola soft drinks use other acids, such as citric acid, instead of phosphoric acid to release the carbon dioxide. The acidity of these soft drinks is enough to cause the loss of some calcium from the teeth. Because this loss is time dependent, rapidly swallowing the liquid instead of keeping it in the mouth can reduce the loss of calcium. It is also a good idea to rinse the mouth with water after consuming the soft drink. Note that it is the acid, not the sugar, that causes the major problem, and so "diet" or "sugar-free" soft drinks are no less hazardous to teeth than are those that contain sugar.

of supplements containing as little as 200 micrograms per day of selenium can lead to toxic symptoms.[24] Take supplements of selenium with extreme caution!

Finally, molybdenum (hard to say, easy to find in foods) does not prevent or cure heart disease or other disorders. In fact, except in patients fed totally through the veins (called *total parenteral nutrition*) with a solution devoid of this mineral, no case of deficiency has been reported.[25]

The importance of mineral balance

A proper concentration of certain minerals is essential to life – too much or too little can cause death. Growing up we may have seen that a saltwater fish would die if we put it in fresh water. Putting a freshwater fish in seawater or even in water containing chlorine results in the same catastrophe. A similar phenomenon occurs in humans: Both too many minerals or too few minerals can be disastrous.

Fortunately for us, the body has a marvelous ability to achieve an ideal mineral content based on its ability to absorb and excrete minerals, provided that we do not abuse the system too much. If the nutrient intake is small, the body can increase its mineral absorption through the gastrointestinal tract and decrease its excretion through the kidneys. If the intake is greater than the amount the body needs, the body has mechanisms to slow down its absorption and speed up its excretion. Luckily for us, our bodies perform this amazing "balancing act" without us having to worry about it! All we need to do consciously is to eat a varied diet. A healthy body obtains the minerals it needs and regulates its internal concentration according to what is optimal for life.

The body's self-regulating mechanisms can be upset by the indiscriminate consumption of supplements of specific minerals. Although each mineral has its own specific functions, you may remember that elements are grouped in families in the periodic table because of the similarity of some of their properties. Because of this similarity, too much of one mineral can interfere with the absorption and utilization of others. Examples of interactions abound. For example, large intakes of zinc interfere with the absorption of copper, and too much copper inhibits zinc absorption. Excessive dietary copper interferes with iron absorption, yet an adequate intake of copper is required for the proper utilization of iron.

Medications can also affect nutrient absorption. For example, laxatives interfere with the absorption of minerals, and for that and other reasons, a constant consumption of them is not a good idea unless they are prescribed by a physician. It won't come as a surprise to anyone who took milk of magnesia as a child that large amounts of magnesium have a laxative effect. But what you may not have known is that when you got diarrhea from milk of magnesia, your absorption of iron, calcium, copper, zinc, and other trace minerals was impeded.

The lesson is: Because minerals interfere with one another, you must be careful about how much of which ones you take as a supplement. Which ones and how much of each in supplemental form should be prescribed by a physician on the basis of clinical evidence. Self-treatment with trace minerals, like vitamins or any other medication, is never wise.

Harmful minerals

Large amounts of minerals, even some of those required, have been found to be dangerous, sometimes deadly, to human or animal life. These findings show the urgent need to remember that "if a little is good, a lot is not a lot better" and that all nutrients are safe or useful to the body only in limited amounts. There is a Latin expression for this: *Sola dosis facit venenum*, or "only the dose makes the poison."

Just because small amounts of some minerals not listed in Table 6.1 can be found in plants and animals, this does not mean that the plant, animal, or human requires these minerals for life. Plant and animal tissues contain boron, aluminum, arsenic, barium, bismuth, bromide, cadmium, germanium, gold, lead, lithium, mercury, rubidium, silver, strontium, titanium, and zirconium. Of these, only boron has been found to be essential to plants; none is known to be essential to animal or human life, and some, even in small amounts, can and do cause death.

There is current public concern about increased environmental exposure to several of the more toxic minerals, such as lead, mercury, and arsenic. Mineral toxicity usually results in mental disorders, resembling schizophrenia, or mental retardation. It is important to remember, however, that in the absence of direct, definitive evidence of mineral toxicity, the occurrence of such mental disorders should not be attributed to excessive intake of minerals.

Lead

Lead poisoning occurs mainly in children between the ages of 1 and 6 years and is most often due to the consumption of lead-containing paint from cribs, toys, walls, or woodwork. The incidence is highest in children living in dilapidated houses. Permanent mental retardation and neurological deficits are common in children who survive lead poisoning. Exposure to lead from food sources has been dramatically reduced in recent years by the virtual eradication of domestically produced lead-soldered food cans.[26] In addition, the Food and Drug Administration continues to monitor levels of lead in foods and has set limits on allowable amounts of lead that can be leached from ceramic, glass, and silver-plated containers. In our opinion, because lead is present in such low concentrations and is poorly absorbed in such small amounts, the fear of lead poisoning from food and water is unwarranted.

Mercury

"Mad as a hatter" is a description made famous in the book *Alice in Wonderland* by Lewis Carroll and is still used today to describe a mental derangement. Years ago, hatmakers indiscriminately used mercury in their trade. That most hatters became "mad" and exhibited permanent neurological damage is now known to be due to mercury toxicity.

The largest source of mercury that can cause epidemic proportions of toxicity today is that from industrial pollution. If industry dumps mercury into waters in which fish live and the fish are subsequently eaten by humans, mercury toxicity can result from eating contaminated fish as happened in the 1950s in Japan.[e] Recently there has been speculation that dental fillings containing mercury amalgam are poisoning the owners. In reality the differences between body loads of mercury in people with and without mercury amalgams are insignificant.[27]

Arsenic

Arsenic is toxic in very small amounts and was once a poison for villainous purposes. Industrial contamination, use in insecticides, and use as an approved additive to animal feeds are sources of small amounts of arsenic in food. That arsenic poisoning is not seen today is a tribute to controlled contamination practices in the United States.

Hair analysis

The fact that heavy metals (particularly lead, mercury, arsenic, and cadmium) do tend to accumulate in hair has given rise to its analysis to determine their presence. Unfortunately, this analysis has been extended to other minerals and vitamins. The American Medical Association Committee on Cutaneous Health and Cosmetics pointed out that the state of the body's health may be completely unrelated to the chemical composition of hair.[28] The committee does not, therefore, recommend hair analysis as a nutrition assessment technique, except possibly for diagnosing poisoning

[e] Reported by E. J. Underwood, "Trace Elements," in *Toxicants Occurring Naturally in Foods*, 2nd ed. (Washington, DC: National Academy of Sciences, 1973), pp. 67–70. Note that cooking does not lessen the toxicity of mercury. Therefore, those who cook their fish are no less apt to be poisoned by mercury than are those who eat *sushi* or *sashimi*.

by minerals such as lead, mercury, arsenic, and cadmium. Even its validity in diagnosing these is questionable.

The hair analysis technique involves analyzing a sample of hair by means of spectrographic analysis. The resulting computer-generated report often lists nutrients (especially vitamins and minerals) that are allegedly deficient, and the report usually further recommends specific supplements, which the practitioner might sell, to treat the identified deficiencies. So-called toxicities of minerals are sometimes noted as well. When the laboratory computer printout indicates that the hair contains too much of any particular mineral, it often diagnoses the person as "poisoned," and the accompanying recommendation often includes advice to treat with EDTA (ethylene diamine tetraacetic acid), a drug that can destroy the kidneys. Any treatment using EDTA should be carried out, if at all, only under the supervision of a physician.

In truth, an analysis of the hair cannot measure vitamin or mineral status, in either the long term or the short term. Because hair contains no vitamins except at the root, which is under the scalp, such an analysis cannot evaluate vitamin status. The composition of hair is affected by environment, age, sex, rate of hair growth, and natural hair color. Dandruff shampoos containing zinc or selenium and hair dyes containing lead can affect hair composition. Hair can also be altered by other treatments, including rinses, sprays, and tonics.[29]

7   Fiber: A nutritional enigma

Fiber is the latest rage in the media and in advertisements and is a major topic for health professionals and scientists. If he were still alive, Sylvester Graham might be disappointed that his treatise on the subject of whole-wheat flour, written in 1839, is not often cited.[a] Sylvester Graham was not the first, however, to promote the use of whole-grain flour. Roman wrestlers must have thought they knew something that the aristocrats who ate refined white bread did not, for they ate only coarse wheat bread, in the belief that it would preserve the strength of their limbs.

We shall see in later chapters that it was Graham who inspired many American health and food reformers, but it took people like Charles W. Post and the Kellogg brothers, John Harvey and Willie Keith, to bring ready-to-eat cereal to our nation's breakfast table almost a century ago. The popularity of high-fiber foods, like whole-wheat bread, has waxed and waned over the intervening decades. During some periods, the medical community was concerned that we consumed too much fiber. We have now gone full circle because there is again considerable interest in fiber, as many people believe that consuming foods high in fiber, such as bran, whole grains, fruits, and vegetables, can prevent and/or treat a variety of diseases. The light is refocused today on the cereal producers, who are bringing back bran.

It used to be called roughage

Fiber is a nutritional enigma. It can be an important component of our diet, although it is not absolutely essential. When fiber is consumed, it is swallowed, but it stays in the digestive tract and never enters the body. That is why it can be described as a "nonnutrient" nutrient.

---

[a] S. Graham, "Lectures on the Science of Human Life" (1839), in R. O. Cummings, *The American and His Food: A History of Food Habits in the United States* (Chicago: University of Chicago Press, 1940), p. 45. Graham advocated the use of whole-wheat flour so strongly that his followers called it *graham flour*. If you check the list of ingredients of the graham crackers of today, you will find graham flour, which is simply whole-wheat flour.

In Chapter 3, we described the digestion and absorption processes, in which complex chemicals in our diet are broken down into their smallest components and absorbed into the cells lining the small intestine. Fiber, however, is complex and is neither broken down by digestive enzymes nor absorbed. In fact, fiber is so complex that it defies description in the chemical sense because it can contain any number of chemicals. Thus we are left with saying that fiber is the part of plants that is not broken down by chemical action in our gastrointestinal tract. It is the indestructible part of food, which, when we eat it, comes through our gastrointestinal tract unscathed and is eliminated through the feces.

Several different chemicals can be part of the substance that we call fiber. *Cellulose* is both the most common form of fiber and the most common carbohydrate. It is a carbohydrate because it is a polymer of glucose, as starch is, but unlike starch, the glucose units are held together by bonds that our digestive enzymes cannot break. Thus it is indigestible. Cellulose is the most common carbohydrate because it is the stuff of which plant cell walls are made. It should come as no surprise, therefore, to learn that it is the basic fiber in fruits, vegetables, and grains.

Hemicellulose is chemically similar to cellulose, and like its chemical cousin, it also is indigestible. Hemicellulose is found in fruits, vegetables, and grains, but to a smaller extent than cellulose is.

Pectin is chemically unrelated to either cellulose or hemicellulose, but it too is indigestible. Pectin is found in fruits, and home canners take advantage of pectin when making jams and jellies because it forms a gel when exposed to heat.

Lignin, which is different chemically from any other fiber component, is abundant in wood. The major dietary sources of it – for those of us who are not termites – are strawberries and pears. Lignified cells can be seen in the flesh of these fruits and is the material that provides the grainy texture. Lignin also is present, although less obviously, in other plants and in grain. Pure lignin is a white fluffy powder that resembles cellulose. Contrary to popular opinion, the inclusion of lignin (or wood pulp) in bread does not result in adding pieces of wood or small splinters that could be harmful or aesthetically distasteful! Other fiber components in our diet include *gums*, *mucilages*, and certain other indigestible carbohydrates.

Two of the most popular words describing fiber are *soluble* and *insoluble*, which may relate to some health benefits. Fibers that are more soluble than their less soluble cousins include pectin, lignin, and gums. These substances are chemically charged, which allows the fiber to bind with other charged compounds, such as bile salts (made from cholesterol) and some vitamins and minerals, and to decrease their absorption. Insoluble fibers such as those found in wheat bran are capable of relieving some of the symptoms of diverticular disease.

The amount and types of fiber vary from one kind of plant to another and may even vary within a species or variety, depending on the maturity of the plant at the time of harvest. As a plant food matures, its fiber and complex carbohydrate contents often shrink, and its sugar content usually rises.

Determining the fiber content of food

Because several different chemicals fit the simple definition of fiber, no simple chemical test can determine its amount in food. Some methods can crudely estimate a food's fiber content by measuring the amount of material that fails to dissolve when the food is heated in acid and alkali. The insoluble material is called, appropriately, *crude fiber*. The acid and alkali conditions used in the laboratory to test for fiber are much harsher than the digestive system, and so these tests underestimate the amount of indigestible material in a particular diet. Therefore another term has been used to describe the amount of material that actually remains undigested in our gastrointestinal tract. It is called *dietary fiber*.

Both terms, crude fiber and dietary fiber, are important to know because either may be listed on the nutrition label on a food package, although neither of them is actually required. Food composition tables usually give crude fiber content, but remember, crude fiber underestimates dietary fiber. If you have crude fiber values, approximate dietary fiber can be estimated by means of simple multiplication. In general, to estimate dietary fiber, multiply the crude fiber content of grains by 5, the crude fiber content of fruits by 4, and the crude fiber content of vegetables, legumes, nuts, and seeds by 3.5.

How much dietary fiber do we eat?

The typical intake of dietary fiber in the United States is in the range of 10 to 20 grams per day. How does this translate into food? The dietary fiber content of several foods is given in Figure 7.1. If we eat six servings of high-fiber foods each day (two at each of three meals), our daily dietary fiber intake will probably be sufficient.

Ready-to-eat and cooked breakfast cereals are often advertised as especially good sources of dietary fiber, and the fiber content of several of them is given in Figure 7.2. A comparison of Figures 7.1 and 7.2 shows, however, that many other foods contain more dietary fiber than do many of these cereals. It is also interesting that the name of the cereal is not necessarily correlated with its fiber content.

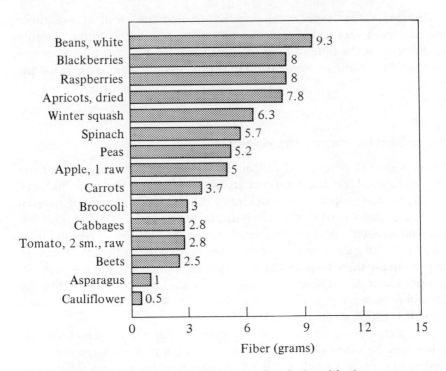

Figure 7.1. Dietary fiber content per serving of selected foods.

What does fiber do?

The one thing that we are sure that fiber does for us is help ensure regular bowel movements. This is not a new discovery. Hippocrates (lived 460 to 377 B.C.), often called the father of medicine, recommended eating whole-wheat bread "for its salutatory effects on the bowels." John Harvey Kellogg, the son of a Battle Creek, Michigan, broom maker, advised consuming fiber because "it would 'sweep' the bowels clean." We now know that fiber helps eliminate waste from the gastrointestinal tract because of its ability to bind water and thus soften the stool. Let's look at what fiber does in some specific diseases and disorders.

Constipation

Constipation is one of the most common chronic digestive complaints in this country, affecting three times more women than men and a significant number of elderly persons. It can be uncomfortable as well as debilitating, and it leads to self-treatment with laxatives and/or a high-fiber diet that may help some people but harm others.

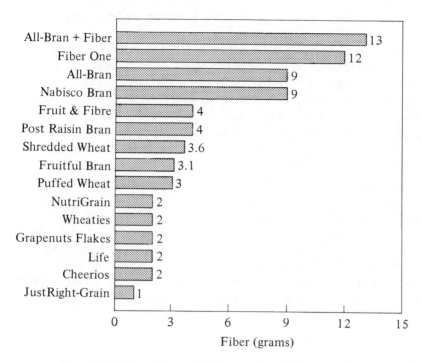

Figure 7.2. Dietary fiber content per serving of selected ready-to-eat cereals.

Epidemiologic studies conducted in the 1960s and 1970s led some researchers to hypothesize that a major cause of constipation is a lack of fiber in the diet. This hypothesis came from the observation that tribespeople in some African communities who consume diets high in fiber are less prone to constipation than are nonvegetarian Americans and Western Europeans. Although a high-fiber diet can alleviate constipation in many people, for most of us the condition is not caused by eating too little fiber.

Constipation can be the result of several factors, not the least of which is simply ignoring the urge to empty the bowels. This practice can blunt the normal reflex to defecate. Constipation is more common in the elderly because as we get older, the muscles surrounding the GI tract become weaker, and so residue moves through the large intestine more slowly. In addition, the elderly are likely to be less physically active, and inactivity can result in constipation, as many long-distance travelers have observed. Drugs – including antacids, blood pressure medications, and cardiac medications – can also contribute to constipation. Additional medical causes of constipation include congenital anomalies, Parkinson's disease, tumors, stroke, renal disease, uncontrolled diabetes, and thyroid problems, among others.

Dietary fiber may reduce constipation in three ways, by its ability to (1) bind water, (2) enhance the bacterial production of matter (including gases) that leads to fecal bulk, and (3) move feces through the gastrointestinal tract in a short time. A fast transit time allows less time for the reabsorption of water from the colon, which results in greater fecal bulk.

Because water is the most abundant component (70 to 80 percent) of fecal waste, fluid intake should not be overlooked as an important component in preventing and treating constipation. Although the amount of water needed depends to a large extent on environmental conditions, most healthy adults require a little more than 4 ounces (½ cup) for every 10 pounds of weight. This usually is equal to 1.5 to 2.5 quarts of fluid daily, which can be obtained from all dietary sources: water, juice, tea, coffee, cocoa, soup, and other liquids and foods. Because dietary fiber increases fecal bulk, the more fiber that is eaten, in foods or fiber-based laxatives, the more fluids that will be required to treat constipation and prevent dehydration. Indeed, if not enough fluids are consumed, constipation can result.

Cancer

In recent years, dietary fiber has been advocated by some on the grounds that it can be used to prevent and/or treat some types of cancer, as well as heart disease. The evidence of its effectiveness in either case is far weaker than the evidence of its efficacy in normal bowel function.[1]

It has been suggested that fiber can protect against colon and rectum (colorectal) cancer. There is a hypothesis, as yet unproven, that fiber can increase fecal bulk and thereby decrease the concentration of carcinogens that may be present in the gastrointestinal tract. According to this hypothesis, the colon may be less exposed to potential carcinogens because fiber dilutes any cancer-causing substances and speeds their transit through the GI tract.

If you believe the advertisements and statements on some cereal boxes, the National Cancer Institute has expressed the belief that eating fiber may reduce the risk of cancer, even though a committee of scientists sponsored by that institute did not find sufficient evidence to justify such a conclusion.[2] In defense of the National Cancer Institute, note that the word *belief*, according to any standard dictionary, implies *faith*, which is not necessarily based on fact. In the case of fiber, the rhetoric implying that it can prevent cancer is much stronger than the evidence.

Heart disease

The role of fiber in preventing heart disease is, in our opinion, on even shakier scientific grounds. In this case, soluble fiber can bind bile acids and prevent their return from the intestine to the liver. Because bile acids are made from cholesterol by the liver, those lost in the feces must be replaced, which can have the effect of lowering the amount of cholesterol in blood. Oats are the most highly advertised source of soluble fiber, but soluble fiber is also present in some other grains and in beans. The problem with this use of soluble fiber is that reasonable amounts of sources of it (like 1 ounce of oatmeal) have a very small, barely detectable effect on blood cholesterol levels. To reduce blood cholesterol levels substantially, enormous quantities must be consumed,[3] which leads to a bloated feeling in most people, as well as gas and abdominal pain in many. Even worse, consuming too much fiber, particularly the soluble variety, can hamper the absorption of many nutrients, especially minerals.

Obesity

A high-fiber diet will neither prevent obesity nor cure it, but high-fiber foods can easily be incorporated into a weight-loss program. Because of the need to chew high-fiber foods more thoroughly, it generally takes dieters longer to eat a meal high in fiber, and therefore they may consume less food because they tend to feel fuller sooner and for a longer time. In addition, if foods high in fiber replace those with more calories, fewer calories may be consumed, and a weight loss may result. The important concept to remember is that a lower intake of calories, not any special properties of fiber itself, is what causes a weight loss.

Diabetes mellitus

The American Diabetes Association recommends that foods high in fiber be included in a balanced and varied diabetic diet. This does not mean that fiber can prevent or cure diabetes. Rather, the association's recommendation is based on the premise that a meal containing fiber, particularly soluble fiber, slows the stomach's emptying time and thus slows the rapid rise in blood sugar that can occur in diabetic patients following the consumption of carbohydrates. In addition, high-fiber diets that are also low in calories may encourage weight loss in those persons who need to lose weight which, in turn, can lead to better control of blood sugar levels. Note that in neither case is the result due to any special properties of fiber.

On the other hand, it is not wise for diabetics to consume a self-prescribed high-fiber diet, because one of the potential consequences of diabetes is a weakening of the muscles surrounding the GI tract. The consumption of diets high in fiber by such patients can lead to intestinal obstruction. Thus, any change in a diabetic patient's diet, including an increase in fiber intake, should be made only after appropriate medical consultation.

Blood pressure

High blood pressure has been purported to be treatable by a high-fiber diet. This assumption is unfortunate, because some people may believe that dietary modification can be substituted for needed blood pressure medication. Self-treatment of hypertension by consuming a high-fiber diet is a dangerous practice. A diet high in fiber does not control blood pressure, although a weight loss, for those who need it, may lower blood pressure. Thus a diet high in fiber and low in calories may be advantageous to those with high blood pressure, but note that it is fewer calories, not fiber, that produces the effect.

As noted previously, sufficient dietary fiber can alleviate the problem of constipation, which may be important for people with high blood pressure. Although constipation does not elevate blood pressure, straining to defecate can raise it. For people who already have high blood pressure, a further increase can cause sudden death from a stroke or heart attack. Straining to defecate may also worsen hemorrhoids, appendicitis, and varicose veins. Thus, a person with hypertension or these other disorders should avoid constipation and straining to defecate. Treatment for each of them is primarily medical, although a high-fiber diet may be a part of the regimen.

How much fiber is too much?

Is it possible to get too much fiber in our diet? It has been known for some time that the answer is a resounding yes! As far back as 1932, medical scientists were concerned that excessive fiber in the diet could cause digestive disorders.[4] It has subsequently been confirmed that eating too much fiber can cause diarrhea and other digestive complaints such as gas, bloating, and pain. Very large amounts of fiber can also cause enlargement and twisting of the large intestine, which may require surgery for correction. Surgery is also a distinct possibility for the correction of unremovable fiber in elderly persons[5] and others who have weak muscles surrounding the large intestine, a disorder called *atonic colon*.

Nutritionally, a high-fiber diet, in amounts substantially greater than 20 to 25 grams daily, depending on the type of fiber, can result in less efficient absorption of calcium, phosphorus, iron, copper, zinc, magnesium, and other trace minerals, because of the binding of these minerals by fiber or chemicals present in fibrous foods. Too much fiber in the form of pectin can also decrease vitamin B_{12} absorption. Finally, if so much fiber is consumed that there simply isn't room in the digestive tract for more nutritious foods – which may happen in the case of children and the elderly – the consequently insufficient ingestion of nutrients, including calories, protein, vitamins, and minerals, may result in overt malnutrition.[6]

How much fiber is enough?

The research is not complete enough to allow a firm recommendation of how much fiber should be consumed. Nutritionists generally assume that for most people, a varied diet, including recommended amounts from each of the four food groups, provides the required nutrients as well as sufficient fiber for proper bowel function. If you want to increase your fiber intake beyond this amount, you have several options.

For example, we showed you in Chapter 1 that even after consuming the appropriate amounts from the four food groups, most of us need to eat other foods in order to meet our caloric needs. One option is to meet the need for these additional calories by eating foods that are high in fiber. You might choose high-fiber snack foods such as dried fruits (prunes or raisins), nuts, seeds, or popcorn in place of high-fat snack foods. These high-fiber foods could also be consumed during meals by adding them to salads, vegetables, or casseroles.

A second option is to substitute some high-fiber foods for lower-fiber foods in your usual diet. For example, you could substitute

> Whole-grain breads and cereals for white bread and more refined cereals and include 1 ounce of bran daily in the diet.
> Fruits and vegetables with skins (fresh, frozen, or canned), for fruits and vegetables that have been peeled.
> A main dish of legumes and whole grains such as white soup beans and cornbread for a meat, fish, or poultry dish once or more often each week.
> Nectars and pulpy fruit juices instead of clear juices, fruit drinks, or carbonated beverages.

A third option is to add fiber supplements to your diet. In effect, in this case, the fiber supplement becomes a drug, and any generalized statements about the use of dietary fiber as a drug to prevent or treat specific diseases should be regarded with caution. Remember that fiber supplements are less likely to be beneficial than is the fiber obtained from an assortment of foods. If you choose fiber supplements, don't overdo it – it is easy to overconsume fiber in the form of pills. Following a diet that is high in fiber and still provides all of the other nutrients (without too many calories) is possible, but you have to work at it. The advice of a registered dietitian can be most helpful to you.

Part III

Foods

Food provides us not only with necessary nutrients, as we have seen in previous chapters, but also with pleasure. The enjoyment of food is an important component of our quality of life. But can you really enjoy eating food while listening to the evening television news tell you that the very items on your plate most likely contains additives and may be laced with pesticides that may have caused the death of thousands of mice and rats? Is our food supply really safe?

As if worrying about what has been added to food through production and processing was not enough, we are told that on the whole, we consume too much of certain natural components of our food – like fat, cholesterol, and sugar – and not enough of others – like fiber. Some health authorities have implored us to change our eating habits on the grounds that doing so might reduce the risk of developing chronic diseases. As a group, we have been reluctant to take this advice. Why? Why do we eat the foods that we do? In the following chapters, we deal with several issues related to food, including food additives, food-borne illnesses, and the use of pesticides as a part of modern food production methods. What are the costs, and what are the benefits? Finally, we look at specific foods that have, over the years, acquired undeserved reputations of being "good" or "bad."

8   Conventional versus organic food production: Assessing the cost–benefit ratio

The terms *organic food* and *organic gardening* entered our vocabulary in a big way in the 1960s as part of the "back to nature" movement. Although organic food production is still with us, it has lost some of its popularity. A much more common reminder of the return-to-nature movement today is the use of the word *natural*, overused and misused *ad nauseam* in media advertisements.

The term organic food is nonsense to the chemist. All food is organic because it is made up of compounds containing carbon. Regardless of the chemical inaccuracy, the term is generally understood to imply a food production method in which animal wastes are used as fertilizers. Agricultural chemicals, including fertilizers, insecticides, and herbicides are not used.

With this definition of organic foods, it takes only a small amount of reflection to realize that organic food production is a description of the way that all food was produced in the United States within the memory of many people who are still not old enough to apply for social security. Until the middle of this century, farmers were forced to practice organic farming, not because of popular demand, but because of necessity. Much of the world's population, particularly in Third World countries, continues to practice organic farming today because they do not have the technology to produce food any differently.

Organic farming: The way it was

Our perception of early America is mostly derived from novels, movies, and a healthy imagination. It is easy to visualize a farm family in the wilderness happily growing their own nutritious food supply without the use of synthetic chemicals such as pesticides and commercial fertilizers. The problem is that these so-called good old days were not so good as our imagination makes them out to be. For most of the time that humans have occupied the earth, they have had a constant struggle to obtain enough food to hold body and soul together. Until recent times, the United States was no different in this respect than the rest of the world. Farmers worked from dawn to dusk just to survive.

Farmers have long realized that harvesting crops from the land year after year depleted the soil of nutrients, which had to be replaced by the addition of fertilizers. Because virtually all farmers kept animals to produce meat, milk, and eggs and to provide the horsepower to plow the fields, a ready source of fertilizer, in the form of animal waste, was always available.

The use of barnyard manure for fertilizer had two major problems. One of these was low nutrient density, meaning that it took a lot of manure to get even a small amount of wanted nutrients. Low calorie density may be desirable in our diet when we are trying to lose weight, but it is not desirable when shoveling tons of manure to fertilize a corn field. Modern farmers typically apply 100 to 150 pounds of nitrogen per acre for corn production. Because barnyard manure is about 1 percent nitrogen on a dry-weight basis, application of this much nitrogen would require spreading 10,000 to 15,000 pounds of manure per acre, or about one-third pound of dry waste per square foot. A 100-acre corn field would require 500 to 750 tons of manure to supply the amount of nitrogen currently used. Most farmers had animals, but not that many, and spreading that much manure over an entire field would be very difficult. In actual practice, the quantity of manure, and therefore the quantity of nitrogen, applied was much less, with a commensurate reduction in crop yield.

The second problem was even worse. Animals were fed grain and hay that had been grown on the farm the previous year. Both sources were contaminated with weed and grass seed, much of which came unscathed through the digestive tract of cattle or horses. Thus, when the manure was spread on the field, the seeds of these pernicious plants were also planted. Often, a larger quantity of weed and grass seed was planted inadvertently than the quantity of corn seed planted deliberately. When the corn seed-lings emerged from the ground following the spring rains, so did the weeds and grasses. If these noxious plants were allowed to remain, they would use the precious water as well as nutrients in the soil. In competition with desirable plants, it seems a law of nature that the weeds will win.

Obviously, such noxious plants had to be removed. Those between the rows could be taken out with a plow, but weeds in the corn row had to be removed by hand, one row at a time. This was done with a torturous device called a hoe. Most farm families had a large number of children to perform this arduous task. Even so, the best they could do was to slow down the growth of the weeds and grasses to enable the corn to get ahead. By harvest time, these unwanted plants had repopulated and produced seed to repeat the cycle next year.

As if nutrient-poor soils and weeds were not enough, along came the insects, in abundance.[a] Most species of insects are either beneficial or innocuous to humans, but the remainder can be devastating to food production. Many insects are very picky about their food source, as indicated by their common names – corn borer, corn rootworm, tomato worm, and potato bug. Others, like the grasshopper, have a voracious appetite for a variety of plants, especially, it seems, for farm crops. Insects provided a constant challenge to farmers, and more often than not, they won the battle.

Only a few semieffective insecticides were available before 1945, and the methods of choice for killing insects were less than desirable. For example, the accepted method for controlling potato bugs was to pick them off the vines one at a time and drop them into a can of kerosene.

If the battle against weeds and insects could be won and if the rain came at just the right time and in just the right amount, a farmer might obtain a yield of 30 bushels of corn or 20 bushels of wheat to the acre. Most of the time, these "ifs" didn't happen. You had to be an optimist to remain a farmer.

Modern farming methods: The way it is today

Many, if not most, farmers of today would argue that you still have to be an optimist to remain a farmer, but the methods of plant food production have changed drastically over the past forty years. Now the use of synthetic chemicals is widespread in the fight against weeds and insects. Chemicals also are used to supply the nutrients needed for optimum yields. Plant breeding has produced varieties that are drought and disease resistant. Mechanization has reduced back pain and labor costs. This technological revolution in agriculture has resulted in ever-increasing yields of food at less cost.

Chemicals are the cornerstone of modern agricultural production. Without them, current levels of productivity would simply not be possible, yet it is the use of chemicals that has been the most controversial part of the technological revolution.

In terms of quantity, most modern agricultural chemicals are used as fertilizers. By chemically analyzing the soil, scientists can advise farmers how much of which nutrients they need to add for the optimum yield of a particular crop. The nutrients are then added in the form of relatively pure, inorganic chemicals. The reason that the addition of these inorganic

[a] Crops grown by today's farmers are still subject to damage – by 1,800 different weeds, 10,000 species of insects, and more than 80,000 diseases caused by 160 species of bacteria, 250 species of viruses, and 8,000 species of fungi. See K. A. Welzel, "Consumer Concerns Are Misplaced, Scientists Say," *Columbus* (OH) *Dispatch*, April 5, 1989, pp. G1–G2.

chemicals is effective is that plants can use only inorganic forms of nutrients. Thus, it is nonsense to supply plants with organic forms of nutrients, such as protein or vitamins. Organic nutrients are of no use to plants until microorganisms in the soil break them down into inorganic forms.

Chemicals are also used to control insects and weeds. Insects have always been a problem in the production of food, and it was no different for American farmers until the chemical industry came to the rescue after World War II with the introduction of DDT. Subsequently, other insecticides have been developed so that farmers now have available a veritable arsenal in their battle against insects. In addition, industry produced chemicals that are effective against another nemesis, weeds. In fact, the chances are good that you use some of these herbicides on your lawn today to kill weeds, particularly dandelions. These chemicals are important to the elimination of plants competing with farm crops for nutrients and moisture.

Less controversial developments in modern-day farming include irrigation, development of new varieties of plants, and mechanization. Mechanization has reduced the cost of food by reducing the cost of labor. Fifty years ago, a typical wheat-harvesting crew consisted of a dozen good men, several boys, and numerous horses to recover a few hundred bushels of the golden grain. Today, one person, driving an air-conditioned combine with stereo music, can harvest that much in an hour. Mechanical corn pickers, cotton pickers, and hay balers have similarly been devised to lower the labor cost of harvesting these crops.

Eggs, milk, and meat

The technological revolution that changed the production of farm crops has had similar effects on the production of animal products. In times past, eggs were plentiful and inexpensive in the spring when chickens, like other birds, felt the urge to fill a nest with eggs to perpetuate the species.[b]

The eggs that we now eat are laid by a hen living alone in a wire cage several feet above the ground. Her diet and the lighting in her cage are manipulated to make the hen think that it is always spring, so that she will lay eggs throughout the year. These chickens never experience the companionship of a rooster. Although this deprivation may damage their psyche, the lack of male companionship has absolutely no effect on the number or the quality of eggs produced. Chickens destined for the family dinner table or fast food restaurants are raised by the millions instead of the dozens, as was once done on individual farms. Today's commercially grown

[b] The practice of placing a glass egg or, lacking that, a white doorknob in nests was not to induce the chicken to lay more eggs. Rather, these "nest eggs" were used to persuade the hen to lay eggs in a nest constructed by the farmer instead of one of her own choosing in a secluded corner of the barnyard.

chickens are ready for market at the tender age of 6 to 7 weeks. The cost, taking inflation into account, is much less today than when fried chicken was the main dish at Sunday dinner for the baby boomers.

Methods of milk production have also changed dramatically. Instead of each farmer's milking a few cows by hand, large dairy herds are now milked by machine. The milk is cooled, transported to processing plants, homogenized, pasteurized, and packaged, all without ever being touched by human hands. When cows bred for milk production are fed a proper diet, they can produce quantities of milk far in excess of those of only a few years ago, and with much less microbial contamination.

America has a worldwide reputation as the home of the cowboy. Actually this romanticized period of our history lasted a relatively short period of time and was not all that successful in producing edible beef. Readers who remember the television shows "Gunsmoke" and "Rawhide" may recall that the basic plot was to herd cattle from their "home on the range" to the railroad terminals at Dodge City, Kansas, and Sedalia, Missouri. From there, the cattle were transported by rail to meat-processing plants in Chicago. The meat was then shipped by refrigerated rail cars to become, among other things, a "New York strip steak." Considering that Marshal Dillon's dinner steak was muscle from an animal that had probably walked the better part of a thousand miles, it is not likely that the final product was all that tender. Muscles tend to get fairly tough after walking across Texas and what is now Oklahoma, not to mention the necessity of swimming across the rivers in between. In contrast, today's beef comes from steers that, like their predecessors, have grown up on pastures. However, in contrast with times past, today's steers are confined and fed grain for several weeks before slaughter. This procedure results in the deposition of fat mixed with muscle fibers that makes the meat more tender, juicier, and, to most people, tastier. This interspersion of fat, called *marbling*, is characteristic of more expensive cuts of beef.[c]

Pork was a favorite meat for American farmers for several reasons, one of which was that pigs could turn table scraps into a tasty product. Methods of producing pork, as well as the pigs themselves, have changed. Pigs are no longer allowed to waste away their summers lazily lying in the mud. They still eat like pigs; that is, they still have voracious appetites, but they do not get as fat as they did in the past, mostly because they have been

---

[c] The grading of beef into the categories such as good, choice, or prime is related, in part, to the amount of fat interspersed with muscle. Much of the beef produced worldwide is grass fed, as opposed to grain fed, and therefore contains less fat. In countries where only grass-fed beef is available, veal, which comes from young calves and is therefore more tender, is much more popular than the meat of older cattle. In recent years, breeds of cattle have been developed in the United States and elsewhere that have less fat in the muscle, in an effort to meet the demand for meat containing less saturated fat. Such breeding has generally resulted in less tender meats.

bred to be leaner. Swine nutritionists and geneticists have combined their efforts to produce more pork protein, and less fat, at a lower cost.

Two of the weapons used by agricultural scientists to increase the production of meat at less cost have led to considerable controversy. These are the use of antibiotics in animal feed and the treatment of animals with hormones. There has been concern by some, and in some cases appropriately so, of the effects of antibiotics and hormones on the safety of the meat produced (see Chapters 9 and 10).

What are the costs of the technological revolution?

The application of science to agricultural production has been hailed by many for what it can do *for* us but has been cursed by others for what it can do *to* us. Critics of the technological revolution in agriculture have argued that it may have lowered the cost of food but that the "price" has been too high. The more extreme view charges that the new methods produce plastic food that has diminished its nutritional value and has loaded it with pesticide residues hazardous to our health. Is there any truth to these charges?

To answer this question, we must recognize that there are at least two different issues involved. The first is the concern that the use of chemical fertilizers produces inferior, less nutritious foods. This charge is not founded on fact and is easily refuted. A second issue is whether modern farming techniques introduce chemical residues into our environment and our food that may be harmful. This issue is not so easily resolved. Modern farm production methods, which rely heavily on synthetic chemicals, cannot be made entirely risk free. Further, mechanization has resulted in much greater use of fossil fuels, and more elaborate packaging has added to landfills. The pragmatic approach is to reduce the risk as much as possible without losing the benefits of the technology.

The surprising laws of nature: The nutritional value of our food supply

You may have heard people say that our food is not as nutritious as it used to be. They believe that this is because in the past the fertilizers were manure instead of chemicals. A second charge is that animals are now fed diets that result in less nutritious products. These assertions are simply not true; they ignore fundamental facts of biology.

The nutritional value of plants

Plants grow for their own sake, not ours. Corn is a corn plant's way of making another corn plant. A potato is a potato vine's way of making another potato vine. The fact that we can eat these seeds is presumably irrelevant to the corn or potato plant. The nutrients in corn or potatoes are put there by the plants in order to provide nourishment during germination and early growth. Vitamins are there because they are needed for the metabolism of the developing plant, not because we need them, although we do. The same can be said for proteins, carbohydrates, fats, and most minerals.[d] Furthermore, any vitamins, proteins, carbohydrates, or fats in plants must be made by the plant itself from inorganic chemicals from the soil and carbon dioxide from the air. The quantity of each of them in the plant is determined by genetics.

It may be tempting to assume that nutrient-deficient soil produces nutrient-deficient plants and plant products. As reasonable as it sounds, however, this assumption simply is not true. If the proper nutrients are not present in the soil, the plant will not respond by producing a nutritionally poor product. Rather, the plant will grow only to the extent that the available nutrients and water allow. If the nutrient deficiencies are extreme, the plant will not grow at all. For example, if the soil does not have enough inorganic nitrogen to make the quantity of protein programmed by the plant's genetic material, the plant simply will not grow, or it will produce less product. The plant does not respond by producing a product with a lower protein content.

Thus, methods of fertilization do not change the nutrient content of plants, although the food that we eat today may be somewhat different from that consumed by our ancestors. The difference is that new varieties of plants are constantly being produced, each of which may contain slightly more or less of some nutrients (because of genetics).

In some cases, the development of new varieties and modern production and distribution methods have changed the taste of food. For example, you may have noticed that tomatoes purchased in the winter do not taste the same as those grown in your own or your neighbor's garden during the summer. Part of the reason for this is that the varieties are different. Tomatoes destined for long-distance shipment have been bred to have thicker skins and thus to suffer less damage during transportation. In ad-

---

[d] Most minerals in plants are present because they are necessary components for plant growth. However, small amounts of some minerals may be taken up by plants and find their way into edible portions by accident. Some of these are in plants not because the plant needs them but because they are incidentally absorbed along with needed minerals present in the soil. This is further discussed in Chapter 6, on minerals.

dition, they are usually picked well before they are ripe so that they can ripen during transport. These two factors combine to result in a product that might remind the consumer of eating red cardboard. Even so, the nutrient content is essentially the same as that of the home-grown variety.

The nutritional value of eggs, milk, and meat

Just as seeds are a plant's way of making another plant, eggs are a chicken's way of making another chicken. The nutrients in the egg are there to sustain the life of the embryo and the newly hatched chicken until the chick is able to consume food by itself. For the most part, the nutrient content of eggs is determined by genetics and not by diet. When a hen is fed a nutrient-deficient diet, the effect is to reduce the number of eggs laid rather than to produce nutrient-deficient eggs. Obviously, because the profit motive of commercial egg producers forces them to maintain high productivity, it is in their own interest to feed their chickens diets that meet all of their nutrient requirements. Thus, the nutritional value of eggs available today is the same as that of eggs from hens scratching in the barnyard that are fed either commercial feed or dinner-table scraps.

One difference between eggs produced by modern methods and those from barnyard chickens is that today's hens have never encountered a rooster. Specialty stores are willing to correct that oversight by selling "fertile" eggs that cost more than the more conventional variety available at the supermarket. Cost, in fact, is the only difference: Fertilization does not affect either the nutrient or the cholesterol content of eggs. Some stores may also sell eggs with brown shells, again at higher prices than for the more common white-shell variety. Eggshell color is strictly a function of the hen's genetic characteristics and, like fertilization, has nothing to do with the nutritional value of the egg.

Milk, which in our society usually means cow's milk, is produced as a source of nourishment for baby calves. The nutrient content of milk is a function of genetics and, for the most part, not diet.[e] When a cow is given an inadequate diet, she produces less milk, but its quality is not significantly affected. Thus, modern dairy farmers give their cows the best possible diet in order to ensure maximum productivity, which raises their profit and lowers the cost to the consumer.

A major difference in the milk available today and that sold a few decades ago is that most milk is now pasteurized and homogenized. Homogenization makes the milk more convenient to use, as the fat droplets are

---

[e] This statement is not entirely true for the fat-soluble vitamins A and D, but these vitamins are usually added to a standard quantity before the milk is sold. The label on the container indicates whether or not the milk has been fortified with them. We recommend buying milk that has been fortified.

dispersed so well that they remain suspended. Because of homogenization, the cream does not rise to the top. Laws that require the pasteurization of milk have been important to public health because the process has virtually eliminated the transmission of disease via milk. Contrary to stories that sometimes circulate, neither homogenization nor pasteurization has any effect on the nutrient content of milk.

Although most of us may not like to think about it, when we eat steak, ham, a drumstick, or a fish fillet, we are eating muscle from what was a living animal. Those muscles were once biochemically active tissue, and the vitamins in those muscles served a function as coenzymes, in the same way that vitamins function in our tissues. These vitamins are still present when we eat the meat of those animals, and they are recycled to meet our vitamin needs. Our digestive processes release the amino acids from the meat, and our tissues make new proteins from them. In this way, an amino acid that was first made in a plant, which was subsequently eaten by a chicken or a pig, now becomes a part of us.

If an animal consumes a diet from which an amino acid is missing, the cells of that animal cannot make a protein that was genetically programmed to contain that amino acid. The cell does not make a protein deficient in that amino acid. Rather, it does not make the protein at all. Because most proteins in the body contain all of the amino acids, protein synthesis virtually stops in the face of an amino acid deficiency. Very simply, a growing animal stops growing.

Are agricultural chemicals a threat to our environment?

In terms of tonnage, fertilizers are the most common agricultural chemical. Can they damage the environment? Yes and no. Do you remember the concern in the 1960s that phosphates, from laundry detergents and farm fertilization, were choking our lakes and rivers by stimulating the growth of algae? The phrase "contains no phosphate" became popular in soap advertisements. Laws were passed to control the time, place, and amounts that fertilizers could be distributed on fields, to minimize the runoff. It was, of course, in the best interest of farmers to cooperate, because fertilizer that was washed out into the river cost them money and did them no good. Occasionally, one reads of fish kills by an inadvertent contamination of water, but these are fairly rare.

Pesticides have been a more difficult political problem. After it became available at the end of World War II, DDT was widely used against insects that devoured farm crops as well as other insect pests, including the ubiquitous housefly and mosquito. Indeed, DDT is credited with virtually eliminating malaria in the United States.[f]

---

[f] Malaria was common in the southern United States until the 1940s, when DDT was used

Several years passed before it was realized that there was an environmental price to pay for the indiscriminate use of DDT, which does not rapidly biodegrade.[g] Many environmentalists fueled the debate over the problem, but the controversy really took off with the publication of *Silent Spring*, a book by Rachel Carson.[1] Public opinion was divided, and extreme views on both sides were expressed. It is not surprising that environmentalists' views of DDT were different from those of people who had had malaria. Views ranged from those wanting laws to prohibit the production and use of all chemicals that interfered with the laws of nature, to those demanding the right to produce and use any chemicals without governmental interference. The eventual answer was one often used in American politics – compromise. Laws were passed to control the production and use of pesticides and other chemicals, and the use of DDT was banned unless given specific approval by the United States Department of Agriculture.

Pesticides and other agricultural chemicals in our food supply

It is one thing to worry about the effects of agricultural chemicals on the birds and bees, but when the concern is with their effects on our health, the issue becomes much more personal. Is it true that our food contains toxic chemicals, some of which might even cause cancer? Yes and no. It is true that residues of some agricultural chemicals can be found in some foods, but only in trace amounts. It is also true that some insecticides are as toxic to animals, as they are insects, and some of them are carcinogenic, but only if they are ingested in amounts much greater than those permitted in food.[h] The prudent approach is to limit our intake of these potentially harmful contaminants. To this end, laws have been passed to limit the use of agricultural chemicals that come into contact with food. Further, laws require that any such chemicals be tested with animals in order to determine the quantity that might be toxic and/or carcinogenic. Food must then be tested to ensure that the quantity of any such contaminants is many times lower than the smallest amount found to cause any health problem (more about this and related issues in Chapters 9 and 10). The point that we want

to reduce, markedly, the population of anopheles mosquitos, the female of which transmits the organism that causes malaria.

[g] Environmentalists quickly realized that DDT killed useful insects, such as honeybees, as well as harmful ones. It took longer to discover that DDT caused many species of birds to lay eggs with soft shells that were easily broken, thereby resulting in fewer hatchlings.

[h] The American Council on Science and Health (ACSH) reports that no deaths have been documented as being caused by synthetic pesticide residues normally found in foods. If synthetic pesticides were to be banned, the ACSH says that the reduction in total cancer risk "would be equivalent to trying to clean up a very sandy beach by removing one or two grains"; Welzel, "Consumer Concerns Are Misplaced."

to make here is that such laws, and the enforcement of them by regulatory agencies, have attempted to lower the risk of chemical use as much as practically possible.

We now have had several years of experience with using agricultural chemicals and enforcing regulations intended to protect our food supply. Regulatory agencies have sometimes bent over backward to protect the public but, in the eyes of some, have been passive or worked to the benefit of industry. Several lessons were learned several years ago regarding this very issue, at the expense of the cranberry industry.

The great cranberry scare

Just before Thanksgiving in 1959, then Secretary of Health, Education and Welfare Arthur S. Fleming announced that a weed killer, aminotriazole, had been found in cranberries from the states of Washington and Oregon.[2] The weed killer had been federally approved for use on cranberries as well as other farm crops, with the condition that it be used in the autumn after harvest. Apparently a few growers had used the chemical in the spring, and it had found its way into the plants and, to some extent, into the berries. Because this was one of the first highly publicized examples of pesticide contamination of our food supply, it is perhaps not too surprising that there was overreaction on all sides.

The federal government did not seek to ban the sale of cranberries, but it might just as well have done so: The government's announcement said that anyone buying cranberries would be doing so at his or her own risk. The timing of the announcement could not have been worse for the cranberry industry. Ordinarily, in those days, about 60 percent of the total annual sale of cranberries came at Thanksgiving and another 20 percent at Christmas. As expected, the holiday season in 1959 was far from merry for the industry! Not until well after those holidays was it established that contamination by the weed killer had affected only a very small percentage of the total crop and that even the cranberries that were contaminated had only a trace of the offending chemical. Scientists at the time pointed out that a human would have to eat 15,000 pounds of contaminated cranberries each day for several years to suffer any ill effects. Even so, most people did without cranberry sauce during the holiday season of 1959. In fact, cranberry sales did not return to prescare levels for several years.

Several lessons were learned from the cranberry scare. The government learned that such a highly publicized, general warning unnecessarily alarmed the public.[i] Almost all of the cranberry crop of 1959 was safe.

---

[i] A similar, highly publicized case occurred in the spring of 1989 when the Food and Drug Administration received a threat from a Spanish-speaking man that Chilean fruit had been poisoned. After an examination of literally tons of fruit from Chile, a total of two grapes

Furthermore, the warning penalized the public as well as the cranberry growers. Consumers who liked cranberry sauce with their Thanksgiving turkey didn't have it. Growers who had used the weed killer inappropriately were penalized, but so were the large majority of cranberry growers who had done nothing wrong (growers were later partly compensated for their losses by the taxpayer). The cranberry industry learned a lesson, because the scare caused them to diversify; they no longer rely on a single product with a single season. Have you heard of cranapple juice? You hadn't before 1959!

Alar alarm: "An apple a day . . ."

Although federal agencies have learned to move with caution to keep from raising undue public alarm, private organizations sometimes do not follow such constraints. The publicity concerning Alar is a case in point.

Except for a few scientists who studied it and some apple growers who used it, most people never heard of Alar before February 26, 1989. On that date, a CBS program, "60 Minutes," reported that Alar, used on apples before harvest, was present in some apples and apple products and that this substance could cause cancer. It was asserted that children were most susceptible to Alar. The primary source of information used in the report was an unpublished analysis from the National Resources Defense Council (NRDC), an environmental group. This televised report and dozens of others that immediately followed erroneously identified Alar as a pesticide. The actress Meryl Streep announced the formation of "Mothers and Others for Pesticide Limits." Publicity quickly led to panic among some, particularly school officials, and cessation of the consumption of apples and apple products by many. Was there reason for such fear?

Alar has been used for almost three decades because it keeps ripe apples on the tree longer, resulting in redder, firmer fruit with better keeping qualities, but the question is, is it safe? Early studies by the manufacturer of Alar – Uniroyal – were sufficiently convincing that government agencies approved its use in the 1960s.

Despite this approval, Alar remained under active investigation. Several studies using rats failed to show that Alar caused cancer, but some reports suggested that when given in massive doses, Alar could cause cancer in mice. The problem was that there is reason to believe that such animal tests are not valid when such toxic doses are given because toxic doses can

were found that contained cyanide, but in amounts so small that it would have caused no harm. The FDA reluctantly felt compelled to go public. News of the threat and the discovery of two contaminated grapes was released on March 13. The result was that many consumers temporarily stopped eating grapes, from any source. The cost of the episode, mostly to the Chilean economy, might reach $50 million. See B. Grigg and V. Modland, "The Cyanide Scare: A Tale of Two Grapes," *FDA Consumer*, November–December 1989, pp. 7–11.

cause cellular damage, thereby resulting in a false positive result.[3] Although government scientists concluded that Alar did not cause cancer when administered in less-than-toxic amounts, the NRDC and other environmental groups were not satisfied. They lobbied the Environmental Protection Agency (EPA) to ban Alar, and the EPA ordered further tests.

On the basis of these additional tests, the EPA calculated that a lifetime exposure to Alar might result in as many as 45 cancers per million population, based on a worst-case scenario.[4] In contrast, the California Department of Food and Agriculture, using the same data but slightly different assumptions, calculated that in the worst-case scenario, the lifetime risk was 2.6 cancers per million population. The California estimate of probable lifetime risk was much lower, 3.5 cases per trillion. This estimate means that the population of the United States would have to be a thousand times greater than it currently is in order to find one tumor due to Alar. In addition, critics charged that even these estimates of risks were exaggerated because they were based on tests that were flawed, in that toxic doses were administered to the mice.

Despite the controversy, the EPA decided to err on the side of safety. On February 1, 1989, the agency announced that it would permit the use of Alar only until July 31, 1990. The NRDC had won a victory, but even so, it apparently decided to go public with its case against Alar. Several reports[5] indicate that the "60 Minutes" broadcast was simply the first step in a publicity campaign orchestrated by a public relations firm. The person who directed the PR effort is quoted as saying that the campaign was designed so that revenue would flow back to NRDC from the public.[6] America was inundated with reports in the news media and on talk shows, of what many scientists believe was a gross exaggeration of the hazards of eating Alar-treated apples.[7]

In the aftermath, Uniroyal suspended the sale of Alar in the United States, but the scare had done its damage. Losses to apple growers have been estimated at $250 million, and many growers declared bankruptcy. Apple processors lost another $125 million. Apple growers in the state of Washington sued CBS and the NRDC, alleging that they published knowingly false statements about the safety of eating apples.[8] The threat of cancer from Alar in the United States, if there ever was one, is history, but so are its benefits to growers and consumers of apples.

Is faith in the system justified?

Since 1959, both consumers and federal agencies have become more sophisticated about the problem of pesticide residues. When accidents happen, and they still do, the local area where the contamination occurs is isolated, and contaminated farm products are removed from the market. Such incidents no longer trigger a nationwide alert, and rightly so.

There are two possible reactions to news reports that pesticides have been found in a food in some part of the country. One reaction is to use this as evidence that our food in general is poisoned and should not be consumed. The other reaction is to use the finding of such contamination as evidence that the system is working and that regulatory agencies are doing an appropriate job. The latter is more realistic. Admittedly, this approach requires a measure of faith, because we as individuals cannot test all of our food for contaminants before we eat it. But it is in our favor that food growers, food processors, and regulatory officials also buy food in supermarkets, just as we do.

Is faith in the system justified? In one respect, we have reason to believe that our system has worked. When tobacco-related cancer is excluded and statistics are corrected for age, the incidence of and mortality from nearly all types of cancer has remained remarkably constant for the past thirty to forty years. (Stomach cancer is an exception to this, in that its incidence has dramatically declined.) Because this coincides with the period of marked increase in the use of agricultural chemicals, including pesticides, it suggests, but does not prove, that pesticides are not a significant factor in causing cancer. We believe that the system has reduced the risk of agricultural chemicals as much as possible. We can only hope, along with you, that the system keeps on working.

Direct benefits of the technological revolution

Few Americans realize that the technological revolution prevented widespread famine in the United States as well as the rest of the world. The 1930s were undoubtedly a gloomy period in American history. The country was in the midst of the Great Depression, and war clouds gathering over Europe and Asia threatened peace in the world. Those who were able to overlook the immediate perils and focus on the long-term future of America's food supply did not like what they saw. The problem was that the production of food, in pounds per acre, had increased little, if at all, since record keeping began at the end of the Civil War. It was only because of the opening of new farmland that food production had kept pace with the ever-expanding population and provided some for export. By the 1930s, almost all of the available productive land was being used. There was every reason to believe that America, "the land of plenty," would be unable to produce enough food for its own use within a few decades, let alone export food for others.

A relatively rapid demise of humanity by starvation was predicted as early as 1800 by an early British economist, Rev. Thomas Robert Malthus

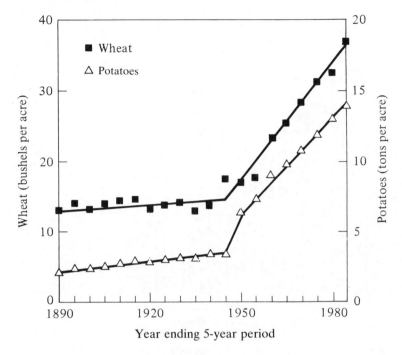

Figure 8.1. Wheat and potato production (average yield, 5-year periods).

(1766–1834).[9] Malthus, writing in a pamphlet entitled "Essay on the Principles of Population," published in 1798, observed that "the passion between the sexes is necessary and would remain" and that food was essential to existence. It was undoubtedly difficult for the critics of those days to argue with those two assertions, just as it would be now. Malthus, however, went further. From these two assertions, he predicted that the population would increase exponentially while the ability to produce food would increase at a much slower rate. Thus, population growth would be limited by the food supply, and the majority would barely survive. Before World War II, the specter of widespread starvation raised by Malthus was threatening to become reality. But this threat has been averted, at least for the foreseeable future, by the technological revolution in agriculture.

Malthus assumed that food production, in quantity per acre, would rise at a slow, linear rate, but this assumption eventually proved to be false (see Figure 8.1). For example, the average yield of potatoes increased by only about 25 percent during the seventy-five years between the end of the Civil War and the beginning of World War II. In 1940, an average acre would produce enough potatoes to feed fifty people; a

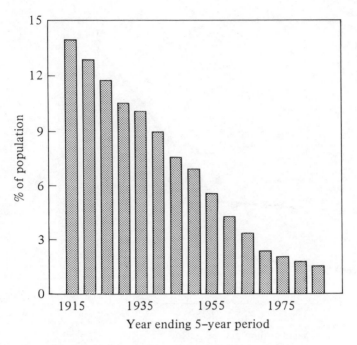

Figure 8.2. Farm workers (average, 5-year periods).

half-century later the same acre would feed five times that many people. Similar dramatic increases in yields of wheat and corn occurred about the same time.

The spectacular rise in production per acre began during the period immediately following World War II when American farmers began to practice scientific agriculture. Scientific agriculture meant a number of changes, including improvement in plant varieties through genetics, but more than anything, it meant a shift away from the organic farming of the past to the greater use of chemical fertilizers, insecticides, and herbicides. These, along with the mechanization that had started earlier with the introduction of tractors, allowed greater production with less labor.

Figure 8.2 shows that there has been a steady decrease in the percentage of the U.S. population engaged in farm work during the technological revolution and, indeed, since 1910. The trend has leveled in the last few years at just over one farm worker for each one hundred members of the population. As any astute student of economics will tell you, greater food production without a commensurate increase in demand, coupled with a reduced labor cost, should result in a lower price for food. And in real dollars, it has.

When corrected for inflation, food prices have steadily fallen during the

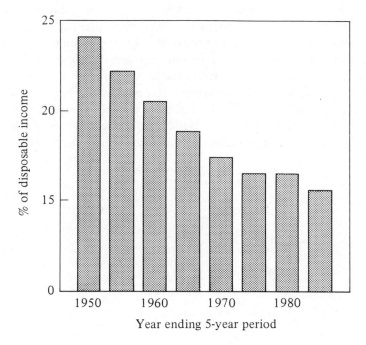

Figure 8.3. Food cost (average, 5-year periods).

technological revolution. One way to correct for inflation is to calculate food costs as a percentage of disposable personal income. Figure 8.3 shows that in these terms, food costs have steadily dropped since the end of World War II. In fact, in real money, the average consumer spent only about 65 percent as much for food in the 1980s as was spent during the Depression years a half-century earlier. Even then, the cost of food was a real bargain for the average person compared with earlier times. A century ago, urban laborers might have to spend 50 to 85 percent of their income for food and, if they had a big family, might still be hungry.[10] The relative decrease in food cost is even more remarkable when one considers that much more of our food is now processed, packaged, and often transported over longer distances than it was before the technological revolution, all of which add to the price.

Cost–benefit ratio

The benefits of the technological revolution in agriculture for the consumer are obvious when you visit the local supermarket – food in abundance at relatively reasonable prices. As a spin-off, there is more food worldwide.

Although the nutritional value of food has not been diminished, there has been a cost. There is no doubt that some of our food today likely contains traces of pesticides that would not have been present in food grown in the 1930s. We have reason to believe that these contaminants do not pose a significant risk to our health, but the risk is not zero. Zero risk would not be possible even if we returned to the food productions methods in use fifty years ago. Can we afford to return to organic farming? We do not think so. Do the benefits justify the potential cost? We believe that they do, but only you can answer that for yourself. In the next two chapters, we will discuss some of the legal efforts to minimize the potential threat to our health.

9   Food laws: Avoiding the chicanery of yesteryear

State and most local governments have health laws and inspectors to enforce them. But how can you be sure that the food you buy in the grocery store or even that supplied to a local restaurant is wholesome? Not so long ago you had no such assurance. Today, because of the passage of several federal "pure food" laws, you do. Unfortunately, too many people are unaware of these measures to protect the consumer from deliberate adulteration of food.

Nosophobia: Fear of our food supply

Although some people may be concerned about the safety of consuming fresh produce because of the chemicals used in modern farm production practices, many more people express a fear of processed foods. A medical term, *nosophobia*, is defined as an abnormal dread of sickness or any particular disease such as cancer. In her book *Toxic Terror*,[1] Elizabeth Whelan asserts that this illness may be the most serious facing our nation because it is producing a population full of healthy hypochondriacs. Dr. Whelan blames the overwhelming fear in our country of cancer and heart disease and the push by many for quick action to eliminate the public health hazards present in daily life. In truth, there is no reason, and no realistic hope, for this quest for zero risk. Pushed too far, it could have the opposite effect because it could result in lowered standards of living and a threat to good nutrition and overall health.[2]

Although nosophobia – and, in particular, the concern that chemicals in our food cause dreaded diseases such as heart disease and cancer – has been called the disease of the 1980s, the fear of disease is obviously not new. Heart disease and cancer are now the first and second causes of mortality, respectively, whereas at the turn of the century they were the fourth and eighth leading causes of death, respectively.[3] There is no reason to believe that these degenerative diseases have moved up on the list because of changes in our food supply or life-style. It is just that in 1900 people were much more likely to die of influenza or pneumonia, tuber-

133

culosis or even gastroenteritis at an age too young for the diseases of older age to get them. The life expectancy of a newborn in 1900 was about twenty-five years less than it is today.[4] There was much more reason to be concerned about the safety of the food supply in these earlier times than there is today.

A justified concern: Early food adulteration practices

Food adulteration has been with us since humans stopped feeding only themselves and started to feed others. Indeed, it is as old as trade itself. Food adulteration was commonplace in the United States well into the twentieth century. At the time of its zenith during the 1800s, 40 percent of samples of ground coffee in New York were fake; 46 percent of candy samples in Boston had mineral coloring added, mainly highly toxic lead chromate; and half of New Hampshire's maple syrup samples were not syrup at all. Before the advent of refrigerated railroad cars, most of the milk sold in New York City was "swill milk." Swill milk was skim milk that had water added. Chalk dust or plaster of Paris was added to restore the white color to the blue liquid. Experiments showed that children given an extra pint of real milk per day increased in height and weight by 20 percent in only seven months.

Tea, the staple drink of Britain, was a target for frequent adulteration long before Americans adulterated Boston Harbor with it on that cold December day in 1773. In the eighteenth century, iron filings, clay, and gypsum were added to increase the weight of tea. Thinning it with leaves was common. To cover up the adulteration, the leaves were colored with molasses, clay, dyes, paints, and even sheep feces.

Food chicanery flourished in early America because the U.S. Constitution guaranteed its citizens the freedom to engage in any practice not specifically prohibited by law. Food was often touted for its ability to cure or prevent certain diseases. In the absence of laws against doing so, mail and newspapers were used to spread untruths. Many newspapers stayed in business because of handsome financial rewards for publishing the "benefits" of food as cures for diseases. The fact that medical practice was so poor at the time was part of the problem. Food poisonings were misdiagnosed.

Drug chicanery was also a problem. Drugs could contain just about anything and could be advertised to cure just about anything. Patent medicines, often consisting of colored water, were sold for the treatment and cure of any and all real and imagined diseases, by hucksters who traveled from town to town by covered wagon and put on "medicine shows." By also providing some type of entertainment, crowds were attracted. Between acts, a miracle cure for cancer, "female problems," dropsy, Bright's disease (a kidney ailment), and male impotence could be bought for a dollar a bottle. Other "medicines" with more active ingredients were available for "quieting" youngsters or wandering husbands who slipped off to the saloon every evening. The cures apparently contained impure and cheap narcotics in amounts large enough to kill small children and slow down many a nightwalker's trips.

Wiley, Sinclair, and Roosevelt

The dawning of the twentieth century ushered in a new era in America. Reform movements were successful in at least reducing the ease with which the unscrupulous could relieve the gullible of their money. In regard to food and medicine, the stars of the reform movement included a physician-chemist, a writer, and a rough-riding, exuberant politician. Their actions culminated in passage of what is popularly known as the Pure Food and Drug Act. This law, officially called the Federal Food and Drug Act, was passed on June 30, 1906, and became effective on January 1, 1907. It was designed to prevent the "manufacture, sale or transportation of adulterated, misbranded or poisonous or deleterious foods, drugs, medicines and liquors."[5] Swill milk wasn't gone, but it definitely was on its way out.

The physician-chemist involved was Dr. Harvey M. Wiley. He worked for the U.S. Department of Agriculture and had the quaint idea that it was the government's responsibility to assure the public that what they ate was safe. Wiley and his "poison squad" of a dozen volunteers set out to discover what the consumer's body could tolerate. Using tests and methods unallowable today, he and his men ingested large amounts of various materials that were being added to food and, not surprisingly, became ill. These findings were published in 1902 and immediately launched a frenzy of controversy. Many of the interpretations of Wiley's discoveries were disputed by other scientists as well as some members of the embryonic food industry, on the grounds that large doses of anything can cause illness. The results of Wiley's studies were not enough to persuade a reluctant Congress to limit the freedoms of food manufacturers and processors. The tradition of "let the buyer beware" remained supreme. It took other events to get the needed legislation.

Fortunately, a few years after Wiley was deliberately eating adulterated food, another star of the reform movement, Upton Sinclair, published a book entitled *The Jungle*, about conditions in the Chicago slaughter houses.[a] Sinclair related horror stories of men falling into cooking vats

[a] Part of *The Jungle* was originally published in serial form in a socialist magazine, *The Appeal to Reason*. Several publishers turned it down because it was too controversial. Doubleday, Page agreed to publish a revised version of it if it could verify the charges. The publishers sent an editor to Chicago who posed as a meat inspector and thereby gained access to the

where lard was produced and, except for the bones, coming out labeled as "pure lard," of rats being ground along with spoiled meat and made into sausage, and of meat – too spoiled for any other use – being canned. When the book was published in 1906, there were outcries from everywhere. The meat-packing industry was outraged and denied the charges. But the press, especially the portion of it that Theodore Roosevelt labeled "muckrakers," publicized the contents of Sinclair's book. A popular ditty in the press at the time went:[6]

> Mary had a little lamb,
> And when she saw it sicken,
> She shipped it off to Packingtown
> And now it's labeled chicken.

Still, *The Jungle* was a novel, and even with the press hammering away at the need for reform and Wiley's reports on the dangers of food adulteration, little might have come of it had it not been for the efforts of a third person, a politician named Teddy Roosevelt. Pure food laws had been introduced into Congress several times over the previous thirty years, only to be bottled up in committee, and Roosevelt was furious.

Roosevelt was known by his political enemies as a "moose on the loose," and indeed, he later started the Bull Moose party when he lost the nomination of the Republican party for a third try at the White House. In 1906, however, as president of the United States, he had firsthand knowledge of what was being sold as canned meat. In fact, Roosevelt had been a witness before a Senate committee investigating what was known as the "embalmed beef" scandal of the Spanish–American War. He testified that he would just as soon have eaten his old hat as the canned beef that was supplied to the soldiers in Cuba under a government contract.[7] Even so, the meat-packing industry would not go down without a fight. A commission, sent to Chicago by the secretary of agriculture to investigate Sinclair's charges, was persuaded that these charges were untrue. Roosevelt sent a second commission to investigate. This time, the observers issued a scathing report confirming the main charges contained in *The Jungle*. Roosevelt skillfully used this information to push through the Pure Food and Drug Act as well as the Meat Inspection Act, both within six months of the publication of Sinclair's book.

The chemist, the writer, and the politician started us on the road of relying on the government to ensure the purity and safety of our food supply. Since then, several modifications and amendments to these original laws have been made (see Table 9.1).

On the whole, these laws have been successful in marshaling the con-

packing plants. He verified Sinclair's charges and found more. The book was released January 26, 1906, and was an immediate success. *The Jungle* was reprinted in 1960 by the New American Library.

Table 9.1. *Food and drug laws*

1906	*Federal Food and Drug Act*, signed into law on June 30, prohibited interstate commerce in misbranded and adulterated foods, drinks, and drugs.
1907	*Meat Inspection Act*
1913	*Gould amendment* enacted, requiring specific quantity information on food packages.
1927	*Food and Drug Administration (FDA)* organized.
1930	*McNary–Mapes amendment* enacted, authorizing standards of quality and fill of containers of canned food.
1938	*Federal Food, Drug and Cosmetic Act* passed, replacing the original Food and Drug Act and adding many new provisions.
1950	*Oleomargarine Act* passed, requiring labeling of colored oleomargarine to differentiate it from butter.
1951	*Delaney Committee* laid foundation for control of pesticides, food additives, and coloring in food.
1958	*Food additives amendment* enacted, requiring manufacturers to prove safety of food additives rather than requiring the government to prove the danger. Included the *Delaney clause*, which reads: "No additive shall be deemed to be safe if it is found to induce cancer when ingested by man or animal, or if it is found, after tests which are appropriate for the evaluation of safety of food additives, to induce cancer in man or animals."
1960	*Color additives amendment* passed, requiring manufacturers to establish safety and allowing the FDA to regulate the safe use of color additives.

Source: Adapted from *Nutrition History Notes,* Vanderbilt Medical Center Library no. 11, June 1981.

fidence of the American consumer in the safety of our food supply. For example, the Food Marketing Institute's annual survey in 1984 found that 88 percent of all shoppers agreed that supermarket food was safe to eat. In a separate poll, 78 percent of the respondents gave a highly or moderately favorable opinion of the Food and Drug Administration (FDA); 72 percent held similar opinions about the Food Safety and Inspection Service, which is responsible for ensuring that meat and poultry products are safe, wholesome, and accurately labeled.[8]

As to the main characters in the drama, 1906 was a banner year for each of them. Theodore Roosevelt received the Nobel Peace Prize that year, not for making peace with the meat packers, but for his part in ending a war between Russia and Japan. Upton Sinclair, whose ambition was to become a successful writer or starve in the process, almost did the latter until publication of *The Jungle*. Although Harvey Wiley was never able to overcome during his lifetime the animosity created by his controversial experiments on the effect of consuming chemicals added to food, he is credited, appropriately, with being the father of modern food laws. He was eventually honored by the issuance of a commemorative postage stamp in 1956, fifty years after the high point in his career and twenty- six years after his death at the ripe old age of 86.

Old errors are hard to break

Wiley's research was seriously flawed in that he forgot an extremely important word that must be considered in any experiments related to toxicity. That word is *quantity*. Unfortunately, most of us continue to make the same error today. We generally believe, for example, that arsenic is a poison and that vitamin C is not. In small amounts, neither is a poison, but in large amounts, both can kill.

Some nosophobes might argue that if a chemical in any amount can cause death, it should not be consumed. If we were to follow that advice, we would not eat, or drink, anything. You could be sure that you would not die of poisoning, but starvation would get you in about two months and dehydration would do you in much faster.

The Delaney clause, included in the food additives amendment passed by Congress in 1958, has caused controversy since it was originally passed, because it forbids the addition to food of any material shown to cause cancer, but it fails to mention anything about quantity. Ronald Deutsch[9] relates an example of how the omission of the word *quantity* has made a world of difference in the effect of the law. A chemical, trichloroethylene (TCE), had been used for years to extract caffeine in the production of decaffeinated coffee. With a name like that, it sounds like it would more likely be a constituent of gasoline than for processing coffee. However, at atmospheric pressure, TCE boils at minus 48.6° F and is practically insoluble in water. This means that TCE is a gas everywhere except at the North and South poles. Such volatility means that only extremely small amounts of it remain in the extracted coffee beans, and even less can be found in brewed coffee. However, scientists at the National Cancer Institute found that when a solution containing TCE was given to mice in large amounts via stomach tube every day for their entire lives, a few mice developed liver cancer.[10] The dosage given the mice is equivalent, in human terms, to the consumption of 50 million cups of decaffeinated coffee per day for several years! Deutsch also explains that other research showed that the consumption of TCE in amounts equivalent to only 100 cups per day did not cause cancer in mice. Nevertheless, TCE is no longer used in the preparation of any food or beverage.

The outcome was better, from the viewpoint of the consumer, for an artificial sweetener, saccharin, and most recently with another artificial sweetener, cyclamate. In the saccharin case, a Canadian study showed that male (but not female) rats developed bladder cancer when saccharin was fed as 7.5 percent of the diet for three generations.[11] If an equivalent dosage were given to an average-sized man, it would be the same as drinking 800 diet colas per day. The FDA threatened to seek a ban on saccharin. However, Congress was lobbied hard by the diabetics of the nation, as well as by many of the rest of us who desire sweetness without calories. In fact, more letters from constituents were received on this issue than on any other in the history of the Congress. The lawmakers responded by passing a law that allowed the FDA to not enforce the Delaney clause in this case. At the same time, the FDA required that warnings of the potential hazards of saccharin appear on the label of sweeteners containing it. It is only because of this legislative action that you can still buy saccharin and products containing it today.

Another artificial sweetener, cyclamate, was banned by the FDA in 1970 amidst one of the biggest health scares in our country. Cyclamate had been accused of causing everything from bladder cancer to birth defects. It was banned mainly because of the results of one study. In this experiment, done by a laboratory in New York, some rats developed tumors when cyclamate pellets were implanted in their bladders. These results could not be replicated in any other laboratory over the next several years. Numerous other countries that had followed the U.S. ban chose to reapprove it. The FDA, however, stood firm until early in 1989 when it finally announced that it had made a mistake in banning the sugar substitute and would likely reapprove its use.[b]

There is always a trade-off

If there is a chance that saccharin might cause cancer, why not ban it? One reason is that many diabetics must limit their intake of simple sugars, including table sugar. The problem is that they, like the rest of us, enjoy tickling their taste buds now and then with food that is sweet. Many more people, who are not diabetic, are concerned with their weight, but those taste receptors, which like to be occupied with something sweet, keep making their presence known to the brain until they are satisfied. The question becomes: Is there enough evidence that saccharin may cause cancer that those people who want to use it should be prevented from

[b] A *Washington Post* article ("Cyclamate Is Safe: FDA Ready to Admit Mistake," also appearing in the *Columbus (OH) Dispatch*, May 16, 1989, p. A1) reported that a group of monkeys at the National Cancer Institute fed the amount of cyclamate that would sweeten 30 cans of diet soda, 5 days a week, for the past 17 years had developed no health problems.

doing so? In this case, Congress has left it up to you to decide whether you want to (1) tell your taste buds to forget it, (2) choose another artificial sweetener, (3) take the minimal risk that saccharin might cause cancer, or (4) not worry about the calories and use plain old sugar to satisfy those taste buds.

Another case, involving nitrite, was easier to decide. For several years, nitrite has been added to foods, particularly to meats. One purpose for adding it to red meat is that it interacts with hemoglobin to maintain the red color. Nitrite has long been known to be toxic in large amounts and indeed has been shown to have been responsible for death in humans, but one must consume a lot of it to be poisoned.[c]

The real concern about nitrite as a food additive came when it was discovered that under some conditions, nitrite could react with certain amino acids to produce chemicals called *nitrosamines*. When fed in high amounts, nitrosamines have been found to produce cancer in animals. Thus, the regulatory agencies had to consider banning the addition of nitrite to food because it could indirectly lead to the production of a carcinogenic agent, even though there was no evidence that the nitrite itself caused cancer. In fact, the conditions in the gastrointestinal tract of humans and animals do not permit the formation of nitrosamines even if nitrite is consumed. Further, most of the preformed nitrosamines in the amounts that might be consumed are destroyed by stomach acid.

If the only purpose for using nitrite was to make meat look better, there likely would have been little opposition to banning its use in food, even in the remote chance that it might cause cancer. However, nitrite has another important purpose. It is one of the best agents available to inhibit the growth of those bacteria, especially in cured meat products, that cause botulism. The trade-off in this case was clear. Though banning the addition of nitrite to food might lower the chances of cancer, it was far more certain that there would have been a higher incidence of death from botulism. The compromise by the FDA was to reduce the amount that could be added to food to no more than just enough to inhibit bacterial growth. To put this decision in perspective, we should point out that vegetables contain relatively large amounts of nitrate, much of which is converted by bacteria in the mouth and intestines into nitrite. The average nitrite intake from

[c] One example of nitrite poisoning is described in *Eleven Blue Men*, by Berton Roueche (New York: Berkley, 1953). In the autumn of 1944, eleven men who had eaten breakfast in a small restaurant in New York City consumed toxic amounts of sodium nitrite when it was accidentally used instead of salt in the preparation of their oatmeal. Each of them had also used generous quantities of the chemical in salt shakers that also contained sodium nitrite instead of salt. Within a very short time, all of the men turned blue in color, a condition known medically as *cyanosis*, accompanied by severe abdominal cramps, retching, diarrhea, rigidity, and an inability to breathe. One of the men died.

food additives is estimated at about 3 milligrams per day, whereas natural food sources contribute up to 100 milligrams daily.[12]

The point of these examples is that the question of whether or not to allow certain chemicals to be added to food often cannot be simply answered. Decisions require some calculation of the cost-to-benefit ratio. We know of no one who advocates adding any chemicals to our food supply in amounts known to be hazardous to human health. Indeed, the prudent approach is that there must be a specific and justifiable reason for adding anything to our food supply. We are fortunate that the FDA and the food laws that have been passed take this prudent approach. Since the passage of the food additives amendment of 1958, the burden of proof of safety has been on the manufacturer.

10   Food processing and additives:
Between farm and table

Have you ever eaten uncooked potatoes or unripened apples? If you ate very much of either, you were likely soon punished by severe abdominal pain. But cooking either of them would have prevented the protestations of your gastrointestinal tract.

You might suppose that cooking destroyed some toxin against which your stomach was rebelling, but this is not the case. Actually, the abdominal pain was caused by the fact that the raw starch in uncooked green apples or potatoes is very poorly digested by the enzymes in your small intestine. Undigested starch then moves into the large intestine, where bacteria feast upon it and produce copious quantities of gas, which results in the abdominal pain. Cooking potatoes or green apples changes the starch into a much more digestible form. This deprives the bacteria in the large intestine of a banquet and prevents the increased production of gas. Had you waited until the apples ripened, much of the starch would have been converted to sugars that can be digested without having to be cooked. These are but two examples of the necessity of "processing," in this case cooking, to make most foods beneficial to humans.

The words *processed food* have gained a bad reputation, though except for a few fruits and vegetables, our food needs to be processed before we consume it. In the broadest sense, processing includes anything done to a food from the time of harvest until it is consumed. Humans have been processing food by cooking it since the discovery of fire. Cooking increases the efficiency of our digestive process to extract nutrients, and it destroys natural constituents in some foods that are harmful to humans.

Other types of processing are also important to our modern food supply and distribution system. Some is done as a means of preserving food. For example, most fruits and vegetables begin to decay the moment they reach maturity because of naturally occurring enzymes that they contain. Decaying fruits and vegetables become excellent media for the growth of microorganisms. If you are to derive optimal taste and nutritional benefit from fruits or vegetables, it is necessary to consume them immediately at the time of ripening or to devise some way to preserve them for con-

142

sumption at a later date. Meat, as soon as it is removed from a living animal, begins to decay, again because of inherent enzymes as well as microbial degradation. Before the middle of the nineteenth century, people solved the problem of preserving these perishable foods, by drying them. They learned that when the water was removed, such foods spoiled much more slowly. Meat was either dried or salted, both of which reduced the amount of water available to degrading enzymes and bacteria.

Of all the foods that our ancestors consumed, cereal grains were the easiest to preserve because they already contained little water. The expression that "bread is the staff of life" was not based on physiological truth but on the observation that grain, from which bread is made, could be preserved from harvest to harvest much better than could other foods. In Asia, rice became a staple no doubt in part because it could easily be stored.

Preserving foods by canning

Canning was invented in the early 1800s at the urging of the French emperor Napoleon Bonaparte, because he needed a way to preserve food for his army, which then occupied most of Europe. In America, home canning got its start at the end of the Civil War,[a] but it only gradually became popular over the next several decades, to become common during the Great Depression when its virtues were extolled by home demonstration agents of the U.S. Department of Agriculture. Home canning reached its peak of popularity during the patriotic days of World War II when almost everyone had a "victory" garden. These were called victory gardens because they had the aim of aiding the war effort by producing enough food to feed the civilian population. The nation's farmers and food processors were busy producing food for the military.

In the heyday of home canning, most families had a pressure cooker, which was necessary in order to elevate the temperature high enough to kill the spores of microorganisms. The canning container was then sealed while still hot to shut out oxygen and prevent the reintroduction of microbial contaminants. Foods high in acidity, such as some fruits and some varieties of tomatoes, could be safely canned by heating them to boiling-water temperature, but other, low-acid foods had to be heated well above

[a] In 1865 the steamboat *Bertrand* set out on the Missouri River heavily laden with provisions destined for the gold mining camps in Fort Benton, Montana. It never made its destination and was found a century later at the bottom of the river. In 1974 the canned food items retrieved from the boat were analyzed and found to be as safe to eat as they had been when canned one hundred years earlier. The food, however, had lost its fresh smell and appearance as well as significant amounts of vitamins C and A. See D. Blumenthal, "The Canning Process: Old Preservation Technique Goes Modern," *FDA Consumer*, September 1990, pp. 14–18.

the boiling point of water in order to reduce the microbial contamination sufficiently. The pressure cooker, first introduced for home use in 1874, provided a means of achieving the necessary high temperature. Although some households in the United States do their own canning, most of us leave this arduous task to industry.

The nutritional quality of food is only minimally lowered by canning if it is done properly. In general, commercial canning probably has less adverse effects than does home canning on the nutrient content of foods, because food companies are more likely to have the proper equipment and technology to achieve high temperatures quickly. In addition, commercially canned foods are much less likely to cause food poisoning. Botulism is one of the more serious examples of food poisoning, in that fatalities from exposure to this toxin range from 30 to 65 percent. Out of 1,780 cases of botulism reported from the beginning of this century until 1963, only 12 percent of them were caused by contamination of commercially produced food.[1]

Preserving food by refrigeration and freezing

Refrigeration of food was not practical until a Maryland farmer, Thomas Moore, obtained a patent in 1803 for a "refrigerator." Actually, it was a very primitive insulated "icebox" that had to be filled with winter ice from ponds. Cutting pond ice by hand was no easy task until an ice cutter, something akin to a plow, was invented in 1827. By 1828, iceboxes were fairly common among the well-to-do in northern cities.[b] Iceboxes were not available to poor people, however, because the box and the ice were too expensive. And as long as it was necessary to rely on winter pond ice, home refrigeration was not practical for those living in the sunbelt regions of the country. But the later development of mechanical refrigeration eventually made the icebox, and then home refrigerators, common nationwide.

The creation of refrigerated railroad cars – which at first meant loading ice into portable iceboxes but which were later cooled by mechanical refrigeration – allowed the shipment of fresh fruits, vegetables, and meat across the country. The Midwest and the South could have clams and lobsters, and the North could have strawberries for four months out of the year instead of only one. Fresh meat became available in population centers around the nation. A meat packer with a name that virtually everyone recognizes, Gustavus Swift, took the lead in distributing his product by means of refrigerated rail cars. Philip Armour swiftly followed.

Refrigeration has several advantages over canning as a method of pre-

---

[b] When ice became available to the rich, ice cream became available also. When ice cream became available to the poor, it was because of the establishment of ice-cream parlors.

serving food. In addition to the fact that less effort is required, foods preserved by refrigeration retain more of the taste and texture of fresh food. Reducing storage temperature to just above freezing slows microbial growth as well as the normal decay processes but does not stop either.

While most of America was reeling from the effects of economic disaster in 1929, a man named Clarence Birdseye was inventing a method to quick-freeze food. His innovation was to place food between two extremely cold metal blocks. Birdseye sold his invention to General Foods in 1932 and thus started a new industry – the preservation of food by freezing.

Many improvements have been made in the technology of rapid freezing since Birdseye's early device, so that for many foods, quick-freezing is one of the most effective methods of preservation. Quick-freezing retains the nutrients as well as taste and color, although the texture of some foods is markedly changed, owing to the formation of ice crystals during the freezing process. Remember, however, that freezing does not necessarily kill microorganisms; instead it virtually stops their growth. Therefore, frozen foods should never be thawed uncovered at room temperature, nor should they be refrozen. Normally, frozen foods should be thawed in the refrigerator. However, if it is necessary to thaw them more rapidly, the defrost setting on a microwave oven or placement in a watertight bag immersed in cold (not hot) water are acceptable methods.

Preserving food by irradiation

Irradiating food as a means of preserving it has been studied since the 1950s, but its use is still quite limited. The idea is simple, but because it means exposing food to radioactive substances, the process generates fear. Actually, irradiation uses either x-rays or a beam of gamma rays from a radioactive substance, usually cobalt-60 or cesium-137. The energy levels of the gamma rays are in the same range as those of x-rays. Depending on the level of exposure, the rays kill some, most, or all of the microorganisms in the food being irradiated. Most often, the amount of radiation used is just enough to reduce the microbial population, similar to the process of pasteurizing milk.

Despite a common misconception, if you serve irradiated foods, you cannot have a candlelight dinner without candles. Irradiated food does not glow in the dark. It does not become radioactive because it never comes into contact with the radioactive substance, only the radiation from it. In this regard, irradiation is comparable to microwave cooking, in that it would be dangerous to us to be directly exposed to microwaves, but there is no risk in eating food heated by microwave energy.

A second concern about irradiating foods is that it might produce chemicals called *radiolytic products*, which may be hazardous to our health.

Food scientists have extensively explored this possibility but have found that irradiation results in no more degradative products than do conventional cooking and processing methods.[2] Furthermore, irradiating food has been found to affect its nutrients no more, and sometimes less, than do conventional methods of preservation.

Scientists agree almost unanimously that irradiation is a safe and effective way to preserve food. Indeed, the benefits and safety of irradiated foods were recognized by an expert panel of the World Health Organization in 1981, which concluded that food exposed to a limited amount of radiation is wholesome for humans.[3] A number of countries have approved irradiation for various uses, ranging from killing insects in grain to sterilizing cooked meat so that it can be kept for long periods without having to be refrigerated. In the United States, the Food and Drug Administration (FDA) has approved only a few uses of irradiation.[4] These include killing insects in wheat, slowing the sprouting of white potatoes, controlling the parasitic worm in pork that causes trichinosis, and extending the shelf life of fresh fruits. The FDA has also proposed using irradiation to control salmonella in poultry products.

Convenience foods

The emphasis in the previous sections has been on preserving foods. The food industry has become much more than a freezing and canning industry, however. Many of the foods that we now buy are convenience foods, that is, formulated foods that require minimum effort to prepare before they are ready to serve. The sale of foods that are not conveniently prepared at home is nothing new. Indeed, at the turn of the century, Henry Heinz got his start by peddling horseradish in a jar in Sharpsburg, Pennsylvania, and he eventually expanded the line to what became the famous "57 varieties." Campbell's soup started at about the same time. What has changed is the contents of the containers.

These early entrepreneurs, as well as later entrants into the food industry, recognized two factors necessary for the success of commercially prepared foods: brand recognition and consumer acceptance. Brand recognition could be achieved by advertisements, many of which appeared in the early days in women's magazines. Now, of course, we also are bombarded by jingles and slogans in television commercials.

Consumer acceptance is perhaps more important than brand recognition. If a consumer buys a product and is dissatisfied with it, the producer will be better served if the consumer does not remember the brand name. In regard to food, acceptance depends on how the food interacts with our senses: taste, appearance, texture, and odor. Acceptance is not related, except in an intellectual sense, to whether the product satisfies our nutritional needs. The food industry has worked diligently to make products that satisfy our senses, which often means adding chemicals to make their product better (as judged by our senses) than the products of competitors or those prepared at home. Does the addition of these chemicals constitute a hazard to our health? To answer this question, it is necessary to consider food additives.

Food additives

The term *food additives* often conjures up visions of mad scientists in a chemistry laboratory inventing synthetic chemicals. We don't often think of the legal definition of a food additive. The food additives amendment of 1958 defined a food additive as "any substance the intended use of which results or may be reasonably expected to result, directly or indirectly, in its becoming a component or otherwise affecting the characteristics of any food."[5] According to this definition, it is clear that any substance can be a food additive whether or not it is synthetic and whether it is intentionally or unintentionally added. Even when a substance is isolated from one food and added to another, it becomes, by definition, a food additive. Most food additives are in fact natural chemicals that may be a natural component of the foods to which they are added. Indeed, when table salt (sodium chloride) is added to foods, it becomes a food additive and must be included on the label of canned or packaged foods, even though the original foods may also contain sodium and chloride. Often food additives are listed on food labels according to their chemical names, which may not be recognized by the average consumer.

Sometimes the requirements of our nation's food laws result in some strange terminology. For example, it might be assumed that the powder available in the grocery store labeled "nondairy creamer" would not contain dairy products. Actually, two of the components contained in the product are isolated from milk: whey and a milk protein, casein. Even though the nondairy creamer contains materials from milk, it is nondairy because the other major ingredients come from other natural sources. It contains corn sugar rather than milk sugar and vegetable fats rather than butter fat. Because nondairy creamer is made from components of various foods, it can be accurately called a synthetic food. It is certainly not a natural food because it does not exist, as such, anywhere in nature. Even so, for those who like cream in their coffee, this synthetic substitute is superior to real cream in at least one respect: It keeps without refrigeration.

Careful reading of the label of nondairy creamer reveals the presence of other substances. One case in point is BHA, which is present as a preservative.

BHA stands for butylated hydroxyanisole. It is a member of a chemical family famous for being "antioxidants," to which vitamins C and E also belong. As this name implies, BHA is added to food to prevent the oxidation of food components, especially fat. Fatty acids, which have one or more double bonds (see Chapter 4), have the unfortunate habit of reacting with oxygen from the air. The products of this illicit affair have a terrible taste and odor and are appropriately described as rancid fat. If you have ever had the misfortune of tasting chicken or hamburger that spent too long dallying in air in a warm climate before it was cooked, you have experienced this phenomenon. Although antioxidants cannot, by law, be added to meat because they might cover up mishandling, resulting in bacterial contamination, they can be added to many other foods.

Guaranteeing a safe and wholesome food supply is the intent of much federal legislation. The food additives amendment put the responsibility on the manufacturer of proving that all food additives were safe. At the same time, the legislation recognized the need for some food additives and the impossibility of testing all of the literally thousands of chemicals in our food supply. As a result, a scientific advisory committee was appointed to examine the evidence for the safety of food additives generally in use at that time, on a case-by-case basis. The list of chemicals considered safe by the expert committee, when used in appropriate amounts, is called the GRAS ("generally recognized as safe") list.

In many cases, the scientists' decision is easy. For example, vitamins and required minerals not only are safe when used in appropriate amounts, but they also are necessary components of our food supply. Even so, the addition of vitamins or minerals to food requires approval by the Food and Drug Administration. Approval is generally denied when a manufacturer wants to add them to foods (such as soft drinks) that would not normally be considered a source of them. Other substances, including sugar, baking soda, acetic acid, spices, and all raw agricultural products are included on the GRAS list because they are natural components of food and have been consumed by humans for years without evidence of harmful effects.

In some cases, however, the decision about the safety of other candidates for the GRAS list is much more difficult.[6] The decision to include purely synthetic substances on this list was made on the basis of extensive studies that indicated that the particular chemical constituted no demonstrable health hazard when included in food in appropriate, specified amounts. At the same time, provision was made to remove chemicals from the GRAS list if subsequent research indicated that their use could result in a health hazard. There are cases in which substances included on the original GRAS list have been subsequently removed.

BHA made the GRAS list on the basis of numerous studies that showed that it was not toxic unless consumed in amounts much larger than would ever be obtained from food.[c] One of the concerns of the law, and indeed of all of us, is that substances added to food should not cause cancer. In the case of BHA, studies showed that it was not carcinogenic in animals and, in fact, inhibited tumor growth.[7] Here then, is a purely synthetic chemical that not only protects our taste buds from the insult of rancid fat but also may reduce the risk of cancer.

Calcium propionate is another preservative found on the GRAS list. Unless you happen to be a biochemist, the name of this chemical is not exactly what one would call a household word, although it is present in almost every household. Calcium propionate is one of the most effective chemicals known for preventing the growth of mold on bread. If the label on the wrapper of the bread you purchase at your local supermarket does not show that calcium propionate has been added, you will likely find the words "no preservatives added." You might think that such a statement means that this bread is better for you than bread to which calcium propionate has been added, but this is not the case. In fact, if you buy bread with "no preservatives added," you had better either (1) eat it fast or (2) develop a taste for green bread. Green (or black) bread mold has a habit of appearing within two or three days after bread is baked unless a mold retardant is added. Because uninvited mold on food is not only aesthetically unappealing but might also be harmful, eating moldy food is not generally a good idea.

Is calcium propionate safe for human consumption? In a word, yes. Chemically, it is the calcium salt of an organic chemical, propionic acid.[d] Calcium is a necessary component in our diet, and the calcium part of calcium propionate simply adds to our calcium intake. The other part of the mold inhibitor, propionic acid, is made and used in our liver as a normal product in the metabolism of certain amino acids. In other words, your liver makes this chemical and uses it, whether or not you eat it. Can your liver distinguish between the propionic acid from food and that synthesized by the liver? No. At reasonable levels of intake, calcium propionate is much safer for the consumer than mold is. In addition, the use of calcium propionate saves money because it reduces food spoilage, the cost of which is passed on to the consumer. The quantity of calcium propionate added is so small that a penny will buy enough of it to protect 100 loaves of bread from mold. Indeed, you can expect to pay much more for

[c] The quantity of BHA added to food is slightly less than four parts per million, which roughly translates into one-eighth ounce per ton of food, or one large needle in a ton of hay. The toxic dose of BHA in rats is 2.5 to 5 grams per kilogram of body weight, according to the *Merck Index* (Rahway, NJ: Merck and Co., 1976). Assuming the same toxicity for humans, it can be readily calculated that an averaged-size man would have to eat 96,000 pounds of food supplemented with four parts per million BHA in order to consume a toxic dose.

[d] The antimold properties of propionate were discovered through the observation that Swiss cheese, which is naturally high in propionate, was resistant to mold.

a loaf of bread with "no preservatives added," because moldy bread cannot be sold, which increases the manufacturer's costs.

BHA and calcium propionate are but two examples of safe preservatives that protect us from potentially harmful substances that can develop naturally in our food. It seems to be a product of human nature, however, to fear the unknown, and to most consumers these chemicals are unknown. You have no doubt seen television commercials that exploit this fear.

Chemicals on the GRAS list have undergone careful scrutiny, but what about other additives in our food? In order to use substances not on this list, manufacturers must provide considerable information to the FDA, including evidence that the substance is safe for the intended use. This is by far the most difficult requirement to satisfy, but it is the most important. Other information that must be provided includes evidence that the proposed additive will accomplish the intended effect and that the quantity to be added is no higher than the minimum amount necessary to do so.

Tests of an additive for safety must be carried out in at least two different animal species over at least two generations, and any effects, including cancer development, reproductive failure, physical defects, and behavior, must be noted. The safe amount that can be added to food is then set at one hundred times lower than the safe level in animal tests. If this safe amount for human food is higher than that needed to accomplish the intended purpose as a food additive, only the smaller amount will be approved. If subsequent research indicates that a substance might have some harmful effect not observed in the original testing, the tests must be repeated, even though the substance may have received earlier approval from the FDA.

The intent of the federal regulations is to reduce the risk of harmful effects of food additives as much as possible. Although it is not possible to lower the risk to zero, manufacturers must prove, beyond a reasonable doubt, that a proposed food additive is safe. Further, food additives are not automatically approved, even if their safety has been established. Criteria have been developed for the acceptable and unacceptable uses of these substances.[8] Some acceptable uses of a food additive are to (1) improve or maintain the nutritional value of a food, (2) enhance quality, (3) enhance consumer acceptability, and (4) improve keeping quality. The use of food additives to deceive the consumer, such as disguising faulty or inferior food processing or concealing damaged or spoiled food, is unacceptable.

Having regulations covering the appropriate use of food additives is one thing, but compliance with those regulations by food manufacturers is another. Occasionally statements are made in the media that the FDA actually tests only a fraction of a percentage of our food to ensure compliance with the regulations. This is true. The FDA expects compliance, just as the Internal Revenue Service expects compliance with the tax laws: It is neither necessary nor possible for the IRS to audit all tax returns, but enough of them are, and the penalty for noncompliance is sufficiently severe, to make most taxpayers volunteer to pay the appropriate amount. In the past, the FDA has had adequate personnel to inspect food-processing plants and to test enough samples to encourage manufacturers to comply with the laws. Unfortunately, with the federal budgetary restraints of the past few years, the FDA is on the verge of losing its enforcement ability,[9] and so we must increasingly rely on voluntary compliance. We can only hope that Congress recognizes that the FDA is too important to the over-seeing of the safety of our food supply that it will not be allowed to suffer from "financial malnutrition."

Substances once thought to be safe that may cause problems

We don't mean to imply that we have achieved 100 percent safety in our food supply. Continued research is essential because there is always the possibility that some chemicals that we think are safe on the basis of our current knowledge will turn out not to be so when we learn more about their effects. Indeed, some chemicals once thought to be safe have been removed from the approved list of food additives, and others are being reinvestigated.

Sulfite, usually in the form of the sodium salt, is one such chemical whose addition to processed food the FDA allows in very limited amounts. Sulfite, which has the property of removing oxygen by reacting with it, can there-fore keep such salad staples as lettuce and spinach from losing their fresh green color and wilting. Thus, some operators of salad bars used to dip their vegetables in a solution of sulfite. The residual sulfite does not cause a problem for most people, but it does cause sometimes serious problems for people who are particularly susceptible to its effects. Because of this, FDA withdrew its approval of using sulfite on raw fruits and vegetables.

A synthetic female hormone, diethylstilbestrol (DES), is another ex-ample. Male animals destined to be meat on the dinner table are often castrated at an early age. Would-be bulls, boars, and roosters are thus converted to steers, barrows, and capons, respectively. The reason for such treatment is that male hormones, including testosterone, make the animal less efficient at depositing fat and thereby reduces the tenderness of the meat. Female hormones, including DES, have the opposite effect. Thus, at one time, DES was routinely added to animal feed to lower food costs and produce a more desirable product. This seemed to be a case in which both producer and consumer benefited – until it was discovered that when women were given relatively large pharmacological doses of DES during pregnancy, their daughters subsequently exhibited a higher incidence of cervical cancer. Could it be possible that the consumption of DES, even the much smaller amount found in meat of animals treated with it, could cause cancer? The FDA decided that the risks were not worth the benefits and thus banned the addition of DES to animal feeds.

The use of antibiotics in animal production is another example of what at first appeared to be a good idea but that, in some cases, turned out not to be. Shortly after World War II, when antibiotics became generally available, it was discovered that when small amounts of antibiotics were added to poultry feed, the animals grew faster and processed their feed more efficiently. During the ensuing four decades, the use of antibiotics became more widespread in the production of animal products. Because of this, meat, milk, and eggs were less expensive than they would have been otherwise. Critics argued that food produced using antibiotics might be less expensive but that it was not risk free.

Over the years, two concerns about the practice of adding antibiotics to animal feeds have been expressed: (1) Antibiotic residues remaining in meat could be consumed by humans, leading to allergic reactions, and (2) antibiotic-resistant strains of some potentially harmful microorganism could develop. As a precaution against these, the FDA has limited the amount and type of antibiotics as well as other antimicrobial drugs in animal feed.[10] The addition of those antibiotics used in human therapy to animal feed is prohibited except by a veterinarian's prescription for the treatment of specific diseases. In such a case, antibiotic treatment must be withheld for a specified period of time before slaughter in order to reduce residues to a safe level in the product. A recent FDA study of antibiotic drug residues in milk reveals little misuse of animal drugs.[11]

Such precautions limited the debate but did not end it, especially with respect to the development of strains of microorganisms resistant to antibiotics. The problem arises because low levels of antibiotics may kill most but not all of a particular strain of microorganism. Those few microorganisms that survive do so because they have enzymes that can either destroy the antibiotic or otherwise resist its effects. These surviving organisms, with less competition from their unfortunate cousins, can then multiply. Fuel to the debate was added when an antibiotic-resistant strain of salmonella, a common bacteria that can cause food poisoning, was found in milk.[12] The FDA is currently investigating this finding and will perhaps reexamine its position on the use of antibiotics in animal feeds.

Food poisoning: What you can't see can hurt you

With the passage and enforcement of our current food laws, it is safe to say that we are in far greater danger from what nature might put in our food than from the additions by humans. Food-borne illnesses are much more common than we realize, as they often go unnoticed or are ascribed to "a touch of the flu." Sometimes, however, they can be quite serious and, in rare instances, fatal, especially in the very young, the very old, and those who are already ill or whose immune systems are suppressed.[13]

A common food-borne illness in the United States in modern times is caused by the ingestion of even a relatively small number of salmonella bacteria. After a short incubation, the symptoms appear, including nausea, diarrhea, abdominal pain, and fever, which for most people abate after two to three days.

Salmonella bacteria are common. We can become infected from water or food or from chewing our fingernails after cleaning the turtle bowl or a chicken before it's cooked. These organisms thrive in the gastrointestinal tract of animals that give us milk, meat, and eggs.[e] Because these foods can easily be contaminated by these animals, it is in our best interest to kill the microorganisms before consuming the foods. Because salmonella bacteria are not killed by either refrigeration or freezing, heat and care are the best weapons against this organism. The risk of salmonella is one of the best arguments that we can give you for pasteurizing milk and against consuming raw milk or eggs and undercooked poultry.

Clostridium perfringens is another bacteria, widely distributed in nature, that can cause illness. The symptoms are similar to those of salmonella infection, but there is a major difference between the two organisms. Although it takes a relatively small number of salmonella bacteria to cause infection, it takes large numbers of clostridium perfringens. Thus, problems with this organism usually come from consuming meat or poultry products held warm for several hours. The obvious way to avoid clostridium infection is to not leave protein-containing foods at room temperature or, if you do, to recook them before eating them.

Salmonella produces illness because of a true infection by the organisms themselves, which can be prevented by killing them with heat. Not all bacteria are so cooperative. If they are allowed to grow in food, some bacteria produce toxic materials that cannot be destroyed by heat. In this case, illness can be prevented only if the organism is not allowed to grow in the first place. For example, when staphylococcus is allowed to grow to large numbers, it produces a heat-stable toxin that causes a relatively minor illness. Symptoms include nausea, vomiting, abdominal pain, and diarrhea within one to six hours after the toxin is consumed. Fortunately, the effects

[e] In fact, salmonella received some major publicity in 1985 when literally thousands of people in Illinois were infected because pasteurized milk became contaminated with raw milk before it found its way to the supermarket. More recently, a survey by the U.S. Department of Agriculture found that more than one-third of the chickens produced in some processing plants were contaminated with significant amounts of salmonella and that some eggs were contaminated as well. See M. Segal, "Invisible Villains: Tiny Microbes Are Biggest Food Hazard," *FDA Consumer*, July–August 1988, pp. 9–11.

of the toxin last only one to two days. Foods commonly involved are potato salads, salads containing meat, cream-filled baked goods, fermented sausages, and cheese. The proper handling of these foods after preparation, including refrigeration, can reduce the growth of the staphylococcus organism and therefore the production of the toxin.

Similarly, *Clostridium botulinum* produces a toxin that is far more dangerous than that produced by staphylococcus. Clostridium's toxin affects nerves even when only a very small amount is ingested. Symptoms of the disease, called *botulism*, develop within twelve to thirty-six hours. The early symptoms include nausea, vomiting, and diarrhea. These are followed by double vision, difficulty in swallowing, inability to talk, and, finally, respiratory paralysis. Botulism is fatal in 30 to 65 percent of cases. Because home-canned foods with a low acid content are the major source of the botulism toxin, it is not surprising that the incidence of the disease has steadily declined since the peak of home canning during the 1940s. Cured meat products such as frankfurters, bacon, bologna, and ham can also support the growth of *Clostridium botulinum*, except that a food additive, nitrite, is used in the production of these foods to prevent sporulation of the organism.

Trichinosis is a food-borne illness that was once much more prevalent than it is today. This disease is not caused by bacteria but by a parasitic worm that finds the muscles of humans, bear, and swine a hospitable environment. Because we don't eat much bear meat, pork is the most common source of this infection for humans. Swine tolerate the presence of the worm well and therefore become carriers of the organism to humans. Humans are much less tolerant. The symptoms of the disease include high fever, itching, swollen eyes, diarrhea, headache, and seething pain in the chest, abdomen, arms, and legs. It is said that victims are so miserable that some wish for death, which often comes, following a coma.

The organism that causes trichinosis has been credited with causing many religions to proscribe the consumption of pork, which is certainly one way of avoiding the disease. However, there are ways to eat pork safely. The most common of these is to cook the meat until well done. (An internal temperature of at least 150° F is slightly higher than the temperature necessary to kill the organism and thus provides a margin of safety.) The organism can also be killed by freezing the pork (for two to three weeks) or salting, smoking, or pickling it. Knowledge and appropriate health laws, such as prohibiting the feeding of uncooked garbage to swine, have reduced the occurrence of this disease.

Potential return of food-borne illnesses

For the most part, the food-borne illnesses experienced in developed nations today are relatively minor annoyances compared with those suffered by previous generations. A one-day bout with the staphylococcus toxin is obviously a nuisance, but it does not compare with the ravages of cholera, typhoid fever, or tuberculosis, all of which can be transmitted by contaminated food and water. It is easy to forget that these diseases plagued the lives of people who are still alive. In fact, the commonly used label "Typhoid Mary" did not enter our vocabulary until the 1920s when a domestic cook, Mary Mallon, was identified as the carrier responsible for at least fifty-one cases of typhoid fever in and around New York City.[14]

Typhoid fever and cholera have been virtually eliminated in our country by means of vaccination, sanitation, and aggressive enforcement of health laws. Human carriers of the organisms causing typhoid fever and tuberculosis are prohibited from being associated in any way with the commercial production, distribution, and preparation of food. The spread of cholera has been held in check because of laws prohibiting the use of human waste as fertilizer in the production of food unless it has been treated to kill harmful microorganisms.

Of all the public health measures for the control of these deadly diseases, the chlorination of water and the pasteurization of milk are among the most effective, as they kill the organisms that cause these and other diseases. Both chlorination and pasteurization are extremely important to the protection of our health. Critics of chlorination have argued that it can lead to the formation of chlorinated hydrocarbons that might be carcinogenic, but the quantity of these produced under any circumstances is very small. It has been suggested that instead of chlorine, it would be safer to use ozone. The problem is that although ozone can kill any microorganisms present, unlike chlorine, it does not remain in the water supply and therefore cannot prevent the growth of organisms introduced by recontamination between the water treatment plants and the time of consumption. Analysis of the cost-to-benefit ratio clearly favors continued chlorination. Unfortunately, in much of the world where these processes are not used, typhoid fever, cholera, and tuberculosis are not relegated to the history books. They still kill today.

Could we do without modern food processing and food additives?

We could obviously return to yesteryear, to a world without modern food processing that did not have, intentionally at least, food additives. But without them, baked goods would become stale quickly; foods with fats and oils would rapidly become rancid and lose their vitamin E; and canned fruits and vegetables would become "mushy." We would have no convenience or fabricated foods. Foods would become much more expensive and less readily available because of spoilage. And starvation due to lack of food, diseases of malnutrition (such as goiter, rickets, pellagra, beriberi, and dental cavities), and food-borne illnesses would be as common as they were in the distant past. We could do without modern food processing and additives. It is doubtful, however, that anyone aware of the facts would want to do so.

11 Foods with reputations: The good, the bad, and the ugly

Foods, like people, develop reputations. Often these reputations are based on innuendo, not fact. For most of us, food is an important part of the quality of life. A few take this to the extreme on both ends of the spectrum. That is, some people only "eat to live," whereas others literally "live to eat."

If the enjoyment of eating is important to you, we do not think that you should be deprived of foods that you like because they have bad reputations, nor do we believe that you should force yourself to eat foods that you dislike simply because they have been said to be good for you.

In this chapter, we discuss some foods with reputations, some good and some bad. Our purpose is to describe what they do and do not contribute to your health from a nutrition standpoint. After learning these facts, the decision of whether to include them among the foods that you eat becomes simply a matter of personal preference as dictated by your senses.

Foods are often described on two different levels, because our consumption of food is usually for two different purposes. One purpose is for enjoyment, and at this level, all of us are our own personal expert. Preferences are often stated by describing a food as good or not good. We have no quarrel with this because it depicts the interaction of specific foods with our senses, including taste, texture, odor, sight, and, if we believe some food commercials, even sound.

A second purpose for eating food is to meet our nutritional needs. Our sensory response to a food does not give us a clue to its nutritional value. To determine the nutritional quality of a food, it is necessary to take it to a chemistry laboratory. This has been done for the consumer, and the results are shown on food labels and in nutrient composition tables (see Chapter 1). It is necessary to rely on intellect, not taste buds, to translate this information into a selection of the suitable types and quantities of various foods.

In our view, it is only logical that the selection of food take into account both purposes – the contribution of food to the enjoyment of life and to the meeting of nutritional needs. Fortunately, our nutrient requirements

157

can be met by so many combinations of foods that there is no reason that the fulfillment of the two purposes should ever be in conflict. This is particularly true for those who have trained their palate to appreciate a large variety of foods. The greater the assortment of foods that are consumed, the better chance that you will have of meeting both objectives.

Health and *junk* are two adjectives often used with the word *food* to imply nutritional value. Frankly, we do not like either of them because both insinuate something that is not true. Both were invented to sell things, books, ideas, or foods. No single food should be called healthy if that term is used to mean that it meets all of our nutritional needs or that it has special properties that will keep us well. Likewise, no food should be called junk if that term symbolizes the lack of any redeeming social value. Despite our objection to these terms, they are so often heard that we deem it appropriate to use them in our discussion of foods with a reputation.

Health foods

The term *health food* is redundant, as food, by definition, is a substance that provides nourishment. Nutrients from foods are essential to sustain life. A hallmark of the language of science is that it is precise. According to these terms, the expression health food defies definition. In popular usage, it presents a moving target. Currently, when we think of health food, we usually think of products available through specialty stores or in sections of supermarkets and pharmacies designated as health, organic, or natural foods. Similar products are also sold door to door and through the mail.

One reason that it is difficult to define health food is because the term is used to describe a philosophy more than a substance. One of the basic tenets of this philosophy is that diseases can be avoided and health achieved by consuming a "proper" diet and adopting an "appropriate" life-style. This is not a new idea. Rev. Sylvester Graham espoused the same conviction a century and a half ago. He preached that by following his recommendations regarding diet and life-style, the dreaded diseases of his day – cholera and tuberculosis – could be prevented or cured. The modern equivalent is that a proper diet can almost guarantee anyone from having a personal confrontation with one of the scariest words in the English language – cancer! As much as we might all wish that this were so (see Chapter 15), Sylvester Graham was, and his present-day counterparts are, wrong.

A second basic tenet of the health food philosophy is that a proper diet is difficult to achieve. Such proponents argue that either ordinary food is not nutritionally adequate or it is contaminated. Therefore, they assert, it is necessary to consume naturally or organically grown foods, preferably containing exotic ingredients.

Are health foods necessarily better for the consumer, as the name implies? If you think the answer is yes, we hope you will consider several facts.

1. In terms of nutritional value, no demonstrable benefits have been shown to accrue from eating health foods in place of conventional foods. For example, crackers, pasta, and bread made with stone-ground wheat are not different nutritionally from these same products made with whole wheat. Using a stone instead of the modern milling process to grind the wheat does not change the wheat's nutrient content. Further, chemical analysis has failed to demonstrate differences in the nutrient content of organically grown foods and that of their conventional counterparts. This should not come as a surprise, because the nutrient content of foods is primarily a function of the plant's genetics, not its environment.

2. Taste panel studies have failed to show any difference in consumer acceptance between organic and conventional foods.[1]

3. One often stated reason for eating organic foods is to avoid chemicals in the food, such as additives and pesticides. As we explained in Chapter 10, it is unreasonable to categorize all additives as bad for the health. Categorically avoiding all of them can invite not only food-borne illnesses but malnutrition as well.

   The argument that organic food is devoid of the pesticides found in regular food is a particularly effective attention grabber because of the widespread fear of these substances. However, it ignores the fact that direct chemical analysis has shown that there is little difference between the amount of pesticide residues in organically and conventionally grown foods.[2] There are two reasons for this. First, as we told you in Chapter 10, the maximum quantity of pesticide residues allowed in food is strictly controlled by law. Thus, conventional foods cannot be sold if they contain more than the small quantity shown to be safe. Second, even when one farmer eschews the use of pesticides, the chances are that neighboring farmers will not.[a] Pesticides from those farms are then distributed by air or water to become incorporated, in trace amounts, in the products grown on the organic farm.

4. Natural does not mean safe. For example, eating bone meal might sound like a natural way to obtain needed calcium. However, bone meal is made, as the name indicates, from grinding the bones of animals. If during their lifetimes, these animals consumed large amounts of toxic minerals, their bones will contain them. Indeed, some samples of bone meal have been shown to contain such large amounts of lead that their consumption has resulted in reported cases of lead poisoning.[3]

5. The words *natural* and *organic* are not legally defined in most states and

---

[a] This is fortunate for the organic farmer because the use of pesticides on neighboring farms reduces the insect population on the organic farm, too. If everyone suddenly decided to farm organic, we would soon be back to the situation before the technological revolution in agriculture, when food production was limited, in part, by insects and plant diseases. It is somewhat analogous to some parents' refusing to have their children immunized against diseases because a reaction to the immunization is more likely than contracting the disease. If that is true, it is only because most other people accept immunization and therefore reduce the chance that unprotected children would be exposed to the diseases.

can therefore be applied to any food, regardless of its origin. Thus, when you buy such food, you have no assurance that it was grown any differently than was conventional food. These terms and our misconceptions about them are commonly used as marketing strategies.

6. Foods sold as health foods are often available in the conventional super-market where they usually can be purchased at considerably less cost than from specialty stores. For example, one company produces pasta "with Jerusalem artichoke flour added," which is sold for about twice the price of conventional pasta. Because both the exotic and conventional pastas are made with semolina (the starch part of durum wheat), doesn't it make sense to consume the conventional product and have the Jerusalem artichoke as a side dish? Note, however, that Jerusalem artichokes, even though they sound exotic, have no unique nutritional properties.[4]

In the final analysis, it is up to you to decide how to spend your money. In our opinion, however, health foods and the health food philosophy do not deserve the positive reputation that the name implies.

Aphrodisiacs and desiccated body parts

According to folklore, the color and shape of certain foods provide insight into what they can do for you if they are eaten. For example, mythology states that oysters are an aphrodisiac because they have the general shape of testicles. Similarly, mushrooms are considered aphrodisiacs because of their phallic shape. It is less clear whether the anti-impotence properties attributed to powdered rhinoceros horn is due to the shape of the horn itself or to the macho image of a rhinoceros. Either way, the myth that rhinoceros horn is an aphrodisiac is a major reason that these poor creatures are on the endangered species list.

Some folklore is less subtle. Because it is widely and erroneously believed that "you are what you eat," there is no point in fooling around with the look-alikes. Why not go for the real thing? If one ascribes to that philos-ophy, it is easy to imagine the origin of the idea that consuming the body parts of animals – and, in the case of cannibals, humans – would provide specific benefits to the consumer. For example, because it was thought that eating brains would make one more intelligent, the leaders of primitive, cannibalistic societies ceremoniously ate the brains of their enemies to obtain such benefits. Similarly, eating the heart of a lion was thought to give one courage.

We might have hoped that these primitive ideas had gone out of fashion long ago, but if that were so, how can we account for the fact that desiccated animal body parts are still on the market? The old idea that one can benefit from eating organs analogous to those that happen to be causing us prob-lems has been given the modern-sounding name of *glandular therapy*.

Labels on the bottles of desiccated tissue and tissue extracts do not make claims for the expected medical benefits that might ensue from ingesting the contents. To do so would legally make the substance a drug, and thus its efficacy would have to be proved. Without the claims, these substances are legally foods, and in practice no claims are necessary. The potential benefits are left to the inspiration of the buyer. After all, it does not require a fertile imagination to perceive the potential advantages of ovarian and uterine extracts (helpfully labeled *female*) or prostate and testicular extracts (labeled *male*). Similarly, the potential benefits from consuming extracts of adrenal gland, pancreas, pituitary, thymus, thyroid, spleen, heart, kidney, and liver are apparent. For those who are not sure which of their many organs need help, they can buy a product containing a combination of these. For customers who may miss the pun, extracts of the green-lipped mussel are labeled as being of value to body builders.

The biological facts of digestion and absorption (see Chapter 3) make nonsense out of "special effect foods," "desiccated body parts," and indeed, the common saying that "you are what you eat" that gave rise to such ideas in the first place. In fact, when these desiccated body parts are eaten, they are broken down into their simplest components (amino acids, simple sugars, and fatty acids) before entering the body. At best, desiccated tissue or tissue extracts are very expensive sources of these nutrients and, at worst, may contribute substances that are harmful.

Other than wasting money for false promises, what harm is there in consuming desiccated body parts? For some people, "glandular therapy" can be hazardous to their health. Consumption of these substances may adversely affect individuals who are allergic to specific glandular materials. Some of these products may also be very high in nucleic acids, which can precipitate gout in people prone to it. Because these glandular materials are often dried at temperatures ideal for bacterial growth, it is not surprising that some products contain a large amount of potentially hazardous bacteria. Note that these perils can be expected from ingesting glandular materials and that the life-threatening dangers are so great that these materials should never be injected.

The greatest danger of these products is that promotional claims for them imply that they can "cure" diseases. If consumers believe this, they may not seek competent medical treatment, or they may stop taking the appropriate medication. It may sound like a good idea to a few, but if a person with insulin-dependent diabetes abandons insulin treatment in favor of consuming pancreas extract, the result is likely to be death. Self-diagnosis and self-treatment are never good ideas. And you'll be acting on your own if you choose these products. No sales clerk or company officer will support your decision should something bad happen. If you have, or think you have, a problem with your glands, you should make an appointment with your physician or a physician specializing in endocrinology.

Herbs and herbal teas

The idea that certain plants and plant extracts are healthful can be traced
to the fact that folk medicine and herbal remedies are a part of world
culture, past and present. Probably every family has at least one cure for
a particular ill that has been passed down through generations. Remember
Aunt Lucy's whiskey, honey,[b] and menthol from peppermint leaves to
treat colds and coughs and to soothe a sore throat?

It is true that many of our modern medicines were originally discovered
in plants, but this does not mean that consuming those plants or extracts
of them is a good idea, for several reasons.[5] The first of these is potency.
For example, ephedrine is a modern drug used in treating a variety of
respiratory disorders. It is found in the brownish green stems of the *ma
huang* shrub that has been used for five thousand years in China and other
parts of Asia to treat asthma, hay fever, and other respiratory problems.[6]
Ephedrine is a chemical cousin of adrenalin (epinephrine) that affects many
physiological processes, including heart rate. Too little ephedrine does no
good, and an excessive intake can cause the heart to beat too fast. How
can anyone expect to obtain the proper dose of this potent chemical or
any other drug, by eating plants or drinking an extract of them? Isn't it
more reasonable to obtain the proper dose of drugs like ephedrine in
products available from a pharmacy,[c] if the drugs are indicated after competent medical advice?

A second problem with using herbs as a source of drugs is purity. If a
plant is a source of one drug, it likely contains other drugs that can have
unwanted effects. It seems inconsistent to us that many people who are
concerned about the chemicals added to foods, which have been thoroughly
examined for safety, are willing to consume large amounts of herbs and
herbal teas containing thousands of chemicals about which little is known.
The rationale may be that if it is natural, it is safe. The fallacy of this
concept is illustrated by the following saying:[7] "There are old mushroom
hunters, and there are bold mushroom hunters, but there are no old, bold
mushroom hunters." This is not to say that herbs and herbal teas are always
dangerous and should never be used. Although we do not believe that they
should be used for the self-treatment of medical problems, seeking out and
consuming the safe ones can be an interesting hobby, if you know what

---

[b] Honey is often but erroneously believed to be "condensed herbs" that are said to be good
for the whole body. Folk medicine remedies frequently suggest that herbs and honey also
be mixed with whiskey, creating an end product called *bitters*.

[c] It is often asserted that drugs obtained from natural sources are superior to those produced
in the laboratory. To believe this is to ignore the progress made in the areas of organic
chemistry and pharmacology over the last century. For example, ephedrine is ephedrine
whether it is isolated from plants or is synthesized in the laboratory.

you are doing. If you plan to munch on the flora of field and stream, it is necessary first to be able to identify the plants. If you plan to eat herbs, whether you pick them yourself or buy them,[d] it is a good idea to obtain an authoritative book, such as *The New Honest Herbal*,[8] that describes their purported uses and, just as important, their dangers. Although common herb teas, such as peppermint,[e] rose hip, orange, spearmint, and others, are commonly drunk and appear to have no major health problems associated with them, you may be surprised to find that many common herbs contain chemicals that can have unfavorable physiological effects in some people.

Coffee, tea, and cola: The caffeine connection

The British are accustomed to their four o'clock tea, and Americans "require" their morning coffee. An active ingredient in both of these beverages is caffeine. The quantity of caffeine in them can vary, of course, depending on how they are made. Colas also contain caffeine. Chocolate has a relatively small amount of caffeine, but it does contain considerable amounts of a closely related chemical, theobromine, which has physiological effects similar to those of caffeine.

Make no mistake about it, caffeine and theobromine are drugs, but to our knowledge, they are not harmful to most people when consumed in moderation. The only known physiological action of caffeine is to enhance and prolong the effects of several hormones. This is important because it means that caffeine does not have primary effects, but rather, its effects are secondary to whatever else is happening, hormonally speaking. This is the reason that caffeine consumption has variable consequences from one individual to another, as well as from one time to another in the same person. As an example, caffeine consumption may, but does not always, result in wakefulness, depending on whether other events have stimulated brain activity.

Because caffeine enhances the action of hormones that regulate, among other things, heart rate, blood pressure, and acid release into the stomach, the consumption of it by people who suffer from these and related problems

---

[d] It might be expected that herbal products offered for sale would be safe, but this is not always true. For example, the Food and Drug Administration has taken action against an herbal product, Herbalife Slim and Trim Formula, that includes mandrake and poke root, both of which are poisonous. Mandrake was once used by Native Americans as a suicide drug. As an FDA journalist wrote, "This diet aid claimed that it will 'keep the weight off indefinitely,' which could prove all too true for those unfortunate enough to consume too much of it" (see T. Larkin, "Herbs Are Often More Toxic Than Magical," *FDA Consumer*, October 1983, p. 6).

[e] Peppermint tea should not be given to infants or very young children, as the menthol may cause choking.

may be proscribed by a physician. In the absence of specific medical disorders that call for avoiding caffeine and related chemicals, the definition of "in moderation" varies considerably because of the differing response to caffeine.[f] In this case, it is best to "listen to your body." If you ingest enough caffeine to increase your heart rate and/or give you a general feeling of nervousness, you have likely exceeded your tolerance level, and so next time it is only prudent to take less.

The use of relatively large doses of caffeine, from pills or beverages, by marathon runners during a race should, in our opinion, be strongly discouraged. The purpose of the caffeine is to give the runner extra energy. It is true that caffeine will work with hormones to increase the release of fatty acids from fat stores during the stress of a race. These fatty acids are then used by the muscles to generate chemical energy. However, a marathon race is, as one might expect, very stressful on the heart. Caffeine can add considerably to that stress by further speeding up the heart rate.

There are numerous other charges against caffeine which, for the most part, are based on suspicion rather than scientific evidence. For example, some observations (not controlled studies) involving a very small number of women were interpreted to suggest that caffeine may contribute to the development of fibrocystic breast disease. This suspicion attracted attention because of widespread public fear that fibrocystic breast disease may be a precursor of breast cancer. Although concern about a suspicious breast lump should be immediately translated into an examination by a physician, there is no basis for assuming a connection between lumpy, fibrous breast tissue and breast cancer. Indeed, it has been concluded that the occurrence of fibrous breast tissue is a normal physiological response to hormonal variations.[9] Further, more extensive studies of much larger numbers of women have failed to find any association between the consumption of coffee, tea, or chocolate and the incidence of fibrocystic breast disease.[10]

Similarly, suspicions that caffeine consumption may be linked to the occurrence of some types of tumors and to birth defects in newborns have not been confirmed by carefully controlled studies.[11] Reports also have appeared suggesting a statistical link between coffee intake and elevated blood cholesterol levels, but the association is very weak.[g] Although ele-

---

[f] Note that the quantity of caffeine (or theobromine) normally tolerated is a function of body size. The amount in 2 cups of coffee or 4 ounces of chocolate candy might be all right for an adult, but the same amount of caffeine or theobromine consumed by a child weighing one-fourth as much would be equivalent to eight cups of coffee for an adult. This may result in considerable restlessness and wakefulness in the child, but weird, uncontrollable behavior is not a normal consequence of these effects.

[g] See, for example, an article entitled "Coffee Intake and Elevated Cholesterol and Apolipoprotein B Levels in Men," by P. T. Williams, P. D. Wood, K. M. Vranizan, J. J. Albers, S. C. Garay, and C. B. Taylor, in *Journal of the American Medical Association* 253 (1985): 1407–11, which reports a correlation coefficient of 0.27. This number may mean little to

vated blood cholesterol has been identified as a risk factor in the development of coronary artery disease, numerous studies have failed to show a link between caffeine consumption and this disease.[12]

If you decide to restrict your caffeine intake, for whatever reason, by consuming decaffeinated coffee, is there reason to fear the chemicals used to remove the caffeine? In our opinion, the answer is no. The chemicals used to extract caffeine legally qualify as food additives, and so the amount remaining in decaffeinated coffee is required by law not to exceed what has been shown to be safe. For example, one chemical that is used is methylene chloride. This may sound exotic and even dangerous, but in fact, it is a highly volatile compound that is present in decaffeinated coffee at a concentration of less than one-tenth of one part per million. This is one hundred times less than what is allowed by the Food and Drug Administration, based on safety. Some companies advertise that they extract caffeine with natural chemicals, such as water. This may sound like a good idea in terms of safety, but it is tricky, as some of the flavor components of coffee are also extracted by water. The success of removing caffeine without appreciably altering the taste can be judged only by you and your taste buds.

Alcohol

Regardless of what habitual imbibers might like to think, alcohol is a food, not a nutrient. It is also a drug. Alcohol has been used as a medicine (internal and external) for centuries. In fact, today many medications, including cold and cough remedies, pain killers, and "vitality tonics," contain alcohol.

In terms of quantity consumed, alcohol is the main mood-altering drug used today. Contrary to popular opinion, it acts as an anesthetic or narcotic rather than as a stimulant. It puts the brain to sleep, beginning with the frontal lobe, progressing to the speech and vision centers, and then to the voluntary muscles. Alcohol causes problems because of this sequence of its effects on the brain. The first casualty is reasoning power, which means the loss of the ability to make appropriate judgments, like whether one is too inebriated to drive. Thus the admonition that "if you drink, don't drive" is a prudent one.

In excessive amounts, alcohol can cause coma and death. It is toxic to the brain, heart, liver, and gastrointestinal tract. Chronic consumption increases the risk for enlargement of the heart (called *cardiomegaly*), high blood pressure and stroke, liver and pancreatic disease, gastrointestinal

the lay public, but the square of it is a measure of the strength of a statistical association. In this case, 0.27 squared is just over 0.07, which means that about 7 percent of the cholesterol-elevating effect may be attributed to caffeine and 93 percent is attributable to other, unknown factors.

ulcers, head and neck cancer, accidents, and male impotence. In terms of sexual performance, alcohol does not deserve the glowing recommendation often conferred on it.

Despite all of its negative attributes, we know of no health reasons (other than during pregnancy or driving or working with machinery) why the consumption of ethyl alcohol in moderation should be avoided.[h] Remember, however, that the amount of alcohol that can be tolerated varies among individuals, depending on several factors, such as body weight. The term "in moderation" is generally defined as the equivalent of the alcohol contained in one to two drinks per day. One drink usually means the equivalent of one-half ounce of absolute alcohol.

Enjoying alcohol but avoiding the unpleasant effects of its consumption is the goal of most social drinkers. Don't forget, however, that alcohol and alcoholic beverages contribute calories. Per unit of weight, alcohol contributes more calories than does starch, sugar, or protein. Hangovers, one undesirable side effect of excessive alcohol consumption, are characterized by a cycle of increased thirst and urination, nausea, vomiting, heartburn, and headaches due to a swelling of blood vessels in the brain. Such effects appear to be caused in large part by the presence of alcohols in addition to ethyl alcohol, called *congeners*. Vodka and gin contain fewer congeners than do other spirits and produce fewer hangovers, whereas bourbon contains the most. Brandy, rum, and Scotch are in between. Hangovers can be treated only with time and sleep. Coffee and exercise do not help get rid of a hangover and, in fact, may make it worse.

Mood food

With the increased use and abuse of mood-altering drugs, it was predictable that sooner or later the idea that foods could be used for "natural" mood alteration would be proposed. If you have been reading some of the more recent magazine and print media articles, you are no doubt aware that this prediction has come true. However, the idea that one can alter one's mood by properly selecting one's food is best characterized by the word *nonsense*. The assertions that such a phenomenon occurs are based on speculation piled on innuendo tottering on suspicion.

Mood is thought to be based in part on the presence of two chemicals in the brain. The first of these is a protein, which has been dubbed a "natural pain killer" because it interacts with the same receptors in the

[h] Alcohol may reduce the risk of heart disease - see S. B. Hulley and S. Gordon, "Alcohol and High Density Lipoprotein Cholesterol," *Circulation* 64 (Supplement 3) (1981): 57–63 – but may increase the risk for breast cancer – see M. P. Longnecker, J. A. Berlin, M. J. Orza, and T. C. Chalmers, "A Meta-Analysis of Alcohol Consumption in Relation to Risk of Breast Cancer," *Journal of the American Medical Association* 260 (1988): 652–56.

brain that morphine occupies when it is administered. This protein, called *endorphin* (from condensation of the two words *endogenous* and *morphine*), is produced by enzymes in the brain and is as much as seventy times more potent, on a weight basis, than is morphine. The second compound is *serotonin*. Little is known about this substance other than that it is produced in the brain from the essential amino acid tryptophan and that its concentration rises during sleep.

The experiments behind the assertion that food can alter mood involved feeding rats various types of food and then measuring changes in the concentration of these two compounds. There are technical problems in the measurement of these substances, because as you might imagine, the biochemistry of the brain is extremely complex. The interpretation of what the results mean in physiological terms is an even more difficult problem. It calls for a giant leap of "nonscience" to speculate on how changes in the concentrations of serotonin or endorphin affect the rat's mood. How can anyone tell whether a rat is in a good mood or a bad mood? Such experiments are obviously impossible to conduct in people, because we doubt that anyone would willingly submit to having his or her brain or even a portion of it removed to allow the determination of endorphin and serotonin.

Despite the difficulty in interpreting the results from rat studies, reports persist that certain foods have predictable effects on mood. For example, around Valentine's Day each year, the speculation is repeated that eating chocolate "puts people in a good mood." The basis for this is the assertion that when rats are fed chocolate, the concentration of endorphin in their brain has been observed to increase. Does this mean that the rat has gone from a bad to a good mood? In fact, because endorphin is regarded as a natural pain killer, it could just as well be concluded that eating chocolate is painful for a rat! Similar types of experiments are the basis for the contention that eating carbohydrates makes one "mellow" and that eating protein makes one "hyper."

Why do we attempt to discover whether food affects mood in rats? Why not go a more direct route by feeding various foods to humans and determining the effects on their mood? The reason that this cannot be done scientifically is that the technical problems are virtually insurmountable. The assessment of mood by self or observers is extremely subjective. To be valid, experiments must be conducted double blind, and it is impossible, for example, to offer only pasta at one meal and only meat at another without the subject's knowing which is which.

The concept of mood foods has little or no biochemical basis at the present time. However, food, or indeed anything else, may affect one's mood if it is thought that it will. It may be a helpful illusion, for example, to think that the consumption of doughnuts may beckon sleep to an in-

somniac, unless the thought of those extra calories causes so much con-
sternation that sleep is impossible.

Yogurt

We suspect that if a group of Americans were asked to name foods that
were "good for you," yogurt would be near the top of the list, along with
milk, orange juice, and whole-grain cereals. The idea that yogurt is a health
food that can increase longevity goes way back to the turn of the century.

In 1907, a book called *The Prolongation of Life* was published. It was
written by a Russian-born scientist by the name of Elie Metchnikoff, who
gained fame while working with Louis Pasteur in the Pasteur Institute in
Paris. The book immediately became a best-seller, apparently for two
reasons. First, everyone then as now was interested in knowing what they
could do in order to live longer. Second, Metchnikoff was awarded the
Nobel Prize in physiology and medicine shortly after his book was published. His Nobel Prize was awarded not for the book but for his work on
the function of white blood cells in the destruction of bacteria. Even so,
the publicity surrounding his award served to authenticate his hypothesis
that you could eat your way to a longer life.

The secret to longevity revealed in Metchnikoff's book was simple – eat
yogurt. He jumped to that conclusion by combining two observations: (1)
It was generally believed that Bulgarians lived longer than did other Europeans, and (2) Bulgarians consumed yogurt in copious quantities. We
now know that Metchnikoff's advice was not only simple but also simplistic.
Longevity is determined by a complicated interaction of genetics and environment. In fact, his discovery apparently did Metchnikoff little good,
as he died at the age of 71, nine years after his book was published. Life
expectancy tables from 1900 showed that on the average, people of his age
(when his book was published) could anticipate living to the age of 73.

Yogurt has no magical properties, but it is a nutritious food for the same
reasons that milk is nutritious. Because yogurt is made from fermented
milk, it should not come as a surprise that the nutrient content of yogurt
is virtually identical to that of milk. The milk proteins are coagulated in
yogurt, giving it the appearance of being more solid, but in fact, even the
water content of the two products is virtually the same. Yogurt is made
by adding cultures of *Lactobacillus bulgaricus* (named after the Bulgarian
people that Metchnikoff studied) and *Streptococcus thermophilous* to pasteurized and homogenized whole or partially skimmed milk. The inoculated
milk is then held between room temperature and 115° F for a few hours,
during which time the bacteria convert some of the milk sugar, or lactose,
into *lactic acid*. It is this acid that causes the coagulation of protein and
gives yogurt the sharp, tangy flavor. One way to avoid the tangy flavor –

for those who don't like it – is to add something like fruit preserves to the plain yogurt, but note that these additions change the nutritional value, especially the caloric content. Yogurt is often thought to be low in calories. To the contrary, it contains about the same as does the milk from which it is made. When fruit preserves are added, the caloric content increases to the point that the combination can rival ice cream.

In fairness to Metchnikoff, we should point out that his advocacy of yogurt was not based on its nutritional properties. In fact, the bare outline of what eventually developed into the field of nutrition had just begun to emerge when he wrote his book. Rather, he hypothesized that the bacteria consumed with the yogurt would be able to "defeat" so-called putrefactive bacteria in the digestive tract, which were widely believed at the time to be the cause of diseases. Both this belief and Metchnikoff's hypothesis were soon proved to be wrong, but yogurt lives on, as does its reputation for being healthful.

Breakfast cereals

Breakfast cereals were invented as health foods a century ago as a part of the vegetarian movement in the United States. To put their development into context, it is necessary to understand the origin of vegetarianism.

The idea that eating cereal grains instead of meat would make one healthier had been around for centuries, but it took a Presbyterian minister, Sylvester Graham, to make the idea popular. Mr. Graham spoke and wrote about the hazards to body and soul if one ate meat. Although health authorities had banned the sale of fresh fruits and vegetables on the grounds that eating them caused cholera, Graham advocated their consumption on theological grounds. He assured his followers that the real causes of cholera were lewdness and chicken pie. Graham concluded that an improper diet was the major cause of most health as well as of the moral problems of the time. Although he preached against consuming meat or alcohol, he saved his greatest condemnation for what he considered to be the worst dietary offender, improperly prepared bread.

In Graham's New England of the early 1800s, bread was made from wheat flour. To produce the flour, wheat was ground between two stones at a water-powered mill. The product did not keep well, however. We now know that when the wheat germ is left with the product, the fat in it can quickly become rancid. Because there was no BHA at that time to use as a food additive to prevent oxidation of the fat (see Chapter 10), the only recourse was to remove the offending component. This was done by straining the flour through bolts of cloth; thus the resulting product was called *bolted flour*. Bolted flour did keep better than the cruder form, but in the process, the outer coating of the wheat – the bran – was lost along with the germ. Graham insisted that to be nutritious, bread had to be made with unbolted flour, or what we would now call whole-wheat flour. This unbolted flour came to be called Graham flour, in honor of the man who was such a strong proponent of its use. Few people today know about the colorful career of Sylvester Graham, although many of his ideas about diet and health are still with us. His name is, however, immortalized in a product familiar to all of us – graham crackers.

Sylvester Graham had many converts to vegetarianism, including a woman named Sister White (née Ellen Hartman), who became a principal figure in the Seventh-Day Adventist church. While traveling in western Michigan as a leader of this religious sect, Sister White decided that the fledgling church needed to build a health spa. The spa would treat the diseases of the faithful by feeding them a diet based on the teachings of Rev. Graham, with an emphasis on whole grains. With the financial help of a wealthy broom maker from Battle Creek named John Preston Kellogg, the Western Health Reform Institute opened for business shortly after the end of the Civil War. The problem was that there was not much business because the spa lacked a physician to oversee the clients' health. Again, Kellogg came to the rescue. He sent his son, John Harvey, to be trained as a doctor at Bellevue Hospital in New York City. At the age of 24, John Harvey Kellogg, M.D., became physician in chief at the Western Health Reform Institute. John Harvey immediately changed the name of the health spa to Battle Creek Sanitarium and hired his younger brother, Will, as its business manager.

Under the innovative leadership of John Harvey Kellogg, The San, as it was called, prospered. Not only were more patients attracted, but more of them were rich. All manner of diseases were treated by what Kellogg considered a proper diet – that is, one very high in fiber – which meant that patients had to consume large amounts of cereal grains and be given many enemas. The idea, prevalent in the medical profession at the time, was that illness was caused by the presence of putrefactive bacteria in the intestinal tract. Kellogg was a strong advocate of this erroneous concept and was convinced that the vegetarian diet advocated by Sister White and Rev. Graham would cure most diseases. This son of a broom maker told his patients that large amounts of fiber would sweep their bowels clean and that water would wash the debris away. The problem was how to get patients to eat enough whole grain to get the amount of fiber that Kellogg thought was necessary. After all, one can eat only so much graham bread and boiled cereal as a major entrée day after day before it becomes boring, and this would not do for the wealthy guests of The San.

The Kellogg brothers solved this problem by developing toasted cereals in a form that was dry and crisp. The first toasted cereal was called Toasted Wheat Flakes. In 1896, John Harvey Kellogg received a patent on the process of producing what he called "flaked cereals." Toasted wheat was only one of many formulated foods concocted at The San. Although toasted cereals were originally intended to be eaten without milk and at all three meals, breakfast cereals, in the form that we know them today, were born.

Breakfast cereals might have remained a novelty served only at The San had it not been for a wealthy businessman from Fort Worth, Texas, named Charles W. Post. Post, who had made his money as a real estate salesman and blanket maker, became a patient at The San in 1891 at the age of 35. Living at The San was expensive, and within a few months, most of his money was gone. Post and his wife thus rented a room in Battle Creek, and he became an outpatient. Ever the salesman, Post proposed to Kellogg that in exchange for treatment and a small share of the profits, he would use his promotional talents to sell toasted cereals to the public. When he was rebuffed, Post decided to go into business for himself.

Post made the fateful decision to invest his savings, all $69 of it, in the production of a coffee substitute. With this money, he purchased 2 bushels of wheat, 200 pounds of bran, and 10 jugs of molasses. The list of ingredients was no doubt familiar to the Kellogg brothers because it was the same ingredients they used to make their coffee substitute, Caramel Coffee, served at The San. Post aggressively marketed his product as a healthy substitute for coffee, under the name of Postum. It became an immediate financial success.

Because Postum was most popular in the winter, Post needed another product to keep his plant busy during the summer. In 1898, he started producing a cereal product that was remarkably similar to another one that had been used at The San for years. He called it Grape-Nuts. With aggressive marketing as a health food, Grape-Nuts soon rivaled Postum for the position as profit leader. By 1900, Charles W. Post was reported to be netting $3 million annually.

Many other entrepreneurs took advantage of the idea that prepared cereals were healthy. For example, as the nineteenth century faded into history, a Denver businessman named Charles D. Perky invented a machine that shredded boiled grains of whole wheat and spun them into fiber. The product of this machine, marketed under the name of Shredded Wheat, was produced in a plant built in Niagara Falls, New York, which just happened to be a favorite honeymoon site. Numerous ways to prepare Shredded Wheat and the healthful properties of it were explained to the newlyweds. It quickly caught on nationally.

In the meantime, the fame of The San spread, and Battle Creek became known for its prepared cereals. By 1904, there were about thirty wheat-flake companies in this small Michigan community. Will Kellogg recognized that a lot of money could be made from marketing the cereals that he and his brother had invented, but Dr. Kellogg refused because he feared the negative effect that this might have on his reputation as a physician. Eventually, John Harvey reluctantly agreed, but only if the advertisements and the box prominently displayed the name W. K. Kellogg and not John Harvey. Indeed, Dr. John Harvey Kellogg's direct involvement in the cereal food business ended in 1906 when Will had accumulated enough stock to control the firm that eventually would be called the Kellogg Company.

As owner of the company, W. K. Kellogg made an important decision to advertise his product as nutritious and tasty rather than as a health food, based on the reasoning that there were more well than sick people. Because of the success of his company, coupled with federal regulations that prevented the advertisement of food as a cure or preventive of specific diseases, the emphasis of the entire industry's advertising shifted, at least until recently.

The claim that breakfast cereals are nutritious was challenged by a civil engineer named Robert B. Choate, Jr., in testimony before the U.S. Senate in July 1970.[13] Choate devised a simple system that he claimed could be used to compare quantitatively the nutritional value of breakfast cereals. According to his system, if one serving of the cereal (without milk) provided 100 percent of the Recommended Dietary Allowance for some nutrient, such as vitamin A, a value of 100 would be assigned. This was done for nine nutrients (protein, calcium, iron, thiamin, riboflavin, niacin, and vitamins A, C, and D). Thus, 900 was the highest possible score. The scores of the sixty breakfast cereals then on the market were published, and forty-two of them scored lower than 100. Nutritionists found this grading system appalling because it overemphasized the role of dry breakfast cereal as a necessary source of protein, vitamins, and minerals, and it contradicted the basic principle that the key to good nutrition is variety.

In Choate's grading system, Nabisco Shredded Wheat was given a score of 12 out of a possible 900, which put it into uncontested last place among the sixty cereals. In contrast, in a rating system devised by Consumers Union[14] in October 1986, Shredded Wheat came out very near the top of fifty-nine cereals. Had Shredded Wheat changed that much in nutritional value in less than two decades? No. But the ratings had changed, not because the cereal was different, but because the rating criteria were different. Choate's ratings were based on what was in the cereal – protein plus eight vitamins and minerals. Although Consumers Union gave high marks to those cereals that provided protein and fiber, it also took into consideration what was not there, namely, sugar, salt, and fat. The vitamin and mineral content was not evaluated.

Although Consumers Union is a highly respected organization, the rating system that it used to evaluate the breakfast cereals makes no more sense than the one that Choate used. Taken to the extreme, the cardboard box used to package the cereal would have a higher score than any of the contents because of the emphasis on fiber and the lack of other components.[i] The system is based on the mistaken assumption that the optimal amount of sugar, salt, and fat in cereal is zero. However, these substances are present as natural components of ingredients or are added, usually in small amounts, to improve the palatability of the product. They are added because cereal companies are quite aware of the results of consumer surveys indicating that a much higher percentage of people select cereals on the basis of taste rather than either nutritional value or even cost.[15] And the quantities of salt, sugar, and fat contributed by the consumption of reasonable amounts of any of the cereals rated are negligible in the context of a varied diet.

In summary, despite their reputation, breakfast cereals are neither good nor bad. They can provide important nutrients, including vitamins, minerals, and fiber, but they, like other foods, are not unique sources of any of these.

Fast food : Getting the most from fast food calories

Our experience and instincts tell us that stereotypes are likely to be misleading, which is certainly true when we try to categorize fast foods. We might automatically think of the "golden arches" when we think of fast food, but fast foods also can describe a veritable cornucopia of restaurants designed to provide rapid service. Some specialize in ethnic foods; others offer specific products; and still others serve complete meals. The variety is so great that it is simply not possible to lump them all together and make any overriding evaluation that correctly describes them all. In general, most fast foods are not bad from a nutritional viewpoint, as they are usually good sources of protein, B vitamins, and calories. They can, however, be low in some nutrients such as calcium and vitamin C. What this means is that when we eat at a fast food restaurant, we need to think about what foods we should select for the other meals of the day.

Let's take an example. Suppose that for lunch, you grab a quick quarter-pound hamburger, medium french fries, and an 8-ounce carbonated beverage. Now compare this with your needs on the basis of the four food groups discussed in Chapter 1. Adults need, each day, two servings from the milk group, the equivalent of 5 to 6 ounces of meat or meat substitute, two fruits, two vegetables, and four servings from the grain group. The

---

[i] If each of the five tested components were given equal weight in a 100-point system, the cardboard box, which is almost 100 percent fiber, would be given a score of 20 for maximum fiber content. The lack of salt, sugar, and fat would add 60 points (20 points each). This would give the box a score of 80, which is 7 points higher than that of the highest-rated cereal. In fact, the box would lose a total of 20 points only because it is not a source of protein.

lunch that was chosen provides two servings from the grain group (the top and bottom of a hamburger bun), 3 ounces of cooked meat (the hamburger patty), one vegetable (french fried potatoes and the addition of ketchup to the french fries; lettuce and tomato on the hamburger could have provided a large part of a second vegetable), no milk serving (unless cheese was added to the hamburger, or a milk shake made with real dairy products was consumed), and no fruit serving. This lunch also contained one serving from the "other" food group (the carbonated beverage).

The lunch met 60 percent of the daily need for the meat group and half of the daily need for both the fruit and vegetable and the grain groups. It provided about 6 grams of dietary fiber, which is more than that contained in a 1-ounce serving of most breakfast cereals (cf. Figure 7.1). Although the meal did not include fruit, it did meet about 20 percent of the RDA for vitamin C (from the potatoes). In order to ensure that the rest of the adult's nutrient needs are met by the foods ingested during the rest of the day, two servings from the milk group, two to three more ounces of meat or meat substitute, two fruits, one vegetable, and two more servings from the grain group should be eaten at breakfast or dinner or as snacks.

The caloric content of this fast food meal is about 560 kilocalories. The proportion of daily caloric needs that this represents depends on several factors, including body size and the amount of physical activity. An estimate of daily caloric expenditure of 2,900 kilocalories for an average adult male and 2,200 kilocalories for an average adult female is reasonable,[16] in which case the lunch provides about 20 and 25 percent of the daily caloric needs of males and females, respectively. It is easy to accommodate the consumption of the additional necessary food groups within the remaining caloric needs and still have room to enjoy consuming calories from the "other" food group. On the other hand, anyone who is attempting to lose weight by restricting caloric intake to 1,200 kilocalories would have consumed almost one-half of his or her daily caloric allotment. Only the dieter can decide whether the lunch was worth the price.

Concern is often expressed that a hamburger and french fries contain too much fat, particularly animal fat. Two of the concerns about fat are (1) that it is a concentrated source of calories and (2) that the intake of too much saturated – relative to unsaturated – fat may increase the blood cholesterol level. The proposed lunch contains 32 grams of fat. Is this excessive? We compared the caloric content of this meal, including the calories from fat, with the daily caloric needs outlined in the preceding paragraph. This leaves the issue of the contribution of such a meal to a person's total saturated fat intake.

Dietary recommendations by both the American Heart Association[17] and the National Institutes of Health[18] suggest that the intake of fat be reduced from the present level of about 35 to 40 percent of total calories consumed to 30 percent, with a distribution of these as 10 percent saturated, 10 percent monounsaturated, and 10 percent polyunsaturated fats. Note that these recommendations suggest a reduction of both total fat and saturated fat from the usual consumption, not their elimination. For those who might wish to follow these recommendations, how does this lunch fit?

In terms of total fat intake, this lunch provides 288 kilocalories as fat, which is about 10 percent of the 2,900 kilocalories needed by the average man, or about one-third of the total dietary calories from fat recommended for those following the diet recommended by the American Heart Association. For the average woman, who requires 2,200 kilocalories, the fat in this lunch provides about 13 percent of total calories, or about 43 percent of her daily allotment of fat.

How does this lunch compare with the recommendations for saturated fat intake? First, there is a widespread misconception that animal fat means saturated fat. It is true that most of the saturated fat in our diet comes from animal sources, but the converse, that all animal fat is saturated, is not true. In fact, an analysis of six cuts of cooked beef, ranging from T-bone steak to round steak, showed that only 42 percent of the total fat was saturated, whereas 48 percent was monounsaturated.[19] This meal thus contributed about 9 grams of saturated fat from the meat. (Although the french fries contributed 11 grams of fat, most of it is unsaturated, as most of the fast food restaurants now use vegetable oil for frying potatoes.) This amounts to about 81 kilocalories, which is less than 3 percent of the total dietary intake of 2,900 kilocalories needed by the average man. It is about one-fifth of the usual saturated fat intake. For men attempting to follow a diet with no more than 10 percent of total calories from saturated fat, this lunch would contribute about 28 percent of their daily allotment of saturated fat. For women, this lunch would contribute about 37 percent of their allotted saturated fat.

It is reasonable for each meal to provide about one-third of one's daily nutrition, and so this lunch clearly does not represent an excessive amount of calories, total dietary fat, or saturated fat for the average man, even those who are attempting to follow the diet recommended by the American Heart Association. In terms of total fat intake, the average woman would need to limit fat intake during the rest of the day to about 40 grams in order to stay within the guidelines of the American Heart Association. On the other hand, the lunch provides only slightly more than one-third of the allotted saturated fat and less than one-third of the daily caloric needs of an average woman. Thus, this fast food lunch does not deserve its reputation for being bad for one's health if the foods for the other two meals of the day are chosen wisely.

When eating out, regardless of whether it is at a fast food or full-service restaurant, it is important to be choosy! We can enjoy fast foods, but we must be sure that our selections fit into a balanced and varied diet. To do this, try the following:

> Choose foods that contribute to meeting the food group recommendations for the day.
>
> Consider how many kilocalories this meal provides. A good but not critical plan is to fulfill about one-third of your calorie needs at each of three meals daily.
>
> Think about what you have already eaten and what you will eat later in the day.
>
> Limit your choices from the "other" food group category (including alcoholic beverages) if you are concerned about your total daily caloric intake.

Sugar and honey

Sugar engenders a love–hate relationship. It is described as good from the perspective of the taste buds, but it is often considered bad in nutritional terms. We have no quarrel with the good part, but there are a lot of things that you should know before you accept sugar's reputation as being bad for health.[20]

A food might be considered bad, from a health standpoint, if it contained substances that were toxic or otherwise had negative physiological effects. It is ironic that although some foods are criticized because they may contain impurities and additives, sugar gets bad marks for being too pure.

On the other hand, a good food might be defined as one that contains all of the nutrients in the proper amounts required by humans. Except for a few commercially formulated medical nutritional products designed to meet all of the nutritional needs of persons with health problems, there are no good foods according to this definition. Foods vary in their content from those that contribute several nutrients to those that contribute only one. Sugar contributes only one, carbohydrate.

One of the persistent charges against sugar is that it affects behavior in adults and, especially, in children. The alleged connection between sugar and behavior suggests that when sugar is eaten, it raises the level of blood sugar (glucose), which causes the release of insulin from the pancreas. Because refined sugar supposedly causes blood glucose to climb too high, too much insulin is released, which then results in the blood glucose's falling too low, a condition called *reactive hypoglycemia*. The decreased blood glucose is then supposed to trigger an adrenalin response that can cause hyperactivity in children and any number of behavioral and mood changes in adults, including difficulty thinking, depression, and irritability. This may sound scientific and may even make a good story, but it is wrong on a number of counts.

First, refined sugar does not cause any more of an increase in blood sugar than does any other equally digestible carbohydrate. Fruit juice or even a baked potato can increase blood sugar just as much. In fact, the relative ability of a food to elevate blood glucose depends more on the composition of the total diet than on the chemical source of the carbohydrate. There has been evidence accumulating in recent years that many diabetics can tolerate a reasonable amount of sugar in a mixed diet. (Diabetics: Check with your physician to see if you qualify.)

Second, true reactive hypoglycemia (rebound low blood glucose) is extremely rare. The usual medical test to determine whether the pancreas is working properly to regulate blood glucose levels is to administer a solution containing high amounts of glucose to fasted patients and then measure their blood glucose levels at several intervals thereafter. In diabetics, blood glucose remains at elevated levels for several hours. In most nondiabetics (70 to 80 percent), blood glucose falls to the pretest levels within two to three hours. In the other 20 to 30 percent of the nondiabetic patients, blood glucose may decrease to a level considered low (below 50 milligrams per 100 milliliters of blood), but except in extremely rare cases, this low blood glucose is not accompanied by clinical symptoms of hypoglycemia (sweating, rapid heartbeat, light-headedness, nausea, and trembling). The American Medical Association and the American Diabetic Association have issued a joint statement advising that a transient low blood glucose level following a glucose load is not sufficient in itself to justify a diagnosis of reactive hypoglycemia.[21] True reactive hypoglycemia is indicative of severe medical problems such as a pancreatic tumor and should be treated as such. Before you assume the worst, we hasten to add that the symptoms of hypoglycemia just described are not unique to this metabolic abnormality. In fact, the great majority of people who exhibit them do not have hypoglycemia at all. Rather, these symptoms can have numerous other causes, including anxiety.

Finally, the proof is in the pudding, as they say, and carefully controlled studies do not support the occurrence of hyperactivity in children, even when the pudding contains refined sugar. In this case, one requisite of carefully controlled clinical studies is that neither the subject nor the evaluator of behavior know whether refined sugar was consumed. The taste of refined sugar must, of course, be masked by some method, such as the use of artificial sweeteners or fruit flavors.

Another type of study compares the clinical evaluations of children with their intake of sugars. In order to be considered controlled, these studies must include normal children along with those diagnosed by professionals or parents as hyperactive or hyperkinetic. Again, to avoid any bias in evaluating behavior, the evaluator must not know which children belong to which group and must not know their dietary intake. The Sugar Task Force of the Food and Drug Administration reviewed and described a number of both types of studies, which led it to conclude, as many others have done in the past, that there is no documented relationship between sugar consumption and hyperactivity or other behavior changes in children or juveniles.[22]

Despite the lack of any evidence, the myth persists that refined sugar causes bizarre, nonsocial behavior.[23] You no doubt have heard that some judges have sentenced juveniles found guilty of delinquency to a diet "devoid of refined sugar and other junk food." Indeed, "the Twinky defense" was used in 1979 by lawyers for Dan White in his trial for the murder of San Francisco Mayor George Moscone and City Supervisor Harvey Milk. During the trial, a psychiatrist made, in our opinion, the preposterous claim that Mr. White's frequent consumption of sugar – especially cake, candy, and soft drinks – was both evidence of a serious mental problem and a factor contributing to his "diminished mental capacity." Whether this testimony had anything to do with the jurors' decision is not known, but it has been alleged that because of it, Mr. White was convicted of the more lenient voluntary manslaughter charge instead of murder.[24]

Another charge that is occasionally leveled against refined sugar is that its consumption can lead to the development of diabetes and heart disease. There is substantial scientific evidence that sugar is not a direct cause of either disorder. We emphasize the word *direct* because obesity is involved in the development of some types of diabetes and may be a factor in heart disease. Thus, sugar could conceivably be considered an unindicted co-conspirator in the development of these diseases to the extent that it contributes to obesity.[j]

It is generally recognized that our appetite for food is regulated by a complex biochemical system that is translated by the brain into either hunger or satiety. At the same time, it is important to note that these signals can be overridden; that is, we can refuse to eat when the biochemical signals say that we are hungry, and conversely, we can choose to eat even when the biochemical signals indicate that we are not hungry. The former situation occurs in patients with eating disorders such as anorexia nervosa. The latter can occur in any of us when we are offered "goodies" that are literally irresistible, even when we have just consumed a large meal. Although we categorically reject the notion that sugar can be addictive, it is obvious that the sweet taste of the stuff is often the reason that it is irresistible.

Similarly, of the numerous other suspicions of negative health effects of

---

[j] In saying this, we do not mean to imply that sugar has a unique biochemical role in the production and deposition of body fat. It does not. Indeed, it is true, as you have been told for years, that excess fat is deposited when caloric intake exceeds caloric output, regardless of the source of those calories. Sugar, refined or otherwise, contributes the same amount of dietary energy on a weight basis as starch and protein do.

sugar, the only one that has stood the test of time and scientific investigation is the role of sugar in causing dental cavities. Indeed, the discussion of sugar in the summary of *The Surgeon General's Report on Nutrition and Health* was only in the context of its role in the development of dental cavities.[25] No other reason for limiting sugar intake was given. Specifically, the report stated: "Sugar: Those who are particularly vulnerable to dental caries (cavities), especially children, should limit consumption and frequency of use of foods high in sugars."[26]

Although there is substantial evidence that sugar can be a threat to dental health, even this must be qualified. Sugar itself does not cause dental cavities. Rather, cavities are produced when microorganisms in the mouth metabolize sugar to produce an acid, called *lactic acid*. The tooth is made of a base containing calcium. You may remember from high school chemistry that acids react with bases to produce salt plus water. In this case, the salt is calcium lactate, which is soluble. When the tooth is exposed to acid, some of the calcium is dissolved, and a tiny hole is left. Over time, the hole grows until it becomes large enough to be identified as a cavity by your dentist.

The bacteria that occupy the mouth are not picky about what they eat. Lactic acid is produced when they metabolize any number of sugars, including those contained in fruit, honey, and milk. They can even use starch to make the acid. In addition to forming acids, bacteria use carbohydrate as a starting material to make a polymer that is attached to the tooth. This material, called *plaque*, traps food and simultaneously forms an excellent environment for the bacteria to grow in. That is why it is important to brush the teeth to remove both the bacteria and this environment after eating, regardless of what has been chewed. (Persons really serious about preventing dental cavities might consider brushing their teeth before eating to reduce the bacterial population.)

From an analysis of the sequence of events leading to dental cavities and plaque formation, it is clear that their development is dependent on how long and how much the bacteria are exposed to usable carbohydrates. For example, refined sugar or naturally occurring sugars (like fruit juice) in soluble form are not particularly cavity producing if they are swallowed directly, especially if the mouth is rinsed with water immediately afterward. On the other hand, holding such solutions in the mouth for extended periods give the bacteria plenty of food with which to create havoc. Before the advent of pacifiers, it was common practice to wrap sugar in a cloth and allow infants to suck on it. This may have calmed the nerves of parents, but it no doubt also provided a continuous banquet for bacteria. Note that allowing a sucker or any type of hard candy to dissolve slowly in the mouth does the same thing.

The assertion that soluble forms of sugar are relatively innocent in causing dental cavities cannot be interpreted as absolving soft drinks of this crime. Carbonated beverages usually contain generous quantities of sugar and therefore qualify as a source of sugar in soluble form, but the drinks also contain acid. Thus, their consumption gives the teeth an acid bath, regardless of whether they contain sugar or are "sugar free." The fact that they are acid and therefore contribute to dental cavities for this reason also negates the facetious argument that they can be rendered innocent by the addition of enough alcohol to kill the mouth bacteria responsible for dental cavities.

One reason that sugar is linked to the development of dental cavities more than are other foods is that this substance has the deplorable habit of becoming sticky after it has been heated. Any carbohydrate material that sticks to the teeth provides a food supply for mouth bacteria as long as it is there. This includes not only sticky candy but also sticky fruits such as raisins and dates.

In sum, sugar does not deserve its reputation as being bad for our health. It is, however, a concentrated source of carbohydrate that provides calories and nothing else. On the other hand, we know of no one who eats handfuls of sugar; instead, it is usually mixed with other ingredients that do supply nutrients. Further, all of us require a source of calories, and there is no reason that sugar cannot be used to provide a reasonable amount of them, assuming that precautions are taken to minimize its contribution to the development of dental cavities. Remember that sugar is a member of the "other" food group. To ensure a balanced diet, it is wise to consume appropriate amounts from the four food groups. Additional calories, if warranted, can be safely obtained from numerous foods in the "other" food group.

Part IV

Nutrition and health

There is no doubt that proper nutrition is necessary to maintain health, but there are limits. In the first chapter in Part IV, we consider what appropriate food choices are known to do and not to do. The critical role of nutrients in preventing specific deficiency diseases is illustrated by the discovery of three vitamins. In contrast, a number of disorders alleged to be prevented by appropriate dietary choices, ranging from aging to premenstrual syndrome, are shown not to be related to nutrition. In the next chapter, we discuss the difficult problem of weight control, including how heredity and nutrition interact to regulate body weight and the relationship of obesity to health problems. Subsequent chapters look at the evidence for whether diet is connected to the incidence of heart disease and cancer.

12   What nutrition can and cannot do for you

In the summer of 1988, physicians at various hospitals around the country observed that some of their patients who were being fed exclusively through a tube that delivered nutrients directly into their bloodstream began to develop classical symptoms of a nutritional deficiency disease called *beriberi* (pronounced berry-berry).[1] Beriberi has long been known to be caused by an inadequate intake of the B vitamin thiamin, but most physicians in the United States have never seen this disease except in a textbook. Investigation showed that thiamin was absent from the nutritional product, and therefore, administration of thiamin to the patients rapidly cured the disease. Although this is a rare, isolated incident, it is a dramatic illustration that nutritional deficiencies can still occur under the right circumstances, as they did in centuries past.

Fortunately for us, it was recognized early in this century that certain diseases were caused by an inadequate intake of specific nutrients. Nutritional deficiency diseases, which had always plagued humankind, were virtually eliminated, at least in the United States, within fifty years after the discovery of vitamins. Scurvy (vitamin C deficiency), rickets (vitamin D deficiency in the young), "nutritional croup" (vitamin A deficiency), goiter (iodide deficiency), beriberi (thiamin deficiency), and pellagra (niacin deficiency) all fell to education, the availability of a varied food supply, and the fortification of staple foods.

The dramatic effect of nutrition on the prevention of specific deficiency diseases led to speculation that many other human diseases and disorders could similarly be prevented by a proper diet. Although there may be some truth to this for chronic diseases such as heart disease and cancer, claims for the prevention of many others are not supported by the evidence. In this chapter, we first consider what nutrition can unequivocally do for you, as illustrated by the discovery of three specific nutritional deficiency diseases, and then we discuss several disorders that are claimed to be, but are in fact not, nutrition related.

183

What nutrition can do for you

Ask any nutritionist whether an appropriate diet is necessary for the prevention of disease, and you will get an enthusiastic, unqualified yes. Virtually all nutritionists agree that an appropriate diet is essential to
preventing nutritional deficiency diseases, because the evidence is overwhelming that they are caused by an inadequate intake of specific nutrients.

The possibility that diet may be related to sickness and death seemed
obvious to people living in the Middle Ages, long before any one suspected
that germs existed. Suddenly and mysteriously, seemingly healthy people
became ill and often died. When deaths were widespread, as happened
during the several centuries of recurring bubonic plague in Europe, people
thought it was punishment from a wrathful God. "God's wrath" was particularly bad during the middle of the fourteenth century when an estimated
40 percent of Europe's population died of the plague. In addition to pious
behavior, the one obvious factor that people could control was diet. With
no explanation for illness other than the wrath of God, it is not surprising
that when people became ill, it was attributed to something they ate.

Ironically, it was the development of the theory that disease was caused
by germs that took diet "off the hook" in the latter part of the nineteenth
century. The widespread acceptance of this theory fostered the belief
among scientists that germs, not an improper diet, were responsible for
sickness and death. In addition, by the end of the nineteenth century,
agricultural chemists had become convinced that food was needed only to
supply protein and a source of calories from carbohydrates and fats. An-
alytical data showed that when the carbohydrate, fat, protein, ash (mineral), and "indigestible matter" (fiber) contents of food were combined,
they accounted for 100 percent of the weight or very close to it. This left
little, if any, room for anything else needed by humans. It never occurred
to these chemists that small amounts of anything could be important, and
this led the scientists of the day to recommend that people buy those foods
that provided the most calories and protein for the money spent.[2]

The agricultural chemist Wilbur O. Atwater, who was so revered that
he has been called the father of American nutrition, gave such advice.
About 1896 he calculated that when a housewife spent ten cents for a half-
pound of beef sirloin, she received 0.08 pounds of protein and 515 kilocalories. The same amount of money could buy 4 pounds of fresh cabbage,
but this yielded only 0.05 pounds of protein and 460 kilocalories. In contrast, ten cents' worth of wheat flour (3.33 pounds) would provide 0.32
pounds of protein and 5,410 kilocalories of energy. The message was clear:
Buy economical flour to make bread, and don't waste money on fruits and
vegetables! This advice was readily accepted by the middle class, and a
diet providing protein and calories from bread and some meat but not fruit

and vegetables quickly became official U.S. government policy. Besides, fruits and vegetables had a bad reputation because they often were eaten by the poor, who had little else to eat, and so they were labeled "second-class foods." Leafy vegetables were called fodder because they were eaten by animals. Worst of all, it was widely believed that the consumption of fresh fruits and vegetables caused cholera.

The laborious task of finding the cause of and cure for nutritional diseases was no doubt made more difficult by the scientific climate of the times. In spite of these problems, progress was made and gained momentum with each success. Nutritional diseases are now so rare in our society that it is easy to forget that they were relatively common occurrences in the formative years of many Americans still alive today. The field of nutrition proudly points to the discovery and demise of these diseases as "their finest hour," which indeed formed the basis for this relatively young science. For the scientists involved in this early work, however, it wasn't easy.

The plague of the sea: Scurvy

Contrary to what we might surmise from folklore, the vitamin C deficiency disease, called *scurvy*, was not a widespread problem[3] even before the economic success of marketing oranges as "liquid sunshine." Epidemics of scurvy actually occurred only during unusual circumstances – sieges in war or during drought, both of which limited the consumption of fruits and vegetables. In 1845, scurvy was one of the notable consequences of the potato famine in Ireland when a potato blight destroyed the one food that provided vitamin C in the population's diet. The one group for which scurvy was a constant occupational hazard was sailors on long voyages. But even for them, the incidence of the disease was quite variable. Some sailors could be at sea for months without developing the disease, whereas others might show symptoms within a few weeks.

Long voyages, of course, became more popular after the exploits of one particularly famous sailor – Christopher Columbus. There is a story that a group of sailors on one of Columbus's voyages developed the symptoms of scurvy – sore and bleeding gums, hemorrhages under the skin, and painful, swollen legs and muscles.[4] The sailors, as well as the disease, had been around long enough for them to know the prognosis. In order to avoid the certainty of a traditional burial at sea and the ignominious fate of being consumed by fish, a merciful Columbus granted their request to be deposited on an island. At least they could die on solid ground. Awaiting death, they ate leaves, fruits, and woodland sprouts. A few months later, Columbus returned expecting to find skeletons and instead found healthy sailors free of the disease. The island, one of the Lesser Antilles, is named Curaçao, derived from the Spanish word for "cure."

James Lind, a Scottish physician, may not have heard this story, but there were plenty of other anecdotes and descriptions of the incidence of scurvy, going back to the earliest recorded history, to allow him to deduce correctly that scurvy could be caused by an improper diet. In his book *Treatise on Scurvy*, first published in 1753,[5] Lind rejected the idea that the disease was different on land and sea, but he overestimated the causative effects of damp air, to which sailors were often exposed. Even so, he concluded that "the cure of the adventitious scurvy is very simple, viz. a pure dry air, with the use of green herbage or wholesome vegetables, almost of any sort; which for the most part prove effectual." The consequences of consuming poisons was, of course, well known, but it was an entirely novel idea that sickness and death could result because of something that was not consumed! This was all the more remarkable because it preceded the concept of vitamins by a century and a half.

The idea was, in fact, so innovative that the response to Lind's prescription was mixed. One person who did pay attention was an English explorer, Captain James Cook. Captain Cook had lost only one man to scurvy out of the 118-member crew of the HMS *Resolution* during his prolonged second voyage (1772 to 1775) to the Pacific. Scurvy had been avoided because Cook stocked his ships with fresh fruits and vegetables at every port he visited. In addition, he fed his crew sauerkraut and germinated grain. On Cook's next voyage, he became the first European to set foot in Hawaii, on January 18, 1778. The natives were friendly, but it turned out, not friendly enough, because Cook was killed about one year later on the island of Hawaii, in what was otherwise "a minor skirmish." Thus, his influence on the British navy to adopt his methods for preventing scurvy was lost. This explains, in part at least, why it was not until 1795 that the British admiralty started requiring that crews of Royal Navy ships be given citrus fruits, often in the form of lime or lemon concentrates preserved with alcohol. Since then, British sailors have been called "limeys."

The beginning of the end of scurvy came, as was the usual case for diseases, when an animal model of scurvy was developed in the laboratory. In the case of scurvy, the animal was the guinea pig. Two Norwegian scientists, A. Holst and T. Frolich, discovered in 1907 that guinea pigs developed symptoms almost identical to those exhibited by humans when fed a severely restricted diet. Fruits and vegetables, as Lind had suggested, would prevent and cure the guinea pigs' disease. This method of using an animal model not only added the expression "guinea pig" to our vocabulary to describe anyone subjected to experimentation, but it also became a powerful tool for examining the amount of the "antiscorbutic[a] factor" or vitamin C in various foods. Even with an animal model, however, it wasn't

[a] *Scorbutic* is derived from the Latin word for scurvy.

until 1932 that two Americans, Charles Glen King and W. A. Waugh, isolated the crystalline material from lemon juice. They quickly concluded that it was the same material that a Hungarian scientist named Albert Szent-Gyorgyi had isolated from adrenal glands four years earlier. After it was crystallized, the chemical structure of this newly discovered vitamin was easily determined, and it was given the chemical name of *ascorbic acid*.

Ascorbic acid, readily synthesized in the laboratory, is chemically identical to the compound that occurs in nature and is so inexpensive that a dollar's worth of the stuff will more than meet one's need for about five years. Better yet, all one needs to do is follow Lind's advice of more than two centuries ago and eat "green herbage or wholesome vegetables of almost any sort." Because we now consume plenty of the foods containing vitamin C, scurvy is spoken of – with the exception of very rare cases – as a dreaded disease only in the past tense.

Sick sailors and crazy chickens: Beriberi

In the 1870s the Japanese navy had a problem with a disease, and it wasn't scurvy. The new problem was a disease given the exotic name of *beriberi*.[6] The name might have suggested that when people had the disease their faces looked like strawberries, but that was not the case. Actually, the disease takes one of two forms. The symptoms of "wet" beriberi are fluid accumulation and heart failure. "Dry" beriberi is a nerve problem leading to paralysis of the lower limbs.

The incidence of the disease in the Japanese navy was high – reaching almost 40 percent in 1879, with a mortality rate of 12 per 1,000. A Japanese naval surgeon, Admiral Takaki, noted that the disease was common among sailors fed predominantly polished rice that had been machine milled and the husk removed.[b] When a diet composed of wheat, barley, beans, milk, and meat was given instead, the beriberi disappeared. Although he thought the preventive factor was protein (vitamins were unknown then), he convinced the naval brass to feed his diet to sailors. They did, and the disease had entirely disappeared from members of the Japanese navy by 1885.

Admiral Takaki published his work in Japanese, which, unfortunately, most of the rest of the world couldn't read. Thus, the incidence of beriberi continued to be high in those cultures whose diet consisted mainly of polished rice.

Beriberi also appeared rather suddenly in the 1870s in the Malayan

---

[b] We now know that beriberi made a sudden appearance as a new disease because of new technology in the form of steam-driven machines to remove the husk from rice. Previous hand methods were more laborious and imperfect in removing the husk. The new polished rice was thought to be superior because it was cheaper and had better keeping qualities.

Peninsula, otherwise known as the Dutch East Indies, and had reached epidemic proportions in some areas by the late 1880s. The Dutch were understandably concerned because it was among the laborers in their tin mines where beriberi was taking its greatest toll. It was the age of discovery of infectious disease in Europe, and so it is not surprising that European medical authorities thought beriberi was another example of such a disease. In 1886, the Dutch government recruited a 38-year-old physician by the name of Christian Eijkman, who had been trained in medical microbiology, to study the disease in the Dutch East Indies.[7] Eijkman had received his education in this new science from the masters of the field, including one of its founders, Robert Koch of Berlin. True to his training, Eijkman established a bacteriology and pathology laboratory to search systematically for the infectious agent.

Actually, there were three distinct ethnic populations living in the Dutch East Indies, in addition to Europeans. Rice was a staple for all three cultures, except that they differed greatly in their preparation of it. The indigenous Malays, living mainly in villages along the seacoast, grew their own rice and ate it after a portion of the husk was removed by means of "home pounding." The Tamil Indians from southern India, most of whom worked on the rubber plantations, "parboiled" their rice before dehusking it. In this process, practiced widely in India, the whole rice is soaked in water and then steamed for 20 to 30 minutes before it is spread out to dry. The steaming process splits the husk so that after it has dried, the husk is easily removed, even by home pounding. The third ethnic group was Chinese laborers, imported by the Dutch to work in the tin mines. The Chinese ate polished rice, imported from Thailand, which was supplied in unlimited amounts by the Dutch to new recruits for the first six months to two years, as sort of a "signing bonus." Beriberi was almost unknown among the Malays and Tamils, but the Chinese laborers were devastated.

Eijkman did not notice these differences in diet and susceptibility to beriberi, at least at first. Because the Chinese laborers were geographically removed from the other groups, the exclusive presence of the disease among them fit the model of a contagious disease, and so Eijkman kept searching, futilely, for an infectious agent.

We will never know whether it was just plain luck (scientists like to call this serendipity) or ingenious scientific observation, but Eijkman found an animal model for the disease right under his nose! The Europeans in the hospital complex where he worked liked to eat chicken more than they did rice. For this reason, they kept a flock of chickens penned up as "meat on the hoof." These chickens were fed table scraps – which in that society meant primarily polished rice. Eijkman noticed that the caged chickens developed a neurological disorder characterized by a "crazed look," staggering, and paralysis, symptoms similar to those of dry beriberi, whereas those chickens running free and scrounging food for themselves remained healthy. When he fed the "crazy" chickens raw, brown rice, they recovered almost immediately.

The recovery of the chickens was enough to persuade Eijkman to drop his search for a germ. Instead, he formed a liaison with the health inspectors and started examining the relationship between the incidence of beriberi and diet. Over the ten years that Eijkman was in the Dutch East Indies, he built the case that beriberi was due to the consumption of polished rather than whole-grain rice. Eijkman published his work in 1897 on the cause of beriberi, but few of its readers were convinced. The new germ theory had already infected the medical establishment in Europe.

Eijkman was, of course, right. The Malays had escaped beriberi because they had left enough of the husks on the rice to provide the "magical" substance that prevented the disease. The Tamils were fortunate to have used the method of parboiling to remove the hulls because the steaming caused the active agent – later known as the vitamin thiamin – to diffuse from the hull into the rice grain. Although Eijkman had discovered that eating polished rice caused the disease, he did not know why.

A giant leap toward the answer was made by another Dutch physician by the name of Gerrit Grijns. His discovery that the factor that prevented beriberi in humans and animals could be extracted from rice polishings with alcohol clearly supported Eijkman's concept of the cause of the disease. The whole story of vital food substances began to emerge when an English physician, named Frederick Gowland Hopkins, reported in 1906 that alcohol could extract several dietary essential organic compounds, including the antiberiberi factor, from dried milk and vegetables.

The antiberiberi factor was finally isolated in 1926 and given the name *thiamin*. It was another ten years before the chemical structure of the vitamin was established by synthesis, and by the time World War II started, it was being produced commercially at a relatively low cost.

The story has a happy ending for Eijkman. He was awarded the Nobel Prize in 1929, which he shared with Hopkins, for the discovery of the cause and treatment of beriberi. The accolades came 32 years after his initial report, and for him, it was in the nick of time. He died in November of the following year in Utrect, Holland. The Nobel Prize is never awarded posthumously.

The story also has a happy ending for the rest of us. Knowledge and inexpensive thiamin have virtually eliminated beriberi except in a few places of the world where polished rice, unfortified with the vitamin, continues to be almost the sole source of food.

Pellagra: The curse of the South[8]

In March 1902, a young Georgia farmer decided to do something about the "spring fever" that he had suffered for the past fifteen years with the coming of warm weather. He made his way to Atlanta where he consulted a physician, Dr. H. F. Harris. The physician became very interested because the symptoms were those of pellagra, a disease that afflicted much of Europe but had not previously been reported in the United States. Dr. Harris gave the farmer some remarkably sound advice, considering the state of knowledge about the disease at the time. His prescription was to move to Indiana and stop eating corn!

Harris reported the case in April at a meeting of the Medical Association of Georgia and described the patient's symptoms: loss of weight, a feeling that his body was on fire, and large blisters on his arms and hands. The patient had experienced unusual poverty and ate bread made with Indian corn. Poverty and corn were two factors that showed up repeatedly in cases of pellagra, as did politics and prejudice. Another constant was that the disease was most common in late winter and spring. Harris's fellow physicians took little note of this single case at the time.

The medical community in the South did take notice, however, of a report made to the Medical Association of Alabama in 1907 that there had been an epidemic of acute pellagra at the Mount Vernon Insane Hospital in Alabama in the summer of 1906, with a mortality rate of 64 percent. Dr. George H. Searcy had diagnosed acute pellagra in 88 inmates of this institution for blacks. Dr. Searcy, like Dr. Harris, attributed the disease to eating damaged corn. Subsequently, pellagra was diagnosed throughout the South in institutions like mental hospitals and prisons. With the publicity, the medical community soon recognized that many patients with pellagra from both city and rural areas had been misdiagnosed as suffering from general debilitation from unknown causes. Whether it was because of the increased incidence or better diagnosis, it was clear that pellagra was spreading throughout the South. There were fewer than 1,000 cases reported in 1907 but 15,870 reported cases of the disease in eight southern states between 1907 and 1911, with 39 percent mortality. The disease was clearly widespread and serious, or would have been considered so under other circumstances.

Unfortunately, the recognition of the pellagra problem occurred barely fifty years after the end of the Civil War. There were many on both sides of the Mason–Dixon line who still had bitter memories of that disastrous conflict. The North considered pellagra to be a problem for the South and often did not appear sympathetic. Indeed, the northern press labeled the South as "the land of hookworm and pellagra." Proud southerners objected to such derision, but the leadership in this region also had less than total concern because pellagra was a disease of poverty and its victims were essentially devoid of political clout. Besides, it was a widely held belief, except by those afflicted, that pellagra was caused by unsanitary conditions that often accompanied poverty. It was often stated by nonvictims that "if those people would take a bath regularly and clean up, the disease would go away."

The U.S. Public Health Service was moved, but not much, by the widespread problem of pellagra in the South. To combat it, in May 1909 it sent a delegation to South Carolina consisting of one man, Dr. C. H. Lavinder. He was given two rooms for a laboratory in the South Carolina Hospital for the Insane. Although he had plenty of patients with pellagra, his "laboratory" had no running water and no natural gas. He was given no clerical help or assistance, expert or otherwise. With this kind of support, it is difficult to make a case that the U.S. government was seriously committed to eradicating this disease.

Despite the prejudice, commissions were appointed by several states to investigate the cause of pellagra. Because it was the "age of the germ," the membership of these commissions was dominated by representatives of the newly emerging field of epidemiology. Practitioners were medical detectives, dedicated to discovering the cause of disease epidemics and preventing their spread. Epidemiology was a growth industry. These dedicated scientists had enjoyed, and would continue for many years to enjoy, victory against such deadly diseases as typhoid fever, scarlet fever, tuberculosis, and cholera.

Pellagra had all the earmarks of another disease that could be overcome by the same methods. The commissions attacked the problem with confidence and enthusiasm, and by 1914, most of them had completed their work. Unfortunately, they invariably arrived at erroneous conclusions, the legacy of which would cloud the issue of the real cause of pellagra for years to come. In retrospect, two lessons could have, and indeed should have, been learned from the work of these state commissions. First, the result of such a group's work depends on its members' training. Second, the probability that a commission or a jury will arrive at an incorrect verdict is directly proportional to the significance of the facts that they do not have.

Two theories regarding the cause of pellagra emerged from these commissions, both of which were wrong. The one with the greater scientific support was that the disease was caused by specific infectious agents. The second theory was that the disease was caused by eating "spoiled corn." In addition, some suspected that both theories were correct, that is, that an infectious agent was the basic cause but that it was transmitted by the consumption of "bad" corn. The idea that pellagra could be caused by eating corn was unsettling, especially to the corn growers and U.S. Department of Agriculture officials. Corn was a major export of U.S. agriculture, and it would never do for potential customers in Europe to believe that American corn could cause such a dreaded disease. To combat this threat to the economy, the Department of Agriculture set minimum standards for exported corn and initiated a corn inspection system. We still have corn inspectors. In addition, politicians, especially those from corn-producing states, insisted that the U.S. Public Health Service resolve the pellagra problem. There was widespread support for this initiative when it became apparent that pellagra was not confined to the South. By 1914, the disease had been diagnosed in thirty-two states.

The political pressure worked. The surgeon general replaced Dr. Lavinder with a team of experts to deal with pellagra. In retrospect, the surgeon general almost made the same mistake that those who had appointed state commissions had made; he recruited an epidemiologist who had achieved notable success in combating infectious diseases to head the investigations. The difference was that he chose one of the best of this new breed of scientists, Dr. Joseph Goldberger.

Goldberger was assigned in March 1914 to be in charge of the pellagra studies of the U.S. Public Health Service. Although Goldberger was to spend the rest of his life studying pellagra, he determined the real cause of the disease in less than three months – diet!

Goldberger published his first paper on pellagra in June 1914, in which he argued against the infectious disease hypothesis. He observed that although pellagra was rampant among inmates in institutions, no cases ever occurred in nurses or attendants, even though they were in close daily contact with pellagrins. He also noted that the inmates ate a different diet than did the staff. But his arguments, like those of Eijkman's years earlier, fell on deaf ears. Critics could point to the state commissions' conclusions, which stated that the "infectious agent" was minimally contagious and that susceptibility to it might be genetically determined. Goldberger continued his work.

Subsequent papers came in rapid succession, in which Goldberger and his coworkers attempted to refute systematically the infectious disease theory and to build their case that an improper diet caused pellagra. They showed that pellagra was prevented and, for those who had the disease, cured when the inmates of institutions were fed the same diet as the staff. (Critics noted: Hadn't "spoiled corn" been suspected before?) Pellagra was produced in volunteer prisoners by restricting their diet and was subsequently cured by feeding them a more varied diet that included milk and fresh meat. (Critics noted: Didn't the varied diet include less "spoiled" corn?) In a particularly repugnant experiment, the disease was shown not to be transmitted to sixteen volunteers (who included Goldberger, his wife, and coworkers) by the consumption of blood, nasal secretions, skin scales, urine, or feces from pellagra victims. (Critics: What about genetic susceptibility?)

Most of the facts that Goldberger used to reach his conclusions were already known to his contemporaries, but they had missed their significance or misinterpreted them and, for the most part, continued to do so even after he had pointed them out. Whereas the others assumed that pellagra was caused by something its victims consumed (an infectious agent, moldy corn, or a combination of the two), Goldberger attributed pellagra to something they did not consume but should have. This was not, of course, a novel idea, even when Goldberger received his pellagra assignment. By then, it had been reported that food contained organic compounds needed for health, and they had even been given the name *vitamines*. The scientists working in this new area were mostly chemists, not physicians, and it appears that the medical community had paid little attention to them. Besides, Goldberger was not talking about the relatively obscure diseases, at least in the United States, of beriberi or scurvy; he was into pellagra and no one else had ever accused that disease of being caused by the lack of some food substance. Goldberger began discussions with leaders of the new field of nutrition and continued to try to establish conclusively that his theory regarding the cause of pellagra was right. He never did. He died in January 1929 at the age of 52, eight years before the antipellagra vitamin was finally found.

Thus, in spite of Goldberger's work, pellagra continued relatively unabated. As the incidence and deaths from pellagra continued to increase, so did public panic. Stories circulated that insects – with a range of candidates from buffalo gnats to mosquitoes to amoebae ingested in contaminated water or vegetables – caused the disease.

The disease was so dreadful, with a death rate averaging about 40 percent, that hysteria ultimately took over. Even though the medical community agreed that the disease was not readily contagious, many hospitals refused admission to any one with pellagra. Victims of the disease were often quarantined and even warned to stay behind screens lest they be bitten by a mosquito that could then transfer the disease to another victim. If not quarantined, the victims of pellagra and anyone associated with them were often ostracized. Children whose parents or siblings had pellagra were not admitted to school.

For every crackpot theory on the cause of pellagra, there were dozens more on how to treat it. Some grocery stores capitalized on the fear of the disease by advertising that they sold only "pure" food and that you could avoid pellagra by buying only from them. Arsenic compounds or castor oil were used by some physicians as specific cures for pellagra, both of which were devastating to weakened victims of the disease.

As with any disease looking for a cure, and even for some that are not, the quacks continued to come out of the woodwork. Mineral spring water for consumption and baths sold well. In Florida patients were treated with "static electricity." They placed their feet on a metal plate, and an electrode was attached to their head. The machine then delivered electricity at the rate of 200 discharges per second, which literally made their hair stand on end but did nothing for pellagra. A mill worker in South Carolina named Ezxba W. Desmond sold a "pellagra cure" called "Ez-X-Ba River, the Stream of Life." Mr. Desmond, backed financially by a group of businessmen, claimed that he was a recovered pellagra victim who had been given the "cure" by a merciful God. His remedy was said to cure pellagra in a matter of weeks. Another similar product, also from South Carolina, was called "Pellagracide." Both products had the following statement on their label: "Guaranteed under the Pure Food and Drug Act, June 30th, 1906." Thus people were led to believe that the products had the blessings of both God and the government, a combination that guaranteed that they would sell like bottled water, which is exactly what they were. The U.S. Public Health Service eventually exposed both products as fraudulent, but not before considerable money had been made from pellagra victims and others hoping to prevent the disease.

Ironically, although pellagra was a disease brought on by the poor diet caused by poverty, the incidence of it declined precipitously at the beginning of the Great Depression. Until then, the cash crop in the South was "King Cotton," but during the Depression, the price of cotton dropped so low that there was no point in growing it. With no money to buy anything, even cornmeal, the farmers used the land to grow food. The result was that their diet became more varied, and with that, the end of pellagra was in sight.

The final battle in determining the cause of the disease came, as it did in the battles against scurvy and beriberi, when an animal model was developed in the laboratory. The "guinea pig" in this case was a dog. The canine equivalent of pellagra, black tongue, provided a means for a University of Wisconsin professor, Dr. Conrad A. Elvehjem, to identify nicotinic acid as the antipellagra factor in 1937, eight years after Goldberger's death. Nicotinic acid and its chemical cousins are now collectively called *niacin*. Inexpensive methods of producing niacin were quickly developed, and with the use of this vitamin in food, pellagra virtually disappeared.

Why nutritional deficiencies are rare today

The three diseases discussed in this chapter, scurvy, beriberi, and pellagra, all were products of new technology. Scurvy developed as a major problem for sailors when the technology of sailing ships allowed long voyages. Beriberi increased to epidemic proportions when new machines were invented that effectively removed the hulls from rice. Pellagra gained a foothold when methods were developed to "improve" cornmeal by removing the germ. It took a while, as we have seen, but eventually the effects of the new technology were overcome with understanding and still newer technology.

Beriberi and pellagra have been virtually eradicated, except in small pockets of the world, by the simple process of adding back the nutrients lost when portions of the whole grain are removed. This process, called *enrichment*, is the addition of thiamin, niacin, riboflavin, and iron to grain products in amounts equal to those lost by processing. Except for products made with the whole grain, enrichment is virtually standard procedure for flour, cornmeal, and some types of rice. The chances are great that if you have white flour, cornmeal, or bread (other than whole grain) in your kitchen right now, the label will tell you that it is "enriched" with thiamin, niacin, riboflavin, and iron.

An inexpensive source of the necessary nutrients for enrichment became available by 1940, but only the largest grain-milling companies bothered to install the expensive equipment required to add them. The situation rapidly changed after the United States entered World War II. During that conflict, the War Department required that grain products (other than those containing whole grains) bought for consumption by the armed services had to be enriched. That meant that any millers who wanted to sell their products to the government, which was virtually all of them, had to install the proper equipment and start adding the prescribed nutrients. The results were miraculous; by 1950 pellagra and beriberi had disappeared in the United States. Similarly, the addition of vitamins A and D to milk and iodide to salt virtually eliminated deficiencies of these nutrients.

What nutrition cannot do for you

In a way, the battle against nutritional diseases was too successful. It confirmed the long-held belief that diet did play a significant role in guarding against illness. But unfortunately, the results were so spectacular that people, understandably, overestimated what vitamins and proper nutrition could do. This made it easy for those who pedaled nutrition products to convince the public that all sorts of ailments could be prevented and/or cured by a judicious selection of nutrients in a bottle. Nutrition "cures" are thus often advocated for such nonspecific symptoms as tiredness, lack of pep, or failure to lose (or gain) weight.

The fact is that deficiencies of specific nutrients result in specific nutrient deficiency diseases. Still, a number of human ailments have repeatedly been shown not to have a nutritional connection, but nutrition products and advice still abound.

Aging

Juan Ponce de Leon explored in 1513 what is now Florida, looking for the fountain of youth. He had no more success than Francisco Coronado did a few years later when he tried to find the fabled cities of gold in the

Southwest. Since then, several people have taken a cue from both of these Spanish explorers and turned promises of a fountain of youth into gold. The fact is that the only way we know to stop the aging process is to die. Given that choice, most of us opt for growing older.

When we think of growing older, both positive and negative images may come to mind. We anticipate a less hectic life of retirement with, we hope, good health and enough time and money to spend as we desire. We hope that our children will be succeeding on their own, and perhaps we may enjoy grandchildren. On the other hand, we often fear poor health due to chronic disease, lack of adequate finances, loss of loved ones, decreased physical capability, diminished sexuality, and the burden that we could become to family, friends, or society. Indeed, the fear of growing old has tempted many to search futilely for "cures." Although the young, who seemed to be blessed with the eternal optimism of immortality, seldom fall prey to "fountain of youth" schemes, this is not true for those of us who find wrinkles and sags that were not there only yesterday. The result can be found in a report by a House of Representatives subcommittee[9] that "the sale of 'youth cures' is the fastest growing segment of current medical quackery. It is apparently the most profitable."

The report discusses several phony "cures" that promise to stop, or even reverse, aging and the physiological changes that accompany it. It is not surprising that of the latter, the two that seem to be of greatest concern are emphasized: wrinkles and sexual dysfunction. The report concludes that "some of the products reviewed were outright dangerous, promising the impossible and promoting unproven remedies, the use of which postponed therapy that might otherwise be effective in treating chronic diseases. Most of the products were simply deceptive, overstated, fraudulent or demeaning."

Severe restriction of food intake has been promoted on the basis of animal studies as one "cure" for aging. It is true that when laboratory rats were fed one-half or less of their normal food intake, their average survival time was longer compared with that of control rats given free access to food. Although such a dietary regime increased longevity in the rats for some as yet unknown reason, this does not mean that it stopped or slowed the aging process. It has certainly not been established that eating less can affect either longevity or aging in humans. Yet books and articles have been written suggesting just that.

Starvation and fasting have been claimed to promote longevity by removing toxic chemicals from cells. This is one of the most blatant nutrition fallacies. Fasting can actually increase the formation of some metabolic products from the degradation of body constituents, and it does increase the excretion of water and minerals. Starvation and fasting do not "cleanse the body"; they cause death! The amount of time it takes to do so varies, depending on age, genetics, body composition, overall health, and environmental factors. Fasting is more likely to cause death in the elderly and the very young than it is in healthy, middle-aged persons.

One theory of aging has it that our genetic material – or nucleic acids, which are present in every cell – undergoes progressive damage over time. The longer we live, the greater the damage will be, and so the more we will age. This theory has never been proved, but nucleic acids have been promoted as "antiaging" chemicals. There are two types of nucleic acids: *RNA*, or ribonucleic acid, and *DNA*, or deoxyribonucleic acid. These form the basis of the genetic code, without which life is impossible. Even if the theory turns out to be correct that aging is caused by damage to these substances, consuming nucleic acids would have absolutely no effect on the process. The reason is that when nucleic acids are eaten, they are degraded to their simplest form before being absorbed. The body can make all of the building blocks that are needed, and even if some from the diet are used, they must be remade into polymer form inside each cell. Thus, the consumption of RNA or DNA is of no benefit to the body, and for some it can cause damage. During the process of excreting two of the building blocks present in both RNA and DNA, a product called *uric acid* is formed. Thus when excessive amounts of RNA and DNA are consumed, more of this product is formed, which can lead to painful gout.

An extension of the theory that aging is caused by damage to our genetic material blames the problem on a group of chemicals called *free radicals*. Free radicals are not terrorists out of jail, as the name implies, but are chemicals with one electron missing. Presumably because being one electron short of a load is an uncomfortable state, the free radical tries to steal one electron from some other chemical. If the reluctant electron giver happens to be a nucleic acid, the loss of that electron will damage our genetic material. And it is argued that damaged genetic material causes not only aging but also cancer. A product containing an enzyme called *super oxide dismutase* (SOD) has been claimed to solve the problem by preventing the formation of free radicals in the first place. The truth is that we have a natural enzyme in our cells that has the effect of reducing free radical formation, and even if it were necessary, there is no way to increase the amount that we do have. All enzymes, including SOD, are protein, and any protein that one eats is digested before it is absorbed. This means that if SOD is eaten, it is an expensive source of amino acids. It has no effect on aging or any other physiological processes. Note that not only would it be dangerous to inject it into the bloodstream but that this also would not work, as SOD could not get into cells where free radicals might be formed.

Other substances that are claimed to prevent aging do not attempt to offer any scientific reasons for their "effectiveness." For example, an herb sold under the name gotu kola has been claimed to "delay aging" and is "good for senility." The House subcommittee report found the claim to be "false and misleading."[10] Multivitamin tablets have been advertised as "antiaging and antistress," often at inflated prices compared with supplements sold at your local drug store (see Chapter 5). Vitamins have not been shown to have any effect on the aging process.

A number of products on the market also claim to cure "impotence" associated with aging. These products, however, are often nothing more than vitamin and mineral supplements, featuring vitamin E (the so-called antisterility vitamin – in mice, not men). A relatively unusual idea has been promoted that the metallic gold in water can treat impotence and increase virility by "exciting" or "stimulating" the male sex glands. Gold has been studied for its requirement by humans, but after years of study no known requirement in any metabolic process has been found.

It is unfortunate that aging is so often feared. With more and more of our society living longer and longer lives, the study of aging (gerontology) has flourished. We can only hope that the more we study, the more we will learn how to maximize the quality of old age and minimize the factors that diminish its quality.

Arthritis

Arthritis is America's number one chronic crippling disease, affecting one in seven Americans and one of every three families. In addition, arthritis may be the nation's most costly disease, estimated by the Arthritis Foundation to cost the economy $25 billion in 1984 in direct and indirect, legitimate and not legitimate costs. Overall, arthritis attacks more women than men and affects persons of all ages. No one knows with certainty what causes arthritis, although heredity, viruses, and injuries are thought to be among its contributing factors. There is no cure for arthritis at the present time, although much of the pain and crippling can be controlled or prevented if proper medical care is implemented early enough.

Literally dozens of arthritis "cures" have been promoted, none of which actually works.[11] Sometimes the "cures" are dangerous in themselves, and all of the self-treatment schemes subject the user to the risk of delaying appropriate medical treatment. Unfortunately, arthritis is a disease that has made many persons rich at the expense of its sufferers, many of whom are poor. It has been estimated that in 1984, Americans spent in excess of $2 billion on questionable arthritis remedies, twenty-five times the amount spent on research to find a cure for the disease.[12] According to the Arthritis Foundation, arthritis quackery succeeds because

1. There is widespread lack of understanding of arthritis.
2. There is no cure at the present time.

3. There is tremendous pain associated with the disease.
4. There are so many people suffering that promoters have a huge market.
5. The symptoms of arthritis come and go like the tide, thereby encouraging people to connect a disappearance with a phony remedy they have been trying.
6. The placebo effect often works, at least temporarily, when people want to get better and believe they will by taking some "remedy."[c]
7. There is little policing of the problem.

Spotting an unscrupulous promoter is not easy. Accurate scientific information may be couched in cleverly written articles that include half-truths, other inaccuracies, and often downright lies. One of the ways to recognize such misinformation is to remember that there is no evidence that arthritis is caused by poor nutrition or that it can be cured by nutrients. In spite of this, so-called dietary cures for arthritis are as legion as copper bracelets and are just as ineffective. Several foods have been falsely accused of causing the disease or falsely promised to cure or prevent it.

Promoters of vitamins and minerals as cures for arthritis claim that a deficiency of one or more of several nutrients causes arthritis and that supplementing them will cure it. It has been asserted at various times that the disease is due to a deficiency of vitamins A, D, E, C, B_6, B_{12}, pantothenic acid, or niacin or the minerals calcium, copper, zinc, iron, lead, nickel, tin, manganese, or molybdenum. Research has found no evidence that arthritis is caused by dietary shortages of any of these nutrients or that supplementation with any of them will cure it.

One of the all-time favorite "cures" for many disorders, including arthritis, is water. It can be hot, lukewarm, cool, cold, or ice; it can be distilled, mineral, or salt; it can be drunk, injected, sprayed on or into various body parts, or body parts can be immersed in it. But most of all, it has to be some type of "special" water that, of course, is more expensive than the mundane stuff. The U.S. Postal Service has taken action against a large number of advertisements for water as a cure-all. One such ad, "Miraculous Water from Lourdes" was hailed by its promoters as a cure for arthritis and even cancer. The water not only failed the test of "miraculous," it had never even seen France, except perhaps in an earlier existence. It was bottled in California. Water is a necessary nutrient for all of us, but it has not been found to be a cure for arthritis or, for that matter, anything else other than thirst and dehydration.

Advocates for the use of dietary fats and oils, such as cod liver oil, in

---

[c] The placebo effect in arthritis has been estimated to be as high as 80 percent. This means that when sufferers are given a treatment that contains no medication, up to 80 percent of the time they will seem to get better. It is not only wrong but cruel to assume that this means arthritic pain is "all in the head." We do not understand the placebo effect, but we do know that its existence does not mean that the pain is not real.

the treatment of arthritis suggest that the disease is a result of "poorly lubricated joints," with an allusion to the need to lubricate the joints on your car. It is insinuated that dietary fats and oils can replace this lost lubrication. In truth, joints are lubricated by a substance called *synovial fluid*, not oil and certainly not fats or oils from the diet.

In some cases, the claim has been made that arthritis is caused by what we do eat rather than what we do not. For example, a New Jersey horticulturist theorized that plants of the nightshade family (which include tomatoes, white potatoes, peppers, eggplants, and tobacco) were the cause of arthritis and therefore that eliminating these foods would cure the disease. In truth, there is no evidence that nightshades, food additives, or food allergies cause arthritis, despite some "arthritis diets" that recommend not eating processed foods, flour, flour products, coffee, tea, wine, beer, or carbonated beverages.

A number of exotic foods, herbs, and spices also have been promoted as arthritis cures.[13] A number of these (including green-lipped mussel extract, gotu kola, pokeweed, aloe vera, ginseng, foxglove, alfalfa, burdock, licorice, pine bark, sassafras, yucca, wormwood, rose hips, allspice, basil, caraway, cayenne pepper, dill, and nutmeg) have been shown to be ineffective, and many have untoward side effects. Others are ineffective and can be very dangerous. For example, wolf herb (*Gordolobos*) is a plant that various Native American tribes make into a tea and drink as a popular remedy for arthritis and other diseases. But the tea contains a toxic compound that has been shown to cause the deaths of some users, including babies, and cirrhosis of the liver in others. Another ineffective remedy, rattlebox, has been found in humans and animals to cause a sudden rise in blood pressure and inflammation of the lung arterial vessels. Drinking it as a tea or eating the seeds can cause death.

Chuifong toukwan is an herbal medication widely advertised to cure arthritis. The pill contains dangerous herb combinations that include potentially lethal ingredients. The product has been implicated as causing an acute blood disorder, called *agranulocytosis*. Drugs in the pills have been changed from time to time, but reports of addiction have been noted. The Food and Drug Administration and the Arthritis Foundation have warned that this product is one of the most dangerous so-called treatments for arthritis to come on the market in many years.

Although some drugs such as aspirin have been shown to alleviate the pain associated with arthritis, no drugs have yet been shown to "cure" the disease, and many can adversely affect health. Before trying any chemical preparation in the hopes of alleviating arthritic pain or its underlying cause, check with your physician for advice. Self-treatment for this malady is always disappointing and can result in deadly consequences.

Acne

For as long as we have had teenagers, we have had acne, but its cause and treatment are still far from being resolved. Probably the most important factor in the development of acne is the increased production of androgen during puberty, which is regulated by heredity. Androgens, which are necessary hormones for the development of sexual characteristics, can play havoc with the face, back, and arms. These hormones increase the production of a fatty secretion of the sebaceous glands, called *sebum*, that fills and often clogs pores in the skin, which, along with bacterial growth, results in unsightly skin blemishes.

There is a widespread belief that certain foods, including chocolate, nuts, fatty foods, sweets, and carbonated beverages, can cause acne or make it worse. There is neither direct evidence nor a biochemical basis for believing that this is true, and many dermatologists discount the effect of these foods.[14]

In the past, it was assumed that because vitamin A is required for normal skin development, it would help a skin problem like acne. This was not only wrong, but an excess of vitamin A can and has caused death. However, a derivative of vitamin A called *tretinoin*, or Retin-A, can be used to treat less serious cases of acne. Because of its side effects, those who use Retin-A should stay out of the sun as much as possible, use sun screens and protective clothing, and avoid sunlamps. Another drug that is also related to vitamin A, generically called 13-cis-retinoic acid or *isotretinoin* (Accutane), has been approved for the treatment of severe acne (see your physician). Accutane, however, can cause miscarriages and birth defects. Therefore women in their childbearing years should avoid pregnancy when taking the drug and for three months after discontinuing it.

The most effective nondrug method of preventing and treating acne is to keep the affected areas as clean as possible and not to use devices (including fingers) to create open sores, because this invites bacterial infection. Eating a varied diet that includes food in appropriate amounts from each of the basic food groups, reducing stress, and obtaining adequate exercise and sleep may also help. This is, of course, good advice for all of us, including teenagers.

Premenstrual syndrome

Although described as early as 1931, premenstrual syndrome (PMS) has undergone a metamorphosis only in recent years. Once an obscure clinical disorder, PMS is now a household word. It seems unlikely that the disorder has changed. It is more likely that recognition and open discussion have increased awareness of it. In the past, women did not discuss issues such as PMS with their physicians (usually male), and physicians were equally reluctant to enter into such discussions. In addition, the medical attitude used to be that such symptoms were not "medical" problems but indicative of a "psychosexual maladjustment."

PMS boasts no specific definition. Rather, it is loosely characterized as a cluster of physical and psychological symptoms typically occurring for about a week before the onset of menstruation. Physical symptoms may include painful or swollen breasts, abdominal pain and bloating, backache, and headache. Psychological symptoms include depression, irritability, tension, anxiety, and hostility. Behavioral changes may include clumsiness, anger, and aggression; bouts of increased physical activity coupled with periods of lethargy; and sometimes changes in libido.[15] Symptoms differ among women and even from cycle to cycle within the same woman. This latter fact can lead one to conclude that some "treatment" was helpful when it was not.

To date, no hard evidence of a specific cause of PMS has been found. It is reasonable to assume that hormones play a role, because postmenopausal women do not experience PMS per se, but this is about all we know with a fair degree of confidence. Clearly, social and cultural factors do affect PMS, but how they do is uncertain. A hormonal theory also has been offered,[16] which suggests that PMS is due to a progesterone deficiency or an abnormal progesterone-to-estrogen ratio.

The introduction of the progesterone deficiency theory into a British court of law resulted in more lenient sentences for two women convicted of a murder committed during the week or so before menstruation.[17] Although this theory is not well supported scientifically and, in fact, is not accepted by most medical authorities, juries or judges often do not know this, and individual responsibility for one's own behavior can thereby be lessened. Not surprisingly, many feminist groups fear the social implications of the British court decision.

A few dietary treatments have been proposed that may alleviate some of the symptoms associated with the menstrual cycle. For example, restricting sodium intake to 1 to 3 grams per day for 7 to 10 days before the onset of menstruation has been recommended for those women who retain fluids prior to menses. Generally, for most women, sodium restriction will not limit fluid retention, because fluid retention is controlled primarily by hormones, not sodium ingestion. In some women, however, sodium restriction before menses may be helpful in this regard. If it is tried and appears to help, there should be no harm in continuing the practice.

Decreasing the intake of caffeine and its chemical cousins has been recommended for PMS sufferers. Sources include foods such as coffee, tea, chocolate, caffeine-containing soft drinks, and several over-the-counter as well as prescription cough and cold remedies. The theory of caffeine restriction is based on the idea that this chemical can aggravate some of the symptoms of PMS, including nervousness, tension, and anxiety, which may be true if these symptoms are caused by the action of certain hormones. Don't expect miracles, but if avoiding caffeine and related compounds seems to help, by all means, do it.

Other dietary remedies have been proposed for PMS, but there is no evidence that any of these actually works. One of the most common assertions is that vitamin B_6 is efficacious, but carefully controlled studies have failed to show that this vitamin is more effective than a placebo is in treating PMS. Vitamin B_6 is often recommended at levels of 500 to 800 milligrams per day, which is 250 to 400 times higher than the Recommended Dietary Allowance (RDA). At that level, this vitamin can be toxic and cause liver damage.

Another assertion is that PMS results from a "cellular deficiency" of magnesium. To combat this, an increased intake of magnesium is sometimes recommended. But again there is no evidence that this is effective in treating PMS. On the other hand, magnesium toxicity, which can occur because of the amounts sometimes suggested for PMS treatment, will unquestionably interfere with normal calcium absorption and metabolism, thereby leading to calcium deficiency. In addition to magnesium supplementation, the consumption of dairy products is sometimes limited to two cups daily, in accordance with the mistaken idea that milk interferes with magnesium absorption. In fact, milk is a good source of magnesium, but it does not have so much that it interferes with the absorption of calcium. Finally, restricting the consumption of refined sugar is often recommended on the grounds that sugar increases the excretion of magnesium in the urine. This is simply not true.

PMS can be an irritating and sometimes painful part of life. There are drugs that can be helpful, and therefore it is only prudent to obtain competent medical advice. On the other hand, self-treatment of this disorder by means of diet is not likely to be of lasting benefit and can be dangerous, especially if too much vitamin B_6 and magnesium are consumed.

Candidiasis hypersensitivity syndrome

Media reports and morning television talk shows have recently referred to a "new" disease among women, called *candidiasis hypersensitivity syndrome*. This "syndrome" has all the earmarks of an invented disorder. Although the yeast in question, *Candida albicans*, also called *monilia*, is normally present in the mouth, urinary tract, and vagina, medical authorities consider the idea that some women have a hypersensitivity to the yeast as speculative and unproven.[18] Believers in this theory blame sensitivity to the yeast for a vast number of "women's problems," including premenstrual tension, headache, abdominal pain, depression, poor memory, fatigue and loss of sexual interest, cravings for sugar and alcohol, and more. According to Stephen Barrett, candidiasis is being erroneously blamed "as an important factor in acquired immune deficiency syndrome (AIDS), rheumatoid arthritis, multiple sclerosis and schizophrenia as well as 'hypoglycemia,' 'mercury amalgam toxicity' and other fad diagnoses."[19]

Those who claim that there is such a disease have a solution – a "proper" diet and antifungal drugs. The prescribed diet, which makes no scientific sense, restricts the consumption of yeast breads, cheese, mushrooms, sugar, white flour, milk, processed foods, and other foods "that contain or provide nourishment for yeast." Supplements of acidophilus ("to keep yeast under control"), vitamins, minerals, coenzymes, and polyunsaturated fatty acids ("to help strengthen the immune system") are often recommended.[20] The other proposed solution consists of antifungal drugs, which are expensive and can be toxic.[21]

At the present time, the consumer should not be misled into thinking that this so-called syndrome is a genuine illness. To date, its diagnosis, laboratory tests, and treatment should be considered experimental.[22]

Spotting the spurious

Medicine has never had more to offer in the diagnosis and treatment of diseases than it does today. But neither have there been more attempts by the unscrupulous to promote unproven claims. Quackery[d] is not only alive and well in our country; it is also growing and becoming highly organized.[23]

How can you tell if someone has a legitimate treatment or is simply taking your money, either out of misguided belief or actual intent to defraud? Answering the following questions[e] will help you separate the sound from the spurious:

1. Is it claimed that the disease or disorder, which has a reasonable-sounding name, is not yet included in general medical textbooks or accepted by traditional physicians because it is so new?
2. Is it claimed that the so-called disorder is due to poor eating and can be treated by a proper diet or supplement?

[d] *Quackery* is defined as promoting health products, services, or practices of questionable safety, effectiveness, or validity for an intended purpose. Victims are not only the desperate and the gullible who buy one diet book or magic diet pill after another. Rather, the majority of quackery's victims are unsuspecting people who tend to believe what they hear the most – whether it be hype from an advertising agency or personal experiences from family members, neighbors, or friends. See S. Barrett, "Common Misconceptions About Quackery," *Nutrition Forum*, June 1987, pp. 41–44.

[e] For more information on these and other tips to spot a health hustler and food quack, consult an excellent book devoted to protecting your life and your money: Stephen Barrett, *The Health Robbers*, 2nd ed. (Philadelphia: George F. Stickley, 1980).

3. Is there a promise for a quick, dramatic, or miraculous cure that involves no hard work on your part or risk to you?
4. Are testimonials presented from persons who say they have been helped or cured by the proposed treatment?

Quackery is not easy to spot, and it is not sold with a warning label! It lives in the promise, not the product. It is targeted to reach you emotionally, where it really sells – by appealing to your vanity, using fear, or offering hope – and with an empty promise of a money-back guarantee!

When it comes to your health, ignorance is *not* bliss. Not only can it separate you from your money, it also can kill. Fighting quackery is not hopeless, though effective control requires a concerted effort on the part of many – educators, publishers, advertisers, legislators, law enforcement officials, and defrauded victims.

You can help defeat quackery by finding out more about it and by joining antiquackery organizations. Excellent sources of antiquackery information include (1) *Nutrition Forum* (Philadelphia, PA); (2) *NCAHF Newsletter of the National Council Against Health Fraud*, Inc. (Loma Linda, CA); (3) *FDA Consumer* (Washington, DC); (4) *ACSH News & Views of the American Council on Science and Health* (New York, NY); and (5) *Consumer Reports* (Boulder, CO). Two effective antiquackery groups that include members from the public and professional communities are the National Council Against Health Fraud, Inc., with chapters in several states, and the American Council for Science and Health.

13   Weight control

It only takes a few minutes of browsing through the literally hundreds of "diet books" in book stores or reading headlines in the well-known "periodicals" available at the checkout counter of the local grocery store to become convinced that Americans are obsessed with fatness. It also takes only a short visit to the mall on a hot summer day to verify that the promises of "sure-fire, guaranteed" methods of weight loss in those publications are false.

In some cases, concern about obesity is justified for health reasons. Each of us is a statistic in someone's book, and according to statistics, 20 to 25 percent of us may have heard our physician say: "You must get some of that weight off or else." Most of us, at one time or another, have looked in the mirror and wondered how, in the relatively short time that we have existed on this planet, our bodies could get into such sad shape. On the other hand, many more people think that they are overweight than actually are. For example, in one study of almost 6,000 men and women aged 14 to 61, 22 percent were found by objective measures to be either moderately or severely overweight, but almost twice as many (41 percent) perceived themselves to be overweight.[1] Not surprisingly, considering the social climate of our time, a higher percentage of women than men erroneously thought that they were too heavy. Of those who believed that they were overweight, whether or not they actually were, 88 percent worried about it at least a little bit.

Weight control, like any other facet of our lives, has both benefits and costs associated with it. Obviously, not everyone will benefit equally from weight loss. Some people may need to gain, not lose, whereas others who are substantially overweight may derive considerable health benefits by losing excess body fat. Most of us find ourselves in between – we may not benefit in terms of health by losing a few pounds, but we still may perceive ourselves as being a bit overweight.

For many people, the costs associated with the process of losing weight are substantial. The task for each of us is to consider the benefits relative to the costs and to decide whether decreasing our body weight is appropriate. In this chapter, we provide information that will allow you to access the cost-to-benefit ratio. The first issue is to determine whether your present weight is inappropriate.

What should you weigh?

From the earliest paintings and statues to the work of present-day artists, the waistline has always been a focal point. It may be some consolation to some of our readers that according to paintings from the Middle Ages well into the nineteenth century, European artists considered fat to be beautiful – in women. In contrast, if a man considered as the American ideal in the early 1800s were around today, he would likely be subjected to court-ordered hospitalization for treatment of self-induced starvation.[a]

Standards have obviously changed from these earlier times for both sexes. Currently, "thin (but not too thin) is in" to a large extent, we suspect, because of television and movie depictions of what is glamorous. To be sure, the popularity of videotapes and books on diet and exercise is not because the featured "star" has a Ph.D. in either nutrition or exercise physiology. Rather, the question is, is the movie star standard suitable for you?

Actually, the only person who is qualified to decide what you should weigh is you! Before some readers respond to that assertion by saying, "Great! Pass the doughnuts," we should give you some standards for comparison and tell you some of the consequences of choosing to be too heavy.

One way to decide what is best for you is to ask yourself two questions:

1. At what weight do I feel the best, physically and mentally?
2. Am I willing to pay the price to achieve that weight?

One way to assess the appropriateness of one's body weight is to consult the various height–weight tables. When the most current height–weight tables were published by the Metropolitan Life Insurance Company, many people felt like leaping for joy! In case you hadn't noticed, the values for desirable height–weight ratios actually went up in 1983. Before you get too excited about this good news, let's put height–weight tables into perspective. They can be a helpful guide, but they were not intended (nor are they correctly used) to tell us what we ought to weigh.

The commonly used height–weight tables from the Metropolitan Life Insurance Company were originally developed in 1942 to identify the weight range at which persons at a given height had the lowest mortality

---

[a] In *Aristocracy in America*, published in London in 1839, Francis J. Grund is quoted by R. O. Cummings in *TheAmerican and His Food: A History of Food Habits in the United States* (Chicago: University of Chicago Press, 1940): "An American exquisite must not measure more than twenty-four inches around the chest; his face must be pale, thin and long; and he must be spindle-shanked or he won't do for a party" (p. 51).

rate. Although labeled "ideal body weights" in its first publication, no evidence existed other than the insureds' mortality rates to justify labeling these weights as ideal. In subsequent revisions and reprintings, therefore, the word *ideal* was dropped.

As an alternative to the use of height–weight tables to determine a reasonable body weight, many health professionals use a simple formula. To calculate a reasonable weight:

For an adult man with a moderately sized frame: Start with 106 pounds for the first 5 feet in height, and then add 6 pounds for each additional inch over 5 feet. This gives an estimate of a reasonable weight, but obviously everyone does not have to weigh this amount to be "reasonable." A "reasonable" range can be calculated by adding 10 percent and subtracting 10 percent.

For an adult woman with a moderately sized frame: Start with 100 pounds for the first 5 feet in height, and add 5 pounds for each additional inch over 5 feet. A "reasonable" range is again calculated by adding and subtracting 10 percent.

For a large-framed person, an additional 10 percent can be added to this range; for a small-framed person, 10 percent can be subtracted from the range.

An example of the reasonable weight for an adult man 5 feet 10 inches tall is calculated as follows:

$$(\text{moderate frame}): \quad 106 + (6 \times 10) = 166 \text{ pounds}$$
$$\text{range} = 149 - 183 \text{ pounds (90 to 110 percent)}$$

$$(\text{large frame}): \quad \text{range} = 165 \text{ to } 201 \text{ pounds}$$

$$(\text{small frame}): \quad \text{range} = 134 \text{ to } 164 \text{ pounds}$$

All of this assumes, of course, that you know your frame size. Fortunately, there are handy ways of estimating it,[2] but it is usually accurate enough to estimate your frame size based on your own intuition.

I may be overweight, but am I obese?

The term *overweight* is applicable to most of us if our weight is between 10 percent and 20 percent above the calculated reasonable weight. Being overweight sounds bad, but being obese sounds even worse. The term *obese* is appropriately applied to those of us who have a considerable amount of excess stored fat. It is often used to describe those people whose body weight is more than 20 percent above reasonable, based on height–weight tables or the calculations just given. A person is correctly called obese, however, only when most of this excess weight is due to excess fat, stored in specialized body cells called *adipose tissue*.

Some people, such as athletes, who are more than 20 percent above a calculated reasonable body weight for height but whose extra weight is due to muscle, not fat, are not obese. Consider a 6-foot-tall football player with a large frame. Calculations suggest that he should weigh about 196 pounds (range: 176 to 216). But it is not unusual to find such an athlete weighing 250 pounds. If you are getting the idea that the use of height–weight tables or calculations of reasonable body weight must be seasoned with a generous helping of common sense and tempered with additional information, you are exactly right. The additional information is a determination of body fat content.

There is a saying among nutritionists that "weight's great, but fat's where it's at!" We are told that the great sculptors of the past, like Michelangelo, approached a piece of granite with tools and a vision that their subject was locked inside the stone waiting for them to release it. Similarly, it has been imagined that each overweight person has a thin one hiding inside, waiting for release. The first job is to find out how much of one's weight is due to the thin interior, composed of water, muscle, and bone (called *lean body mass*) and how much is composed of fat.

The most accurate method of determining the amount of fat in a person would be to grind up him or her and analyze the remains, but this is what chemists call destructive testing and therefore is not recommended. A less accurate but more desirable method is *underwater weighing*. This method takes advantage of the fact that fat tends to float in water but the lean body mass portion is less buoyant. In the test, a person is weighed out of the water and then is strapped in a seat and weighed while completely immersed in water. Because air in the lungs increases buoyancy, the subject empties his or her lungs of air by breathing out as much as possible and holding the breath in this fashion for two to three seconds while at the same time being weighed. One is not in danger of drowning, but for obvious reasons the test is wisely not done on persons with limited lung capacity due to lung disease, those afraid of water, small children, or pregnant women. After several mathematical calculations, the person's percentage of body fatness can be estimated with reasonable accuracy, depending on the expertise of the tester and the cooperation of the testee.

Other methods to estimate body fat content have been developed, but these have variable accuracy. For example, a recently developed technique, called *electrical impedance*, has been used to estimate body fat content. This procedure is based on the fact that components of lean body mass contain water and therefore offer less resistance to the flow of electrical current than does fat tissue, which contains less water. A machine is used to measure the resistance to a flow of small, harmless electrical impulses through a section of the body, usually the forearm. The results are then used to calculate the amount of fat relative to lean body mass. The validity depends on the skill of the operator and the proper calibration of the equipment, as well as other factors. For example, if the subject is perspiring during the test, conductivity will be greater, and thus the apparent fat content will be less.

Another technique that is less invasive than underwater weighing, but also less accurate for determining the degree of body fatness, is the "pinch test." A crude version of this test can be done by anyone, with the aid of a friend who acts as the "pincher." To do this, allow your arm to hang by your side and have another person pull the skin of the back of the arm away from the muscle about midway between the shoulder and elbow. If the thickness is more than one inch, it means that there is a substantial amount of underlying fat. This amateur method gives a crude measure indicating whether the "pinchee" is "fat" or "not fat."

Specially trained health professionals armed with a tape measure and calipers (mechanical hand-held pinchers), can perform a scientific version of the pinch test. By measuring the thickness of skin and underlying fat stores at various parts of the body and comparing the results with standardized tables, the percentage of total body fat can be estimated.

It is relatively easy to identify people who are clearly obese, and because of the health problems that this can engender, they should be under the care of a physician. For people who are marginally overweight, they should consider obtaining a professional assessment of the percentage of their body fat before they attempt to lose those extra pounds. Many people assume, based on a comparison with height–weight tables or the old self-assessment-in-the-mirror test that they have entirely too much fat. Analysis can provide information as to whether they have a fat problem and, if so, allow them to set realistic goals to solve it. If you are interested in having your percentage of body fatness determined, the following organizations either may have equipment to perform the test or can tell you where to obtain reliable services:

> Universities, departments of:
>   Health and Physical Education
>   Nutrition and/or Dietetics
> Hospitals, departments of:
>   Nutrition, Dietetics, or Food Service
>   Health Promotion or Cardiac Rehabilitation
> Registered dietitians (R.D.s can be found by checking the yellow pages
>   of your local telephone directory)

The fees for such tests are usually nominal.

It might be assumed that the ideal fat content of the human body is zero or close to it, but this is not the case, as all cells have membranes that contain fat. On average, a suitable body fat percentage is 20 to 25 percent for women and 15 to 20 percent for men.

Consequences of excess body fat

There seems to be a public perception that those who are thin are somehow healthier than are those who are overweight, even by a little bit. The facts do not conform to this perception, however. Although having substantial amounts of excess fat is associated with negative health consequences, it is generally agreed that being marginally overweight – defined as being no more than 20 percent above a reasonable body weight – has little, if any, adverse effect on health or longevity.[3] In contrast with the idea that being thin is healthier, there is evidence that people who are substantially underweight have a higher risk of earlier mortality than do those closer to a reasonable body weight. This is particularly true for older people. That is, elderly people who are moderately overweight generally have longer survival rates than do their thinner counterparts.

On the other hand, when body weight exceeds 120 percent of reasonable, the risk of acquiring diseases and disorders rises, and this includes heart disease, diabetes, gallbladder disease, and cancer, as well as all-cause mortality. In general, for those who are more than 20 percent overweight, the more excess fat they are carrying, the greater their risk of negative health consequences will be.

In addition, obesity, particularly in its more severe forms, can have social repercussions, such as discrimination in employment and promotion, college admission, and, in some cases, even by physicians who may find it difficult to sympathize with an obese patient's problems. Such prejudice can probably be attributed to the public perception that obesity is a direct and exclusive result of the commission of one of the "seven deadly sins," gluttony, even though the scientific evidence clearly shows that in most cases, this is incorrect.[4]

Reducing fat stores: The nature of the problem

Once we decide that we have too much extra body fat, the question then is, what can we do about it? The answer is deceptively simple. In terms of weight control, our destinies are guided not so much by the stars as by the laws of thermodynamics. In particular, the first law, which states that energy can be neither created nor destroyed, provides a solution for reducing excess deposits of body fat. Anyone above the age of 12 has heard dozens and perhaps hundreds of times that weight control is simply a matter of energy balance. If energy intake is less than energy expenditure, body weight will be reduced.

The energy intake part is not complicated; it is simply the number of calories consumed. As to energy expenditure, only three things can happen to the calories in a food that is consumed and absorbed: (1) They can be used directly to produce chemical energy for physical activity and normal metabolic processes; (2) they can be released from the body as heat;[b] or

---

[b] In fact, most of the energy consumed is dispelled as heat. For example, if we are maintaining

(3) they can be stored (primarily as fat). To maintain body weight in an adult, it is necessary to consume the exact number of calories expended. On the other hand, when calorie (energy) expenditure exceeds calorie consumption, body fat is lost. Nutritionists are fond of telling us this. However, as most of us know, the solution is much easier stated than accomplished. On the theory that knowing the enemy is important to winning any battle, let us first explore some of the intricacies of body weight control.

Nature is on the side of body weight control

Because so many of us have such difficulty controlling our body weight, it may sound strange to assert that our body has built-in systems to balance energy consumption with energy expenditure. Nevertheless, it does. In fact, without such systems, our problems with weight control might be considerably worse. Consider that the average person consumes about 1,000 pounds of food per year. This means that between the ages of 20 and 40, the average person consumes 10 tons of food and yet gains only 10 to 15 pounds over that period. This suggests we have a rather efficient mechanism for balancing energy intake with energy used.

It is indeed fortunate that we have this built-in regulatory system because if we had to exert even tighter control over what we eat, virtually all of us would fail miserably. For example, very few people calculate how much butter (or margarine) to spread on bread, but starting at the age of 20, if you moved the knife over just a bit each day so that you would use the equivalent of an extra teaspoon of fat, there would be about 75 pounds more of you to help celebrate your fortieth birthday! On the other hand, assuming a daily caloric need of 2,000 kilocalories, you would lose about 45 pounds over that same time period for each 1 percent that you under-estimated your daily energy needs. This amounts to 20 kilocalories per day, the equivalent of a spoonful of sugar.

For some people, this built-in regulatory mechanism works very well. You surely know some of them; they can eat whatever and whenever they want, with minimal consequences to their body weight. Other people have a continuous, mostly losing, battle with excess body fat. And then there is the majority who have intermittent (again, mostly losing) battles with a few extra pounds. Why doesn't the built-in system work for the latter two groups? It probably does, at least for most of them, but the problem is that their system is set to store more fat than they want.

our body weight while consuming 2,500 kilocalories per day, virtually all of those 2,500 kilocalories will be dissipated from our body as heat. If for some reason they did not, our body temperature would increase by about 96° F to a walloping 195° F. Physical activity uses up energy primarily because it increases heat output from the contraction and relaxation of muscles.

What determines how the system is set? Why do some individuals tend to store more fat than others do? There are speculative ideas that attempt to answer these questions. We do not know that any of them are true. Rather, we present them as a logical framework for considering the problem of weight control. As you read them, keep in mind that one basis for developing these ideas was to explain why it is so difficult to control body weight.

Body fat: Programmed by genetics?

The available evidence can readily be interpreted to indicate that humans, as well as other higher animals, have a built-in regulatory system to balance caloric intake with caloric expenditure. If this is true, the obvious question is, how does it work? A theory was developed years ago that, simply stated, asserts that we are programmed to store a certain amount of fat in our body. Because fat is stored in cells of specialized tissue, called adipose tissue, the theory is called the *adipose set-point theory*.

According to this theory, the body has some mechanism to determine and regulate the amount of fat it stores. This amount, called our *set point*, can be defended in two ways, by regulating our caloric intake or by regulating the efficiency of our metabolism, that is, how many of the consumed calories are stored as fat, compared with how many are released as heat.

Regulating the first of these, caloric intake, has been studied extensively and found to be extremely complex. Caloric consumption appears to be regulated, at least in part, by a balance between being hungry (appetite) and not hungry (satiety). These biochemical regulatory mechanisms, thought to be centered in the brain and other tissues, can obviously be overridden. That is, one can eat when not hungry or refuse to eat when hungry, but the adipose set-point theory suggests that when the body's fat content drops below the programmed set point, a biochemical message is sent to the regulatory centers, which is translated by the brain into "I am hungry!" We are thereby encouraged to consume more food, which will replenish our fat stores.

Although overconsumption of calories can obviously lead to increased fat deposition, there is substantial evidence that human obesity is more likely associated with increased metabolic efficiency. The adipose set-point theory suggests that the adipose set point can be defended by regulating the amount of energy expenditure. Although we can, with varying degrees of success, consciously control the number of calories we consume, we can control only one of the ways that calories are expended: in physical activity. The contraction and relaxation of muscles always require the expenditure of chemical energy, most of which is released from the body as heat. We can choose to increase – or decrease – the contraction and relaxation of voluntary muscles. Except for those few individuals in our society who are continuously engaged in hard physical labor, most of our energy expenditure is for processes over which we have no control and, for the most part, of which we are not even aware. This energy expenditure, known collectively as *basal metabolic rate*, includes the energy required for heartbeat, breathing, maintenance of an appropriate ionic environment in the cells, and the energy released during normal cellular metabolism. The chemical energy is released as heat.

The adipose set-point theory proposes that the body could defend the programmed amount of body fat by altering the basal metabolic rate. For example, if you were preprogrammed to weigh an appropriate amount and if you ate more calories than you expended, an increased basal metabolic rate would get rid of these extra calories as heat, thereby preventing weight gain. On the other hand, if you ate too few calories, a decreased basal metabolic rate would result in less heat loss and conserve calories for fat deposition. This process is thought to be controlled by genetics. In studies of adults[5] and infants,[6] a reduced rate of energy expenditure can be measured in overweight adults or predicted in infants born to overweight mothers.

Because some of the energy-using processes included in the basal metabolic rate, like heartbeat and breathing, seem to be relatively constant, how can heat output vary so much among individuals and from one time to another? A possible answer was discovered a few years ago in animal studies. It has long been known that animals have a specialized tissue, called *brown fat* or *brown adipose tissue*, which is capable of producing substantial amounts of heat. Early research emphasized the importance of this tissue in maintaining body temperature when the animals were exposed to cold. Brown fat has the capability of burning carbohydrate and fat, and instead of trapping the energy from them in chemical form as other tissues do, the energy is released as heat. Part of this heat is used to maintain body temperature. The discovery that caused such excitement was that the quantity and activity of this specialized tissue in animals could vary and therefore play an important role in determining the efficiency with which these animals utilize dietary energy.

The surprise came when evidence began to accumulate that the heat produced by brown adipose tissue could be increased in laboratory animals by, of all things, overeating! That is, adult rats normally consume sufficient calories to increase their weight gradually. When the rats were induced to overeat, it was discovered that a large proportion of the extra calories they consumed were expended as heat rather than deposited as fat. This phenomenon is called *diet-induced thermogenesis*.[7] Could it be that humans have the same mechanisms?

Brown fat has long been known to be present in human infants, presumably to maintain body temperature, but more recent evidence indicates that it also is present in adults. Because adults have some of this specialized tissue, there has been speculation that it also is important to the regulation of heat production in humans as a part of their built-in system to balance caloric intake with caloric expenditure. But many scientists question this assertion, pointing out that although most of us have "white fat" (the regular adipose tissue) in abundance, it is doubtful that we have enough of the brown variety to make a significant difference in heat loss. Which side of the argument is right will have to be settled by more research. Nevertheless, the concept of diet-induced thermogenesis (whether it occurs because of the activity of brown fat or some other unknown mechanism lurking under our skin) is consistent with and could conceivably be a part of the built-in system to regulate caloric intake and output, called the adipose set-point theory.

We should emphasize that the adipose set-point theory has not been proved. It does, however, have many attractive features, not the least of which is that it provides a logical framework for continued research, as any good scientific theory should. Further, it explains many of the observations that have been made concerning weight control. Some people are under the weight that they would like to be. Many people, who wish they had that problem, are surprised to learn that it is just as difficult for some people to gain weight as it is for others to lose it.

Some people have no difficulty regulating their body weight. The built-in system to balance energy intake with energy output is a decided advantage for people who are satisfied with their weight and fat content. On the other hand, for people who are not satisfied with the amount of their stored fat, the existence of a built-in system to balance caloric intake with expenditure is decidedly bad news. For them, it is unfortunate that their body has its own independent, and probably genetically determined, idea of how much fat to store.[8]

The adipose set point could also account for a phenomenon observed by most people who have succeeded in losing a substantial amount of body fat: As they lose weight, it becomes more and more difficult for them to lose additional weight. That is, for a person who is 80 pounds overweight, it is easier to lose the first 20 than it is the last 20 pounds. Note that this also means that a person trying to lose "only" 10 or 20 pounds will have a difficult job of taking it off and keeping it off. An important reason for this is that most people find that as they lose weight, their energy expenditure drops. Part of this is due to the decreased energy needed to transport a smaller body, but part is due to increased energy efficiency, meaning less heat output. This apparent decrease in basal metabolic rate means that more weight can be lost only by further reducing caloric intake and/or increasing physical activity. The latter is probably a better idea, as there is evidence that physical activity can decrease the extent to which the basal metabolic rate is reduced by losing weight.

Some of our colleagues in the field of nutrition may argue that people trying to lose weight should not be told that there are biochemical mechanisms working against them, because it may be so discouraging. On the other hand, anyone who has tried to lose weight already knows that it is difficult. In fact, if "cure" is defined as losing excess weight and keeping it off for five years, the cure rate for obesity is depressingly low – much lower than the cure rate for most types of cancer. Why is weight control so hard if it is a simple matter of caloric balance? The adipose set-point theory simply tries to explain why it is so difficult – and sets the problem squarely on the shoulders of heredity.

Survival of the fattest

There is now abundant evidence that genetics plays a major role in regulating body fat stores. At one time not so long ago, it was widely believed that the tendency for overweight parents to have overweight children was due primarily, if not exclusively, to behavioral and environmental factors. For example, it was assumed that parents were overweight because of inappropriate eating behavior, which was passed on by example to their offspring. We now know that parents pass on more than behavior; they also pass on their genetic heritage.

This does not mean that people with a weight problem should blame their parents or even grandparents. The problem goes back much further. A persuasive argument can be made that the human tendency to store fat can be attributed to the value of stored fat for the survival of our distant ancestors. According to this reasoning, it is quite likely in the early history of humans that there were periods when food was in abundance and other periods when it was not so easily available. This was particularly true for early humans, who were hunters and gatherers. This variation in food supply was a likely impetus for the formation of societies of people who became planters and harvesters. Even then, there is little doubt that there were periods of feast followed by periods of famine, as surely as night follows day. Survivors of this gastronomical roller coaster were those who could efficiently store enough nutrients in their body during the feast to make it through the famine. Less efficient individuals – those in whom more of the energy was expended as heat instead of going into storage – were more likely to have succumbed to starvation before reaching sexual maturity and obviously therefore could not pass on their genes to future generations. To paraphrase, this analysis argues that there is a natural law for "survival of the fattest."

There may have been another, more subtle, psychological factor that increased the gene pool for fat deposition. In many primitive, and some not so primitive, societies, fat was considered beautiful and desirable. Thus, individuals with more than adequate fat deposits were likely to be more desirable mates and therefore had a greater chance to pass on their genes to future generations.

Finally, physiology played a role in the conspiracy. When the body fat content of women drops below a minimal level – notably in athletes such as long-distance runners and gymnasts – ovulation, and therefore the menstrual cycle, stops. This phenomenon reflects a relationship between fat stores and circulating hormone levels. It presumably can be attributed to the need of a certain level of fat to maintain a fetus through pregnancy. At any rate, women who have less than these minimal fat stores are incapable of reproduction.

Thus, survival, psychology, and physiology of reproduction provide genetic pressure toward the storage of a minimum amount of fat. Is there also genetic pressure to set a maximum limit on fat storage? The answer is very likely yes – but the upper limit by our standards may be very high. It is not uncommon to find individuals weighing 300 pounds or more, but it is uncommon to find those weighing in excess of 500 pounds. In part, an upper limit to fat storage can be attributed to the fact that obesity predisposes one to a variety of maladies, including diabetes. Impotence is a common consequence of diabetes, and infertility is associated with obesity in women. In addition, it is not difficult to imagine that massively obese individuals could neither keep up in the travels of nomadic tribes nor move well enough to find food and water by themselves.

Regardless of the validity of this reasoning for genetic pressures toward fat storage in our ancestors, animal and human studies have made it clear that there is a major hereditary component in the regulation of body weight. For example, in studies of identical and fraternal twins, it was reported that on a scale of 0 percent (no genetic involvement) to 100 percent (determined exclusively by genetics), the heritability of obesity was estimated to be as much as 88 percent. Indeed, the hereditary influence is so strong that it has been said that the simplest solution for weight control is to choose your parents properly. Because it is impossible to do that, those who inherited genes that predisposed them to excess fat deposition need to know that although heredity may make it more difficult, it is not impossible to control body weight. The body cannot store calories as fat if they are not consumed.

The most important ingredient in weight reduction: Motivation

Now that you know several hypothetical reasons for why it is difficult to get rid of excess body fat, we shall give you the good news. If you are overweight, you can win the battle against excess fat! Regardless of your heredity, adipose set point, or built-in system for regulating caloric balance, all tissues of your body must have a source of calories for survival. If you do not consume as many calories as your body uses, the extra must come from stored energy, including fat.

The challenge facing anyone who attempts to lose weight is a formidable one: In general, the more weight you want to lose, the greater the challenge will be. Because the battle will be difficult to win and may last for an extended period, the most important ingredient for success is motivation.

Motivation is not only important to the initiation of a weight-loss program; it also must be sufficiently high to sustain efforts for however long it takes to get the weight off and keep it off. To assess motivation, anyone considering beginning a weight reduction program would do well to answer – honestly – the following questions:

1. Why do I want to lose weight?
    There are any number of acceptable answers to this question. For example, for those who are substantially overweight, concern for health could provide significant motivation because of the many health problems related to obesity. For some, improved self-image may also provide sufficient motivation. Answers such as "I want to please others (spouse, parents, friends, supervisor, physician)" should be honestly judged as to whether this reason will sustain motivation through an extended period. In general, motivation based on your desires is more easily sustained than that based on the wishes of others. Answers that have a built-in time limit (such as "I want to be slim for my class reunion") may supply motivation until the big day, but what will happen after that? If other reasons for sustaining weight loss are not found, return to the previous weight is a likely prognosis.
2. How much weight do I want to lose?
    Any goal that is set must be realistic, or your motivation will give way to discouragement. For people who have a large amount of weight to lose, it is usually a good idea to set several intermediate, reachable goals. When the first goal is achieved, they then should decide whether and how soon to begin working toward another goal.
3. How fast do I expect to reach my overall goal?
    Again, the rate of weight loss must be realistic. A reasonable goal for weight loss is between 1 and 2 pounds per week maximum. Losing weight more rapidly is difficult and may cause physiological damage. If you have 25 pounds to lose, set your overall goal to do so in six months. Although you may achieve it sooner, for motivational reasons it is better to overestimate how long it will take than to underestimate it.

    It is important to think in the long term, not the short term. It is only natural for dieters to want to know how they are doing, but weighing themselves too often can destroy their motivation. This is particularly true at the beginning of a diet. Any reduction in caloric intake rapidly lowers the amount of protein and carbohydrate (glycogen) stored in the body (see Chapter 4). Because a large amount of water is also stored with them, it is not uncommon to lose weight quickly in the first three or four days of dieting. The rate of loss may be much less, however, during the next few days. This phenomenon has defeated many dieters who make the mistake of weighing themselves daily. Success may breed success, but there is a flip side. Weighing yourself more often than once each week may suggest failure when you are in fact succeeding.

4. Will I be happy with my appearance and image when I reach my goal?

Do not be surprised if losing weight does not achieve that youthful appearance that you may have had before you gained it. One problem with the deposition of excess fat is that it stretches the skin, and it may have been stretched so much that when the fat is removed by dieting, it hangs loose. Although exercise can help by improving the tone of underlying muscles, it might also be necessary to undergo plastic surgery (tummy tucks and face lifts) to achieve the appearance that you want, especially if you have lost a lot of weight. Successful dieters may find that with their new appearance, they take on a new image, both in their own eyes and in the eyes of others. This will likely require some psychological adjustments. Are you ready for these?

5. Is this an opportune time?

Be careful with this one because it always is possible to find some reason that now is not the right time. If you do that, there may never be a "right time." On the other hand, there are some legitimate reasons for postponing weight reduction. For example, dieting is a strain on the psyche of everyone involved, and if you are already into a stressful situation (e.g., recently married or divorced, recent family death or illness, or new job pressures), this may not be a good time to start a weight-reduction program, especially if you are one of those whose appetite increases when you are under stress.

If you are in the middle of a weight-reduction program when an unavoidable external stress occurs, you might well consider adjusting your caloric intake to maintain your body weight at its present level until things calm down again. This may delay achievement of your goal, but it is better than "going off the wagon," eating everything in sight, and regaining the weight that you already have lost.

If you have considered all of these factors and decide to proceed with a weight reduction program, what are your options? One is to buy a magazine or book containing the latest diet and follow the advice. Unfortunately, for the most part, these diets are not effective in removing excess fat and keeping it off. If they were effective, there would be no reason to invent another one next week or next month, just in time for a new issue of the periodical. Nutritionists call these diets "fad" diets. There are dozens of them and therefore dozens of reasons that in the long run, they are ineffective.

Fad diets: "Free weight loss" – you get what you pay for

An article appeared in the January 1974 issue of *Family Circle* magazine with the title of "My Amazing Cider Vinegar, Lecithin, Kelp, B_6 Diet." It sent shivers of excitement through the dieters of America and shudders of disbelief through professional nutritionists. The article was written by Mary Ann Crenshaw, described as a "beauty writer." She made no claim to being a nutritionist.[c] Her formula was to take supplements of lecithin, kelp, and vitamin B_6, drink vinegar, and consume a 1,000-kilocalorie diet. She claimed that "her four little friends" helped her lose 12 pounds in two weeks.

Did the "little friends" have anything to do with the weight loss? Obviously not; it was the low-calorie diet and not the supplements that resulted in the weight loss. And yet after this issue of *Family Circle* hit the newsstand, people stood in line to buy lecithin, vitamin B_6, kelp pills, and, of all things, "dehydrated vinegar."[d] The products are still available, along with reprints of the article. The reprints that we have seen carry the following statement: "This article is offered for [its] entertainment, cultural and educational value. . . . [It is] specifically not related, and should not be related by the reader, to any products sold in this store."

The public response to this "secret of weight loss" can tell us several things. First and foremost, much of the public still has not gotten the message that the real secret of weight loss is lowering caloric intake to a level below caloric expenditure and that no additional gimmicks are necessary or, in the long run, helpful. Indeed, many gimmicks are dangerous. It is also apparent that much of the public has misunderstood the message that nutrition information should be obtained from a health professional with training in nutrition or dietetics. Even though most fad diet articles and books contain a disclaimer to "see your doctor," they unfortunately foster a "do-it-yourself" attitude.

One gimmick that has been around for a long time is the low-carbohydrate diet. This diet first appeared shortly after the Civil War as a treatment not for obesity but, rather, for diabetes. (This was long before insulin was discovered.) Reincarnations of the diet have appeared regularly over the intervening century. Titles and authors vary, but each one, along with the accompanying publicity, has one common trait: Each incorrectly implies that the culprit causing excess fat is carbohydrates, not calories.

Books describing the low-carbohydrate diet have enjoyed success because the diets are effective, or seem to be – at least for a while. One reason for the appearance of success is that at the start of a weight-reducing program, any restriction of caloric intake rapidly decreases the amount of carbohydrates and proteins stored in the body, along with the water stored with them. The fewer carbohydrates that are in our diet, the faster these stores will be depleted. Note, however, that most of this rapid weight loss

[c] In fact, the article is replete with nutritional misinformation. For example, it asserts that lecithin is a source of two vitamins, choline and inositol. In fact, lecithin does contain choline, but not inositol. But neither choline nor inositol is a vitamin for humans.

[d] Vinegar, by definition, is a solution of acetic acid in water. Because acetic acid is volatile, "dehydration" removes it along with the water. "Dehydrated vinegar" pills resemble "dehydrated water" pills, except for a few contaminants found in both.

is not due to the loss of fat but to the loss of bound water; true fat is lost much more slowly. Therefore, this rapid weight loss is regained just as rapidly when caloric intake, including carbohydrates, returns to predieting levels. A weight-control program is successful only if it takes weight off and keeps it off.

It is not clear whether low-calorie diets that severely restrict carbohydrate intake are more effective in the long term than are those in which more of the calories come from carbohydrates. Although fat deposition does depend on the blood insulin level, which in turn depends to a large extent on the blood sugar concentration and hence carbohydrate consumption, hormone levels do adapt to a low-carbohydrate intake over time. For example, tissues adapt to a lower insulin level by becoming more sensitive to insulin. Thus, it is likely that the longer a low-calorie diet is consumed, the less important the number of calories coming from carbohydrate will become.

One advantage of restricting carbohydrate intake while reducing calories is that such a diet increases the concentration of substances in the blood called *ketone bodies*, which may depress the appetite. Thus, reducing carbohydrates to the point that it increases ketone body formation may help curb the urge to eat.

If low-carbohydrate diets have some advantages, are there reasons that they should not be followed? There have been so many books describing low-carbohydrate diets for weight control that it is fairly easy to find people who swear that they have lost literally hundreds of pounds following such a diet. Therein lies part of the problem. Most of us do not have hundreds of pounds to lose. People who use these diets may lose considerable weight, but as soon as they return to their old eating habits, they plump right back. These types of diets often result in a yo-yo effect. By their very nature, they do not encourage the establishment of eating behaviors that will keep weight off for an extended period.

In addition, low-carbohydrate diets can be dangerous to the health. The ketone bodies can cause problems. In the first place, they are acids, and when acids are excreted in the urine, they take minerals with them. The loss of potassium can be significant, and therefore, these diets should be undertaken only with careful medical supervision.

The excretion of ketone bodies can cause another problem as well. When excessive amounts of one of them are excreted through the kidneys, this interferes with the excretion of another compound called *uric acid*. When uric acid is not excreted properly, it can result in gout, the symptoms of which include painful joints. Because one of the first joints affected is that of the big toe, it can truly be said, both literally and facetiously, that low-carbohydrate diets cause a pain in the big toe.

Finally, it can be a fatal mistake to binge on carbohydrates after a long period of following a low-carbohydrate diet. Over time, the body adapts to decreased carbohydrate intake, and a sudden influx of carbohydrates can lead to a heart attack. There is only one way to protect yourself from this: Do not binge on carbohydrates after following for a week or more any diet low in carbohydrates. Reintroduce carbohydrates slowly when going off such a diet.

There are other diets that are low in carbohydrates, although their names may not indicate that they are. One thing to keep in mind is that any diet that severely limits food intake is likely to be low in carbohydrates. Some commercial weight-loss products give dieters only about 300 to 500 kilocalories per day – far below any adult's caloric needs. Some of these, called *liquid protein diets*, which were introduced in the 1970s, were blamed for a number of deaths.[9]

In our opinion, self-treatment with any diet that severely limits caloric intake is fraught with dangers and therefore should not be attempted. The use of very low calorie diets can be medically justified in the case of morbidly obese patients who otherwise have not been able to lose weight, but they should be used only for limited periods and, even then, only under direct medical supervision.

Other fad diets attribute special properties to certain foods. The best-known example of this is the grapefruit diet. With this diet, you can supposedly eat whatever you want, provided that you eat a grapefruit first. If the diet works at all for those who stick to it, it is only because after three days of eating grapefruit, it may be impossible to look at one and retain an appetite. Success cannot be attributed to the grapefruit's containing substances that either depress the appetite or cause weight reduction. Yet there are dehydrated grapefruit extract pills on the market, often advertised by simply saying "You know about the famous grapefruit diet. Now here is a grapefruit pill."

Another scheme to sell fad diets and associated products is to make up disorders associated with being overweight. For example, have you heard of cellulite? This substance, alleged to be composed of fat, water, and toxic wastes, has been held responsible for the lumpy, bumpy, dimply bulges on various parts of the anatomy, especially on the hips and thighs of women. It is said that cellulite is "fat gone wrong" and that it is resistant to removal by means of dieting and exercise. The fact is, though, cellulite does not exist. It is a made-up term, coined in European salons and spas in the early 1900s to sell a product.[10] It became well known in the United States in 1973 with the publication of a book by the same name, written by a Frenchwoman who owned a beauty salon in New York City.

When biopsies are taken of so-called cellulite tissue and normal fat tissue, no differences can be observed. The bulgy, waffled appearance of skin is readily explained by the expansion of fat cells to the point that the strands of fibrous tissue connecting the skin to deeper tissue layers become stretched and unable to hold the fat close to the tissue layers. This is more evident in women than in men because the outer layers of skin in women are thinner and therefore more likely to reveal bulging fat cells underneath. And these layers become even thinner and less elastic with age.

For a disorder that does not exist, selling the idea of cellulite and products to cure it has been remarkably successful. Rolling machines, creams, vitamin and mineral supplements, enzymes, hormones, vibrators, muscle stimulators, whirlpool baths, thermal treatments, and massage all have been touted as cures. The fact is that because cellulite is no more and no less than excess fat, the only cure is weight loss and exercise. No special miraculous drug or nutrient can alter that fact.

Weight-reducing pills and other magical elixirs

In 1959, Mead Johnson and Company started marketing a product called *Metrecal* intended to help people lose weight. It appeared to be an excellent idea. Metrecal was a nutritionally complete diet in cans, each of which contained 225 kilocalories. The idea was that a person trying to lose weight could consume four cans per day, which would give them all of their necessary nutrients and a total of 900 kilocalories. Because this caloric intake is below the needs of almost all adults, the company could correctly promise that following this plan would slowly but surely result in weight loss. Many people successfully used the product for weight loss, but for too many people, Metrecal did not work. It was eventually withdrawn from the market, not because the promise was untrue, but because too many people misunderstood the plan and misused the product. Despite protestation and clarifications by the company, it was widely assumed that Metrecal contained some secret ingredient that caused weight loss. People were so convinced of this that they thought they could eat anything and still lose weight as long as they also consumed Metrecal. They therefore ate their regular meals and then drank Metrecal in addition. The result was predictable: weight gain, not weight loss.

The simple truth is that there are no magic potions that can rid the body of excess fat. There are drugs, however, that can temporarily reduce appetite and therefore help get one through short periods of difficulty when lowering one's caloric intake.

Amphetamines have been found to depress appetite in some people for the relatively short time of a few days to a few weeks, after which the body adapts, and the drug becomes less effective in promoting additional weight loss. Amphetamines are available only by prescription because they are dangerous and habit forming. The reason that amphetamines are dangerous is that they are chemically and physiologically related to a hormone, adrenalin, and can therefore produce side effects similar to the effects of too much of this potent substance. Side effects include a jittery feeling, increased sweating, and increased heart rate. An overdose of amphetamines can be fatal. Because amphetamines are addictive, it is not a good idea to continue their use over long periods, and because of the side effects, a decision to use amphetamines should be carefully considered.

There are a number of other appetite-suppressing drugs available by prescription. All of them have side effects and work only for limited periods. This means that these drugs cannot be used as a substitute for motivation to stick to a low-calorie diet for weight control. Your physician might suggest them, however, to help you over short, particularly difficult periods.

Phenylpropanolamine (PPA), often combined with caffeine, is a non-prescription drug used in many diet pill preparations. Claims for it exceed performance, however. It is related chemically to amphetamines and therefore has some of the appetite-suppressing activity as well as some of the side effects of its more potent cousin. Sudden withdrawal of PPA after long-term use may result in anxiety and depression. Continuing to take large amounts of these pills after their beneficial effect has worn off is not only useless and expensive but also can be dangerous.

Studies of both animals and humans have shown that PPA can inhibit appetite, but only for a few days. Therefore, its use may help dieters get past a particularly difficult period, but it cannot be expected to help for long. PPA was given a backhanded endorsement by a Food and Drug Administration (FDA) report a few years ago, which called it the most effective nonprescription appetite suppressant available. This was not so much a statement on how effective this drug is as it was on how ineffective other drugs are. Unfortunately, even this limited statement has been used by advertisers to claim that PPA has been found effective by government scientists.

Anesthetic-type pills, containing topical anesthetics such as lidocaine or benzocaine, are purported to dull the taste buds and thereby decrease appetite. This might sound like something that would work, but the regulation of appetite is far more complex than simply a response to the taste of food. Therefore, it is not surprising that controlled studies have shown that these pills have no appetite-suppressing effect. There is always the possibility of a short-term placebo effect, but it takes more than a numb tongue to inhibit appetite in the long run.

Sugar-containing pills are alleged to raise blood glucose to a level that will inhibit appetite. Although blood glucose may be one factor in appetite regulation, the system is far more complex than this single component. Laboratory tests on animals and humans have failed to show a reduction in appetite with these pills, compared with a placebo. In fact, rather than being helpful in weight loss, they can add weight, as they contribute calories.

Fiber-containing pills are also advertised as appetite suppressants. The argument is that when the contents of these pills combine with water, they swell and trick the stomach into thinking it is full of food. There are pressure receptors in the stomach that are part of the short-term appetite regulation system, but even though the fiber in these pills (usually cellulose or its chemical cousins) does have water-holding capacity, it does not swell to an extent that can cause satiety. To take more than the recommended quantity because "the more I take, the fuller I'll feel" is an unwise practice. Consumption of too much fiber can be hazardous. Fiber alters gastric motility, and of greater concern, the intestinal tract can become obstructed, which may require surgery to relieve. One such high-fiber product containing guar gum, sold under the trade name of Cal-Ban 3000, was recalled by the FDA after a number of people suffered injuries to their digestive tract.[11] Specifically, at least seventeen people experienced obstruction in the esophagus, presumably because the tablets became lodged in the throat and absorbed water.

Spirulina is a natural substance promoted as a weight-loss wonder. It is a species of blue-green algae, high in protein and some vitamins and minerals, believed to be a food source of the Aztec Indians. Claims have been made that it inhibits appetite because of its phenylalanine content. Phenylalanine is an amino acid found in protein, but it has not been demonstrated to be effective as an appetite suppressant. Because algae are single-celled organisms, they are rich in nucleic acids that can cause kidney stones or gout when ingested in large amounts by persons susceptible to these disorders. Once promoted as the "food of the future," these algae are expensive to harvest, hard to digest, and unpalatable, and they cause gastrointestinal problems, including nausea, vomiting, and anorexia. Spirulina has also been touted as a nutritional supplement, but it does not contribute any nutrients required for our nutritional well-being that are not also present in normal, tastier, and less expensive foods.

Other chemicals have been or are being sold with claims that they have a more direct effect on weight loss than mere suppression of appetite. *Starch blockers* were sold as substances that inhibited the essential enzyme in the gastrointestinal tract responsible for digesting starch. The idea was that if you took starch blockers, you could eat your favorite starch-containing foods; the starch would not be digested; and the calories would go right on through. There were at least three things wrong with this. First, there was little evidence that these substances actually inhibited starch digestion enough to make a difference. Second, if starch digestion were inhibited in the small intestine, the bacteria in the large intestine would have a feast, resulting in abdominal pain, gas, and diarrhea. Third, if starch digestion were inhibited so that the glucose from it could not be absorbed, you could expect to feel as hungry as you would have if the starch had not been consumed. Courts have ruled that starch blockers are drugs, not food, and therefore to be legal, must undergo the drug testing required by the FDA.

Glucomannan comes from the konjac root, which has been used as food for centuries in Asia. This substance allegedly speeds up the transport of food through the digestive tract, resulting in poor absorption and increased excretion of potential calories from food. In truth, both the FDA and the American Medical Association have stated that it is useless for weight reduction.

Several hormones are claimed to have a direct effect on fat metabolism and therefore being effective as weight-loss aids. *Human chorionic gonadotropin* (HCG), a hormone from the urine of pregnant women, has been given by injection to persons for weight loss. HCG by itself is ineffective, but when accompanied by the 500-kilocalorie diet that is often also given, it may result in significant weight loss as well as protein malnutrition. FDA requires that all labeling and advertising of HCG state that it has not been demonstrated to be effective or safe in the treatment of obesity. The use of *thyroid hormone* alone or as an adjunct to weight-reduction diets and exercise is inappropriate and dangerous, especially because of adverse effects on the heart. The gastrointestinal hormone *cholecystokinin* has been shown to decrease food intake but has not been proved effective for weight control.

Two naturally occurring amino acids, *arginine* and *ornithine*, have been singled out as being able to remove fat by stimulating the release of growth hormone. The FDA has stated that there are no data to support this claim, which is fortunate, because if these pills did what the manufacturers claimed, they could be dangerous. Excessive amounts of growth hormone in adults, whether taken in pill form or made in excessive amounts by the body cause diabetes mellitus. It does not result in weight loss except what may be secondary to diabetes. A deficiency of an essential amino acid, lysine, is a more likely result of the consumption of excessive amounts of these two amino acids because they can interfere with the absorption of lysine that is required for growth.

Finally, prescriptions for *diuretics* are sometimes requested from physicians by persons trying to lose weight. Pounds can be lost as a result of taking diuretics, but it is because of increased water excretion. As soon as the drug is withdrawn, back comes the water – and the weight. Contrary to popular opinion, diuretics do not reduce fat stores or cause fat loss. There are medical disorders for which diuretics are appropriately prescribed by physicians, but weight loss is not one of them. In general, the possible damage from side effects on fluid and electrolyte balance are not worth the temporary loss of weight (as water) that they cause.

Spotting weight-reduction schemes that you don't want to buy

Based on our present state of knowledge, it appears likely that as long as there is an abundance of food, there will be people with excess stores of fat. It is even more likely that as long as there are people who are overweight, there will be others who promise a "cure." There is no easy way to control weight. When a "cure" sounds too good to be true, it probably is. Be wary if diets claim

> Instant weight loss.
> To have been discovered by nonprofessionals in their spare time or accidentally by "scientists" in some foreign country.
> That you can eat as much as you want and still lose weight.
> That a product will "burn up" or "melt" fat.
> That certain foods have "magical properties" or require that foods from one or more of the basic food groups be left out of your diet.
> That you must take expensive dietary supplements such as vitamins, minerals, or protein powders.
> That no effort on your part is required.

In addition, you would do well to consider the qualifications of the promoters of weight-loss diets or devices. Just as the impressive credentials of the promoters do not always mean that you are getting your money's worth, we can almost guarantee that if the promoters do not have legitimate credentials in the field of nutrition, you will, at the least, be given misinformation. Nutrition is much too complicated and involves the study of too many fields for anyone to master the subject without formal training.

Effective methods for losing weight

Weight reduction seems simple enough. If fewer calories are consumed than are expended, body weight will fall. Unfortunately, for the reasons that we have discussed in this chapter, this is easier stated than done. Because permanent weight loss is rarely successful as a do-it-yourself project, most people find that professional support is helpful, if not essential. In general, the more excess fat you have, the greater your need will be for professional help.

For those who would like to lose only a few pounds, the simplest approach is to continue to eat a variety of foods, but in smaller portions. In addition, substituting lower-calorie vegetables for foods high in fat may be a good idea. As we showed you in Chapter 1, it is relatively easy to obtain all of the necessary nutrients from the four food groups and still maintain a caloric intake of approximately 1,200 kilocalories. Consultation with a registered dietitian who can help you plan menus and give you advice on eating behavior will probably be useful. A relatively small but consistent reduction in caloric intake, particularly when combined with a physically active life-style, will eventually produce the desired effect. Patience is an essential ingredient. Restricting caloric intake to less than 1,200 kilocalories, without medical advice and monitoring, is not recommended because of the potential health risks.

For those who are substantially overweight, professional help is necessary. There are, however, a number of options available from which to choose. Some professional organizations, such as Weight Watchers, have very effective weight-loss programs. In addition, some physicians and registered dietitians specialize in weight reduction. These professionals often collaborate with other professionals who have expertise in behavioral modification and exercise. Successful multifaceted weight-control programs, either individually planned or administered in a group setting, usually include the following components:[12]

1. Sound medical advice, including regular monitoring and follow-up.
2. Nutrition education, including a sound low-calorie food plan.
3. Behavioral modification.
4. A physical activity program.

Totaling the costs and benefits of losing weight

In considering the problem of excess body fat, there is obviously a continuum, ranging from people who are not actually overweight but think they are, through those who are slightly or moderately overweight, to those who are severely to massively obese. Just as obviously, the costs, in terms of the effort required, and the potential benefits of reducing body weight have an equally wide range.

Those who perceive themselves as being too heavy, even though they are not – which appears to describe a fairly large number of people[13] – would not derive any apparent health benefits from losing weight. For those who are close to a reasonable body weight but worry about being too heavy, a realistic assessment by objective measures of body weight and body fat content by a health professional may be a sound investment.

People who are slightly to moderately overweight, as determined by objective measures, appear to derive few, if any, health benefits from losing weight but may "feel better," both physically and mentally, by diminishing their fat stores. These benefits must be weighed against the costs, in terms of effort, needed to take off those extra pounds. The amount of effort involved is not trivial, for the reasons described in this chapter, but the goal, with patience, can be achieved.

Those who are severely to massively obese can expect to derive substantial health benefits from decreasing excess body fat stores. The amount of effort required to reduce body weight significantly, and subsequently to maintain a lower weight, is substantial, but so are the potential benefits. Consultation with health professionals can be helpful in determining both the costs and the benefits of losing weight.

Despite the tremendous advances by the scientific community, the reasons that some people become massively obese are not well understood. Although research has shown that the problem is multifaceted, there is little doubt that for many people, if not most, heredity plays a major role. This does not mean that those who have such an inheritance are forever destined to be obese, but it does mean that for them, the task of losing substantial amounts of excess fat becomes more difficult. It is important to understand that for some people, a significant weight loss may require heroic efforts, such as hospitalization and a near-starvation diet for an extended period. Some people may legitimately decide that the benefits do not outweigh the economical and the physical costs. The decision is a personal one, which, in our opinion, deserves respect.

14　Diet and heart disease

If a large number of people on the street were asked to name the principal cause of heart disease, it is likely that most of them would mention cholesterol. The media and advertisers have certainly raised our collective conscience regarding cholesterol, but it is still another example of why twenty-second news spots or commercials do not really educate the public. By hammering away with the message that cholesterol is "the villain," publicity has oversimplified the disease so much that it is often misunderstood. It would be gratifying to be able to confirm the impression that the disease would go away if we all ate the right foods. Unfortunately, that isn't true. Heart disease is far too complicated to have such a simple solution.

At the present time, heart disease is the major cause of death in the United States. Out of every one hundred people who die each year, about forty die of some type of heart disease. Each of us would like to know what we, and those around us, can do to avoid becoming one of these statistics. In this chapter, we will tell you what is known about the most common form of heart disease and review the evidence concerning the role of diet in the development and treatment of it.

We would like to make it clear from the beginning that there has been intense debate in the scientific and medical community for several years, mostly out of public view, about diet and heart disease. One side of the controversy argues that heart disease is basically a medical problem.[1] Proponents of this view propose that susceptible segments of the population be screened and that those who are or are suspected to be at increased risk for heart disease be further evaluated by a physician. Depending on the results of the evaluation, the physician might institute treatment designed to lower blood cholesterol levels by means of dietary modification and/or drugs. Self-diagnosis and treatment are discouraged.

The other side of the controversy argues that in addition to being a medical problem for some, heart disease is also a public health problem, amenable to public health measures.[2] Proponents of this view recommend, in addition to aggressive medical treatment for persons at high risk, that

230

all Americans above 2 years of age modify their diet in an attempt to reduce blood cholesterol levels. A major impetus for this approach is that if it works, it may lower our nation's burgeoning health care costs. That is, any reduction in the incidence of heart disease obtainable simply by self-implemented dietary changes would lower treatment costs with no financial cost, as food expense is not a part of the health care budget. Opponents of this view argue that the available evidence indicates that the great majority of us will receive little or none of the promised benefits of dietary modification and that the proposed dietary changes may decrease the quality of life for many of those who follow the advice.

It can be seen from this that although both sides of the controversy agree that some people might lower their susceptibility to heart disease by changing their diet, there is a glaring divergence of opinion about who those people are and how much they can expect to benefit from doing so. The controversy revolves around the answer to two questions. First, how important is blood cholesterol level to determining the incidence of heart disease? Second, how much, if any, can the blood cholesterol level be changed by means of dietary modification?

Risk factors for heart disease

In 1949, a study began in the small Massachusetts town of Framingham to observe the effects of people's life-styles, diet, and medical characteristics on the development of heart disease. This study, which is continuing, is attempting to identify those traits that are statistically associated with the development of heart disease. These have come to be known as *risk factors* because a person having these characteristics is at a statistically greater chance of developing the disease than are those persons without these characteristics. Although there is some variation in the list of these risk factors, depending on the source, the following are usually included:[a]

> Male sex (before the age of 55).[b]
> Positive family history of heart disease.
> Diabetes mellitus.
> High blood pressure.
> Cigarette smoking.
> Physical inactivity.
> High blood cholesterol levels.

Note that this is a list of characteristics having a statistical association with heart disease, but this does not mean that they are (or are not) causes of

[a] Obesity is sometimes included, but it may not be an independent risk factor. That is, diabetes, high blood pressure, and high blood cholesterol levels, which are considered to be primary risk factors, can occur because of obesity.

[b] Just as many women die of heart disease as men do, but women are not nearly as susceptible until after menopause.

it. That is, many people with one or more of the characteristics associated with heart disease do not develop it, and on the other hand, people with none of these characteristics die of the disease. Of all the deaths that occur each year from heart disease, only about half of them can be attributed to the presence of known risk factors.[3] The lesson is that the presence of risk factors does not mean that heart disease will be the cause of death of those who have them, but the absence of them does not mean immunity from the disease, either.

In retrospect, it can be argued that it was unfortunate that the word *risk* was used in describing characteristics that have a statistical association with heart disease. Most of us associate the word risk with danger, but the word has little meaning until a probability value is connected to it. For example, all of us run the risk of being killed by an automobile. There is even a risk, albeit extremely low, that couch potatoes, engaged in their favorite activity, will be hit by an automobile coming through the front window of their house, but it is doubtful that the probability is high enough to encourage them to change their behavior. On the other hand, joggers crossing a busy intersection at rush hour run a much greater risk of losing a battle with an automobile. Our point is that because we cannot avoid all risks, common sense demands that we assess the probabilities of dangers associated with that behavior and weigh them against the benefits derived from our behavior. In the issue of diet and heart disease, those who have blood cholesterol levels well above average, particularly if they also have other risk factors, should seek competent medical advice to assess the benefits of a change in behavior. Those with more moderate blood cholesterol levels who might be contemplating self-imposed dietary modification need to decide whether its costs will diminish the risk of heart disease enough to justify the effort. In order to make that decision, it is helpful to know several basic facts about heart disease.

Coronary artery disease

By far the most common form of heart disease, accounting for between 20 to 25 percent of all deaths annually, is not a disease of the heart muscle at all, at least initially. Rather, it is a problem of the blood vessels in the heart and is more properly called *coronary artery disease*. In this disease, there is a narrowing of the arteries in the heart. Normally the arteries in the heart, as well as those that carry blood to various parts of the body, are very smooth, open tubes.

In coronary artery disease, a bump, called a *plaque*, forms in the wall of the blood vessel. The plaque reduces both the size of the blood vessel and blood flow. The owner of the plaque does not likely know that it is present until the blood vessel becomes sufficiently constricted to decrease the nutrient and oxygen supply to a section of the heart. At that time, some people may experience a pain in the chest, indicating that something is wrong. This chest pain usually, but not always, occurs during periods of exercise, emotional stress, or even after a heavy meal. Moderately inadequate coronary circulation, accompanied by transient pain, is called *angina pectoris*, or simply *angina*. Chest pain can be caused by any number of conditions and disorders in addition to angina, but the consequences of angina can be sufficiently severe that it is a good reason to make an appointment with your physician, the sooner the better. Some individuals with blockage severe enough to restrict the blood flow to the heart significantly may experience only shortness of breath or fatigue instead of pain, whereas others, perhaps as many as half, feel no symptoms at all.

One reason that angina should be diagnosed and treated as soon as possible is that disaster can occur if a blood clot comes along and occludes the constricted area of the blood vessel. When this happens, heart tissue being nourished by the artery can be deprived of oxygen and nutrients, resulting in the death of the cells in that section of the heart, within several minutes. When heart cells die, they never regenerate. This catastrophic event, which results in damage to heart muscle, is called a *myocardial infarction*, or simply a *heart attack*. The severity of the heart attack depends on how many cells are affected, how much blood is able to get past the clot, and how long the cells are deprived of oxygen and nutrients. One of the most effective treatments for a heart attack is to inject drugs that cause the clot to be dissolved. The sooner the clot is removed, the better the chance of survival will be. Cardiac rehabilitation seeks to strengthen those heart muscle cells that survived the heart attack, to enable them to take over the function of the ones that died.

Once a plaque is formed, the only known method to remove it is by physical means. A technique has been developed, called *angioplasty*, in which a small balloon is inserted into a blood vessel. Then, when the balloon is inflated, the outer smooth muscle cells are pushed outward to make more room and to open the artery somewhat. This approach cannot be used on everyone and has some dangers associated with it.[c] Further, in about one-third of patients, the plaque reblocks the artery within a year, and so the process must be repeated.

Another method to deal with the offending plaque is a much more complicated procedure, called *coronary bypass* surgery. This procedure requires major surgery in which an unobstructed blood vessel is taken from

---

[c] If the plaque is too large, too hardened, or in some vulnerable arteries, the procedure is not used. About 3 to 5 percent of patients in whom the procedure is attempted require immediate bypass surgery because the artery completely closes immediately after angioplasty. See E. Zamula, "Balloons to Bypass Bypass Surgery," *FDA Consumer*, May 1988, pp. 24–27.

some other part of the body, often the thigh, and used to bypass the section of the heart artery that has the plaque. If two sections of artery are bypassed, it is called a *double bypass*; three replacements, a *triple bypass*.

It is so difficult to remove plaques once they are formed[d] that the obvious solution is to prevent their formation in the first place. The problem is that no one actually knows how to do this because it is not known, with any degree of certainty, why they form. What is in a plaque, however, may be one clue.

What is in a plaque?

If you ask anyone what is in a plaque, most likely they will tell you cholesterol, because of the publicity that this compound has received. Cholesterol is present, but a plaque is not just a blob of cholesterol; it is a lot of other things, too. Figure 14.1 shows the anatomy of a normal blood vessel and a plaque.

Most of the physical space in a plaque is made up of smooth muscle cells that normally lie underneath the artery wall but, for some reason, have multiplied. In addition, another specialized type of cell, called a *foam cell*, is present. These cells are engorged with fatty material, including cholesterol. Some cholesterol also fills in the spaces between these cells. Finally, as the plaque matures, calcium salts are deposited. This hardens the plaque, which accounts for the name *atherosclerosis*; *sclerosis* is derived from a Greek word meaning "to harden." It seems reasonable to expect that when all of the facts are eventually known, the scenario of plaque development must account for all of these components.

The injury theory of plaque formation

One scenario that accounts for the composition of plaque, called the *injury theory*, has recently been developed. The theory is based on experimental observations showing that a physical injury to the inside of an artery can result in the formation of a plaque. For example, when a balloon is inserted and inflated in a chimpanzee's artery and then drawn through the artery, the surface of the artery is injured. A plaque will form at the site of injury, much like scar tissue on a wound.

---

[d] It has been reported that drug therapy decreased plaques in a small percentage of selected patients (see D. H. Blankenhorn, S. A. Nessim, R. L. Johnson, M. E. Sanmarco, S. P. Azen, and L. Cashin-Hemphill, "Beneficial Effects of Combined Colestipol–Niacin Therapy on Coronary Atherosclerosis and Coronary Venous Bypass Grafts," *Journal of the American Medical Association* 257 [1987]: 3233–40). However, the prospects of reversing plaque formation in most people by dietary or drug therapy are not encouraging (see J. F. Oliver, "Serum Cholesterol – The Knave of Hearts and the Joker," *Lancet*, November 14, 1981, pp. 1090–95).

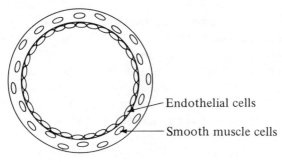

Endothelial cells

Smooth muscle cells

Normal blood vessel

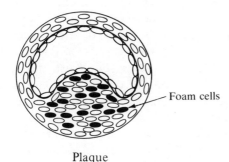

Foam cells

Plaque

Figure 14.1. Anatomy of a normal blood vessel and a plaque.

During the past few years, research has led to the discovery of the sequence of events that leads to atherosclerotic plaque formation after such an arterial injury.[4] A simplified version of this complex sequence goes like this: After the surface layer of the artery is injured, specialized cells involved in blood clotting, called *platelets*, congregate at the site where the underlying protein has been exposed. When these platelets gather to "seal over" the injured area, they secrete a protein, called *platelet-derived growth factor* (PDGF), that causes the underlying smooth muscle cells to multiply and move to the site of injury.[e] This is the start of the formation of scar tissue and accounts for the large concentration of smooth muscle cells in the plaque.

[e] Essentially the same sequence of events occurs when you cut your skin. If you cut your finger enough for it to bleed, for example, platelets will congregate at the cut and function as a part of the blood-clotting system. At the same time, the platelets secrete PDGF, which causes the skin cells to multiply and move into the injured area. This is the reason that a small cut will seal itself virtually overnight, but you may note a "bump" (or scar tissue) at that site for some time. Saliva contains growth factors similar to PDGF, which is presumably why dogs find it advantageous to "lick their wounds."

In addition to platelets, the foreign protein exposed by injury attracts another type of blood cell, called *macrophages*. The normal function of these cells is to patrol the bloodstream on a "search and destroy mission"; that is, they seek out foreign proteins like those in bacteria and destroy them. These macrophages congregate at the site of physical injury to the artery, where along with platelets, they also secrete PDGF as well as other cellular growth factors that cause smooth muscle cells to multiply. The macrophages become filled with fatty material, including cholesterol, and are transformed into foam cells.

The accumulation of platelets, smooth muscle cells, and foam cells in response to injury to the interior of the artery covers the injury site and leaves a bump that can continue to grow and mature. With maturation, more cholesterol and calcium ions are deposited, and the site hardens.

There is evidence that a plaque can develop in humans when there is physical injury to the interior of the artery. Indeed, after bypass surgery, plaques often reform at the site where the new section of artery is attached. It is difficult to imagine, however, how such physical injury could occur in our arteries in the absence of surgery. This has led to the idea that perhaps a similar sequence of events could occur because of chemical injury. There are known cases in which the interior of an artery can undergo such a chemical injury,[f] which, like physical damage, results in plaque formation, presumably because of essentially the same series of events. There is a suspicion, far from proven, that the constituents of cigarette smoke can cause chemical injury to arteries. It has also been suggested that very high blood sugar levels, like those that can be found in people with poorly controlled diabetes mellitus, can result in chemical injury to arteries.[5] If the latter is true, it could account for the fact that diabetics are more susceptible to heart disease than are nondiabetics, although diabetics typically have higher levels of blood cholesterol than normal, attributable again to the consequences of high blood sugar levels.[6] Although the injury theory is attractive because it accounts for the components of a plaque, we wish to emphasize that it is far from proven that it alone accounts for, or is even a major cause of, the development of arterial plaques.

One obvious question is, can cholesterol itself cause chemical injury to the artery wall? Animal studies suggest that very high concentrations, in the range of five to ten times the normal level of cholesterol in blood, can

[f] For example, when the amino acid homocysteine is present at much higher than normal levels, it has been shown to cause chemical damage and lead to plaque formation in the arteries of animals. Abnormally high concentrations of this amino acid occur in humans who have a very rare genetic defect in which the enzyme that normally metabolizes this amino acid is missing. Persons with this disorder often die of coronary artery disease at an early age. See J. W. Hurst, *The Heart*, 6th ed. (New York: McGraw-Hill, 1986), p. 1343; J. H. Stein, *Internal Medicine*, 2nd ed. (Boston: Little, Brown, 1987), pp. 2064–65.

result in chemical injury and thus lead to plaque formation.[7] Although most of us will never have concentrations of blood cholesterol as high as those that can be induced in animal studies, a few people do have such high levels because of a genetic defect, and they do experience heart attacks much more often than do the rest of us.

In 1985, Drs. Michael S. Brown and Joseph L. Goldstein won the Nobel Prize[g] in physiology and medicine for their study of people with such a genetic disorder.[8] The inherited trait prevents or limits the removal from the blood of one of the particles that carries cholesterol. Persons who inherited a defective gene from both parents (homozygous) – occurring once in a million births – have, from birth, six to ten times the normal amount of blood cholesterol and often have heart attacks even in childhood. Persons who inherited the defective gene from only one parent (heterozygous), occurring once in 500 births, typically have twice the normal level of cholesterol and begin to have heart attacks at 30 to 40 years of age. This is not to say that heart disease is strictly a problem of inheriting these particular defective genes. In fact, these genetic defects are relatively rare and account for only about 5 percent of the heart attacks that occur in people under 60 years of age and a much smaller percentage of overall heart deaths. It is not known whether people with the genetic defect develop plaques because a high level of cholesterol has injured the arteries or whether some other mechanism is involved. Studies of people with the genetic disorder do indicate that extremely high levels of cholesterol in blood are associated with the development of heart disease. The question facing most of us is whether more moderately high levels of cholesterol increase our risk of heart disease.

Blood cholesterol and the risk of heart disease

We have told you that high blood cholesterol is one of the many risk factors for heart disease. The continuing debate raging in the scientific community is primarily over one word when it comes to blood cholesterol level: How high is high? Figure 14.2 shows a graph, based on data from several studies, of the relationship between blood cholesterol levels and the development of coronary artery disease in men 40 years old or older.[9] We have superimposed the approximate percentage of people with blood cholesterol values above the indicated level, to relate risk to the normal range of blood cholesterol values.

Note that the risk for heart disease begins to increase significantly when

---

[g] Cholesterol holds the record for the most decorated chemical in history. Brown and Goldstein were the twelfth and thirteenth recipients of the Nobel Prize for their study of it.

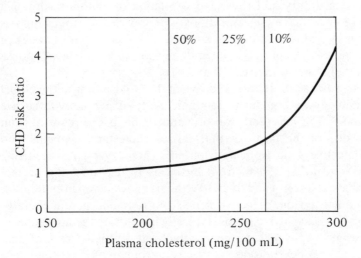

Figure 14.2. Coronary heart disease risk related to blood cholesterol.

blood cholesterol exceeds about 240[h] and continues to increase as the values rise. Such data are the reason that there is substantial agreement that those with blood cholesterol levels above 240 – particularly if they are males under the age of 60 and also have other risk factors – should seek competent medical advice. Most of the debate centers on whether those of us with lower cholesterol levels would benefit from trying to limit our risk. These data suggest that there is little difference in risk for heart disease, regardless of blood cholesterol level, if it is below 240.

In 1980, the Food and Nutrition Board of the National Academy of Sciences looked at the information in Figure 14.2 as well as other data available to them at the time. They concluded that most of us would not be able to lower our risk of heart disease enough to justify recommending changing the fat and cholesterol level of our diet. Instead, they admonished Americans to adjust their caloric intake to maintain an appropriate body weight.[10] Essentially, the Food and Nutrition Board said, in 1980, that the theory that improper diet caused heart disease had not been scientifically proved.[i] Instead, the board recommended that rather than attempting self-

[h] Cholesterol values are usually reported as the amount in milligrams per 100 milliliters (or 1 deciliter) of blood, abbreviated as mg/dL. We use this convention in this book.

[i] This was a position that drew an immediate response from critics. In effect, the Food and Nutrition Board said that if we maintain an appropriate body weight, there was insufficient scientific evidence to recommend that we quit eating bacon and eggs. The opposition disagreed. The ensuing brouhaha resulted in a congressional investigation. One major charge was that the money used to print the committee report was supplied by the "food industry." The food industry is not, of course, monolithic. Some segments of it would have profited from public acceptance of the report, and other segments would have suffered. See "Erup-

treatment by means of dietary modification, "persons with a positive family history of heart disease and other risk factors such as obesity, hypertension and diabetes" should have their blood lipids examined, "and if any are abnormal, therapy should be undertaken under a physician's guidance." In other words, it is recommending that you see your doctor if you are worried about heart disease!

What would a physician have recommended at the time of the Food and Nutrition Board's report? The position of the American Medical Association (AMA) was made clear in 1983.[11] That organization advised medical intervention, including dietary modification, for those patients with a blood cholesterol level above 260, corresponding to the upper 10 percent of the total population. A decision to modify diet for those patients between the 75th and 90th percentiles would be made on a case-by-case basis, depending on the exposure of the patient to other risk factors. Thus, the AMA's position in 1983 was very close to that of the Food and Nutrition Board, with both concluding that heart disease is a medical problem and not amenable to public health measures such as dietary modification by everyone. Note, however, that the position of the AMA and many physicians changed dramatically in subsequent years at the urging of the National Institutes of Health (NIH).

About the same time that the Food and Nutrition Board report appeared, the Nutrition Committee of the American Heart Association (AHA) reached a very different conclusion, not because of new data but because of a different philosophy.[12] The philosophical statement in the introduction of the AHA's committee report informs the reader that although many questions about heart disease remain to be answered, the public deserves the best advice available at the time. In other words, the AHA committee was willing to make recommendations on the basis of less definitive evidence than that required by the Food and Nutrition Board. The AHA Nutrition Committee agreed with the board and the AMA that active medical intervention should be instituted for individuals whose blood cholesterol level was much higher than normal, but with its more relaxed "rules of evidence," it did not stop there. It recommended that all adults attempt to lower their blood cholesterol level by modifying their diet. In other words, the AHA committee viewed heart disease as not only a medical problem but also a public health problem.

A conference was convened at the National Institutes of Health in December 1984 to consider recommendations regarding the diet-and-heart controversy. The consensus report of the conference[13] agreed with the recommendations of the groups in regard to what should be done for those who had very high blood cholesterol levels. The report defined those individuals with blood cholesterol levels in the highest 10 percent as "high risk" (greater than 260), whereas those between 25 percent and 10 percent (240–260) were designated "moderate risk" (see Figure 14.2). For these two groups of patients – if additional diagnostic tests so indicated – diet therapy to reduce blood cholesterol and normalize weight was advised and, if necessary, following this with drug therapy to try to bring down blood cholesterol levels.

With respect to those patients with a blood cholesterol level between 200 and 240, the consensus conference report went much further than did the previous groups: It recommended that virtually all of those persons above the age of 2 years try to lower their blood cholesterol levels by means of dietary modification.[j] This recommendation was met with howls of protest from many quarters. The report was criticized by some scientists for exaggerating the evidence that dietary modification by the entire population, including children, would lower the incidence of heart disease.[14] The Nutrition Committee of the American Academy of Pediatrics (AAP) had already pointed out[15] that the safety of diets with reduced calories, fat, and cholesterol for children had not been established, stating that "an increase in cereal grains at the expense of animal protein with a decrease in density of essential nutrients . . . might pose health risks to children." It turned out that the AAP statement was prophetic; there are reported cases of malnutrition in children whose parents had been feeding them a "healthy low-fat diet."[16] Fortunately, the publicity advocating stringent diets for children has subsided. We encourage parents not to impose on their children low-fat, low-cholesterol diets as a preventive measure without their pediatrician's advice.

The NIH Consensus Conference and the AHA Nutrition Committee argued that the type of data shown in Figure 14.2 represent risk of older men and therefore do not show the risk of long-term exposure to high blood cholesterol levels. They asserted that exposing the arteries to even modest levels of blood cholesterol over a lifetime could result in increased risk. Even though comparisons of blood cholesterol levels and heart disease among populations of different countries could be used to justify this assertion, such evidence is far from proof. What these proponents of the diet–heart theory needed was additional evidence to bolster their case. A report appeared in 1986 that seemed to do just that, at least at first glance. Careful reading of the report, however, showed that it revealed another complicating factor in the whole issue – the age effect.

---

[j] In 1984, the National Heart, Lung and Blood Institute, one of the constituent institutes of the NIH, launched the National Cholesterol Education Program for the purpose of educating the public about the relationship of dietary fat, saturated fat, and cholesterol to high blood cholesterol levels. Individuals with a blood cholesterol level above 200 mg/dL were urged to attempt to lower it by means of dietary modification. The AMA and many physicians endorsed the program.

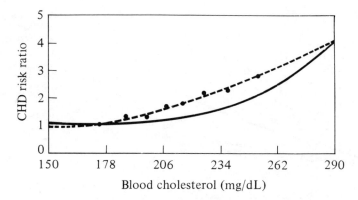

Figure 14.3. Relative risk for coronary heart disease in men of all ages above 39 years (solid line) and in men between the ages of 35 and 57 years (dashed line).

Cholesterol, heart disease, and age

This new analysis reexamined the relationship between blood cholesterol and the risk of death from heart disease.[17] In the process, it provided clear evidence that the importance of elevated blood cholesterol as a risk factor for heart disease is greatest in middle-aged men and decreases with increasing age.

The data in Figure 14.3 offer a strong indication that age makes a difference in the importance of cholesterol as a risk factor for heart disease.[18] The dashed line in this figure represents the relative risk of heart disease at various levels of blood cholesterol in men aged 35 to 57, based on an analysis of a whopping 356,220 men. The solid line represents the risk of heart disease versus blood cholesterol for men at all ages above 39. When men older than 57 were included, the importance of cholesterol as a risk factor was diminished except at very high blood levels. More direct evidence of the age effect on the importance of cholesterol as a risk factor for heart disease is shown in Figure 14.4. For men aged 40 to 44 at the start of the six-year study, there was a perceptible increase in risk of heart disease with each incremental increase in blood cholesterol above 181. Blood cholesterol level became less and less important as a risk factor for heart disease as the men's age increased. Indeed, there is now considerable evidence indicating that high blood levels of cholesterol in men above the age of 60 are not associated with a higher risk of heart disease[19] Although there are fewer data available, it has similarly been concluded that elevated blood cholesterol level does not predict heart disease in women above the age of 50[20] or 60.[21] The lessons from these reports are clear: Elevated blood cholesterol is an important risk factor for premature heart disease, and the

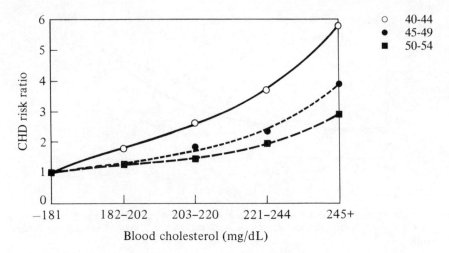

Figure 14.4. Decreasing effect of blood cholesterol as a CHD risk factor with increasing age.

benefits of lowering blood cholesterol are considerably fewer in older men than they are in middle-aged men.[22]

The observation that elevated blood cholesterol is of greater concern to middle-aged men than to any other group does not mean that middle-aged men are more susceptible to heart disease than older men are. In fact, only about 13 percent of men who eventually die of heart disease do so "prematurely," that is, before the age of 55. The other 87 percent die when they are older, with almost half of those deaths occurring after the age of 74. In women, 70 percent of those who die of heart disease do so after the age of 74. Thus, the diminished importance of cholesterol as a risk factor for heart disease in older people does not mean that they are not likely to die of the disease. What it does mean is that when we pass age 45, whether we will or will not eventually die of heart disease depends less and less on our blood cholesterol level.

It seems to us that a large part of the public's confusion about blood cholesterol and heart disease is due to a failure in media reports and advertisements to differentiate between premature heart disease and the disease that appears in older people. As we have seen, age does make a difference in the importance of elevated blood cholesterol as a risk factor. Yet most of the clinical studies that have tried to determine the possible relationships between blood cholesterol and heart disease have been conducted using young to middle-aged men with very high levels of blood cholesterol. That is, by selecting such subjects from literally hundreds of thousands of candidates, these studies specifically tried to determine the effects of lowering blood cholesterol level on the incidence of premature heart disease in men whose blood cholesterol level put them at high risk for heart disease. We now shall describe two such major studies completed relatively recently.

Intervention to prevent premature heart disease in "high-risk" men

The Framingham study, referred to earlier, described the characteristics that are associated with the development of heart disease but did not try to change them. In contrast, intervention trials attempt to change some parameter in subjects to see whether the change alters the incidence and progress of the disease.

One such study, the Multiple Risk Factor Intervention Trial, is widely known by the acronym MR FIT. As the name implies, it tried to change several known risk factors at the same time, in order to determine whether such an approach would lower the incidence of death from heart disease.[23] The $100 million, seven-year project involved 12,866 men, aged 35 to 57, selected from a total of over 350,000 original recruits. Criteria for selection were the presence of multiple risk factors, including smoking, high blood pressure, and a blood cholesterol level above the 90th percentile. Diabetics, those with a history of heart attack and those with very high blood pressure or very high blood cholesterol (above 350) were excluded. Half of the men were assigned to a control group, and the other half were assigned to a treatment group. The control group received "usual" medical care (which meant only periodical medical examinations), and the treatment group received intense medical care. Intense care meant counseling to stop smoking, medical treatment to lower blood pressure, and dietary modification to conform to the diet recommended by the American Heart Association (low total fat, low saturated fat, more polyunsaturated fat, and low cholesterol).

Dietary modification by the treated group resulted in an average reduction in blood cholesterol of 6.7 percent, as well as a reduction in the magnitude of other risk factors. Despite the apparent success in changing risk factors, intervention failed to have any effect on deaths from either heart disease or any other cause. Specifically, the control and treated groups had incidences of 19.3 and 17.9 heart deaths per 1,000 subjects, respectively, a difference so small that statistically it could have been due to chance alone. The number of deaths from all causes was also equal between the two groups: 40.4 deaths per 1,000 subjects in the control group and 41.2 deaths per 1,000 in the treated group. Although this study did not prove that intervention, including dietary modification, would cut the number of heart disease deaths, neither did it disprove it. Indeed, as far as proving or disproving the hypothesis, MR FIT was a "wash."

Another major study that attempted to prove that lowering blood cho-

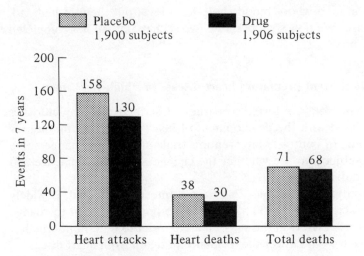

Figure 14.5. Heart attacks or deaths in the Lipid Research Clinic (LRC–CPPT) trial.

lesterol levels prevents heart disease went by the name of Lipid Research Clinic Coronary Primary Prevention Trial, abbreviated LRC-CPPT.[24] It was labeled a "primary prevention" trial because it involved subjects who had not previously had a heart attack. As with the MR FIT study, the primary criteria for selection were that subjects had to be relatively young (35 to 59 years) and had to have a high blood cholesterol level, in this case equal to or greater than that found in the upper 5 percent of men. Using these criteria, 3,806 were selected after screening more than 400,000 age-eligible men.

All subjects were given a diet patterned on that recommended by the American Heart Association, which restricted the intake of dietary fat, saturated fat, and cholesterol while increasing dietary polyunsaturated fat. After several months of eating the modified diet, half of the men received a placebo, and half received a drug that was found in previous studies to lower blood cholesterol. Note that the experiment did not test the effect of the diet, as all of the participants ate the same modified diet; rather, it tested the effect of the drug. As expected, the drug worked: In the seventh year, blood cholesterol levels averaged 277 in the placebo group and 257 in the drug-treated group, an average difference of 8.5 percent.

With such a difference in blood cholesterol, a decrease in the risk of heart disease would have been expected, as the participants chosen had such a high level of blood cholesterol that any reduction should have lowered their risk for heart disease. As shown in Figure 14.5, drug treatment did cut both the number of heart attacks and the number of deaths from heart disease, but as in the MR FIT study, lowering the blood cholesterol had virtually no effect on mortality from all causes. Critics of the report – and there were many of them – pointed out that the amount of reduction in the number of both heart attacks and heart deaths was surprisingly small, considering the subject selection process. For each 1,000 participants, drug treatment resulted in only about two fewer heart attacks per year and one less heart death every other year. Although the statistical analysis used in the report indicated that the reductions could be attributed to drug therapy, it was noted that such decreases could have been attributed to chance alone instead of to drug treatment, by the more usual methods of statistical analysis.[25]

In addition to the scientific report, scientists involved in the study took the relatively unusual step of holding a press conference to present their findings directly to the public;[k] part of the press conference was reported on national television. Statements made at the press conference drew strong criticism from some scientists, whereas others defended them.[26] One major area of disagreement was the same issue that has been debated for years. Researchers argued at the press conference that the results of their study implied that the "benefits of [blood] cholesterol lowering extend to: other age groups, women, [those with] lower levels of blood cholesterol, and dietary reduction of blood cholesterol." Numerous opponents[27] vigorously objected to this statement. The critics asserted that there is no way that the results of a study of a drug, not diet, in middle-aged men with very high blood cholesterol levels could be extrapolated to demonstrate beneficial effects of diet modification in women, children, and men of other ages or even to men of the same age with lower blood cholesterol levels.

Although it was widely hoped that this $155 million LRC-CPPT study would settle the issue of diet and heart disease "once and for all," it was not to be. Instead, it served only to fuel the debate within the scientific community. That debate spilled over into the public arena when an article entitled "The Cholesterol Myth" was published in the September 1989 issue of *The Atlantic*.[28] This article pointed out that (1) it is very difficult to reduce blood cholesterol substantially by means of dietary modification; (2) drugs that lower blood cholesterol can have devastating side effects;

[k] The press briefing was held at the National Institutes of Health on January 12, 1984. A verbatim report issued by the scientists at that press conference was published in *Nutrition Today*, March–April 1984, pp. 20–25. It was from this press conference that the rule of thumb that "for each 1 percent increase in blood cholesterol, there was a 2 percent increase in risk" was derived from the study of men whose initial blood cholesterol level was above 265. The relationship is very likely not true for those whose blood cholesterol level is average or below (see Figure 14.2). Yet media reports have extended the applicability to virtually all of us. For example, an article on drug treatment for high cholesterol states that "recent studies show that for each one-percent increase in cholesterol above the 200-milligram mark, there is a two-percent increase in risk of heart disease." See I. Ross, "A New Drug That Fights Cholesterol," *Reader's Digest*, December 1987, pp. 91–94.

Table 14.1. *Percentage of deaths from heart disease, cancer, and stroke in the United States versus Japan, 1984*

Cause	United States	Japan
Heart disease	37	20
Cancer	22	25
Stroke	8	19
Total	67	64

and (3) there is little evidence that reducing blood cholesterol levels prolongs the life of most people.

Blood cholesterol and changes in life expectancy

Recall that in both the MR FIT study and the LRC-CPPT intervention trial, the number of deaths from all causes was not changed by changing the blood cholesterol level. In the LRC-CPPT study (Figure 14.5), the lack of difference in overall mortality was attributed to an unusually large and inexplicably high incidence of deaths by accidents and violence in the control group, which almost exactly offset the decrease in mortality from heart deaths. Was the lack of effect of intervention a fluke? Perhaps, although this has been a general trend in such studies. Indeed, when the results of nineteen diet/drug trials involving 36,000 persons were combined, it was found that although the number of coronary deaths was statistically lower, the number of deaths from other causes rose, and so the overall death rate was not affected by intervention.[29] It has been reported "that in each of five studies linking dietary changes to reduced mortality from heart disease, such reductions were balanced by increases in deaths from other causes; life expectancy therefore remained unchanged."[30] The writer went on to point out that "this observation suggests that the effects of our interventions are analogous to stewards rearranging the deck chairs on the *Titanic*." It is interesting that even in studies involving men who were at high risk for developing heart disease, intervention changed the cause of death more often than it changed its incidence.

The NIH consensus conference report, discussed earlier, emphasized that Japanese in Japan, on the average, had lower blood cholesterol levels than did Americans and a lower incidence of deaths from heart disease. As Table 14.1 illustrates,[31] the smaller number of heart deaths was essentially balanced by an increase in the number of deaths from cancer and strokes. It is not known, of course, how many of the deaths in each category were influenced by diet. Such data may simply reflect that humans have reached their genetic potential for longevity.[32]

A report by W. C. Taylor and colleagues[33] took a different approach to determining benefits that might be derived from reducing blood cholesterol level by means of dietary modification. The authors used the data from the Framingham project, as well as other sources, to calculate the amount of time that might be added to life expectancy by reducing blood cholesterol levels. They assumed that using dietary modification to lower blood cholesterol was not associated with death from causes other than heart disease, an assumption that may be overly generous in view of the results of many clinical studies, as discussed earlier. To measure the amount of reduction in blood cholesterol level that might be achieved by dietary modification, the authors used the data from the MR FIT study, which indicated that on the average, consumption of the American Heart Association diet resulted in a 6.7 percent decrease in blood cholesterol level. Calculations were made for men and women of various ages with and without other risk factors such as high blood pressure or smoking.

The number of weeks that could be added to life expectancy by reducing blood cholesterol by 6.7 percent for men without other risk factors ranged from less than a week to 5 weeks, depending on the age at which they started the dietary modification and their initial blood cholesterol level. There was a virtual absence of effect in men who started the dietary modification at age 60, which reflects the lack of effect of blood cholesterol level on the risk for heart deaths in older men. For women who did not have other risk factors, calculated increased life expectancy ranged from 3 to 13 weeks, depending on age and initial cholesterol values. Although critics have charged that the change in life expectancy reported in this paper underestimates the benefits that might be expected,[34] later work confirmed that a modest reduction in blood cholesterol level does have a minimal effect on life expectancy for most people.

A study conducted by S. A. Grover and colleagues used a computer model to calculate the effect of reducing blood cholesterol level on life expectancy and the delay in onset of heart disease symptoms.[35] The researchers assumed that blood cholesterol level could be lowered by an average of 5 percent by means of dietary modification. The results of the study, shown in Table 14.2, carry a high degree of credibility because the computer model used was verified using actual results from clinical trials. Calculations indicate that men who did not have other risk factors could expect to increase their life expectancy by 11 to 117 days by means of dietary modification, depending on their age and blood cholesterol level at the time of intervention. Women without other risk factors could expect to gain 15 to 69 days in life expectancy.

Table 14.2. *Increase in life expectancy and delay of onset of appearance of coronary heart disease symptoms in persons who do not smoke cigarettes and have normal blood pressure when blood cholesterol is lowered by 5 percent by means of dietary modification*

	Original blood cholesterol level					
	220		240		300	
			Days added to			
	Life expectancy	Heart disease symptom free	Life expectancy	Heart disease symptom free	Life expectancy	Heart disease symptom free
Males						
35	51	131	62	161	117	274
45	40	102	51	120	91	193
55	26	58	29	69	51	99
65	11	22	11	26	22	32
Females						
35	29	77	37	88	69	135
45	29	69	33	77	58	117
55	22	51	26	58	44	84
65	15	33	18	37	26	51

Source: Adapted from S. A. Grover, M. Abramowicz, L. Joseph, C. Brewer, L. Coupal, and S. Suissa, "The Benefits of Treating Hyperlipidemia to Prevent Coronary Heart Disease: Estimating Changes in Life Expectancy and Morbidity," *Journal of the American Medical Association* 267 (1992):816–22.

Critics have argued that even though a reduction of blood cholesterol level may have minimal effects on life expectancy, dietary modification may significantly delay the onset of heart disease symptoms. Grover and colleagues calculated the number of additional days that people could expect to remain free of heart disease symptoms if their blood cholesterol were reduced by 5 percent. Table 14.2 shows that if a 35-year-old male with a blood cholesterol level of 300 followed a cholesterol-lowering diet for the remainder of his life, he could expect to have an additional 274 days without heart disease symptoms; a 65-year-old male with a similar blood cholesterol level would delay his heart disease symptoms by 32 days. In women, the delay in onset of heart disease symptoms ranged from 33 to 135 days, depending on age and blood cholesterol level at the time of intervention.

In these reports, it was assumed that dietary intervention would lower blood cholesterol level by only 6.7 percent (Taylor et al.) or 5 percent (Grover et al.), based on the results of numerous clinical trials. Note that some participants in these clinical trials experienced a reduction in blood cholesterol level of 10 percent or more, in which case a somewhat greater effect (although not doubled) on life expectancy and the delay in the onset of heart disease symptoms would be anticipated. On the other hand, an average reduction of 5 percent in blood cholesterol level means that for each person who achieved a 10 percent reduction by means of dietary modification, another individual experienced no change in blood cholesterol concentration in response to dietary modification. Calculations show that when greater changes in blood cholesterol level are achieved through aggressive medication and diet therapy, greater benefits can be expected but that their magnitude depends on age and blood cholesterol level at the time of intervention. Young (35-year-old) males with blood cholesterol levels approaching 300 gain the most benefits from aggressive therapy, whereas 65-year-old members of either sex with blood cholesterol levels of 220 add only 18 to 25 days of life and delay the onset of heart disease symptoms by only 40 to 55 days when blood cholesterol levels are reduced to 200.

Before you try to find yourself among the statistics in Table 14.2, let us hasten to add that the calculations assume the absence of two other risk factors for heart disease – cigarette smoking and high blood pressure (i.e., diastolic pressure of 100 mm Hg or greater). The presence of these two additional risk factors approximately doubles the increase in life expectancy and delay in onset of heart disease symptoms that can be expected from a 5 percent reduction in blood cholesterol. That is, people who smoke cigarettes and have high blood pressure have more to gain from dietary modification than do people who do not have these risk factors. On the other hand, not smoking and controlling high blood pressure increase lon-

Table 14.3. *Months added to life expectancy in persons with high risk for heart death*

Age	Cholesterol reduction[a]	Cessation of smoking	Blood pressure reduction[b]
Females			
20	4	37	19
40	9	37	26
60	11	23	22
Males			
20	4	70	24
40	7	63	34
60	2	32	24

[a]Reduction of blood cholesterol of 6.7 percent assuming that initial value was in the upper 10 percent of population.
[b]Reduction of systolic blood pressure of 14.3 percent, assuming that initial value was in the upper 10 percent of the population.
Source: Adapted from W. C. Taylor, T. M. Pass, D. S. Shepard, and A. L. Komaroff, "Cholesterol Reduction and Life Expectancy," *Annals of Internal Medicine* 106 (1987): 608.

gevity more than does reducing blood cholesterol level. The paper by Taylor and colleagues includes information that may help to put the diet–heart controversy into perspective with respect to these other risk factors (Table 14.3). Note that in this analysis, not smoking and lowering blood pressure reduce not only the risk of heart disease but also the risk of two other leading causes of death, strokes and cancer. This explains, in part, the apparent greater benefits of cessation of smoking and reduction of blood pressure.

Achieving the desirable level of blood cholesterol

The NIH consensus conference defined a blood cholesterol level of 200 as "desirable" for individuals 40 years of age and up.[36] In the eyes of the public, this desirable level soon became maximum for the prevention of heart disease.[37] We have already presented arguments for and against recommending dietary modification for those with cholesterol levels below 240. What we wish to address here are some of the problems associated with achieving a level of 200.

One of the practical problems is that methods for quantitatively determining blood cholesterol do not give reproducible values even in clinical settings, never mind those that take place in the mall. Repeated measurements in an individual over time, using optimal laboratory methods, might be off as much as 25 or even 50 points.[38] This means that individuals might well find that one test indicates their measured cholesterol level to be in the high-risk category, whereas the next day it may be at the "desirable" level of 200.

A second problem is that although desirable and average levels were established using the Lipid Research Clinic (LRC) method, it has been reported that two methods most often used to measure blood cholesterol clinically overestimate the values by 8 percent and 15 percent.[39] This means that a patient who had a desirable LRC value of 200 could be informed that his or her level was either 216 if measured with the Technicon SMAC method or 230 if measured with the DuPont aca method. The lesson is simple – before you worry about your cholesterol value's being too high, determinations should be repeated on three or four blood samples taken over time and the values compared with the normal range found using the same method.

Finally, even by LRC methods, most people over the age of 40 have cholesterol values above 200.[40] Almost 70 percent of men above age 45 and about 80 percent of women above age 60 have blood cholesterol levels above that level. The results of a number of clinical trials indicate that most of us can expect a reduction of 5 to 10 percent in our blood cholesterol level from modifying our food intake to conform to the prudent diet recommended by the American Heart Association. This means that statistically, about half of us above the age of 45 will not be able to lower our blood cholesterol to 200 by dietary means, short of heroic efforts of severe dietary restrictions. Don't be too discouraged if you try to do so and fail. You will have a lot of company. Why is it so difficult to lower the blood cholesterol by means of diet? The answer is not simple.

Cholesterol: What it does, where it goes, and where it comes from

Cholesterol has such a bad reputation that most people are surprised to learn that cells in our bodies make it. Even more surprising, the amount that is made depends on how much is consumed. In most of us, the less that is consumed, the more the body will make! If cholesterol is so bad for us, why do we make it? Cholesterol performs several important functions that are essential to life.

Most of the cholesterol in our bodies occurs as a component of membranes that surround each cell and of membranes of particles that occur inside cells. If you think about how many individual cells you contain, it is obvious that this is where most of the cholesterol in the body can be found. In addition, cholesterol is the starting material for making vitamin D when skin is exposed to sunlight. Cholesterol is also converted into hormones, including sex hormones. Finally, cholesterol is used to make *bile acids*.

Bile acids are the chemicals secreted into the small intestine in bile that work as detergents to allow proper digestion and absorption of dietary fats (see Chapter 3). Although about 90 percent of the bile acids are recycled back to the gallbladder to be used again, about 10 percent of them are not reabsorbed and are thus eliminated in feces. This conversion to bile acids and their elimination in the feces is the main way in which cholesterol is removed from the body.

The cholesterol that is in the body comes from one of two sources: diet or synthesis. Meat, milk, and eggs contain cholesterol because membranes in the cells of animals, like ours, contain it. For the average person, these foods contribute about one-fourth, whereas synthesis, mostly in liver, contributes three-fourths of the cholesterol needed to replace that lost as bile acids each day. Whether cholesterol comes from the diet or is made in the liver, it must be transported through the blood to the cells that need it. Because cholesterol, like fat, is not water soluble, it must be associated with protein before it can enter the blood. Particles formed by the association of lipids (triglyceride and/or cholesterol) with proteins are called *lipoprotein* particles. There are five different types of lipoprotein particles in the blood of humans.

Cholesterol: How it is carried in the blood

Two of the types of lipoprotein in blood help transport fat from digestive processes and are not thought to be involved, at least not directly for most of us, in heart disease.[1] When lipids (triglyceride and cholesterol) are shipped out of the liver, the transport particle is called a *very low density lipoprotein* (VLDL), because it has a very high percentage of fatty material, which makes it buoyant. After this particle makes its way through the blood to the fat storage cells, some of the triglyceride is removed, thereby making it more dense (less buoyant) than the VLDL particles and changing its name to a *low-density lipoprotein* (LDL). Note that it is triglyceride, not cholesterol, that is removed for deposition in fat cells, and so VLDL and LDL have the same quantity of cholesterol per particle, but the cholesterol makes up a higher percentage in the LDL particle. Therefore, LDL particles are said to be "cholesterol rich." It is high levels of LDL

---

[1] One of these lipoprotein particles, called a *chylomicron*, is responsible for carrying fat and cholesterol from the small intestine to the fat storage cells, as described in Chapter 4. When some of the fat is removed from chylomicrons for deposition in the fat storage cells, the smaller, denser lipoprotein that is left over, called a *chylomicron remnant*, returns to the liver for disposition. Thus, both chylomicrons and chylomicron remnants contain cholesterol, but in this form the cholesterol is delivered to the liver.

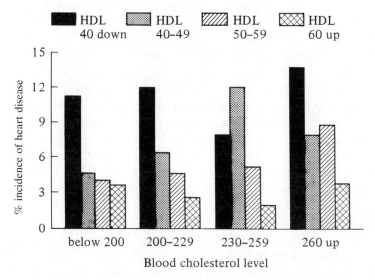

Figure 14.6. Effect of HDL on risk of high blood cholesterol.

particles that are thought to be associated with the development of artery plaque.

Finally, during the process of depositing triglyceride from VLDL particles to form LDL particles, still another lipoprotein particle, more dense than any of the others, is formed. This one, which can also be made in the liver, is called a *high-density lipoprotein* (HDL) particle. HDL particles contain cholesterol, but in contrast with LDL, high levels of HDL are thought to protect against plaque formation. When media reports differentiate "bad" from "good" cholesterol, what is meant is LDL cholesterol and HDL cholesterol, respectively. On the average, most of the cholesterol in blood after an overnight fast is present in LDL (65 percent), and HDL (25 percent) and VLDL account for the rest. The cholesterol in VLDL is generally thought to be neither "good" nor "bad" – it is neutral.

Protective effect of HDL cholesterol

The different effects of LDL and HDL cholesterol on the risk for heart disease have obviously complicated efforts to assess risk on the basis of total blood cholesterol level. Although considerable emphasis is often placed on the relationship between risk and total blood cholesterol level (see Figures 14.2 and 14.3), even total cholesterol levels above 260 may not be associated with high risk if the HDL cholesterol also is elevated.

Figure 14.6 shows the interaction of HDL cholesterol and total blood cholesterol on the four-year incidence of coronary heart disease in 4,200 men and women above the age of 48.[41] According to this analysis, subjects with HDL-cholesterol levels below 40 had an almost equally high risk of heart disease whether total blood cholesterol level was below 200 or above 260. On the other hand, subjects with HDL-cholesterol levels of 60 or above had a relatively low risk for the disease, regardless of blood cholesterol levels. It was only for those who had HDL-cholesterol levels between 40 and 60 that risk generally increased with rising blood cholesterol. These data indicate that people who are concerned about their blood cholesterol level should have a "lipoprotein profile" test. Such a test determines the amount of both LDL and HDL in blood, the ratio of which provides a much better estimate of heart disease risk than does total cholesterol level alone. A lipoprotein profile is considerably more expensive than the measurement of total cholesterol, but it is likely to be worth the cost for people who are worried about their cholesterol.

Only about 25 percent of men and 10 percent of women above the age of 45 have low HDL-cholesterol levels (below 40), whereas between 10 and 25 percent of men and about 50 percent of women have high levels (above 60).[42] Although a few behaviors have been identified that raise the HDL level by at least a small degree (not smoking, exercising, and consuming moderate amounts of alcohol), the quantity of HDL in blood is primarily determined by genetics.[43] It has been suggested that HDL particles may be protective because they pick up cholesterol from arteries and carry it back to the liver for disposal. However, this explanation appears less likely than the possibility that high HDL-cholesterol levels simply mean that the whole system of cholesterol transport is working normally.[44]

Do not be misled by the statement that HDL protects against heart disease. It cannot be said that HDL cholesterol prevents the disease any more than it can be said that LDL cholesterol causes it. People who have high HDL-cholesterol levels may have heart attacks, whereas those with low levels may not. What can be said is that if blood HDL cholesterol is high, elevated blood cholesterol is much less important as a risk factor for coronary artery disease. Conversely, a low HDL cholesterol means that total blood cholesterol, in the form of LDL, becomes much more important as a risk factor. That is why it is important to measure the ratio of LDL to HDL cholesterol by means of a lipoprotein profile before you become overly concerned about a high blood cholesterol level.

Lowering blood cholesterol by means of drugs

For people who need to lower their blood cholesterol level and even for people who may not need to but want to, there are two basic choices: dietary modification or drugs. A number of drugs can lower blood cholesterol levels, especially combined with dietary modification, but their effectiveness varies with each person. Unfortunately, virtually all of the cholesterol-lowering drugs have unwanted side effects for some people and therefore should never be self-prescribed. For example, despite suggestions in the popular press that the B vitamin niacin is an effective way to lower blood cholesterol levels, niacin should not be consumed in large amounts unless prescribed by a physician. The reason is that in large amounts, niacin acts as a drug that produces uncomfortable side effects in most people (feeling flushed, itching skin) and liver damage in some. People taking large amounts of niacin should periodically have liver function tests.

In addition to side effects, drugs that lower blood cholesterol levels are relatively expensive when administered to large numbers of patients.[45] The minimal effect of the drug used in the LRC-CPPT study of heart attack deaths prompted one scientist to suggest that "those with high cholesterol levels must ask themselves whether they would be willing to pay $150 per month for 7 to 10 years for an unpleasant medication that would reduce their chances of dying [due to a heart attack] from 2 percent to 1.6 percent."[46] A subsequent report estimated that the cost of the particular drug used in that study, even when consumed by large numbers of patients at high risk from heart disease, would range from $36,000 to $1 million per year of life saved, depending on the age at which the subject started taking the drug.[47]

The problems with blood cholesterol–lowering drugs have prompted most health authorities to suggest that dietary modification be attempted before drug therapy is instituted. Unfortunately, because the blood cholesterol level is regulated primarily by genetics, it is difficult to change it appreciably by means of diet. Further, the effectiveness of dietary modification, like that of drugs, varies considerably from one person to the next.

How to lower blood cholesterol by means of diet

There are essentially two ways to modify a diet to reduce blood cholesterol level. The first way is simple but not easy (see Chapter 13): Reduce your calorie intake. We told you in the previous section that cholesterol is carried in blood in lipid-containing particles (VLDL), whose principal task is to transport triglyceride from the liver to fat cells for deposit, at which time LDL particles are produced. If you consume fewer calories, there will be fewer of both types of particles in your blood and therefore less cholesterol. This method is obviously advantageous to people who are overweight, because an added benefit is weight loss.

The second way is easier but not simple. It involves dietary manipulation to reduce (but not eliminate) the intake of saturated relative to unsaturated fats. This decrease in the ratio of saturated to unsaturated fats has been shown repeatedly to lower blood cholesterol levels. A ratio of 1:1:1 of saturated:monounsaturated:polyunsaturated[m] fats, which is recommended by the American Heart Association, has been found in various clinical studies to result, on the average, in a 5 to 10 percent reduction in blood cholesterol levels. Generally, this means eating fewer fats from animal sources (which are about half saturated and half monounsaturated) and eating more fats from vegetable oils (which are usually high in polyunsaturated fat).

We, along with other groups, caution against an overzealous consumption of polyunsaturated fats because as we shall see in Chapter 15, eating too much of these may be associated with a higher risk for cancer and other disorders, such as gallstones. Thus, the Nutrition Committee of the American Heart Association[48] and the Committee on Diet and Health of the Food and Nutrition Board of the National Academy of Sciences[49] recommends that no more than 10 percent of total calories be obtained from polyunsaturated fats. The latter group suggests, in fact, that the consumption of polyunsaturated fats not be increased above the 7 percent of calories that our average diet currently supplies. It would seem foolish to consume an excessive amount of polyunsaturated fat in an effort to prevent heart disease if doing so resulted in other medical problems.

Indeed, the American Heart Association recommends reducing fat intake from the present 37 percent of calories to about 30 percent and making up the difference in calories with carbohydrates. In biochemical terms, this makes little sense because it has repeatedly been shown in animal studies that if calories are provided as carbohydrates instead of fats, the liver can use the carbohydrates to make the same kind of fat that is in pork or beef. Clinical studies of humans indicate that exchanging carbohydrates for fats, without changing the proportion of saturated to unsaturated fat, does not affect blood cholesterol levels.[50] However, the American Heart Association's recommendation does make sense from another standpoint. That is, if the total amount of fat in the diet is decreased by eating less saturated fat, the ratio of saturated to unsaturated fat will increase without overconsuming polyunsaturated fat. One of the results of such a recommendation, however, is that most of us will need the help of a registered dietitian to answer the question, What should I eat for dinner?

The simple idea that we can lower our blood cholesterol by shifting the composition of the fat in our diet has become more and more complicated. For example, recent evidence indicates that substituting monounsaturated fat for saturated fat is as effective as substituting polyunsaturated fat for saturated fat in lowering blood cholesterol.[51] In fact, monounsaturated fat may be a better choice because although polyunsaturated fat lowers both LDL and HDL cholesterol, monounsaturated fat lowers LDL without low-

---

[m] See Chapter 4 for the definition of these three types of fat.

ering HDL. Finally, it now appears that all saturated fat is not equally guilty in raising blood cholesterol; one common form actually reduces it.[52] If all of this sounds like there is a lot more to be learned about dietary fats and blood cholesterol, we agree.

In relation to its reputation, decreasing the amount of cholesterol in the diet is, for most of us, probably the least effective way to lower blood cholesterol.[53] The reason is simple. The average person consumes about 450 milligrams of cholesterol each day, but of that no more than one-half is absorbed into intestinal mucosal cells.[54] Because each of us eliminates daily about 1,000 milligrams of cholesterol as bile acids, this means that our tissues (mostly liver) normally make about four times what we get from our diet.

In addition, biochemical studies in animals indicate that the synthesis of cholesterol by the liver is subject to what is called *feedback control*. This means that the more cholesterol that comes from diet, the less that will be made. Conversely, if less cholesterol is eaten, our liver will make more of it. In general, long-term studies have not found an effect of dietary cholesterol on blood cholesterol, whereas short-term studies do tend to find such an effect, probably because the feedback control system does not operate rapidly. This means that if you usually eat two eggs daily and suddenly stop eating any, there may be a decrease in blood cholesterol for a relatively short time, but after that it will likely return to the level that it was when you were eating the eggs. Note, however, that some individuals may have less than complete feedback control; in their cases dietary cholesterol may increase blood cholesterol levels. Further, many of the blood cholesterol–lowering drugs are effective only when dietary cholesterol intake is restricted.

There have been reports, accompanied by loads of publicity, suggesting that fiber may lower the blood cholesterol level. The type of fiber that supposedly does the trick is "soluble" fiber, found in certain foods, including fruit, beans, peas, and oats. Such news has placed oats among the hot topics for some consumers and cereal manufacturers. Oat bran was added not only to foods such as bread and muffins but also to other products, ranging from potato chips to beer.

It is true that in some studies, oat fiber has been found to lower blood cholesterol levels, but the amount it takes to cause a significant reduction is very large. That is, even when combined with a high-fiber, low-cholesterol diet, it is necessary to consume the amount of soluble fiber equivalent to about one and one-half quarts of oatmeal per day in order to achieve a 10 percent reduction in blood cholesterol level. A 1-ounce serving of oatmeal daily can be expected to reduce blood cholesterol by about 2 to 3 percent.[55] The effectiveness of soluble fiber as a blood cholesterol–lowering agent has varied, depending on a number of factors, including the amount added to the diet, the initial level of blood cholesterol in subjects, and other components of the diet.[56] Thus, the efficacy of consuming soluble fiber in order to lower blood cholesterol is open to serious question.[57] However, we know of no reason that moderate amounts of oats should not be included as a part of a varied diet, especially by those who like them. We would caution, however, that it is possible to eat too much fiber (see Chapter 7).

Finally, the consumption of fish oils has been touted as a way to prevent heart attacks. The idea that fish fat might decrease the risk of heart disease came from epidemiological studies of people, like Eskimos and some Japanese, who habitually consume coldwater fish.[58] Considerable research has led to the conclusion that eating fish lowers the risk of heart disease because fish contain polyunsaturated fats called *omega–3*s. These differ chemically from plant polyunsaturated fats but may share their ability to lower blood cholesterol. However, they may lower the risk of heart disease for another reason. Recall that a blood clot is often responsible for triggering a heart attack in patients who have plaques in their arteries. Omega–3 fatty acids inhibit the blood-clotting process and therefore decrease the chance of a heart attack. In addition, according to the injury theory of plaque formation, platelets (white blood cells) congregate at the site of injury that supposedly initiates plaque formation. Omega–3 fatty acids cause the platelets to be less "sticky" and thus may interrupt the formation of plaque at an early stage. This same property leads to prolonged blood-clotting time[59] and, with the overconsumption of omega–3 fatty acids, spontaneous bleeding. Indeed, although Eskimos and Japanese do have lower rates of heart disease, both populations have relatively high rates of cerebrovascular disease ("strokes") that may be due to cerebral hemorrhage.[60] Thus, the potentially harmful side effects of omega–3 fatty acids are sufficiently large that consuming too many of them is not a good idea. We therefore caution against taking the "purified" omega–3 fatty acids available in drugstores because it is too easy to consume too much of them. It is a much better idea to get fish fats from eating fish once or twice a week.

Dietary modification and the quality of life

We have attempted to tell you what is known about heart disease so that you can assess the benefits you might gain from a self-imposed dietary modification to lower your blood cholesterol. The next question is, what are the costs? Proponents of dietary modification say, in effect, that we can change our diet without running nutritional risks and it might help, so why not?[61] Opponents of recommending sweeping dietary modification based on the conflicting data we currently have express "concern about promising tangible benefits from controversial recommendations that alter people's lives and habits."[62] Another question therefore is, how important are the favorite foods on your list of those things that add to your "quality of life"? Quality of life, by its very nature, is an individual, subjective judgment that cannot be quantified in the laboratory. You are the only one who can define it for you.

People choose foods for a variety of reasons, but for most of us, a major one is enjoyment. Although it may not bother some people to give up bacon, eggs, and whole milk for breakfast in favor of foods containing less cholesterol, less saturated fat, more fiber, and more polyunsaturated fat, others may abhor the trade. In fact, when 3,890 members of the U.S. armed forces were given a list of 378 foods and asked to indicate their preference, the top twelve, in order, were:[63]

1. milk
2. grilled steak
3. eggs-to-order
4. corn-on-the-cob
5. orange juice
6. strawberry shortcake
7. French fried potatoes
8. fried chicken
9. ice cream
10. milk shake
11. bacon
12. spaghetti and meat sauce.

Note that in order to comply with the diet recommended by the American Heart Association, the consumption of most of these foods would have to be limited. Although this list reflects the food preferences of a selected group of young men and may not reflect the preferences of the wider population, it is likely that many of us would find some of our favorite foods included. Each of us must answer the question, is there sufficient evidence of benefit from a self-imposed dietary modification to justify altering our eating habits? One way to approach this question is to ask:

1. If I change my diet and then scientists find out years down the road that it made no difference in risk for heart disease, how disappointed will I be?
2. If I do not change my diet and then find out years down the road that altering my diet could have decreased my risk for heart disease, will I regret my decision?

It is a tough decision, but in the end, you are the only one who can make it.

15   Diet and cancer

It has been said that *cancer* is one of the scariest words in the English language. Currently, cancer is the cause of about 20 percent of the deaths occurring annually in the United States. It is no wonder that there is a high degree of public interest in studies that attempt to determine the cause of and ways to prevent cancer. One question that has been debated for decades in the scientific community is whether cancer is a product of our genetic heritage, our environment, or a combination of both.

The idea that cancer is related to environment – defined in the broadest sense to include the water we drink, the food we eat, and the air we breathe – comes primarily from the study of the incidence of various types of cancer in people of different countries and in groups who have migrated from one area of the world to another.[1] In general, patterns of various types of cancer differ from one country to another, but when immigrants migrate to a different country, the incidence pattern tends to become, within a few generations, similar to that of the new host country.

If it is accepted that environment plays a role in the development of cancer, how important to the process are food choices versus other components of our environment, such as industrialization? Although media reports, advertisements, and pronouncements by various environmental groups imply that cancer is a product of America's modern industrial society, the available evidence simply does not fit that conclusion.[2] The fact is that though our society has become increasingly industrialized, the per capita incidence of non-tobacco–related cancer, at a given age, has not changed during this century, except for stomach and uterine cancer, both of which have decreased. Although the actual number of cancer cases has risen, this can be attributed to the fact that there are more of us and the average age of the population continues to go up. Because the incidence of cancer, like heart disease, increases with age, it is not surprising that the total number of cancer cases has also climbed. The lack of change in the age-specific, per capita incidence of cancer in this country at the same time that we have become an industrialized society supports the conclusion that industrialization does not cause cancer.

The same conclusion can be reached by looking at the incidence of cancer in other industrialized countries like Czechoslovakia compared with non-industrialized countries like New Zealand. The incidence of cancers of the breast and large intestine in Czechoslovakia are much lower than the incidence of these cancers in New Zealand.[3] These are, of course, general observations spread over the entire population, and they do not mean that industrial pollution should never be of concern, for two reasons. First, pollutants could be associated with cancer risks in specific geographical sites within countries. Second, there may be a lag time of several years between the exposure to cancer-causing agents and the actual development of cancer. Recent contaminations may not translate into increased cancer rates for years.

Still, the age-specific incidence data in the United States and elsewhere suggest not only that cancer cannot generally be attributed to industrialization, at least in a simple way, but also that modern agricultural production and processing methods, with their heavy reliance on synthetic chemicals, have not contributed to an increase in cancer incidence. Rather, if our food choices affect the incidence of cancer, it is more likely attributable to long-standing eating habits. In order to consider objectively whether specific foods or food components can cause or prevent cancer, it is necessary first to examine what is known and not known about the disease.

The nature of cancer

Normally, cells divide only under certain circumstances. Although some cells in adults, such as those in skeletal muscle and the nervous system, are not capable of dividing, others, like the epithelial cells that line the inside of the intestine and the skin surface, are continually manufactured to take the place of cells that are continually lost. Epithelial cells, as well as cells in bone marrow, actively divide throughout life, but the process is carefully controlled. Liver cells retain their ability to multiply but do not normally do so except in response to injury. Tumors appear when cells in an organ or tissue multiply inappropriately, without the usual constraints.

Abnormal growths, or *tumors*, that are confined to their original location are classified as *benign*, and those that invade surrounding tissues or migrate to different tissues are *malignant*, or *carcinogenic*. Cancers that arise in epithelial cells, called *carcinomas*, can occur in any of several tissues, including those of the lung, breast, intestine, skin, pancreas, and liver and account for over 90 percent of cancer deaths. The remainder of cancers are those associated with blood cell formation (*leukemias*, *lymphomas*, or *myelomas*) or with fibrous tissue or bone (*sarcomas*).

In recent years, a number of proteins that regulate cellular multiplication have been identified. These proteins, which can either increase or decrease the rate of cellular division, are products of the message carried by the cell's genetic material, DNA. Thus, the DNA within each of the body's ten trillion cells ultimately regulates cellular multiplication. Because we inherit from our parents the basic information found in our DNA, it would be easy to conclude that cancer is predestined by our heredity, but cancer is not that simple.

Although defective DNA appears to be behind the development of cancer, our DNA structure may have been altered well after our birth by any of a number of agents, such as viruses or chemicals from our environment.[a] This damage to the DNA, which ultimately results in cancer, is called *initiation*. When the DNA structure is altered, it is called a *mutation*, and substances that cause such a change are called *mutagens*.

Cancer cells are not initiated solely by external agents. Indeed, there is clear evidence that cancers can arise in the apparent absence of any external initiator in animals as well as in humans. This implies that initiation can also be spontaneous, as it is assumed to be a prerequisite for the development of cancer. The incidence of spontaneous cancers in animals can be increased by selective breeding, and the number of such spontaneously initiated cancer cell clusters rises with age in experimental animals.

As the name implies, initiation is only the first step in the process that ultimately can result in detectable cancer. That is, defective DNA within a cell may lie dormant for years until something happens to cause that cell to multiply. This process of cells multiplying that carry defective DNA, called *promotion*, can occur as a result of any of several factors, including repeated injury or chronic irritation of tissue[4] or the action of various hormones in the body or of chemicals from the environment.[5] Finally, in addition to initiation and promotion, there appears to be a third step, called *progression*, in which what may have been a benign tumor is transformed into a malignant cancer. Progression, like the other two steps, can be the response to any of several factors by means of mechanisms that are not yet well understood.

If the sequence of events that results in cancer can have so many different scenarios, why isn't cancer much more common than it is? Even though we humans carry the possibility of cancer in our genes, fortunately we also have defense mechanisms against it. One of the first lines of defense is that each cell contains DNA-repair enzymes that can seek out and repair defective DNA. Their importance is illustrated by the disaster that can occur when they are not functioning.[b] The DNA-repair mechanism is not, how-

---

[a] The human hereditary unit contains between 50,000 and 100,000 genes, a few of which are known to be precancer genes (proto-oncogenes) that can be converted into cancer genes (oncogenes) by means of mutation.

[b] For example, the hereditary disease xeroderma pigmentosum occurs because a DNA-repair enzyme is missing in skin cells. This enzyme normally repairs the damage done to DNA

ever, a fail-safe system, for a variety of reasons, such as the fact that some mutations, which lead to the formation of a precancer cell, are so subtle that the repair enzymes do not recognize that the DNA is defective. Further, cancers are *clonal*; that is, they arise from a single parent cell. Thus, if the defective DNA in only one cell escapes repair, the progeny of that cell can become a cancer.

Our immune system also has a second line of defense against cancer. Cancer cells are not normal cells, and each of us carries both specialized cells and specific proteins in our blood whose function is to seek out and destroy abnormal cells. Again, several lines of evidence indicate that this is an important protection against cancer, including the fact that patients taking drugs to suppress their immune system have a higher risk for cancer. Unfortunately, this defense also is not foolproof, because cancer cells have various ways of escaping detection by the immune system. For example, some cancer cells cover their surface with carbohydrates, as normal cells do, which allows the cancer cell to masquerade as a normal cell and not be detected by the immune system.

Does heredity play a role in cancer?

It is well established that individuals who have a family history of breast or colon cancer have a substantially higher risk for cancer at these sites.[6] Further, selective breeding can produce strains of animals with a higher incidence of cancer.[7] Both observations suggest that heredity plays some role in cancer, but it may not be a simple one. That is, heredity might affect the incidence of cancer by any of several mechanisms.

The simplest mechanism would be for a defective gene to be passed from parents to offspring, which appears to be the case for an inherited defect that usually leads to colon cancer.[8] Even though this inherited defect is rare, there is evidence that the more common form of colon cancer – which does not follow a simple inheritance pattern – is due to damage to the same gene,[9] presumably occurring after conception. It clearly is possible that heredity could affect susceptibility to such postconceptual damage.

Heredity could influence cancer incidence in a number of other, more subtle ways. For example, the incidence of breast cancer is influenced by circulating levels of estrogen, prolactin, and other hormones that could vary according to heredity. Further, there are many examples of substances that are not carcinogenic in themselves but become carcinogenic after metabolic alteration within the body. The activity of enzymes that catalyze such reactions and, for that matter, the activity of enzymes that can detoxify a carcinogen can differ from one person to the next, depending on genetics.

by ultraviolet light. Those persons with a genetic defect in which the repair enzyme is missing usually die at an early age, often from a particularly virulent form of skin cancer.

Finally, both the activity of DNA-repair enzymes and the effectiveness of the immune system are genetically determined. Any or all of these mechanisms might account for why each of us has varying proclivities to cancer.

Testing for carcinogens in food and drink

The search for cancer-causing agents (carcinogens) in our environment has been actively pursued for decades. The complex nature of cancer has substantially complicated the lives of scientists who attempt to determine whether chemicals in our environment cause cancer. Unlike simple toxicity tests, in which a substance is or is not toxic at a specified dose, carcinogenicity is not easily determined, because a substance may act at any of the three stages of cancer development.

Several rapid, relatively inexpensive laboratory tests have been developed to determine whether a chemical is a mutagen and causes DNA damage. The most widely used of these is called the *Ames test*, named for its developer, Bruce Ames, a biochemist at the University of California. Although laboratory methods have been used to screen synthetic chemicals used in food production and processing, such as pesticides and food additives, the test results have not been able to conclude that a substance is not carcinogenic. For example, these tests are designed to determine whether a substance can damage DNA but not to detect substances that promote the growth of tumor cells. Further, the chemical being tested may not itself be carcinogenic but may be converted in the body to a product that is. Therefore, animal tests must be used to obtain more definitive information.

Animal tests for carcinogens, usually with mice and rats, take longer and are considerably more expensive than simpler laboratory tests, but the results are considered more reliable if they are conducted properly.[c] Generally, after various doses of the chemical under study are administered to test animals, sometimes over several generations, the animals are killed, and their tissues are examined for tumors. Animals that receive identical treatment but do not receive the test chemical (called *control animals*) must be maintained for the same length of time to account for spontaneous tumors that presumably would occur at the same rate in control and test

[c] Animal tests for carcinogens are not valid when the substance is administered in toxic amounts; see B. N. Ames and L. S. Gold, "Too Many Rodent Carcinogens: Mitogenesis Increases Mutagenesis," *Science* 249 (1990): 970–71. The reason is that when enough of a substance is given to cause death of cells, the remainder of cells in a tissue multiply, thereby increasing the probability of spontaneous tumors' developing. Thus, it is the dose, not the substance, that may be carcinogenic. Critics have charged that the experiments suggesting that Alar caused cancer were flawed because cancer appeared in mice only when toxic doses were administered. See J. D. Rosen, "Much Ado about Alar," *Issues in Science and Technology*, Fall 1990, pp. 85–90.

animals. From such experiments, a dose response curve is constructed to estimate the relative strength of a compound to cause cancer. Generally, substances that damage DNA do so at a relatively low dosage, and thus the tolerance of them in food or water is set extremely low, often at zero (i.e., below detection limits).

Is cancer caused by foods we consume?

Although laboratory screening procedures and animal tests have been valuable tools in the study of carcinogens, the ultimate question is whether a substance causes cancer in humans. Obviously, a suspected carcinogen cannot ethically be administered to humans. Thus, most of the studies that try to relate diet to cancer in humans have been done by epidemiologists, not laboratory scientists. Such studies try to relate, statistically, dietary patterns and cancer incidence in defined population groups.

Though the approach is simple, the conduct of such studies and the interpretation of results are not. For example, consider a comparison of cancer incidence and dietary patterns between two different countries. The cancer incidence can easily be compared, assuming no difference between the two countries in diagnostic ability, but how can the dietary patterns be assessed? One way is to find the per capita consumption based on food disappearance data. To do this, the amount of a food produced in a country is added to the amount of that food imported minus the amount exported. The resulting value divided by the total population provides an estimate of per capita consumption. This is a crude estimate at best because it does not take into account waste or other uses of the food (e.g., animal feed) and clearly does not factor in either geographical or individual differences in the consumption of that food.

Attempts to calculate more accurately the eating patterns within households or by individuals by means of interviews are also fraught with difficulties. Because there is substantial evidence that cancer may not develop for years after exposure to a carcinogen, dietary patterns of several years ago may be more relevant than those of last week. To obtain the necessary information, subjects could be asked about dietary patterns of the distant past or about recent dietary patterns, assuming that they haven't changed over time. But the first approach might provide a wrong assessment because of a faulty memory, and the second because of an erroneous assumption.

Although the goal of studies that attempt to relate dietary patterns to the incidence of cancer is laudable, the difficulties encountered in the conduct and interpretation of such studies are enormous. Several factors add to the complexity of the problem, including

1. The fact that cancer is not one disease but many that develop in stages.
2. The probability that there is a genetic susceptibility.

3. The long latency period between exposure to a potential carcinogen and the development of the disease.
4. The difficulty in establishing actual dietary intakes of large numbers of people.
5. The limitations of epidemiological studies.[d]

What is the overall risk of cancer from the foods we eat? Could we change our risk for cancer if we changed our diet? Unfortunately, at the present time, no one knows the answers to these questions, although there have been attempts to quantify the role of diet by combining estimates from epidemiological studies.

One such attempt, which has been widely quoted, was published in 1981. In it, the authors compared (1) the deaths from various types of cancer before the age of 65 years within and between countries, (2) migrants versus compatriots who remained in their native land, and (3) the incidence of cancer within populations over time. Interpretation of the data required a number of assumptions, the most important (and, critics suggest, the most dubious) of which was that the differences between the lowest and highest death rates represented "avoidable" cancer. Based on these assumptions, the authors estimated that "it may be possible to reduce U.S. death rates by practicable dietary means by as much as 35 percent," but they cautioned that the figure was highly speculative. They suggested that the value may be as low as 10 percent but that a 70 percent reduction "may ultimately be achievable, although this certainly cannot be expected in the near future."[10]

This analysis may have introduced a bias by excluding data on deaths from cancer in individuals older than 65 years. Because animal studies have shown that the incidence of spontaneous cancer rises with age, excluding older people may have emphasized environmental factors and deemphasized internal causes. In any event, critics have pointed out that it is virtually impossible to separate the effects of diet from other variables in this type of study. That is, populations may differ genetically and also be subject to different risks from other environmental and life-style factors, and the

---

[d] A. R. Feinstein, "Scientific Standards and Epidemiologic Methods," *American Journal of Clinical Nutrition* 45 (1987): 1080–88. Feinstein, a professor of medicine and epidemiology at Yale University, points out that there are rigorous "rules of evidence" in epidemiology just as there are in other scientific disciplines but that these are often violated. One type of violation is to change the hypothesis being tested after the data are analyzed. For example, if a researcher finds no relationship between a particular diet and the incidence of cancer, he or she might be tempted to subdivide the experimental population into categories (e.g., sex, race, age). If enough subdivision takes place, the laws of probability make it likely that in at least one of these, by chance, the diet will appear to be statistically associated with cancer. Feinstein calls this approach "torturing the data until it confesses," and such epidemiological literature is often cited to support the relationship of diet to the incidence of cancer.

differences in detection, diagnosis, and classification could affect the results.[11]

The Committee on Diet, Nutrition and Cancer[12] acknowledged the difficulties in estimating the importance of diet in cancer incidence. It concluded that although the available evidence suggests that the cancers of most major sites are influenced by dietary patterns, there are insufficient data to quantify the contribution of diet to the overall cancer risk or to determine the percentage of reduction in risk that might be achieved by dietary modification.

If dietary factors are involved, they might cause an increased incidence of cancer because of effects at any or all three levels of cancer development: initiation, promotion, and progression. Components in our food that have such effects could be those chemicals added during production and processing, natural nonnutritive substances in food, or one or more of the nutrients that we require in our diet. Let's look at the issues concerning each of these dietary factors.

Are carcinogens being added to food?

Surveys show the remarkably disparate views of food scientists and members of the general public regarding factors that affect the safety of our food supply.[13] Whereas experts are mainly concerned about the natural constituents of food, like microbial contaminants, consumers are most concerned about synthetic chemicals, such as pesticides and food additives, often fearing that they might cause cancer. Why do scientists consider that the use of synthetic chemicals in food production and processing represents a minimal risk to health? The reason is that these chemicals have undergone a myriad of laboratory tests and animal trials that measure their ability to cause cancer, birth defects, and other human disorders. Although these tests – or, for that matter, any test – cannot prove that a substance is safe, the results of such tests put the risks into perspective.

After a chemical is tested, federal agencies use the data to settle on a level that is legally tolerated in food. This tolerance level, calculated on the basis of a worst-case scenario, is deliberately set low. In this regard, federal agencies take the conservative approach – some say too conservative – and err on the side of safety. Indeed, animal studies indicate that some food additives, like BHT, appear to protect against cancer when administered in amounts much higher than those ordinarily consumed, although they are not added for that purpose (see Chapter 10). The fact that the incidence of non-tobacco–related cancers, when corrected for age, has remained constant or, in the case of stomach and uterine cancer, has decreased since the advent of synthetic chemicals for food production and processing is corroborative evidence that the system has worked well.

Natural carcinogens in food

This is not to say that food does not contain carcinogens. Although we can regulate the introduction of synthetic chemicals into foods, we have much less control over the chemicals that nature puts into them. In fact, natural foods contain literally thousands of chemicals, most of which have not even been identified, much less tested for their ability to produce cancer. Still, a number of naturally occurring chemicals of plant or microbial origin have been shown to be carcinogenic in animal trials when pure forms of the substances are administered in relatively high doses. One of the most potent of these is a substance produced by certain molds, called *aflatoxin*. Although there is evidence that aflatoxin may be responsible for a high incidence of liver cancer in parts of Africa and Asia, the amount of this potent carcinogen in food is monitored in the United States, and the tolerance for it is set so low that it represents a minimal risk.[14] Similarly, the numerous other known carcinogens naturally occurring in food are present at levels far below the amount necessary to induce cancer in animals. Although the consumption of foods containing these carcinogens represents some level of risk, however small, there is no way to avoid them short of not eating anything. Zero risk is simply not obtainable.

In addition to the body's defense systems against the spread of cancer, there are other protective mechanisms against low levels of potential cancer-causing agents. For one, remember that the membranes of the mucosal cells that line the gastrointestinal tract are very picky about which substances they will permit to enter (see Chapter 3). Although required nutrients or chemically related substances are readily absorbed, only very small amounts, if any, of most other chemicals at the low concentrations found in food are taken in. On the other hand, when artificially large amounts of a substance are administered, as in an animal trial, there is a greater chance that the gastrointestinal tract will be overwhelmed and a significant amount of the substance will be absorbed. Similarly, although DNA repair enzymes and the immune system may counter the effects of small amounts of a carcinogen, a flood of damage may overpower these protective systems.

Caffeine is a nonnutritive chemical that, in contrast with most other nonnutrients, is readily absorbed from the intestinal tract, because it is chemically similar to components of RNA and DNA. There is a widespread public belief that caffeine causes mischief, perhaps because Charles W. Post, in order to sell a coffee substitute, Postum, made false claims almost a century ago that many human disorders were caused by caffeine.[15] Media reports have often magnified public concern that drinking beverages containing caffeine, particularly coffee, can cause cancer. For example, a very preliminary report,[16] never substantiated, that suggested that caffeine consumption may increase fibrocystic breast disease was widely reported. As a result, many women cut their intake of caffeine in coffee and its chemical cousins, theobromine and theophylline found in chocolate and tea, in the mistaken belief that these substances might also cause breast cancer. In fact, of the several studies of breast cancer and coffee intake, none has found any relationship between them, but these studies have received little public attention.[17]

A similar scare occurred in 1981 when an epidemiological study concluded that coffee consumption was associated with an increased incidence of pancreatic cancer.[18] Even though the evidence was weak, the conclusion was widely quoted by the media. Five years later, the same group of scientists published another paper in which they reported that the first conclusion was a mistake – coffee was not associated with increased risk of pancreatic cancer.[19] A more recent review of the available evidence concluded that caffeine does not constitute a health hazard when consumed in reasonable amounts by healthy people.[20]

Are any nutrients carcinogenic?

Although most nonnutrients in food are not absorbed, nutrients that are required by the body are allowed entry, and most are actively absorbed. Are any of these carcinogenic? The Committee on Diet, Nutrition and Cancer of the National Academy of Sciences, reviewed the available evidence concerning this question and decided that there was insufficient evidence to indict carbohydrates, proteins, vitamins, or required minerals as being carcinogenic.[21] On the other hand, fats have fallen under suspicion on the basis of several lines of evidence.

Fat consumption and cancer

One of the first indications that fat might play a role in the development of cancer came unexpectedly in 1971 from a study conducted at the Veterans Administration Hospital in Los Angeles.[22] It obviously is unethical to feed a diet to humans that is expected to cause cancer, and this was not the purpose of the experiment. Rather, the subject of the study was heart disease, in which approximately 400 men (whose average age was 65 years) were given a control diet that corresponded to the usual American diet at the time, with about 40 percent of the total calories from fat. Another 400 men of equivalent age were given a diet with a comparable amount of fat, but a much higher percentage of the fat was polyunsaturated.

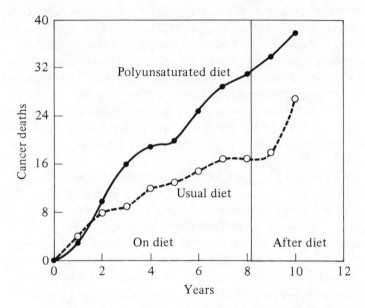

Figure 15.1. Deaths from cancer in men over the age of 65 years fed the "usual" American diet (dashed line) or a diet high in polyunsaturated fat (solid line). *Source:* M. L. Pearce and S. Dayton. "Incidence of Cancer in Men on a Diet High in Polyunsaturated Fat," *Lancet,* March 6, 1971, pp. 464–7.

The results of the study were fascinating. Blood cholesterol, as expected, fell in those fed the experimental diet, and there was a slightly lower incidence of death from heart disease. But the overall death rate was essentially the same in the control and the experimental groups. In this study, many of the additional deaths in the group fed the polyunsaturated fat diet were caused by cancer (see Figure 15.1). Note that the total fat intake between the control and experimental group was the same – the difference was the amount of saturated and polyunsaturated fat.

The VA Hospital study did not prove that polyunsaturated fats caused cancer in these men, particularly because subsequent epidemiological investigations have led to much less clear-cut results. Still, there is evidence from animal studies that ingesting polyunsaturated fats increases the incidence of cancer, particularly when the total amount of fat in the diet is relatively low. Because of the possibility that an excessive intake of polyunsaturated fats might lead to cancer and other disorders such as gallstones in susceptible individuals, the Committee on Diet and Health of the National Research Council recommends that the intake of them not be increased above their present level in our diet of about 7 percent of calories.[23] Thus, attempts to lower blood cholesterol by the wholesale substitution of plant oils for saturated fats found in animal products is probably unwise.

Other studies have focused on the effect of total dietary fat on cancer. Trials with animals usually involve treating mice or rats with a mutagen in order to initiate cancer, after which the animals are fed various levels of fats in the diet to determine the ability of fat to promote tumor formation. It is also typical in such studies to compare marked differences in dietary fat content in order to maximize any effect. For example, when one group of animals is fed a diet in which 10 percent of total calories is derived from fat, and the other group obtains 40 percent of its calories from fat, the higher level of dietary fat will often be associated with a higher incidence of tumors, particularly in the breast and colon. It is not clear how relevant this result is to humans, that is, whether more modest differences in fat content that could reasonably be expected in human diets would correspond to detectable differences in tumor incidence.

Epidemiological studies of humans have produced mixed results, perhaps in part because of the complexities in the conduct and interpretation of such studies. In general, positive statistical correlations have been found between per capita fat consumption (usually based on disappearance data) and the incidence of both breast and colon cancers in large populations (e.g., between countries), but when individuals are studied (case-controlled studies), statistical associations are generally much weaker or nonexistent. This is particularly true for comparisons between total fat intake and breast cancer. In epidemiological studies in general, it is difficult to control for other variables that may affect results. For example, a lower intake of dietary fat presumably means that there is a compensatory increase in other dietary components that may contain factors that protect against cancer. Further, such studies generally are not able to control for total calorie intake. Indeed, some scientists assert that it is not total fat but total calories that is associated with a higher incidence of cancer.[24] That argument is supported by the observation that there is a positive statistical association between obesity (defined as more than 20 percent above reasonable body weight) and breast cancer, particularly in postmenopausal women.

The available evidence is sufficient to raise suspicion that both the quantity and the type of dietary fat may be related to cancer, but it is far short of proof of such an association. Still, many health organizations recommend reducing the consumption of total fat intake from its current average of 36 percent of total calories to 30 percent, with no more than 10 percent of calories coming from polyunsaturated fats, on the grounds that this may lower the incidence of both cancer and heart disease. It is far from clear how effective this dietary modification might be in preventing cancer for most people, but those persons with a personal or family history of breast or colon cancer may benefit from eating less fat.

Does eating fiber prevent cancer?

Of all the elements in food that may have a protective effect against cancer, fiber has received the most public attention, perhaps because of advertisements for products featuring it. The idea that fiber might protect against colorectal cancers came from early observations that cancers of the large intestine are relatively rare in Africa, where the inhabitants' diets are customarily high in fiber. Subsequent epidemiological studies of humans produced mixed results, in that some studies suggested that fiber had a protective effect against colon cancer, whereas others showed no such association. Similarly, although some animal trials indicated that dietary fiber did protect against colon cancer induced by the deliberate administration of known carcinogens, other studies failed to confirm this. And still other trials suggested that fiber strengthened the carcinogenic effect of certain mutagens.

These disparate results prompted the Committee on Diet, Nutrition and Cancer to report in 1982 that it had "found no conclusive evidence to indicate that dietary fiber (such as that present in fruits, vegetables, grains and cereals) exerts a protective effect against colorectal cancer in humans."[25] The Committee on Diet and Health of the National Academy of Sciences reached essentially the same conclusion in 1989: "Evidence for a protective role of high fiber intake per se for cancer, CHD [coronary heart disease], or other diseases must be regarded as inconclusive."[26]

In the meantime, *The Surgeon General's Report on Nutrition and Health*, issued in 1988, put the possible relationship between fiber intake and cancer in a slightly more positive light: "While *inconclusive*, *some* evidence also *suggests* that an *overall* increase in intake of foods high in fiber *might* decrease the *risk* for colon cancer" (emphasis added).[27] We have italicized the limiting words to emphasize that this statement is not a ringing endorsement of the idea that eating fiber can prevent cancer.

Despite the lack of definitive evidence, the National Cancer Institute has clung to the hope that ingesting fiber might reduce the risk of cancer, as stated on the back of some cereal boxes. The consumption of fiber from a variety of sources is, of course, consistent with good nutrition practices, but it is possible to get too much (see Chapter 7). Thus, the habitual use of fiber supplements for treating specific medical disorders is not recommended without physician's advice.

Will eating fruits and vegetables prevent cancer?

Nutritionists have long advocated eating fruits and vegetables both because they add to the enjoyment of eating and are important sources of nutrients that complement those supplied by the other food groups (see Chapter 1). In recent years, there have been increasingly vocal advocates for eating more of these foods on the grounds that in addition to their traditional roles, they may also lower the risk of developing cancer. Will eating fruits and vegetables provide some protection from cancer? Perhaps, although direct evidence from human epidemiological studies is sparse and relatively weak, and evidence from animal studies is difficult to translate into human terms.

A number of epidemiological studies have tried to relate the consumption of vegetables that are high in beta carotene to a lower risk of developing cancer at various sites.[28] Although several of these studies, conducted in various parts of the world, indicated that increased consumption of these vegetables was statistically associated with a lower incidence of cancer, particularly lung cancer, others failed to find such a relationship. Similarly, some (although not all) studies indicated that persons with lung cancer have lower levels of carotene in their blood than their healthy counterparts do. This could mean that not eating enough carotene-containing vegetables increased their susceptibility to lung cancer, but it could also reflect a decreased intake of these types of vegetables as a result of the cancer. Because vegetables are a complex mixture of literally thousands of chemicals, it is not clear even in those cases in which an increased intake of vegetables appeared to provide some protection whether their protective effects were due to beta carotene or to other components.

Studies of animals to determine whether pure beta carotene protects against carcinogens have not cleared up the issue. That is, in some experiments, the administration of beta carotene to animals appears to provide some protection, but it takes enormous doses, in human terms, to do so.[29] For example, the administration of beta carotene to mice at a level equivalent in human terms to the consumption of 3 pounds of carrots per day had no effect on the development of skin cancer induced by ultraviolet radiation, whereas the administration of ten times that amount (equivalent to eating 30 pounds of carrots per day) delayed the appearance of, but did not prevent, skin cancer. Similarly, large doses failed to protect against carcinogen-induced cancers of the respiratory tract in hamsters, or cancers of the colon and rectum in rats. On the other hand, other studies indicated that such large doses gave some measure of protection against various other carcinogen-induced cancers, perhaps because they strengthened the immune system. Taken together, the evidence from animal studies indicates that beta carotene, in amounts normally consumed, provides minimal if any protection against cancer.[e] It is more likely that if green leafy and deep orange vegetables offer some protection against cancer, it is because of components other than beta carotene.

The search for other nonnutritive components of foods that might protect

---

[e] Carotene supplements are not recommended because the evidence that it protects against cancer is so weak. See *Diet and Health* (Washington, DC: National Academy Press, 1989), p. 695. Besides, although beta-carotene is much less toxic than is its animal counterpart, vitamin A, even relatively low levels of consumption of it cause the skin to take on the color of carrots.

against cancer has occupied many scientists for years, but as with many of the other aspects of this disease, the results have been difficult to interpret. Still, in large measure, the proposition that certain fruits and vegetables can provide some protection against cancer comes from those animal studies in which pure chemicals known to be present in these foods are fed to rats or mice, usually in conjunction with the administration of known carcinogens. For example, the administration of a chemical found in broccoli and its relatives, indole carbinol, has been found to inhibit carcinogen-induced mammary tumors in rats.[f] Although this might suggest that eating these vegetables could protect against human breast cancer, the real world is not so simple.

Indole carbinol protected against the particular carcinogen used in this study because it activated a set of oxidative enzymes in cells of the body that converted the carcinogen into an inert chemical. The problem is that the same set of oxidative enzymes can also convert other chemicals, initially inert, into potent carcinogens.[30] Thus, whether activation of the oxidative enzymes by indole carbinol from cruciferous vegetables protects against cancer or increases its incidence depended on which type of potential carcinogens was ingested.

The hypothesis that the consumption of certain foods might protect against cancer is further clouded by the fact that foods are so complex, some of which can have opposing effects. For example, although broccoli contains indole carbinol, which may be anticarcinogenic under some conditions, it also contains a compound similar to dioxin, which is carcinogenic when administered to animals in high doses.[31] The presence of both anticarcinogens and carcinogens in broccoli has led to conflicting reports in the media. Some reports have emphasized the presence of anticarcinogens and imply that eating broccoli may protect against cancer,[32] whereas others emphasized the presence of carcinogens and imply that eating broccoli can cause the disease.[33] In fact, there is no definitive evidence that the amount of either type of chemical that would be absorbed when a reasonable amount of broccoli is consumed would be enough to make any difference in preventing or causing cancer. In more general terms, there is no rational reason to fear that the putative carcinogens in any fruits or vegetables represent more than a very minimal risk for developing cancer. On the other hand, it is not reasonable to conclude on the basis of the available evidence that fruits or vegetables represent a living drugstore that can protect us from cancer or any other human disorder, with the exception of bona fide nutritional deficiency diseases.

[f] Broccoli, cabbage, cauliflower, and brussels sprouts are members of the mustard family. They are called *cruciferous* vegetables because of their cross-shaped stalks.

Competing philosophies concerning the food–cancer connection

Despite a lack of definitive evidence, in 1982 the Committee on Diet, Nutrition and Cancer of the National Academy of Sciences recommended changes in the diet that included eating less fat and more grains, cereals, fruits, and vegetables.[34] These recommendations, echoed in 1989 by the Committee on Diet and Health, were widely reported in the media, but the reports did not make it clear that these were interim recommendations based, for the most part, on preliminary interpretations of the available evidence.[35] Specifically, the introduction to the Committee on Diet, Nutrition and Cancer's report states:

The public often demands certain kinds of information before such information can be provided with complete certainty. . . . The public is now asking about the causes of cancers that are not associated with smoking. What are these causes, and how can these cancers be avoided? Unfortunately, it is not yet possible to make firm scientific pronouncements about the association between diet and cancer. We are in an interim stage of knowledge similar to that for cigarettes 20 years ago. Therefore, in the judgment of the committee, it is now time to offer some interim guidelines on diet and cancer.[36]

The issuance of interim dietary recommendations is not without critics. A more conservative approach was adopted by the Food and Nutrition Board of the National Academy of Sciences:

Any public official considering a new public health program for disease prevention must evaluate the potential effectiveness of the proposed action before recommending its adoption. If there is uncertainty about its effectiveness, there must be clear evidence that the proposed intervention will not be harmful or detrimental in other ways. In the cases of diseases with multiple and poorly understood etiology, such as cancer and cardiovascular disease, the assumption that dietary change will be effective as a preventive measure is controversial. . . . Authorities who resist recommendations for diet modification express legitimate concern about promising tangible benefits from controversial recommendations that alter people's lives and habits.[37]

These pronouncements represent opposite views in a heated debate that has raged within the scientific community for years, mostly out of public view, about the validity of making dietary recommendations on the basis of preliminary evidence. A reasonable case can be made by proponents of both sides of the controversy. Activists argue that the proposed dietary recommendations, which might help reduce the incidence of chronic diseases, cannot hurt because they do not put people who follow them at risk for nutritional deficiencies. In contrast, those who resist making sweeping dietary recommendations contend that premature judgments that may have to be reversed later not only undermine the credibility of the scientific/

medical community but also can adversely affect the quality of life for people who are persuaded to give up their favorite foods.

Is there a cost to acting on preliminary information that turns out to be wrong? Consider the report that coffee consumption was associated with an increase in cancer of the pancreas,[38] only to be retracted five years later.[39] How many people gave up drinking coffee during those intervening five years because of fear of pancreatic cancer? How many of the 125,000 people who found out that they had cancer of the pancreas during those five years assumed that their disease was self-inflicted? How many of the 125,000 people who died of the disease during that period assumed that they had caused their own demise because they drank coffee? How many of their friends and relatives made the same assumption? We don't know what the actual costs were, but it seems to us that for many, they were great.

Words in scientific reports are chosen very carefully. Unfortunately, something is often lost when they are paraphrased in the media. You can rest assured that if and when there is a real breakthrough in the fight against cancer, it will get more than twenty seconds of airtime. In the meantime, when you hear of another food to avoid or to eat to prevent cancer, consider the words describing the benefits with as much care as was used when they were chosen. Then ask yourself how much it will cost you in terms of your quality of life to follow that advice.

Conclusion: Nutrition, chronic diseases, and the quality of life

The field of nutrition has come a long way since it started in the early years of the twentieth century. Research has now firmly established that humans require certain nutrients in order to live. Research has also shown what those nutrients do to protect us from several diseases, called *nutritional deficiency diseases*, when we do not consume enough of them. More important, there is no longer any doubt that these nutrients can be found in a variety of foods, and so obtaining them does not need to be incompatible with enjoying one's meals. Indeed, for most people, the pleasure of eating their favorite foods is an important part of the quality of their life.

In recent years, the hypothesis that food choices might affect the incidence of some chronic diseases has received substantial publicity. Some scientists believe that there is sufficient evidence to warrant recommending that virtually all of us change our eating habits. Other scientists are equally convinced that the benefits claimed by those who have made these recommendations are empty promises for most of us.

Although each side of the dispute can point to specific pieces of evidence to support its view, we have tried to make it clear in this book that the issues involved are exceedingly complex. The hypothesis remains controversial – and indeed, the jury is still out in settling the dispute.

Because controversy breeds headlines, publicity regarding the debate will undoubtedly continue for the foreseeable future. To keep the media reports in perspective, it is important to recognize that the truth is best revealed by viewing the entire fabric, in which each experiment represents a thread, added one at a time. A single thread, even though it may make headlines, cannot show the entire picture.

It seems apparent that even if the risk of chronic diseases can be affected by dietary modification, the potential benefits will vary for each of us. Some persons may profit from changing their diet in order to lower their blood cholesterol level, whereas others would not, just as an obese person may benefit more than a thin person would from eating less. At the same time, the costs of changing our eating habits will differ for each of us. Although some people may not mind giving up or cutting down on their favorite foods, for others, doing so would mean a significant loss from their quality of life.

Believing that the public wants to have information that will help them make their own choices about living longer or living better, we have tried, in the preceding chapters, to point out the trade-offs in substituting one way of eating for another. The idea that foods contribute not only to our nutritional well-being but also to our quality of life, was aptly encapsulated by Naavi Morreim: "Life needs a certain amount of cheesecake."[1] Another idea, that foods should be enjoyed and not feared, is also cleverly illustrated in the following poem, reprinted from a book by Michael J. Gibney:

> They brush and they floss
> with care every day,
> But not before breakfast
> of both curds and whey.
>
> He jogs for his heart
> she bikes for her nerves;
> They assert themselves daily
> with appropriate verve.
>
> He is loving and tender
> and caring and kind,
> Not one chauvinist thought
> is allowed in his mind.
>
> They are slim and attractive
> well dressed and just fun.
> They are strong and well-immunized
> against everything under the sun.
>
> They are sparkling and lively
> and having a ball.
> Their diet? High fiber
> and low cholesterol.
>
> Cocktails are avoided
> in favour of juice;
> Cigarettes are shunned
> as one would the noose.
>
> They drive their car safely
> with belts well in place;
> at home not one hazard
> ever will they face.
>
> 1.2 children they raise,
> both sharing the job.
> One is named Betty,
> .2 is named Bob.

And when at the age of
two hundred and three
they jog from this life
to one still more free,

They'll pass through those portals
to claim their reward
and St. Peter will stop them
"just for a word."

"What Ho" he will say
"You cannot go in.
This place is reserved
For those without sin."

"But we've followed the rules"
she'll say with a fright
"We're healthy" –
"Near perfect" –
"And incredibly bright."

"But that's it" will say Peter,
drawing himself tall.
"You've missed the point of living
By thinking so small."

"Life is more than health habits,
Though useful they be
It is purpose and meaning,
and grand mystery."

"You've discovered a part
of what makes humans whole
and mistaken that part
for the shape of the soul."

"You are fitter than fiddles
and sound as a bell,
Self-righteous, intolerant
and boring as hell."[2]

Appendix A

Recommended dietary allowances[a] (revised 1989); designed for the maintenance of good nutrition of practically all healthy people in the United States

Category	Age (years) or Condition	Weight[b] (kg)	Weight[b] (lb)	Height[b] (cm)	Height[b] (in)	Protein (g)	Fat-Soluble Vitamins Vita-min A (μg RE)[c]	Vita-min D (μg)[d]	Vita-min E (mg α-TE)[e]	Vita-min K (μg)
Infants	0.0–0.5	6	13	60	24	13	375	7.5	3	5
	0.5–1.0	9	20	71	28	14	375	10	4	10
Children	1–3	13	29	90	35	16	400	10	6	15
	4–6	20	44	112	44	24	500	10	7	20
	7–10	28	62	132	52	28	700	10	7	30
Males	11–14	45	99	157	62	45	1,000	10	10	45
	15–18	66	145	176	69	59	1,000	10	10	65
	19–24	72	160	177	70	58	1,000	10	10	70
	25–50	79	174	176	70	63	1,000	5	10	80
	51+	77	170	173	68	63	1,000	5	10	80
Females	11–14	46	101	157	62	46	800	10	8	45
	15–18	55	120	163	64	44	800	10	8	55
	19–24	58	128	164	65	46	800	10	8	60
	25–50	63	138	163	64	50	800	5	8	65
	51+	65	143	160	63	50	800	5	8	65
Pregnant						60	800	10	10	65
Lactating	1st 6 months					65	1,300	10	12	65
	2nd 6 months					62	1,200	10	11	65

[a]The allowances, expressed as average daily intakes over time, are intended to provide for individual variations among most normal persons as they live in the United States under usual environmental stresses. Diets should be based on a variety of common foods in order to provide other nutrients for which human requirements have been less well defined. See text for detailed discussion of allowances and of nutrients not tabulated.

[b]Weights and heights of Reference Adults are actual medians for the U.S. population of the designated age, as reported by NHANES II. The median weights and heights of those under 19 years of age were taken from Hamill et al. (1979) (see pages 16–17). The use of these figures does not imply that the height-to-weight ratios are ideal.

Water-Soluble Vitamins							Minerals						
Vitamin C (mg)	Thiamin (mg)	Riboflavin (mg)	Niacin (mg NE)^f	Vitamin B$_6$ (mg)	Folate (µg)	Vitamin B$_{12}$ (µg)	Calcium (mg)	Phosphorus (mg)	Magnesium (mg)	Iron (mg)	Zinc (mg)	Iodine (µg)	Selenium (µg)
30	0.3	0.4	5	0.3	25	0.3	400	300	40	6	5	40	10
35	0.4	0.5	6	0.6	35	0.5	600	500	60	10	5	50	15
40	0.7	0.8	9	1.0	50	0.7	800	800	80	10	10	70	20
45	0.9	1.1	12	1.1	75	1.0	800	800	120	10	10	90	20
45	1.0	1.2	13	1.4	100	1.4	800	800	170	10	10	120	30
50	1.3	1.5	17	1.7	150	2.0	1,200	1,200	270	12	15	150	40
60	1.5	1.8	20	2.0	200	2.0	1,200	1,200	400	12	15	150	50
60	1.5	1.7	19	2.0	200	2.0	1,200	1,200	350	10	15	150	70
60	1.5	1.7	19	2.0	200	2.0	800	800	350	10	15	150	70
60	1.2	1.4	15	2.0	200	2.0	800	800	350	10	15	150	70
50	1.1	1.3	15	1.4	150	2.0	1,200	1,200	280	15	12	150	45
60	1.1	1.3	15	1.5	180	2.0	1,200	1,200	300	15	12	150	50
60	1.1	1.3	15	1.6	180	2.0	1,200	1,200	280	15	12	150	55
60	1.1	1.3	15	1.6	180	2.0	800	800	280	15	12	150	55
60	1.0	1.2	13	1.6	180	2.0	800	800	280	10	12	150	55
70	1.5	1.6	17	2.2	400	2.2	1,200	1,200	320	30	15	175	65
95	1.6	1.8	20	2.1	280	2.6	1,200	1,200	355	15	19	200	75
90	1.6	1.7	20	2.1	260	2.6	1,200	1,200	340	15	16	200	75

^{c}Retinol equivalents. 1 retinol equivalent = 1 µg retinol or 6 µg β-carotene. See text for calculation of vitamin A activity of diets as retinol equivalents.
^{d}As cholecalciferol, 10 µg cholecalciferol = 400 IU of vitamin D.
^{e}α-Tocopherol equivalents. 1 mg d-α tocopherol = 1 α-TE. See text for variation in allowances and calculation of vitamin E activity of the diet as α-tocopherol equivalents.
^{f}1 NE (niacin equivalent) is equal to 1 mg of niacin or 60 mg of dietary tryptophan.
Source: Committee on Dietary Allowances, Food and Nutrition Board, *Recommended Dietary Allowances*, 10th ed. (Washington, DC: National Academy of Sciences, 1989).

Appendix B

Estimated safe and adequate daily dietary intakes of selected vitamins and minerals[a]

Category	Age (years)	Vitamins	
		Biotin (μg)	Pantothenic Acid (mg)
Infants	0–0.5	10	2
	0.5–1	15	3
Children and adolescents	1–3	20	3
	4–6	25	3–4
	7–10	30	4–5
	11+	30–100	4–7
Adults		30–100	4–7

Category	Age (years)	Trace Elements[b]				
		Copper (mg)	Manganese (mg)	Fluoride (mg)	Chromium (μg)	Molybdenum (μg)
Infants	0–0.5	0.4–0.6	0.3–0.6	0.1–0.5	10–40	15–30
	0.5–1	0.6–0.7	0.6–1.0	0.2–1.0	20–60	20–40
Children and	1–3	0.7–1.0	1.0–1.5	0.5–1.5	20–80	25–50
adolescents	4–6	1.0–1.5	1.5–2.0	1.0–2.5	30–120	30–75
	7–10	1.0–2.0	2.0–3.0	1.5–2.5	50–200	50–150
	11+	1.5–2.5	2.0–5.0	1.5–2.5	50–200	75–250
Adults		1.5–3.0	2.0–5.0	1.5–4.0	50–200	75–250

[a] Because there is less information on which to base allowances, these figures are not given in the main table of RDA and are provided here in the form of ranges of recommended intakes.

[b] Since the toxic levels for many trace elements may be only several times usual intakes, the upper levels for the trace elements given in this table should not be habitually exceeded.

Source: Committee on Dietary Allowances, Food and Nutrition Board, *Recommended Dietary Allowances*, 10th ed. (Washington, DC: National Academy of Sciences, 1989).

Notes

Introduction

1. D. M. Hegsted, "Nutrition: The Changing Scene," *Nutrition Today*, July–August 1985, pp. 16–25.
2. S. Pell and W. E. Fayerweather, "Trends in the Incidence of Myocardial Infarction and in Associated Mortality and Morbidity in a Large Employed Population, 1957–1983," *New England Journal of Medicine* 312 (1985): 1005–11.
3. Food and Nutrition Board, National Research Council, National Academy of Sciences, *Toward Healthful Diets* (Washington, DC: National Academy Press, 1980). Reprinted in *Nutrition Today*, May–June 1980, pp. 7–11.
4. *The Surgeon General's Report on Nutrition and Health: Summary and Recommendations* (Washington, DC: U.S. Department of Health and Human Services, Public Health Service, DHHS [PHS] Publication no. 88-50211, 1988).
5. W. C. Taylor, T. M. Pass, D. J. Shepard, and A. L. Komaroff, "Cholesterol Reduction and Life Expectancy," *Annals of Internal Medicine* 106 (1987): 605–14.
6. See a series of letters to the editor and replies by W. C. Taylor et al., *Annals of Internal Medicine* 107 (1987): 420–22.
7. Committee on Diet, Nutrition, and Cancer, *Diet, Nutrition, and Cancer* (Washington, DC: National Academy Press, 1982), p. 1.
8. See Chapter 11 for more information about this and other myths about food.
9. Chapters 5 and 6 discuss vitamins and minerals, respectively, and tell you what they will and will not do for you.

Chapter 1

1. *Recommended Dietary Allowances*, 9th ed. (Washington, DC: National Academy of Sciences, 1980), p. 127.
2. C. F. Adams, "Nutritive Value of American Foods in Common Units," *Agricultural Handbook 456* (Washington, DC: U.S. Government Printing Office, 1975).
3. A. E. Harper, " 'Nutrition Insurance' – A Skeptical View," *Nutrition Forum* 4 (1987): 33–37.
4. R. Passmore, "How Vitamin C Deficiency Injures the Body," *Nutrition Today*, March–April 1977, pp. 6–11, 27–31.

Chapter 2

1. M. E. Lowenberg, E. N. Todhunter, E. D. Wilson, M. C. Feeney, and J. R. Savage, *Food and Man* (New York: Wiley, 1968).

283

2. J. T. Dwyer, E. M. Andrew, I. Valadin, and R. B. Reed, "Size, Obesity, and Leanness in Vegetarian Preschool Children," *Journal of the American Dietetic Association* 77 (1980): 434–9.
3. P. C. Dagnelie, F. J. Vergote, W. A. van Staveren, H. van den Berg, P. G. Dingjam, and J. G. Hautvast, "High Prevalence of Rickets in Infants on Macrobiotic Diets," *American Journal of Clinical Nutrition* 51 (1990): 202–8.
4. P. C. Dagnelie, W. A. van Staveren, F. J. Vergote, P. G. Dingjam, H. van den Berg, and J. G. Hautvast, "Increased Risk of Vitamin B_{12} Deficiency in Infants on Macrobiotic Diets," *American Journal of Clinical Nutrition* 50 (1989): 818–24.
5. For example, see L. Robertson, C. Flinders, and B. Godfrey, *Laurel's Kitchen* (Petaluma, CA: Nilgiri Press, 1977); and F. M. Lappé, *Diet for a Small Planet* (New York: Ballantine, 1975).
6. Report of the Nutrition Committee, American Heart Association, "Rationale of the Diet–Heart Statement of the American Heart Association," *Circulation* 65 (1982): 839A–54A; "Dietary Guidelines for Healthy American Adults. A Statement for Physicians and Health Professionals by the Nutrition Committee, American Heart Association." *Circulation* 77 (1988): 721A–24A.
7. National Institute of Health Consensus Development Conference Statement, "Lowering Blood Cholesterol," *Nutrition Today*, January–February 1985, pp. 13–16.

Chapter 3

1. "The Prepared Mind," *Nutrition Today*, September–October 1971, pp. 28–36. Despite Beaumont's singular contribution to science, his name never became a household word. Scientists have not forgotten him, however: The headquarters of the Federation of the American Societies of Experimental Biology in Bethesda, Maryland, is named Beaumont House.

Chapter 4

1. J. C. Waterlow, "The Assessment of Protein Nutrition and Metabolism in the Whole Animal, with Special Reference to Man," in H. N. Munro, ed., *Mammalian Protein Metabolism*, vol. 3 (New York: Academic Press, 1969), pp. 325–90.

Chapter 5

1. W. O. Atwater and C. Woods, *The Chemical Composition of American Food Materials*, U.S. Office of Experiment Stations Bulletin no. 28, 1896.
2. R. O. Cummings, *The American and His Food: A History of Food Habits in the United States* (Chicago: University of Chicago Press, 1940), pp. 112–13.
3. M. L. Stewart, J. T. McDonald, A. S. Levy, R. E. Schucker, and D. P. Henderson, "Vitamin/Mineral Supplement Use: A Telephone Survey of Adults in the United States," *Journal of the American Dietetic Association* 85 (1985): 1585–90.
4. National Research Council, *Diet and Health: Implications for Reducing Chronic Disease Risk* (Washington, DC: National Academy Press, 1989).
5. J. Pearson, "Nutrition-related Health Practices and Opinions," *Nutrition Program News*, USDA, September–December 1972, pp. 1–4. See also "The Vitamin Pushers," *Consumer Reports* 51 (1986): 170–75.
6. V. Herbert, *Nutrition Cultism: Facts and Fictions* (Philadelphia: George F. Stickley, 1980), pp. 15–73.

7. Ibid., pp. 107–20.
8. Ibid., p. 179.
9. H. A. Guthrie, "Supplementation: A Nutritionist's Point of View," *Journal of Nutrition Education* 18 (1986): 130–32.
10. J. N. Hathcock, D. G. Hattan, M. Y. Jenkins, J. T. McDonald, P. R. Sundaresan, and V. L. Wilkening, "Evaluation of Vitamin A Toxicity," *American Journal of Clinical Nutrition* 52 (1990): 183–202.
11. J. A. Olson and R. E. Hodges, "Recommended Dietary Intakes (RDI) of Vitamin C in Humans," *American Journal of Clinical Nutrition* 45 (1987): 693–703.
12. L. Pauling, *Vitamin C and the Common Cold* (New York: Bantam, 1971).
13. T. R. Karlowski, T. C. Chalmers, L. D. Frenkel, A. Z. Kapikian, T. L. Lewes, and J. M. Lynch, "Ascorbic Acid for the Common Cold: A Prophylactic and Therapeutic Trial," *Journal of the American Medical Association* 231 (1975): 1038–42.
14. E. T. Creagan, C. G. Moertel, J. R. O'Fallon, A. J. Schutt, M. J. O'Connell, J. Rubin, and S. Frytak, "Failure of High-Dose Vitamin C (Ascorbic Acid) Therapy to Benefit Patients with Advanced Cancer: A Controlled Trial," *New England Journal of Medicine* 301 (1979): 687–90.

Chapter 6

1. R. O. Cummings, *The American and His Food: A History of Food Habits in the United States* (Chicago: University of Chicago Press, 1940), p. 122.
2. Ibid., p. 123.
3. O. Walden, "The Relationship of Dietary and Supplemental Calcium Intake to Bone Loss and Osteoporosis," *Journal of the American Dietetic Association* 89 (1989): 397–400.
4. Ibid.
5. *Recommended Dietary Allowances*, 9th ed. (Washington, DC: National Academy of Sciences, 1980), p. 127.
6. Ibid., pp. 127–28.
7. Ibid., pp. 125–33.
8. K. M. Hambidge, P. A. Walravens, R. M. Brown, J. Webster, S. White, M. Anthony, and M. L. Roth, "Zinc Nutrition of Preschool Children in the Denver Head Start Program," *American Journal of Clinical Nutrition* 29 (1976): 734–38.
9. M. A. Johnson and S. E. Kays, "Copper: Its Role in Human Nutrition," *Nutrition Today*, January–February 1990, pp. 6–14.
10. M. Steinbaugh, "Nutritional Needs of Female Athletes," *Clinics in Sports Medicine* 3 (1984): 661–62.
11. M. L. Watson and C. Palmer, "Position of the American Dietetic Association: The Impact of Fluoride on Dental Health," *Journal of the American Dietetic Association* 89 (1989): 971–74.
12. Ibid.
13. Ibid.
14. Report of the Nutrition Committee, American Heart Association, "Rationale of the Diet–Heart Statement of the American Heart Association," *Circulation* 65 (1982): 839A–54A.
15. J. H. Laragh, "Two Forms of Vasoconstriction in Systemic Hypertension," *American Journal of Cardiology* 60 (1987): 826–36.
16. F. C. Luft, "Dietary Sodium, Potassium and Chloride Intake and Arterial Hypertension," *Nutrition Today*, May–June 1989, pp. 9–14.

17. T. J. Moore, "Overkill," *The Washingtonian*, August 1990, pp. 64–67, 194–204.
18. J. Z. Milfer, M. H. Weinberger, S. A. Daugherty, N. S. Fineberg, J. C. Christian, and C. E. Grim, "Heterogeneity of Blood Pressure Response to Dietary Sodium Restriction in Normotensive Adults," *Journal of Chronic Diseases* 40 (1987): 245–50.
19. Food and Nutrition Board, National Research Council, National Academy of Sciences, *Toward Healthful Diets*, reprinted in *Nutrition Today*, May–June 1980, pp. 7–11; "Dietary Guidelines for Healthy American Adults: A Statement for Physicians and Health Professionals by the Nutrition Committee, American Heart Association," *Circulation* 77 (1988): 721A–24A; U.S. Department of Health and Human Services, Public Health Service, *The Surgeon General's Report on Nutrition and Health: Summary and Recommendations* (Washington, DC: U.S. Government Printing Office, 1988).
20. See Senate Select Committee on Nutrition and Human Needs, *Dietary Goals for the United States* (Washington, DC: U.S. Government Printing Office, 1977).
21. Luft, "Dietary Sodium, Potassium and Chloride Intake and Arterial Hypertension."
22. D. Farley, "Top 10 Laboratory Tests: Blood Will Tell," *FDA Consumer*, July–August 1989, pp. 22–27.
23. H. Spencer, L. Kramer, and D. Osis, "Do Protein and Phosphorus Cause Calcium Loss?" *Nutrition Today*, January–February 1989, pp. 33–35.
24. *Recommended Dietary Allowances*, p. 163.
25. F. H. Nielsen and W. Mertz, "Other Trace Elements," in *Present Knowledge in Nutrition*, 5th ed. (Washington, DC: Nutrition Foundation, 1984), p. 610.
26. A. Greeley, "Getting the Lead Out," *FDA Consumer*, July–August 1991, pp. 26–31.
27. "Alleged Dental Amalgam Toxicity . . . Are Dental Fillings Poisoning People?" *National Council Against Health Fraud Newsletter*, September–October 1985, pp. 3–4.
28. L. Fenner, "Hair Analysis? May As Well Be Bald," *FDA Consumer*, April 1983, pp. 16–17.
29. K. Hambidge, "Hair Analyses: Worthless for Vitamins, Limited for Minerals," *American Journal of Clinical Nutrition* 36 (1982): 943–49.

Chapter 7

1. For an excellent review of fiber and its relationship to diseases, see K. L. Roehrig, "The Physiological Effects of Dietary Fiber – A Review," *Food Hydrocolloids* 2 (1988): 1–18.
2. Committee on Diet, Nutrition and Cancer, Assembly of Life Sciences, National Academy of Sciences, *Diet, Nutrition and Cancer* (Washington, DC: National Academy Press, 1982), p. 134.
3. J. W. Anderson and N. J. Gustafson, "Hypocholesterolemic Effects of Oat and Bean Products," *American Journal of Clinical Nutrition* 48 (1988): 749–53.
4. G. Cowgill and W. Anderson, "Laxative Effects of Wheat Bran and 'Washed Bran' in Healthy Men," *Journal of the American Medical Association* 98 (1932): 1866–75.
5. S. G. Cooper and E. J. Tracey, "Small-Bowel Obstruction Caused by Oat-Bran Bezoar," *New England Journal of Medicine* 320 (1989): 1148–49.
6. M. T. Pugliese, M. Weyman-Daum, N. Moses, and F. Lifshitz, "Parental

Health Beliefs as a Cause of Non-organic Failure to Thrive," *Pediatrics* 80 (1987): 175–82.

Chapter 8

1. R. Carson, *Silent Spring* (Boston: Houghton-Mifflin, Company, 1962).
2. *U.S. News & World Report*, November 23, 1959, pp. 44–45.
3. B. N. Ames and L. S. Gold, "Too Many Rodent Carcinogens: Mitogenesis Increases Mutagenesis," *Science* 249 (1990): 970–71.
4. J. D. Rosen, "Much Ado About Alar," *Issues in Science and Technology*, Fall 1990, pp. 85–90.
5. J. Beck, "Some Pesticide Scare Stories Rotten to Core," *Columbus* (OH) *Dispatch*, October 1, 1990, p. 7A; K. Smith, "Alar: One Year Later – A Media Analysis of a Hypothetical Health Risk," *American Council on Science and Health, Special Report*, March 1990.
6. Smith, "Alar – One Year Later."
7. D. E. Koshland, "Scare of the Week," *Science* 244 (1989): 9.
8. "Revenge of the Apples," *Wall Street Journal*, December 17, 1990, p. A8.
9. M. Kleiber, *The Fire of Life* (New York: Wiley, 1961), p. 329.
10. R. O. Cummings, *The American and His Food: A History of Food Habits in the United States* (Chicago: University of Chicago Press, 1940).

Chapter 9

1. E. Whelan, *Toxic Terror* (New York: Jameson Books, distributed by Kampmann and Co., 1985).
2. A. J. Barsky, "The Paradox of Health," *New England Journal of Medicine* 318 (1988): 414–18.
3. A. Leaf, "The Aging Process: Lessons from Observations in Man," *Nutrition Reviews* 46 (1988): 40–44.
4. S. Jonas, *Medical Mystery, the Training of Doctors in the United States* (New York: Norton, 1978).
5. R. O. Cummings, *The American and His Food: A History of Food Habits in the United States* (Chicago: University of Chicago Press, 1940), pp. 100–1.
6. R. B. Downs, "Afterword," in Upton Sinclair, *The Jungle* (New York: NAL, 1960), p. 348.
7. Ibid., p. 344.
8. These survey and poll results were reported by L. L. Gast, then associate administrator of the Food Safety and Inspection Service, U.S. Department of Agriculture, in *Nutrition News*, October 1985, pp. 9–11.
9. R. M. Deutsch, *The New Nuts Among the Berries* (Palo Alto, CA: Bull, 1977), pp. 317–18.
10. Ibid., p. 317.
11. D. L. Arnold, C. A. Moodie, H. C. Grice, S. M. Charbonneau, B. Stavric, B. T. Collins, P. F. McGuire, Z. Z. Zawidzka, and I. C. Munro, "Long-Term Toxicity of Ortho-toluenesulfonamide and Sodium Saccharin in the Rat," *Toxicology and Applied Pharmacology* 52 (1980): 113–52.
12. Food and Nutrition Board, *Toward Healthful Diets* (Washington, DC: National Academy Press, 1980).

Chapter 10

1. J. M. Jay, *Modern Food Microbiology* (New York: Van Nostrand, 1970), pp. 219–31.

2. Council for Agricultural Science and Technology, "Ionizing Energy in Food Processing and Pest Control. I. Wholesomeness of Food Treated with Ionizing Energy," Report 109 (Ames, IA: Council for Agricultural Science and Technology, 1986).
3. World Health Organization, "Wholesomeness of Irradiated Food," Report by a Joint IAEA/WHO Expert Committee, Geneva, October 27–November 3, 1980; *Technical Report Series* no. 659 (Geneva: WHO, 1981).
4. D. Blumenthal, "Food Irradiation. Toxic to Bacteria, Safe for Humans," *FDA Consumer*, November 1990, pp. 11–15.
5. Committee on Food Protection, Food and Nutrition Board, *The Use of Chemicals in Food Production, Processing, Storage, and Distribution* (Washington, DC: National Academy of Sciences, 1973), p. 27.
6. Select Committee on GRAS Substances, Life Science Research Office, Federation of American Societies for Experimental Biology, "Evaluation of Health Aspects of GRAS Food Ingredients: Lessons Learned and Questions Unanswered," *Federation Proceedings* 36 (1977): 2527–56.
7. Committee on Diet, Nutrition and Cancer, Assembly of Life Sciences, National Academy of Sciences, *Diet, Nutrition and Cancer* (Washington, DC: National Academy Press, 1982), p. 360.
8. Committee on Food Protection, Food and Nutrition Board, *The Use of Chemicals in Food Production, Processing, Storage, and Distribution*.
9. Department of Health and Human Services, Food and Drug Administration, "Food Labelling; Health Messages and Label Statements; Reproposed Rule," *Federal Register*, February 13, 1990, pp. 5176–92.
10. "Antibiotics and the Foods You Eat," *FDA Consumer Memo*, DHEW Publication no. (FDA) 73-6001, 1973.
11. "Study Reveals Few Traces of Antibiotics in Milk," *FDA Consumer*, July–August 1990, p. 3.
12. "Superbugs May Have Tainted Milk," *FDA Consumer*, March 1988, pp. 2–3.
13. A. Hecht, "The Unwelcome Dinner Guest: Preventing Food-borne Illness," *FDA Consumer*, January–February 1991, pp. 18–25.
14. C. Carey, "Mary Mallon's Trail of Typhoid," *FDA Consumer*, June 1989, pp. 18–20.

Chapter 11

1. H. Appledorf, W. B. Wheeler, J. A. Koburger, "Sensory Evaluation of Health Foods: A Comparison with Traditional Foods," *Florida Agricultural Experiment Stations Journal Series* no. 5328, 1974.
2. S. P. Gourdine, W. W. Traiger, and D. S. Cohen, "Health Food Stores Investigation," *Journal of the American Dietetic Association* 83 (1983): 285–90.
3. C. W. Marshall, *Vitamins and Minerals: Help or Harm?* (Philadelphia: George F. Stickley, 1985), p. 175.
4. *Composition of Foods: Raw, Processed, Prepared*, Agriculture Handbook no. 8, U.S. Department of Agriculture, Superintendent of Documents (Washington, DC: U.S. Government Printing Office, 1963).
5. S. Snider, "Beware the Unknown Brew: Herbal Teas and Toxicity," *FDA Consumer*, May 1991, pp. 31–33.
6. L. Aikman, *Nature's Healing Arts from Folk Medicine to Modern Drugs* (Washington, DC: National Geographic Society, 1977).
7. T. Larkin, "Herbs Are Often More Toxic Than Magical," *FDA Consumer*, October 1983, pp. 4–11.
8. V. E. Tyler, *The New Honest Herbal* (Philadelphia: George F. Stickley, 1987).

9. S. M. Love, R. S. Gelman, and W. Silen, "Fibrocystic 'Disease' of the Breast: A Non-Disease?" *New England Journal of Medicine* 307 (1982): 1010–14.

10. F. Lubin, E. Ron, Y. Wax, M. Black, M. Fumaro, and A. Shitrit, "A Case-Control Study of Caffeine and Methylxanthines in Benign Breast Disease," *Journal of the American Medical Association* 253 (1985): 2388–92.

11. Report of the Council on Scientific Affairs, American Medical Association, "Caffeine Labeling," *Journal of the American Medical Association* 252 (1983): 803–6.

12. T. R. Dawber, W. B. Kannel, and T. Gordon, "Coffee and Cardiovascular Disease: Observations from the Framingham Study," *New England Journal of Medicine* 291 (1974): 871–74. Also, two letters to the editors by M. G. Kovar, R. Fulwood, and M. Feinleib, *New England Journal of Medicine* 309 (1983): 1249; and R. B. Shekelle, M. Gale, O. Paul, and J. Stamler, *New England Journal of Medicine* 309 (1983): 1249–50.

13. *Newsweek*, August 3, 1970, pp. 57–58; *Time*, August 17, 1970, p. 57.

14. "Ready-to-eat cereals," *Consumer Reports*, October 1986, pp. 628–36.

15. Ibid., p. 630.

16. Committee on Dietary Allowances, Food and Nutrition Board, *Recommended Dietary Allowances*, 10th ed. (Washington, DC: National Academy of Sciences, 1989).

17. Report of the Nutrition Committee, American Heart Association, "Rationale of the Diet–Heart Statement of the American Heart Association," *Circulation* 65 (1982): 839A–54A.

18. Lipid Metabolism–Atherogenesis Branch, National Heart, Lung, and Blood Institute, National Institutes of Health, "Science Press Briefing: Lipid Research Clinics Coronary Primary Prevention Trial Results," *Nutrition Today*, March–April 1984, pp. 20–25.

19. Select Committee on Nutrition and Human Needs, U.S. Senate, *Dietary Goals for the United States* (Washington, DC: U.S. Government Printing Office, 1977). The same source shows that pork fat such as that in bacon is, on average, 37 percent saturated and 47 percent monounsaturated. On average, about 11 percent of the fat in bacon is polyunsaturated and comes from the diet of the pig.

20. An excellent, comprehensive (216 pages, 922 references to the scientific literature) report on the consumption and health aspects of sugar has been prepared by the Sugar Task Force of the Food and Drug Administration: W. H. Glinsmann, J. Irausquin, and Y. K. Park, "Evaluation of Health Aspects of Sugars Contained in Carbohydrate Sweeteners," *Journal of Nutrition*, supplement, November 1986. This report forms the basis of much of our discussion here.

21. R. A. Rizza and J. E. Gerich, "Statement on Hypoglycemia," *Diabetes Care* 5 (1982): 72–73.

22. W. H. Glinsmann et al., *Evaluation of Health Aspects of Sugars*, pp. S102–4.

23. D. A. Gans, "Sucrose and Unusual Childhood Behavior," *Nutrition Today*, May–June 1991, pp. 8–14.

24. Dan White served a five-year jail sentence, was released in 1984, and committed suicide in 1985 (*People Magazine*, November 4, 1985, pp. 46–47).

25. *The Surgeon General's Report on Nutrition and Health: Summary and Recommendations*, U.S. Department of Health and Human Services, Public Health Service, DHHS (PHS) Publication no. 88-50211, 1988.

26. Ibid., p. 15.

Chapter 12

1. "Deaths Associated with Thiamine-deficient Total Parenteral Nutrition," *Morbidity and Mortality Weekly Reports*, January 27, 1989, pp. 43–46.

2. R. O. Cummings, *The American and His Food: A History of Food Habits in the United States* (Chicago: University of Chicago Press, 1940), pp. 127–31.
3. World Health Organization, *Conquest of Deficiency Diseases*, Basic Study no. 24 (Geneva: WHO Distribution and Sales Unit, 1970).
4. J. de Castro, *The Geography of Hunger* (Boston: Little, Brown, 1952).
5. The book was reprinted under the title of *Lind's Treatise on Scurvy*, ed. C. P. Stewart and D. Guthrie (Edinburgh: University of Edinburgh Press, 1953) and includes additional notes on scurvy and vitamin C.
6. World Health Organization, *Conquest of Deficiency Diseases*.
7. "Biographical Notes from the History of Nutrition," *Journal of the American Dietetic Association* 29 (1953): 8.
8. Much of the information found here is derived from two sources: E. W. Etheridge, *The Butterfly Caste: A Social History of Pellagra in the South* (Westport, CT: Greenwood Press, 1971); and M. Terris, *Goldberger on Pellagra* (Baton Rouge: Louisiana State University Press, 1964). Biographical information on Goldberger also can be found in the *Journal of the American Dietetic Association* 29 (1953): 673.
9. *Quackery – A $10 Billion Scandal*, A Report by the Chairman of the Subcommittee on Health and Long-Term Care, Select Committee on Aging, House of Representatives, 98th Cong., 2nd sess., comm. pub. no. 98–435 (Washington, DC: U.S. Government Printing Office, 1984).
10. Ibid.
11. Ibid.
12. Ibid.
13. Ibid.
14. S. Snider, "Acne: Taming That Age-old Adolescent Affliction," *FDA Consumer*, October 1990, pp. 17–19.
15. R. M. Rose and J. M. Abplanalp, "Premenstrual Syndrome," *Hospital Practice* 18 (1983): 129–41.
16. K. Dalton, *The Premenstrual Syndrome and Progesterone Therapy* (London: Heinemann, 1977).
17. Rose and Abplanalp, "Premenstrual Syndrome."
18. Executive Committee of the American Academy of Allergy and Immunology, "Candidiasis Hypersensitivity Syndrome," *Journal of Allergy and Clinical Immunology* 78 (1986): 271–73.
19. S. Barrett, "Candidiasis Hypersensitivity," *Nutrition Forum*, November 1987, pp. 84–85.
20. Ibid.
21. J. P. Quinn and F. R. Venezio, "Ketoconazole and the Yeast Connection," *Journal of the American Medical Association* 255 (1986): 3250.
22. The American Academy of Allergy and Immunology (611 E. Wells Street, Milwaukee, WI 53202) will provide professional information on candidiasis upon request.
23. "Dr. Victor Herbert Launches Major Lawsuit Against American Quack Association, et al.," *National Council Against Health Fraud Newsletter*, March–April 1988, p. 1.

Chapter 13

1. A. L. Stewart and R. H. Brook, "Effects of Being Overweight," *American Journal of Public Health* 73 (1983): 171–8.
2. P. G. Lindner and D. Lindner, *How to Assess Degrees of Fatness* (1972), Cambridge Scientific Industries, Inc., 101 W. Virginia Ave., Cambridge, MD, 21613; R. A. Frisancho, "New Standards of Weight and Body Composition

by Frame Size and Height for Assessment of Nutritional Status of Adults and the Elderly," *American Journal of Clinical Nutrition* 40 (1984): 808–19.

3. A. E. Harper, "Transitions in Health Status: Implications for Dietary Recommendations," *American Journal of Clinical Nutrition* 45 (1987): 1094–1107.
4. Committee on Diet and Health, Food and Nutrition Board, National Research Council, "Obesity and Eating Disorders," in *Diet and Health: Implications for Reducing Chronic Disease Risk* (Washington, DC: National Academy Press, 1989).
5. E. Ravussin, S. Lillioja, W. C. Knowler, L. Christin, D. Freymond, W. G. H. Abbott, V. Boyce, B. V. Howard, and C. Bogardus, "Reduced Rate of Energy Expenditure as a Risk Factor for Body–Weight Gain," *New England Journal of Medicine* 318 (1988): 467–72.
6. S. B. Roberts, J. Savage, W. A. Coward, B. Chew, and A. Lucas, "Energy Expenditure and Intake in Infants Born to Lean and Overweight Mothers," *New England Journal of Medicine* 318 (1988): 461–66.
7. J. Himms-Hagen, "Brown Adipose Tissue Thermogenesis: Interdisciplinary Studies," *FASEB Journal* 4 (1990): 2890–98.
8. Committee on Diet and Health, Food and Nutrition Board, National Research Council, "Genetics and Nutrition," in *Diet and Health: Implications for Reducing Chronic Disease Risk*.
9. M. Apfelbaum, J. Fricker, and L. Igoin-Apfelbaum, "Low and Very Low Calorie Diets," *American Journal of Clinical Nutrition* 45 (1987): 1126–34.
10. L. Fenner, "Cellulite: Hard to Budge Pudge," *FDA Consumer*, May 1980, pp. 4–7.
11. "Guar Gum Diet Products Under Investigation," *FDA Consumer*, October 1990, p. 3.
12. A. J. Stunkard, "Conservative Treatments for Obesity," *American Journal of Clinical Nutrition* 45 (1987): 1142–54.
13. Stewart and Brook, "Effects of Being Overweight."

Chapter 14

1. Food and Nutrition Board, National Research Council, National Academy of Sciences, *Toward Healthful Diets* (Washington, DC: National Academy Press, 1980); reprinted in *Nutrition Today*, May–June 1980, pp. 7–11.
2. National Institutes of Health, "Consensus Development Conference Statement: Lowering Blood Cholesterol"; reprinted in *Nutrition Today*, January–February 1985, pp. 13–16.
3. Food and Nutrition Board, *Toward Healthful Diets*.
4. The following two articles provide more information: R. Ross, "The Pathogenesis of Atherosclerosis – An Update," *New England Journal of Medicine* 314 (1986): 488–500; and A. Leaf and P. C. Weber, "A New Era for Science in Nutrition," *American Journal of Clinical Nutrition* 45 (1987): 1048–53.
5. K. L. Roehrig, *Carbohydrate Biochemistry and Metabolism* (Westport, CT: AVI Publishing, 1984), pp. 133–44.
6. U. Steinbrecher and J. Witztum, "Glycosylation of LDL's to an Extent Comparable to That in Diabetes Slows Their Catabolism," *Diabetes* 33 (1984): 130–34.
7. Ross, "The Pathogenesis of Atherosclerosis"; and Leaf and Weber, "A New Era for Science in Nutrition."
8. M. S. Brown and J. L. Goldstein, "A Receptor-mediated Pathway for Cholesterol Homeostasis," *Science* 232 (1986): 34–47.
9. S. M. Grundy, "Cholesterol and Coronary Heart Disease – A New Era," *Journal of the American Medical Association* 256 (1986): 2849–58.

10. Food and Nutrition Board, *Toward Healthful Diets*.
11. Council on Scientific Affairs, "Dietary and Pharmacologic Therapy for the Lipid Risk Factors," *Journal of the American Medical Association* 250 (1983): 1873–79.
12. Report of the Nutrition Committee, American Heart Association, "Rationale of the Diet–Heart Statement of the American Heart Association," *Circulation* 65 (1982): 839A–54A.
13. National Institutes of Health, "Consensus Development Conference Statement."
14. G. Kolata, "Heart Panel's Conclusion Questioned," *Science* 227 (1985): 40–41.
15. Committee on Nutrition, American Academy of Pediatrics, "Toward a Prudent Diet for Children," *Pediatrics* 71 (1983): 78–80.
16. M. T. Pugliese, M. Weyman-Daum, N. Moses, and F. Lifshitz, "Parental Health Beliefs as a Cause of Non-organic Failure to Thrive," *Pediatrics* 80 (1987): 175–82.
17. J. Stamler, D. Wentworth, and J. D. Neaton, "Is Relationship Between Serum Cholesterol and Risk of Premature Death from Coronary Heart Disease Continuous and Graded?" *Journal of the American Medical Association* 256 (1986): 2823–28.
18. J. B. Allred, C. R. Gallagher-Allred, and D. F. Bowers, "Elevated Blood Cholesterol: A Risk Factor for Heart Disease That Decreases with Advanced Age," *Journal of the American Dietetic Association* 90 (1990): 574–76.
19. M. F. Oliver, "Prevention of Coronary Heart Disease – Propaganda, Promises, Problems, and Prospects," *Circulation* 73 (1986): 1–9; W. C. Taylor, T. M. Pass, D. S. Shepard, and A. L. Komaroff, "Cholesterol Reduction and Life Expectancy," *Annals of Internal Medicine* 106 (1987): 605–14.
20. W. B. Kannel, W. P. Castelli, T. Gordon, and P. M. McNamara, "Serum Cholesterol, Lipoproteins, and the Risk of Coronary Heart Disease: The Framingham Study," *Annals of Internal Medicine* 74 (1971): 1–12.
21. D. Shurtleff, "Some Characteristics Related to the Incidence of Cardiovascular Disease and Death: Framingham Study, 18 Year Follow-up," in W. B. Kannel and T. Gordon, eds., *The Framingham Study: An Epidemiological Investigation of Cardiovascular Disease: Section 30* (Washington, DC: U.S. Department of Health, Education and Welfare, 1974, DHEW Publication no. [NIH] 74–599).
22. Council on Scientific Affairs, "Dietary and Pharmacologic Therapy for the Lipid Risk Factors."
23. The Multiple Risk Factor Intervention Trial Research Group, "Multiple Risk Factor Intervention Trial: Risk Factor Changes and Mortality Results," *Journal of the American Medical Association* 248 (1982): 1465–77.
24. Lipid Metabolism, Atherogenesis Branch, National Heart, Lung, and Blood Institute, Lipid Research Clinic Program, "The Lipid Research Clinics Coronary Primary Prevention Trial Results: I. Reduction in Incidence of Coronary Heart Disease," *Journal of the American Medical Association* 251 (1984): 351–64.
25. R. A. Kronmal, "Commentary on the Published Results of the Lipid Research Clinics Coronary Primary Prevention Trial," *Journal of the American Medical Association* 253 (1985): 2091–93.
26. The views of twenty-seven scientists, representing both sides of the issue, were published in *Nutrition Today*, September–October 1984, pp. 22–29.
27. For example, see E. H. Ahrens, "The Diet–Heart Question in 1985: Has It Really Been Settled?" *Lancet*, May 11, 1985, pp. 1085–87; R. A. Kronmal, "Commentary on the Published Results of the Lipid Research Clinics Coronary

Primary Prevention Trial," *Journal of the American Medical Association* 253 (1985): 2091–93; and M. F. Oliver, "Prevention of Coronary Heart Disease – Propaganda, Promises, Problems and Prospects," *Circulation* 73 (1986): 1–9.

28. T. J. Moore, "The Cholesterol Myth," *The Atlantic*, September 1989, pp. 37–70.
29. See R. E. Olson, "Mass Intervention vs Screening and Selective Intervention for the Prevention of Coronary Heart Disease," *Journal of the American Medical Association* 255 (1986): 2204–7; M. F. Oliver, "Strategies for Preventing Coronary Heart Disease," *Nutrition Reviews* 43 (1985): 257–62.
30. M. H. Becker, "The Cholesterol Saga: Whither Health Promotion?" *Annals of Internal Medicine* 106 (1987): 623–26.
31. A. E. Harper, "Transitions in Health Status: Implications for Dietary Recommendations," *American Journal of Clinical Nutrition*, suppl. vol. 45, pp. 1094–1107.
32. Ibid.
33. Taylor et al., "Cholesterol Reduction and Life Expectancy."
34. See a series of letters to the editor and replies by Taylor et al. in *Annals of Internal Medicine* 107 (1987): 420–22.
35. S. A. Grover, M. Abramowicz, L. Joseph, C. Brewer, L. Coupal, and S. Suissa, "The Benefits of Treating Hyperlipidemia to Prevent Coronary Heart Disease: Estimating Changes in Life Expectancy and Morbidity," *Journal of the American Medical Association* 267 (1992): 816–22.
36. National Institutes of Health, "Consensus Development Conference Statement."
37. I. Ross, "A New Drug That Fights Cholesterol," *Reader's Digest*, December 1987, pp. 91–94.
38. "Measuring Cholesterol Is as Tricky as Lowering It," *Science* 238 (1987): 482–83. Also see S. D. Filn, "A Prudent Approach to Control of Cholesterol Levels," *Journal of the American Medical Association* 258 (1987): 2416–18.
39. D. W. Blank, J. M. Hoeg, M. H. Kroll, and M. E. Ruddel, "The Method of Determination Must Be Considered in Interpreting Blood Cholesterol Levels," *Journal of the American Medical Association* 256 (1986): 2867–70.
40. The distribution of blood cholesterol values with age is given in the following: Ad Hoc Committee to Design a Dietary Treatment of Hyperlipoproteinemia, "Recommendations for Treatment of Hyperlipidemia in Adults," *Circulation* 69 (1984): 1065A–90A.
41. W. P. Castelli, R. J. Garrison, P. W. F. Wilson, R. D. Abbott, S. Kalousdian, and W. B. Kannel, "Incidence of Coronary Heart Disease and Lipoprotein Cholesterol Levels: The Framingham Study," *Journal of the American Medical Association* 256 (1986): 2835–38.
42. Ad Hoc Committee, "Recommendations for Treatment of Hyperlipidemia in Adults," p. 1071A.
43. A. Nicoll, N. E. Miller, and B. Lewis, "High-Density Lipoprotein Metabolism," *Advances in Lipid Research* 17 (1980): 53–106.
44. S. Eisenberg, "High Density Lipoprotein Metabolism," *Journal of Lipid Research* 25 (1984): 1017–58.
45. A. S. Brett, "Treating Hypercholesterolemia: How Should Physicians Interpret the Published Data for Patients?" *New England Journal of Medicine* 321 (1989): 676–79.
46. Becker, "The Cholesterol Saga: Whither Health Promotion."
47. G. Oster and E. M. Epstein, "Cost Effectiveness of Antihyperlipemic Therapy in the Prevention of Coronary Heart Disease," *Journal of the American Medical Association* 258 (1987): 2381–87.

48. Report of the Nutrition Committee, American Heart Association, "Rationale of the Diet–Heart Statement of the American Heart Association."
49. Committee on Diet and Health, Food and Nutrition Board, National Academy of Science, "Executive Summary. Diet and Health: Implications for Reducing the Chronic Disease Risk," *Nutrition Reviews* 47 (1989): 142–49.
50. M. Z. Nichaman and P. Hamm, "Low-Fat, High-Carbohydrate Diets and Plasma Cholesterol," *American Journal of Clinical Nutrition* 45 (1987): 1155–60.
51. S. M. Grundy, "Monounsaturated Fatty Acids, Plasma Cholesterol and Coronary Artery Disease," *American Journal of Clinical Nutrition* 45 (1987): 1168–75.
52. A. Bonanome and S. M. Grundy, "Effect of Dietary Stearic Acid on Plasma Cholesterol and Lipoprotein Levels," *New England Journal of Medicine* 318 (1988): 1244–48.
53. D. McNamara, "Impact of Dietary Cholesterol on Serum Cholesterol," *Nutrition Close-Up* 6 (2) (1989): 3–5.
54. Food and Nutrition Board, *Toward Healthful Diets*.
55. L. V. VanHorn, K. Liu, D. Parker, L. Emidy, Y. Liao, W. H. Pan, D. Giumetti, J. Hewitt, and J. Stamler, "Serum Lipid Response to Oat Product Intake with a Fat-modified Diet," *Journal of the American Dietetic Association* 86 (1986): 759–64.
56. J. W. Anderson and N. J. Gustafson, "Hypocholesterolemic Effects of Oat and Bean Products," *American Journal of Clinical Nutrition* 48 (1988): 749–53.
57. J. F. Swain, I. L. Rouse, C. B. Curley, and F. M. Sacks, "Comparison of the Effects of Oat Bran and Low-Fiber Wheat on Serum Lipoprotein Levels and Blood Pressure," *New England Journal of Medicine* 322 (1990): 147–52.
58. H. O. Bang, J. Dyerberg, and H. M. Sinclair, "The Composition of the Eskimo Food in North Western Greenland," *American Journal of Clinical Nutrition* 33 (1980): 2657–61.
59. J. E. Kinsella, "Dietary Fish Oils," *Nutrition Today*, November–December 1986, pp. 7–14.
60. R. N. Podell, "Nutrition, Platelet Function and Disease," *Postgraduate Medicine* 73 (1983): 269–71.
61. D. M. Hegsted, in U.S. Senate, Select Committee on Nutrition and Human Needs, *Dietary Goals for the United States*, December 1977, p. xv.
62. Food and Nutrition Board, *Toward Healthful Diets*.
63. B. M. Gordon, "Why We Choose the Foods We Do," *Nutrition Today*, March–April 1983, pp. 17–24.

Chapter 15

1. Committee on Diet, Nutrition and Cancer, Assembly of Life Sciences, National Research Council, National Academy of Sciences, *Diet, Nutrition, and Cancer* (Washington, DC: National Academy Press, 1982).
2. Ibid., p. 21.
3. Ibid., p. 23.
4. "Teaching About Cancer," Public Education Department, American Cancer Society, 1975, p. 15.
5. H. C. Pitot and Y. P. Dragan, "Facts and Theories Concerning the Mechanisms of Carcinogenesis," *FASEB Journal* 5 (1991): 2280–86.
6. R. M. Morse and W. A. Heffron, "Preventive Health Care in Family Practice," in R. E. Rakel, ed., *Textbook of Family Practice* (Philadelphia: Saunders, 1990), pp. 223–46.

7. Pitot and Dragan, "Facts and Theories Concerning the Mechanisms of Carcinogenesis."
8. W. F. Bodmer, C. J. Bailey, J. Bodmer, H. J. R. Bussey, A. Ellis, P. Gorman, F. C. Lucibello, V. A. Murday, S. H. Rider, P. Scambler, D. Sheer, E. Solomon, and N. K. Spurr, "Localization of the Gene for Familial Adenomatous Polyposis on Chromosome 5," *Nature* 328 (1987): 614–16.
9. E. Solomon, R. Voss, V. Hall, W. F. Bodmer, J. R. Jass, A. J. Jeffreys, F. C. Lucibello, I. Patel, and S. H. Rider, "Chromosome 5 Allele Loss in Human Colorectal Carcinomas," *Nature* 328 (1987): 616–18.
10. R. Doll and R. Peto, "The Causes of Cancer: Quantitative Estimates of Avoidable Risks of Cancer in the United States Today," *Journal of the National Cancer Institute* 66 (1981): 1191–1308.
11. M. W. Pariza, *Diet and Cancer* (Summit, NJ: American Council on Science and Health, 1985), p. 8.
12. Committee on Diet, Nutrition and Cancer, *Diet, Nutrition, and Cancer.*
13. K. Lee, "Food Neophobia: Major Causes and Treatments," *Food Technology* 43 (1989): 62–64, 68–73.
14. Committee on Diet, Nutrition and Cancer, *Diet, Nutrition, and Cancer.*
15. R. M. Deutsch, *The New Nuts Among the Berries* (Palo Alto, CA: Bull, 1977).
16. J. P. Minton, M. K. Foecking, D. J. T. Webster, and R. H. Mathews, "Caffeine, Cyclic Nucleotides and Breast Disease," *Surgery* 86 (1979): 105–9.
17. For example, see F. Lubin, E. Ron, Y. Wax, M. Black, M. Funaro, and A. Shitrit, "A Case-Control Study of Caffeine and Methylxanthines in Benign Breast Disease," *Journal of the American Medical Association* 253 (1985): 2388–92.
18. B. MacMahon, S. Yen, D. Trichopoulos, K. Warren, and G. Nardi, "Coffee and Cancer of the Pancreas," *New England Journal of Medicine* 304 (1981): 630–33.
19. C-C. Hsieh, B. MacMahon, S. Yen, D. Trichopoulos, K. Warren, and G. Nardi, "Coffee and Pancreatic Cancer (Chapter 2)," *New England Journal of Medicine* 315 (1986): 587–89.
20. D. E. Grobbee, E. B. Rimm, E. Giovannucci, G. Colditz, M. Stampfer, and W. Willett, "Coffee, Caffeine and Cardiovascular Disease in Men," *New England Journal of Medicine* 323 (1990): 1026–32.
21. Committee on Diet, Nutrition and Cancer, *Diet, Nutrition, and Cancer.*
22. M. L. Pearce and S. Dayton, "Incidence of Cancer in Men on a Diet High in Polyunsaturated Fat," *Lancet*, March 6, 1971, pp. 464–67.
23. Committee on Diet and Health, Food and Nutrition Board, National Research Council, *Diet and Health: Implications for Reducing Chronic Disease Risk* (Washington, DC: National Academy Press, 1989), p. 672.
24. See symposium proceedings, "Calories and Energy Expenditure in Carcinogenesis," *American Journal of Clinical Nutrition*, January 1987, supplement.
25. Committee on Diet, Nutrition and Cancer, *Diet, Nutrition, and Cancer.*
26. Committee on Diet and Health, *Diet and Health: Implications for Reducing Chronic Disease Risk*, p. 303.
27. *The Surgeon General's Report on Nutrition and Health: Summary and Recommendations*, U.S. Department of Health and Human Services, Public Health Service, DHHS (PHS) Publication no. 88-50211, 1988.
28. R. G. Ziegler, "Vegetables, Fruits, and Carotenoids and the Risk of Cancer," *American Journal of Clinical Nutrition* 53 (1991): 251S–9S.
29. N. I. Krinsky, "Effects of Carotenoids in Cellular and Animal Systems," *American Journal of Clinical Nutrition* 53 (1991): 238S–46S.
30. D. W. Nebert and F. J. Gonzalez, "P450 Genes: Structure, Evolution and Regulation," *Annual Reviews of Biochemistry* 56 (1987): 945–93.

31. "Broccoli, Peanut Butter May Carry Carcinogens," *Columbus* (OH) *Dispatch*, February 13, 1988, pp. A1–A2.
32. "Wonders of the Vegetable Bin," *Time*, September 2, 1991, p. 66.
33. "Broccoli, Peanut Butter May Carry Carcinogens."
34. Committee on Diet, Nutrition and Cancer, *Diet, Nutrition, and Cancer*.
35. Committee on Diet and Health, *Diet and Health: Implications for Reducing Chronic Disease Risk*.
36. Committee on Diet, Nutrition and Cancer, *Diet, Nutrition, and Cancer*, p. 1.
37. Food and Nutrition Board, National Research Council, National Academy of Sciences, *Toward Healthful Diets* (Washington, DC: National Academy Press, 1980; reprinted in *Nutrition Today*, May–June 1980, pp. 7–11.
38. MacMahon et al., "Coffee and Cancer of the Pancreas."
39. Hsieh, MacMahon, et al., "Coffee and Pancreatic Cancer (Chapter 2)."

Conclusion

1. H. Morreim, in D. T. Zallen and M. L. Brown, "Food Fights: Deciding About Diet and Disease," *American Journal of Clinical Nutrition* 52 (1990): 944–45.
2. M. J. Gibney, *Nutrition, Diet and Health* (Cambridge: Cambridge University Press, 1986), pp. 150–51.

Index

absorption: definition, 41; process of, 44–6

acne, 201

adipose tissue: brown, 214, 215; fat storage in, 52, 208

aging, 195–8

agricultural chemicals, 117, 118, 123

Alar scare, 126, 127

alcohol, 165, 166

amino acids: absorption of, 59; dietary essential, 10, 16; imbalance, 34, 35; in proteins, 10; supplements, 35

anemia: iron deficiency, 88, 90, 91; sports, 89; in vegetarians, 33

antibiotics, in animal feed, 152

aphrodisiacs, 160

arsenic, 101

arthritis, 198–200

ATP, 49, 50

basic food groups, 14; fruits and vegetables, 18; grains and cereals, 18; meat and meat substitutes, 16, 17; milk and milk products, 15, 16; "other" group, 21

beriberi, 183, 187–9; *see also* thiamin

bile acids: and cholesterol excretion, 257; in fat digestion, 57

bioflavonoids, 64, 65

biotin: food sources, 73; function of, 73

blood lipids: cholesterol in lipoproteins, 252–4; from fat digestion, 57, 58

blood sugar (glucose), 50

caffeine: and birth defects, 164; and blood cholesterol, 164, 165; and cancer, 164; in coffee, tea, and cola, 163; effects of, 163, 164; and fibrocystic breast disease, 164, 269

calcium: availability, 33, 87, 88; excessive intake, 87, 88; food sources, 15, 84; function of, 84; and osteoporosis, 86, 87; supplements, 34, 88

Calories, definition of, 10, 49

cancer: and fat consumption, 269–71; and fiber consumption, 108, 271, 272; and fruit and vegetable consumption, 272–4; and heredity, 263, 264; nature of, 261–3; relation to environment, 260, 261

cancer and diet, 260–76

candidiasis hypersensitivity syndrome, 203, 204

carbohydrates: absorption of, 51, 54; conversion to fat, 58; digestion of, 50, 51, 54; metabolism of, 52–4; simple sugars, 50; starch, 50

carcinogens, testing in food and drink, 264–9

carnitine, 64

carotene: and cancer, 273; excessive intake, 75

cellulite, 222, 223

cellulose, 51, 104

cereals, breakfast: history of, 169–72; nutrients in, 172, 173

chloride: food sources, 84, 93; function of, 84, 93

chlorination of water, 155

chocolate: and acne, 201; caffeine and theobromine in, 163

cholesterol: function of, 79, 251, 252

cholesterol, blood: and coffee consumption, 164; effect of dietary fiber, 109, 257, 258; effect of fish oils, 258; effect of type of fat on, 255–7; errors in measurement, 250, 251, and heart disease, 230, 231, 237–40; (and age) 241–3; importance of liver synthesis, 257; and life expectancy, 246–50; lowering, (by diet) 255–8, (by drugs) 254, 255

cholesterol, dietary: effect on blood cholesterol, 257; sources, 252

chromium: food sources, 85; function of, 85, 98

coenzymes, function of, 66, 67

coffee: with caffeine, 163; decaffeinated, 138, 165

constipation, 47, 106–8

convenience foods, 146, 147